LEE & HIS
ARMY IN
CONFEDERATE
HISTORY

Civil War America

Gary W. Gallagher, editor

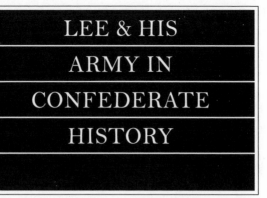

Gary W. Gallagher

The University of North Carolina Press

Chapel Hill & London

© 2001

The University of North Carolina Press

All rights reserved

Designed by Richard Hendel

Set in Monotype Bell

by Tseng Information Systems

Manufactured in the United States of America

The paper in this book meets the guidelines for

permanence and durability of the Committee on

Production Guidelines for Book Longevity of the

Council on Library Resources.

Library of Congress Cataloging-in-Publication Data

Gallagher, Gary W.

Lee and his army in Confederate history /

by Gary W. Gallagher.

p. cm. — (Civil War America)

Includes index.

ISBN-13: 978-0-8078-2631-7 (cloth : alk. paper)

ISBN-10: 0-8078-2631-6 (cloth : alk. paper)

ISBN-13: 978-0-8078-5769-4 (pbk. : alk. paper)

ISBN-10: 0-8078-5769-6 (pbk. : alk. paper)

1. Lee, Robert E. (Robert Edward), 1807–1870—Military

leadership. 2. United States—History—Civil War, 1861–

1865—Campaigns. 3. Confederate States of America.

Army. 4. Confederate States of America—History.

I. Title. II. Series.

E467.1.L4 G29 2001

973.7′3′0092—dc21 2001027126

10 09 08 07 06 6 5 4 3 2

Once again for Eileen Anne, who always understands

CONTENTS

Preface ix
Acknowledgments xv
Essay Credits xvii

Robert E. Lee and the Army of Northern Virginia have engaged my interest for nearly forty years. As a young person drawn to the Civil War, I read Douglas Southall Freeman's *R. E. Lee: A Biography* and *Lee's Lieutenants: A Study in Command.* Freeman's works, together with many of the participants' accounts to which his footnotes led me, created a sense that Lee and his army held center stage in the Confederate drama. Indeed, the military conflict in Virginia seemed synonymous with the Civil War as a whole, and Lee emerged as a fabulously gifted soldier whose only weaknesses—including excessive amiability with lieutenants—represented outgrowths of his personal virtues. Subsequent exposure to studies by Thomas L. Connelly and other revisionist historians tested my early reading of Confederate military affairs. These scholars emphasized the importance of the Western Theater and averred that Lost Cause writers such as Jubal A. Early had distorted the record by vastly inflating Lee's abilities and wartime stature.

My own research over the years indicated that Freeman might have been closer to the mark than many of those who insisted Lee and his army had been overrated. Various kinds of Confederate testimony bespoke a national focus on Lee and his operations. Considerable evidence also supported the Lost Cause idea that superior northern numbers and resources played a fundamental role in the Confederate defeat. That Lost Cause warriors sometimes argued from positions of strength not only helps explain why their writings have been tenaciously influential but also raises an important concern. Can we accept part of what Lost Cause authors said about Lee and his army without also lending a measure of authority to their denial of slavery's centrality to secession and the Confederacy, their romantic portrayal of a united white South battling to the end, and their blatant distortions regarding other aspects of the war?

The essays in this collection explore the relationship between Lee's operations and Confederate national morale, the quality and nature of his generalship, and the thorny problem of how best to handle Lost Cause writings about the Army of Northern Virginia and its commander. The four essays in Part I grew out of a belief that most historians of the Civil War, whether pursuing military or nonmilitary topics, have accorded surprisingly little attention to the ways in which Confederates in uniform and behind the lines reacted to Lee's famous campaigns. Hindsight tells us one thing, but the contemporary record often reveals something very different. I offer four case studies to gauge the impact, at the time, of Lee's activities. I selected three battles that seem uncomplicated in this respect: Antietam and Gettysburg, a pair of defeats that ended Lee's two invasions of the North, and Fredericksburg, an apparently unequivocal victory. For my fourth topic, I canvassed sentiment in the winter and spring of 1864, a period typically portrayed as a time of waning will in the Confederacy.

I based my findings almost entirely on letters, diaries, newspapers, and other wartime sources—as distinct from postwar accounts informed by full knowledge of how the war unfolded. I drew on the writings of more than 300 witnesses, among them soldiers and male and female civilians. Although I tried to find evidence from a broad spectrum of society representing various geographical regions, my sample was not scientifically constructed. My conclusions thus should be considered suggestive rather than definitive.

Having offered that caveat, I will say that Confederates often responded differently to news from the battlefront than we have come to assume. They relied on fragmentary accounts from relatives and friends in the army, often inaccurate reporting in newspapers, and rumors spread behind the lines. Most did not see either Antietam or Gettysburg as a military disaster; a number expressed some unhappiness with the outcome of Fredericksburg; and many exhibited a tenacious belief in ultimate victory during the winter and spring of 1864. The essays in Part I collectively accentuate the importance of relying on evidence from the time, rather than reading backward with all we know about the war's outcome, to fathom the complexity of attitudes and morale at specific times. They also underscore a remarkable faith among soldiers and the citizenry in Lee and the prowess of his army. Well before he and his troops marched toward Pennsylvania in June 1863, the Confederate people looked to them as the nation's best hope for winning independence. That conception of Lee and the Army of Northern Virginia in turn cushioned reaction to Gettysburg and fed optimism in early 1864.

Other historians have reached conclusions quite different from mine. Knowing eventual defeat awaited the Confederacy, many scholars have taken their cue from Union opinions about military operations. Northern soldiers and civilians in September 1862 and July 1863 typically considered Antietam and Gettysburg successes (although some demurred from the prevailing views), which lends credence to the argument that these battles marked major mileposts along the road to Appomattox. Similarly, northerners manifested a strong expectation that Ulysses S. Grant would achieve success against Lee as the spring campaigning season approached in 1864.

How can we account for strikingly divergent Confederate and Union reactions to the same events? Were white southerners engaged in self-delusion? Did they proclaim false optimism in a desperate effort to maintain national resolve in the face of an obviously failing struggle for independence? Some newspapers friendly to the Davis administration undoubtedly tailored their editorials and coverage of events to boost morale. Just as surely, some Confederates wrote letters to relatives designed to buck up spirits. But I believe it is a mistake not to accept roughly at face value a good part of the written record. The notions that participants often failed to record their true opinions and that we, at a distance of more than a century and a third, can detect what they really thought strike me as highly problematical. Northerners and Confederates simply perceived some events differently and responded accordingly.

When assessed within the context of the time, Confederate reactions to Antietam and Gettysburg and optimism in the spring of 1864 seem plausible. After all, military events in the Eastern Theater during the nine months following Antietam included important Confederate victories at Fredericksburg and Chancellorsville followed by Lee's second invasion of the North. Would anyone appraising the situation in late June 1863, when the Army of Northern Virginia roamed across the Pennsylvania countryside seemingly at will, insist that Antietam had delivered a fatal blow to southern hopes for success? Similarly, the Army of the Potomac mounted no serious threat in Virginia for almost ten months after Gettysburg; and when the combatants renewed their struggle during the Overland campaign, Lee and his army amply justified the confidence their countrymen and countrywomen had voiced that spring. By the late summer of 1864, Abraham Lincoln and countless others in the North despaired over their prospects for victory, and Gettysburg represented scarcely more than a receding memory of triumph.

Defeat fundamentally altered Confederate thinking about Gettysburg and other wartime events. Painfully aware that they emerged from the conflict a conquered people, many white southerners looked back to find points at which their fortunes might have taken another direction. Gettysburg proved a natural candidate for such retrospective speculations. It had marked the deepest penetration into the United States by a major Confederate army, claimed more casualties than any of the war's other battles, and ended the remarkable run of victories Lee had crafted during the preceding year. Lost Cause authors especially relished Gettysburg because it allowed them to absolve Lee of responsibility for failure by blaming James Longstreet (very few accounts written in the aftermath of Gettysburg had mentioned Longstreet in this light). If "Old Pete" had attacked as ordered on July 2, they insisted disingenuously, Lee would have won the battle and marched on to national victory in 1863. Thus did former Confederates create a postwar literature that, unlike the bulk of their wartime writings, buttressed the notion of Gettysburg as a clear turning point.

The three essays in Part II focus on Lee's generalship. I am intrigued by various dimensions of the Lee myth—not just from the perspective of revisionists such as Thomas L. Connelly and Alan T. Nolan, who have attacked what they consider a hagiographic literature, but also as one mindful of how admirers have insisted that their hero's faults as a general represented exaggerations of his personal virtues. The first of these essays takes issue with what I see as a flawed interpretive tradition. Nourished by the writings of both critics and admirers, it presents Lee as a throwback to an earlier style of leadership ill suited to a modern mid-nineteenth-century conflict between democratic societies. The second essay in Part II addresses the idea that Lee was too much of a gentleman to make hard decisions about his top lieutenants. It argues that the Overland campaign, and especially the two weeks of fighting and maneuvering around Spotsylvania Court House in mid-May, highlighted Lee's willingness to deal firmly with his corps commanders.

Lee also has been criticized for granting some subordinates too much latitude and failing to exercise a tight rein at critical moments. The third essay in Part II engages this topic obliquely in the course of examining Jubal A. Early's role in the Chancellorsville campaign. Events of May 1–4, 1863, provide an instructive example of Lee's giving Early wide discretion and then stepping forward to take control when Lafayette McLaws, another senior subordinate, failed in a crucial moment at Salem Church. Generally pleased with Early's performance in a difficult, semi-independent role at Chancellorsville, Lee nevertheless exerted a firm hand after the battle when "Old Jube" pursued a controversial exchange with William Barksdale that threatened to taint the Confederate victory.

The single essay in Part III examines Lee, Early, and Douglas Southall Freeman as shapers of how Americans have understood Confederate military history. All three men argued within the Lost Cause tradition. Early and Freeman presented Lee as the most important and talented Confederate general, awarding his campaigns clear primacy among Civil War operations. They highlighted his disadvantage in human and material resources and asserted that northern numbers largely determined Confederate defeat. In doing so, they skirted the fact that it took superb leadership by Abraham Lincoln and Ulysses S. Grant to ensure decisive use of northern means. Yet despite according too little weight to the difficulty of applying Union power effectively, Early and Freeman grounded many of their claims about numbers, Lee's ability, and the effect of his army's campaigns in solid evidence. This essay asks whether it is useful—or desirable—to separate veracious Lost Cause arguments from the transparently false ones relating to the institution of slavery and other aspects of Civil War era history.

Six of these pieces first appeared in volumes of the Military Campaigns of the Civil War series published by the University of North Carolina Press. As editor of that series, I planned my contributions with the intention of eventually gathering them in a volume devoted to Lee and his army during the war and in the historical literature. I slightly revised each of the six and added the two on Lee as a modern soldier and on him and his army in public memory to round out the book. As a collection, these essays represent a step in my continuing effort to comprehend how military and civilian affairs intersected during the Civil War, where Lee and his army fit within the larger story of the Confederacy, and how Americans have interpreted their great national crisis.

ACKNOWLEDGMENTS

Several friends helped with the preparation of these essays. Joseph T. Glatthaar, George C. Rable, and T. Michael Parrish read parts of the text and offered suggestions for improvement. William A. Blair, Keith S. Bohannon, Peter S. Carmichael, Thavolia Glymph, Robert E. L. Krick, Robert K. Krick, Robert Sandow, and Joan Waugh shared material turned up during their own research and recommended additional avenues of investigation. Edward L. Ayers proved especially helpful in prodding me to revise my approach to the last essay. I hasten to add that these able and generous scholars do not agree with all of my arguments. I also wish to thank Mary Tyler Freeman McClenahan, whose friendship has been a delight over the past several years and who kindly allowed me to use a photograph of her father. The dedication recognizes my continuing debt to Eileen Anne Gallagher. Her patience with my obsession about Civil War history and cheerful participation in untold conferences, seminars, and battlefield tours continue to astonish me.

ESSAY CREDITS

All but the last essay in this volume have been published elsewhere. Each of those previously published has been revised, some more substantially than others, and several titles have been slightly altered. I thank the publishers who granted permission to reprint the essays in their revised forms.

"The Net Result of the Campaign Was in Our Favor: Confederate Reaction to the 1862 Maryland Campaign" was originally published as "The Net Result of the Campaign Was in Our Favor: Confederate Reaction to the Maryland Campaign," in Gary W. Gallagher, ed., *The Antietam Campaign* (Chapel Hill: University of North Carolina Press, 1999), 3–43.

"The Yanks Have Had a Terrible Whipping: Confederates Evaluate the Battle of Fredericksburg" was originally published in Gary W. Gallagher, ed., *The Fredericksburg Campaign: Decision on the Rappahannock* (Chapel Hill: University of North Carolina Press, 1995), 113–41.

"Lee's Army Has Not Lost Any of Its Prestige: The Impact of Gettysburg on the Army of Northern Virginia and the Confederate Home Front" was originally published in Gary W. Gallagher, ed., *The Third Day at Gettysburg and Beyond* (Chapel Hill: University of North Carolina Press, 1994), 1–30.

"Our Hearts Are Full of Hope: The Army of Northern Virginia and the Confederacy in the Spring of 1864" was originally published as "Our Hearts Are Full of Hope: The Army of Northern Virginia in the Spring of 1864," in Gary W. Gallagher, ed., *The Wilderness Campaign* (Chapel Hill: University of North Carolina Press, 1997), 36–65.

"An Old-Fashioned Soldier in a Modern War?: Lee's Confederate Generalship" was originally published as "An Old-Fashioned Soldier in a Modern War?: Robert E. Lee as Confederate General," in *Civil War History* (December 1999): 295–321. Reprinted by permission of the Kent State University Press.

"I Have to Make the Best of What I Have: Lee at Spotsylvania" was originally published as "I Have to Make the Best of What I Have:

Robert E. Lee at Spotsylvania," in Gary W. Gallagher, ed., *The Spotsylvania Campaign* (Chapel Hill: University of North Carolina Press, 1998), 5–28.

"Fighting the Battles of Second Fredericksburg and Salem Church: Lee and Jubal A. Early at Chancellorsville" was originally published as "East of Chancellorsville: Jubal A. Early at Second Fredericksburg and Salem Church," in Gary W. Gallagher, ed., *Chancellorsville: The Battle and Its Aftermath* (Chapel Hill: University of North Carolina Press, 1996), 36–64.

Part One

LEE'S

CAMPAIGNS

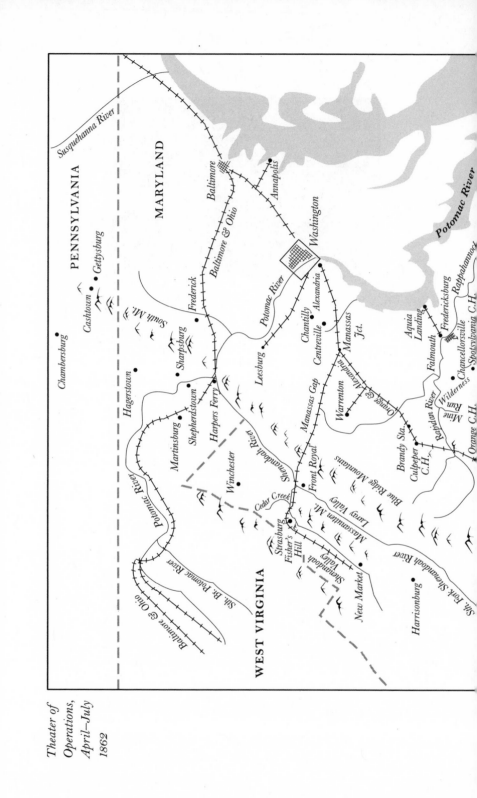

Theater of Operations, April–July 1862

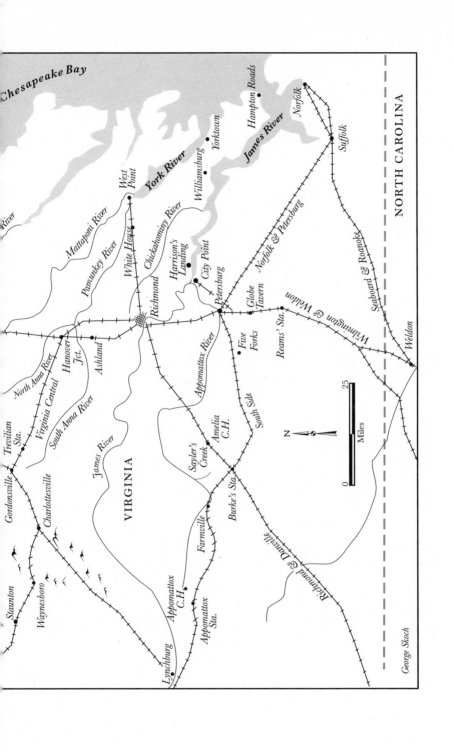

Chesapeake Bay

NORTH CAROLINA

Norfolk

Hampton Roads

Suffolk

Yorktown

Williamsburg

James River

York River

West Point

Seaboard & Roanoke

Mattaponi River

Pamunkey River

White House

Chickahominy River

Norfolk & Petersburg

Harrison's Landing

City Point

Weldon

River

Richmond

Petersburg

Globe Tavern

Wilmington & Weldon

North Anna River

Hanover Jct.

Ashland

Appomattox River

Five Forks

Reams' Sta.

Virginia Central

South Anna River

Trevilian Sta.

James River

VIRGINIA

South Side

N

25

Miles

Gordonsville

Charlottesville

Sayler's Creek

Amelia C.H.

Burke's Sta.

0

Staunton

Waynesboro

Farmville

Richmond & Danville

Appomattox C.H.

Lynchburg

Appomattox Sta.

George Skoch

THE NET RESULT

OF THE CAMPAIGN

WAS IN OUR FAVOR

Confederate Reaction

to the 1862 Maryland

Campaign

The roads leading from Sharpsburg to Boteler's Ford choked under the strain of men, vehicles, and animals during the night of September 18, 1862. Trudging through a sheltering fog that helped mask their movement toward the Potomac River, Confederate soldiers hoped that an enemy who had been quiescent all day would remain so for a few hours longer. A North Carolina chaplain, carried along through the predawn Maryland darkness on this martial tide, left a vivid impression in his diary: "Though troops and wagons have been passing all night, still the roads and fields were full. Ram! Jam! Wagons and ambulances turned over! One man was killed by the overturning of an ambulance." An artillerist described a more orderly withdrawal, mentioning especially that Robert E. Lee "stood at the ford in Shepherdstown and gave directions to the teamsters and others, showing a wise attention to details which many men in less elevated positions would think beneath their notice." By eight o'clock on the morning of September 19, all were safely across the Potomac onto Virginia soil.[1]

Thus ended a fifteen-day campaign in Maryland that represented the final act of a drama begun eighty-five days earlier with Confederate assaults at the battle of Mechanicsville outside Richmond. These twelve momentous weeks had witnessed Lee's offensive victory over George B. McClellan in the Seven Days and an equally impressive thrashing of John Pope's Army of Virginia at Second Manassas, which together shifted the strategic focus in the Eastern Theater from Richmond to the Potomac River. Surging across the national frontier into Maryland less than a week after Second Manassas, Lee and his army had hoped to make the strategic reorientation even more striking. Dramatic events in the gaps of South Mountain, at Harpers Ferry, and amid the rolling countryside near Sharpsburg had punctuated Lee's foray north of the Potomac—and would dominate the thinking of most contemporary observers and later critics who sought to judge what the Army of Northern Virginia had won or lost.

Historians typically have assessed the Maryland campaign from the perspective of its long-term impact, looking back with later events in mind to label it a major turning point that foreshadowed Confederate defeat. Writing in the mid-1950s, Clement Eaton touched on the two factors most often mentioned in this connection: Lincoln's preliminary proclamation of emancipation and Europe's decision to back away from recognition of the Confederacy in the autumn of 1862. "The checking of the Confederate invasion at Antietam . . . was disastrous to the cause of Southern independence," wrote Eaton. "The retreat of Lee not only gave Lincoln a favorable opportunity to issue his Emancipation Proclamation but it also chilled the enthusiasm of the British government to recognize the independence of the Confederacy." Nearly two decades earlier, Robert Selph Henry had argued similarly in his widely read history of the Confederacy, pointing to Antietam and suggesting that "On the seventeenth day of September in 1862 the decline of the Confederacy began." Clifford Dowdey, who in the 1950s and 1960s inherited Douglas Southall Freeman's mantle as the leading popular writer about Lee and his army, added his voice to this chorus, stating bluntly, "Politically, the war ended at Sharpsburg for the Confederacy. That was the last chance the Southern states had really to win independence."[2]

More recent historians have continued this interpretive tradition. James M. McPherson's magisterial history of the conflict reminded readers that the battle of Antietam "frustrated Confederate hopes for British recognition and precipitated the Emancipation Proclamation. The slaughter at Sharpsburg therefore proved to have been one of the war's great turning points." In summary comments about

Antietam from his overview of the Civil War era, Brooks D. Simpson asserted that "most people, North and South, American and European, interpreted a pitched battle followed by a Confederate withdrawal as a defeat." The result was diminished chances for European recognition and Lincoln's opening for the proclamation—a conclusion Charles P. Roland echoed in his insightful survey of the Civil War.[3]

A decade ago, I summarized the impact of the Maryland campaign on Confederate fortunes in similar terms: "Lee went north and fought, avoided a series of lurking disasters, and found refuge in the end along the southern bank of the Potomac River. But the military events of mid-September 1862 bore bitter political and diplomatic fruit for the Confederacy. The nature of the conflict changed because of Lee's Maryland campaign." No longer a contest to restore the status quo ante bellum, "the new war would admit of no easy reconciliation because the stakes had been raised to encompass the entire social fabric of the South. The war after Antietam would demand a decisive resolution on the battlefield, and that the Confederacy could not achieve."[4]

The understandable desire to highlight the broad implications of the Maryland campaign has left another important question relatively neglected, namely: How did Confederates at the time react to Lee's campaign in Maryland? Did the operations of September 1862 engender hope? Did they cause Confederates to lose heart at the thought that their struggle for independence had taken a grim turn downward? Did the campaign provoke a mixed reaction? In short, what impact did Lee's foray across the Potomac have on his men and on their fellow Confederates?

A survey of military and civilian testimony during the period following Lee's retreat from Maryland underscores the challenge of assessing the relationship between military events and popular will during the Civil War. Although any such survey is necessarily impressionistic, it is worthwhile searching letters, diaries, and newspaper accounts for patterns of reaction.[5] Examined within the context of what people read and heard at the time, and freed from the powerful influence of historical hindsight, Confederate morale assumes a complex character. Rumors and inaccurate reports buffeted citizens long since grown wary of overblown prose in newspapers. Knowing they often lacked sound information, people nonetheless strove to reach satisfying conclusions about what had transpired.

As the autumn weeks went by, they groped toward a rough consensus that may be summed up briefly. The Maryland campaign did not represent a major setback for the Confederacy. Antietam was at worst a bloody stand-off, at best a narrow tactical success for Confederates who beat back heavy Union assaults and then held the field for another day. "Stonewall" Jackson's capture of 12,000 Union soldiers and immense matériel at Harpers Ferry and A. P. Hill's stinging repulse of Union forces at Shepherdstown on September 20 marked unequivocal high points of the campaign. McClellan's inaction throughout late September and October demonstrated how badly his army had been damaged, and Lincoln's emancipation proclamation betrayed Republican desperation and promised to divide northern society. Reconciled to the fact that the war would not end anytime soon, most Confederates looked to the future with a cautious expectation of success.[6]

In one important respect, the Maryland campaign served as the coda to a different kind of watershed than most historians have described. Lee and his army emerged from Maryland as a major rallying point for the Confederacy. Their operations between July and September began the process that, within another eight months, would make them the focus of Confederate national sentiment. Starting in the autumn of 1862, white southerners increasingly contrasted Lee's and Jackson's successes in the Eastern Theater with repeated failures in the Western Theater, concluding that prospects for victory would rest largely on the shoulders of Lee and his lieutenants and on the bayonets of their soldiers. Better attuned to Confederate sentiment than many later historians would be, Edward A. Pollard of the *Richmond Examiner* touched on this point in his wartime history of the Confederacy. "The army which rested again in Virginia had made a history that will flash down the tide of time a lustre of glory," wrote Pollard in 1863 of the aftermath of the Maryland campaign. "It had done an amount of marching and fighting that appears almost incredible, even to those minds familiar with the records of great military exertions." The "remarkable campaign . . . extending from the banks of the James river to those of the Potomac," concluded Pollard, "impressed the world with wonder and admiration."[7]

Newspapers supplied most Confederates outside Lee's army with their initial impressions about the Maryland campaign. As is always the case, such accounts must be read with the understanding that editors often tried to shape public opinion as well as inform readers about what had transpired. During the initial phase of reporting, editors typically took the stance that Sharpsburg ranked among the bitterest of engagements and, though perhaps not a clear southern victory, reflected well on Confederate prowess. Six days after the battle, for example, Charleston's *Mercury* admitted that accounts of fighting at Sharpsburg were "meagre and somewhat contradictory, but all agree in representing it to have been the most bloody and desperately contested engagement of the war." The outnumbered Confederate army had "again illustrated its valor and invincibility by successfully repelling the repeated onsets of the enemy." The *Charleston Daily Courier* noted that "All accounts agree in representing that the fight of Wednesday was closely contested," adding that a reliable witness quoted General Lee as saying he "looked upon the struggle of that day as favorable to our arms." Richmond's *Dispatch*, which had the largest circulation among the capital's newspapers, took a bit more optimistic view: "[I]t is evident that we were victorious on Wednesday. We acted on the defensive. The enemy tried a whole day to drive us from our position. He utterly failed. We held our position, and slept on the ground, ready to renew the contest the next day." Even less restrained was the *Richmond Enquirer*, which breathlessly announced that "the battle resulted in one of the most complete victories that has yet immortalized Confederate arms."[8]

The capture of Harpers Ferry received wide coverage and almost universal praise,[9] as did the battle of Shepherdstown. Little remembered now, the latter loomed much larger in September 1862 and satisfied Confederate yearnings for offensive victories. In reporting on Shepherdstown, the *Richmond Weekly Dispatch* described how a Union column had crossed at Boteler's Ford in pursuit of the Army of Northern Virginia, only to be driven back by A. P. Hill's outnumbered division: "Our forces poured the grape and canister into them as they crossed the Potomac, and the slaughter was terrible." Fleeing Federals fell in such profusion that the "river was black with them." The *Charleston Daily Courier* termed the fight "a severe engagement . . . in which the Yankees were almost annihilated. They were driven into the river, shot down by hundreds, and those who survived taken prisoner." Peter W. Alexander, among the best of the Confederate military correspondents, reported "additional particulars . . . of the affair at Shepherdstown" for the *Savannah Republican* on September 23. Quoting a Federal surgeon, Alexander stated that "about 2,000 Federal infantry attempted to cross after us, and out

*Artillery covering the Union retreat at the battle of Shepherdstown on September 20, 1862. Confederates applauded this engagement as a bloody debacle for George B. McClellan's Army of the Potomac. (*Frank Leslie's Illustrated Newspaper, *October 25, 1862)*

of that number only ninety lived to return. Such as were not killed and drowned, were captured." [10]

Lee's decision to seek shelter south of the Potomac after Sharpsburg provoked far more disagreement among editors than the apparently uncomplicated Confederate successes at Harpers Ferry and Shepherdstown. The *Charleston Mercury* somewhat sarcastically called the crossing at Boteler's Ford a "movement which, to the unmilitary eye, with no more subtle guide than the map, would certainly resemble a retreat." Richmond's *Dispatch* disagreed, emphasizing "the wearied and almost starving condition of our men," and rationalizing the withdrawal as "made necessary not by any reverse in battle, but by the stern exigency of the absence of commissary supplies." The *Enquirer* reported that "McClellan's army was too badly used up on Wednesday . . . to perform any rapid movement for strategic effect." As a consequence, continued this pro-Davis administration paper, the "movement of a portion of our forces to the South side was purely a matter of precaution, to provide against possible contingencies." Seldom has more nebulous language been used to place a positive gloss on an army's retreat (the degree to which the *Enquirer* achieved its goal cannot now be determined).[11]

Newspapers also argued about Lee's goals in entering Maryland. The *Enquirer* claimed that "our distinguished General projected the movement into Maryland as a cover to his march against Harper's Ferry, and for the purpose of drawing McClellan out of Washington." Having established a standard by which to evaluate Lee's operations, the paper added: "He has entirely succeeded. Harper's Ferry has fallen, and McClellan enticed sixty-five miles from Washington, has been defeated." With an eye toward those who questioned the retreat on September 18, the *Enquirer* concluded that "Such glorious triumphs should teach our people the utmost reliance on General Lee, and make them easy even when they do not understand his movements."[12]

In Charleston, the *Mercury* would have none of this, noting dismissively that that the *Enquirer* "professes, in a soothing article, to believe that Lee contemplated only the capture of Harper's Ferry in his advance into Maryland." The *Mercury* suspected more had been intended, and less accomplished. For one prominent Confederate, at least, the *Enquirer's* position carried the day against the *Mercury*. According to the *Southern Confederacy* of Atlanta, Vice President Alexander H. Stephens considered the capture of Harpers Ferry to have been "Lee's principal object in going into Maryland, . . . [and] one of the most brilliant achievements of the war." The battle of Sharpsburg was "only an *incident* to the main object, in which our forces were victorious, though the victory was dearly bought."[13]

All of the newspapers discussed the problem of straggling among Lee's soldiers. "Candor compels me to say," admitted one correspondent from the field, "that the straggling and desertion from our army far surpasses anything I had ever supposed possible." Although editors strongly deplored the absence of stragglers at Sharpsburg, where comrades in the laggards' units fought bravely and fell in profusion, most expressed at least some sentiment similar to that in a piece written for the *Savannah Republican*. "A fifth of the troops are barefooted; half of them are in rags, and the whole of them insufficiently supplied with food," wrote this observer on September 19 from near Smithfield. "Men in this condition cannot be relied on to the same extent as when they are properly clothed and subsisted. The best soldiers, under such circumstances, will straggle on the march and in battle." The *Dispatch*, which shared some of this compassion for worn-out soldiers, nevertheless suggested that if "only as many as five thousand of the stragglers who left their colors and lingered behind had been present, McClellan's rout would have been irremediable" on September 17.[14]

During the first two weeks of October, newspapers drew on extensive reporting from correspondents in the field, letters from soldiers, and coverage in the northern press to render generally optimistic final verdicts about the campaign. The *Richmond Whig* touched on themes repeated in many other papers. Northern sheets such as New York's *Times* and *Tribune*, observed the *Whig*, no longer claimed Antietam as a great victory for McClellan. Indeed, many northern correspondents "deny outright that it was a Federal victory at all; and all of them admit the immense loss sustained by McClellan's army, and its shattered condition after the action." The *Whig* also stressed three other points: Lee's men had occupied the field through September 18, withdrawn in perfect order to the Potomac, and held their position along the river ever since. The *Charleston Daily Courier* joined numerous papers in stressing the odds against which the Confederates had contended: "Seventy thousand men, weary and weak with labors and marches, and fasting for fifteen hours, struggled with two hundred thousand, and after repulsing the heavy columns hurled upon them, remained masters of the battle ground." McClellan's immobility supported the idea that Lee had bested his opponent in Maryland. If "General McClellan had not been severely beaten and his army demoralized," suggested a piece in the *Richmond Dispatch*, "it is very natural to suppose he would not have hung so closely to the Maryland shore for the past three weeks."[15]

Among the more restrained sets of conclusions appeared in the *Charleston Mercury*, which lamented the "moral and political consequences" of the campaign for the people of Maryland. Other papers also had raised the issue of Lee's failure to liberate Maryland from the yoke of Lincoln's tyranny. Yet even the *Mercury* reckoned that in "prisoners and arms, we got greatly the advantage of the enemy, as we did in the casualties sustained by the respective armies. Considered apart, therefore, from the effect upon Maryland of our retreat across the river, the net result of the campaign was in our favor."[16]

Lincoln's preliminary emancipation proclamation spurred generally optimistic responses from the Confederate press. In light of emancipation's eventual role in weakening the southern war effort, this reaction might strike modern readers as disingenuous. How could Confederates interpret the proclamation as anything but a crushing blow to their hopes of maintaining an effective national military resistance? A number of editors undoubtedly sought to put the best face on the situation. They also had at hand, however, encouraging news from the pages of northern newspapers, which provided ample details about Democrats and others unhappy at the prospect of risking white lives for black freedom. Southern papers insisted that weakness arising from indifferent Union performances on the battlefield had pushed Lincoln toward precipitate action. The president had "at last shaken the rod of terror he refrained from raising till the cause he is engaged in should be compassed about with such perils that it became desperate," stated one editor, who continued: "The South rejoices in the publication of his emancipation proclamation. It cannot do us any harm; it will do us great good. It breeds divisions in his own borders; it will compose differences and produce a greater unanimity throughout these Confederate States." Another editor saw in the proclamation indication "of a current of distrust" in the North, "a distrust swelling even to desperation," while a piece in the *Enquirer* characterized the proclamation as a measure out of step with most northern civilians and soldiers. Lincoln had surrendered the government "into the hands of the Abolitionists," suppressing "the last lingering hope of a restoration of the Union, even on the part of those who sustained his Administration under the honest belief that he was endeavoring in good faith to accomplish that end." [17]

Newspaper coverage of the Maryland campaign suggests the extent to which popular expectations had risen for Lee and his army. More than one editor chided readers, who remained enthralled by the Seven Days and Second Manassas, for lamenting the absence of an unequivocal victory north of the Potomac. Too many Confederates were "cast down" by Lee's withdrawal from Maryland, remarked the *Charleston Daily Courier*, which asked rhetorically: "Was not Southern prowess as splendidly illustrated at Sharpsburg as it was before Richmond or on the plains of Manassas?" The *Richmond Dispatch* reminded readers that just a few months earlier, "at a time when our city was actually beleaguered by the enemy," citizens had manifested great fortitude. Since then, Lee's generalship had created a situation where "people are disappointed because we did not gain a victory as decisive as those around Richmond and at Manassas."

Confederates simply could not "expect such victories always." The *Richmond Daily Enquirer* joined other papers in placing the Maryland campaign within the larger chronology of events since Lee took charge of the Army of Northern Virginia. The Confederate commander had outwitted McClellan on the Chickahominy, made a fool of Pope at Manassas, and bested "Little Mac" again by capturing Harpers Ferry. Viewed against this record, the retreat to the south bank of the Potomac meant little. The difference between that position and one on the north bank amounted to "an hour's march" and no more.[18]

In a widely published dispatch from Winchester dated September 26, Peter W. Alexander elevated Lee's army to a singular position among Confederate forces. "No army on this continent has ever accomplished as much or suffered as much," affirmed the native Georgian, "as the Army of Northern Virginia within the last three months.— At no time during the first Revolutionary war—not even at Valley Forge—did our forefathers in arms encounter greater hardships, or endure them more uncomplainingly." Alexander's invocation of the Revolutionary War anticipated innumerable Confederates who later would compare Lee and the Army of Northern Virginia to George Washington and the Continental army. Lest anyone underestimate how vital Lee and his soldiers had become, Alexander explicitly spelled out their role as the nation's primary defenders: "The army in Virginia stands guard this day, as it will stand guard this winter, over every hearthstone throughout the South. The ragged sentinel who may pace his weary rounds this winter on the bleak spurs of the Blue Ridge, or along the frozen valleys of the Shenandoah and Rappahannock, will also be your sentinel, my friend, at home."[19]

The civilians to whom Alexander addressed his comments watched the autumn's campaigning with great interest. They poured through newspapers, lingered over letters from relatives in the army, and plotted the respective armies' geographic positions. Moods and attitudes on the home front fluctuated as new information became available. By mid-October, most people had reached their ultimate conclusions about the campaign. Some pronounced it a mistake; but the majority seem to have favored the positive side of the scales, taken comfort in the overall record Lee's army forged between June and October, and looked toward the winter with cautious confidence in Confederate prospects for success.

Inconsistent early reports about the fighting on September 17 left many people on edge. "I have waited for time to clear the mists that lie around our recent actions on the Potomac," wrote a North Carolina diarist on September 25, "but even now I cannot tell if what I record is correct." Four days later this woman accused "the authorities in Richmond" of suppressing news about casualties, which she considered "a bad sign for us!" From near Richmond, the old fire-eater Edmund Ruffin complained that "reports from our army in Md. & on the Potomac, & those from the northern papers, are so contradictory that it can scarcely be recognized that they speak of the same actions." A Georgian believed that even bad news was preferable to maddening uncertainty, arguing that Jefferson Davis should bend every effort to make public the results of big battles. "Our nation has by past acts," he averred, "demonstrated the fact that with astonishing composure it can bear alike the joys of success and the disheartening influences of reverses." The Davis administration should not withhold "authentic information in reference to past occurrences and accomplished facts"; to do so left people dependent on "the uncertain reports of letter-writers and the lying statements of Northern presses . . . for a knowledge of the true status of affairs." [20]

Precise casualty figures for Sharpsburg never reached the Confederate home front, leaving citizens certain only that the fighting had been costly. A quartet of diarists from Virginia, Georgia, and Louisiana reflect a consensus that the battle had been bloody and far from decisive. Lucy Rebecca Buck, whose family lived near Front Royal, described "a most terrific battle at Sharpsburg, Maryland in which we had nearly been defeated but had succeeded in driving the enemy from the field and then slowly fell back ourselves." A native of Maine long resident in Georgia, Dolly Lunt Burge wrote with other Confederate families in mind: "This month, the 17th & 18th has been fought the bloodiest [battle] of the war. My heart sickens when I think of it & the affliction it has brought upon thousands and thousands of our countrymen."

Youthful Sarah Morgan wondered about the impact on her own circle. "Our army, having accomplished its object, recrossed the Potomac, after what was decidedly a drawn battle," she observed from her vantage point in the Trans-Mississippi. "Both sides suffered severely. Hardly an officer on either side escaped unhurt. . . . I expect the list will contain the names of many friends when it comes." From Lynchburg on September 22, William M. Blackford claimed "a victory to our arms" in "one of the bloodiest and best contested" engagements of the conflict. Two days later, this father of five Confederate soldiers revised his earlier statement, remarking that the "weight of evidence is to the effect that we have been in the main victorious." The Federals, added Blackford, "as usual, claim a victory and publish lying bulletins as they did in the fights around Richmond." [21]

Stonewall Jackson's success at Harpers Ferry and A. P. Hill's tidy victory at Shepherdstown stood out as elements of the Maryland campaign that helped offset doubts about Sharpsburg. "We have had a glorious victory at Harper's Ferry," cheered the daughter of a merchant in Orange, Virginia, "with but slight loss to ourselves—a number of *prisoners, guns, small arms, horses, servants*, & stores of all sorts." Mary Fielding of Limestone County, Alabama, whose brother served in the 9th Alabama Infantry of Cadmus M. Wilcox's brigade, noted that the "surrender of Harper's Ferry clears the Shenandoah valley of Yankees"; closer to the scene, a diarist near Paris, Virginia, reported "quite a victory at Harper's Ferry yesterday—several thousand taken prisoner and several hundred contrabands." Anne S. Frobel, whose section of Fairfax County had been occupied by Federal troops for much of the war, seemed to take special comfort from Jackson's seizure of large numbers of runaway slaves. "We have just heard of the recapture by the Confederates of Harper's ferry," she wrote on September 17, "with 12000 yankees, and immense quantities of ordnance, ammunition, commissary stores and a large number of Contrabands, which in yankee parlance means negro." The Yankees admitted all of these facts, stated Frobel, who then asked rhetorically: "[I]f they acknowledge such a great loss what must the reality be." [22]

While Harpers Ferry conjured images of prisoners and loot, the action at Shepherdstown conveyed more gory—but probably no less satisfying—images of dead Federal soldiers floating in the Potomac. Two witnesses captured the essence of what most Confederates had to say about Shepherdstown. "On the 19th a division of the enemy crossed over to Shepherdstown. Jackson captured or killed the whole of them," stated a woman in Fredericksburg, Virginia, with typical hyperbole. "The Potomac was damned up with their bodies." Another diarist estimated that "Ten thousand Yankees crossed at Shepherdstown, but unfortunately for them, they found the glorious Stonewall there." Combat erupted near Boteler's Mill, and Jack-

Harpers Ferry, a photograph looking across the Potomac from the Maryland side of the river. Stonewall Jackson's capture of more than 12,000 Federal soldiers at Harpers Ferry marked a frequently mentioned high point of the campaign for Confederates. (National Archives)

son's troops "totally routed" the enemy, "as we succeeded in driving a good many of them into the Potomac. . . . The account of the Yankee slaughter is fearful."²³

As in these two accounts of Shepherdstown, Stonewall Jackson dominated many of the more enthusiastic descriptions of Confederate successes in Maryland. He was the Confederacy's most famous officer in the summer and autumn of 1862, and his fellow citizens embraced the idea that he smashed Yankee opponents at will. Three soldiers outside the Army of Northern Virginia wrote typical passages about the dour Virginian's exploits. On September 29, a captain in Texas informed his wife of recent news about Harpers Ferry, which he called "another of Stonewall Jackson's victories," before closing with a rousing "Huzzah for Stonewall. he's the man of the times." Enthusiasm trumped accuracy when a sergeant serving in Mississippi described the fight at Shepherdstown: "[N]ews is rattling over the wires of victories again of Stonewall Jackson over Burnside killing and capturing his whole army save 2000. . . . Stonewall was ordered to fall on Burnside while crossing and rumor says he dammed up the River with the slain." A private in the 10th Texas Infantry employed inelegant language to make a similar point. "[M]ore good news from the other side of the river —," wrote Benjamin M. Seaton, "the report says that Stonewall Jackson has gained another battle and McClenan lost 18,000 kild and woned in crossing the river — a considerable loss on their side." [24]

"Jeb" Stuart's slashing cavalry raid into Pennsylvania in mid-October added another bright vignette to many civilians' overall picture of the Maryland campaign. Carried out while Lee's army remained defiantly along the Potomac frontier, it reinforced the idea that McClellan was a timid commander and reassured citizens who favored offensive action. One man compared it to Stuart's first ride around McClellan during the Peninsula campaign, calling it "not less brilliant than the grand round in June," and pointing out that "This was the enemy's country." In Richmond, where he documented reaction to the war in his famous diary, War Department clerk John B. Jones termed the raid "a most brilliant affair" that yielded much "public property" captured or destroyed. "The Abolitionists," wrote Jones with obvious satisfaction, "are much mortified, and were greatly frightened." [25]

In contrast to such hopeful expressions, Maryland's anemic response to Lee's army engendered feelings of disappointment and anger. Many Confederates were torn between an inclination to criticize Maryland for not doing more and a desire to give residents of a sister slave state the benefit of the doubt. Some blamed tepid support among Marylanders for Lee's decision to abandon the state after just two weeks. "Our army returned to Va after this battle [Sharpsburg]," wrote one woman in this vein, "as they were unprepared for an advance into Pennsylvania and could not be sustained in that unfriendly part of Maryland." Conditioned by newspaper accounts to believe that only Federal bayonets held Maryland in the Union, many Confederates had invested considerable hope in the prospect of wooing another state to their slaveholding republic. Reports of a cold reception for Lee's veterans prompted a number of these people, including Ada Bacot, a volunteer nurse in Charlottesville, to suggest that Maryland's cause was not worth the expenditure of Confederate blood: "I fear Maryland is not going to come to our relief, a few of her sons may be loyal but not so many that we might risk our army in her borders." After Sharpsburg, a disappointed Bacot looked to providence rather than to Maryland. "God help us," she wrote, "we can do nothing of ourselves." Others put the case with more bitterness, as when a Louisiana woman described "great disappointment over Maryland. . . . There has been but little enthusiasm and few recruits. Well, let the Old Bay State go, if her people had rather be slaves in the Union than masters in the Confederacy. They must abide by their choice." [26]

For Confederates who had doubted the propriety of invading the North, Maryland's behavior confirmed that the South should do no more than defend its own borders. A Georgia clergyman alluded to the popular clamor for invasion that had risen in the wake of Lee's victories in July and August. Attempting to carry the war to the Federals "in the most favorable moment and upon the most favorable soil—at least one upon which the people were, to a good degree, at least, so friendly as not to rise upon us," Lee had marched into Maryland. There he found that he "could advance but a little way" because the "people did not come to his standard." This individual looked upon the whole episode "*as a special providence in our behalf*," and hoped "this taste of invasion will be satisfactory—at least for the present. . . . The Maryland pear certainly is not ripe yet." [27]

Most Confederates seem to have emulated their newspaper editors in viewing Lincoln's emancipation proclamation as a potentially positive development. At a distance of more than a century and a third it is impossible to know whether people believed one thing and wrote another, but considerable testimony suggests that many white southerners expected emancipation to weaken the Union war effort. Some looked to fissures behind the lines in critical northern states, as when a Virginia physician pronounced it "more than probable" that Lincoln's action would "redound to our benefit, in . . . that it will produce dissentions among his own followers, as it has already done in New York." Diarist Catherine Edmondston, scrutinizing the war from her home in eastern North Carolina, discerned that "Evidences of division at home appear in the Northern journals—the Emancipation Proclamation meets with some bitter opponents & M Clellan is like to have a fire in his rear." Pennsylvania-born Josiah Gorgas, the Confederacy's resourceful ordnance chief, initially considered the proclamation worthy of notice only "as showing the drift of opinion in the northern gov." A few days later, however, he recorded that Lincoln's action triggered "marked opposition at the north, & is denounced by the democrats generally." [28]

Unhappiness in the Union army relating to emancipation impressed some Confederates as particularly noteworthy. The northern press served as the primary source for information about this topic in late September and early October. "General McClellan has issued a mild general order cautioning the troops against political discussion," observed a man who relied on Union newspaper accounts: "It is a very significant production and goes to corroborate the report that great trouble exists in their camps on account of the war becoming one for the abolition of slavery." Witnesses such as Cornelia Peake McDonald and Anne S. Frobel reached similar conclusions based on firsthand testimony from the enemy. Thrown together with Federals in Winchester, McDonald observed, "There seems no doubt now that the Yankee army is disgusted with the war, now that the real object of it has been made manifest, and many go so far as to say that they will fight no longer if the fight is for the freedom of the negroes." As if to clinch her point, she added that "Some of their soldiers have said so in my presence." In occupied Fairfax County, Frobel wrote that "Lincoln's recent proclamation has caused great dissatisfaction" among troops loyal to McClellan. They feared Lincoln would replace their hero with John C. Frémont, and "that does not accord at all with the wishes of the army." Northern soldiers said the proclamation would "put a speedy termination to the war"—welcome words to Frobel, yet she knew "they talk a great deal of what they know nothing about." [29]

In late September, John B. Jones prophesied that Lincoln's measure would "intensify the war, and add largely to our numbers in the field." A subsequent passage in his diary highlighted outrage over the proclamation and hope that it might spawn a crisis of command in the Army of the Potomac—sentiments voiced frequently

In the wake of Antietam, many Confederates portrayed Lincoln's preliminary Emancipation Proclamation as detrimental to the Union cause. This view persisted for months, as indicted in this cartoon from Punch *republished in slightly altered form by the* Southern Illustrated News. *It depicts Lincoln trying to persuade an aloof freedman to join the army: "Why I du declare it's my dear old friend Sambo! Course you'll fight for us Sambo. Lend us a hand, Old Hoss, du!"* (Southern Illustrated News, *March 14, 1863*)

across the Confederacy. "Yesterday in both Houses of Congress," Jones wrote, "resolutions were introduced for the purpose of retaliating upon the North [for] the barbarities contemplated in Lincoln's Emancipation proclamation." Meanwhile, he continued, the "Abolitionists of the North want McClellan removed." Believing that a change of generals would discomfit the most famous Union army, Jones found himself in the odd position of aligning himself with the abolitionists: "I hope they may have their will."[30]

Just before news of Sharpsburg spread across the South, a man from Lynchburg lauded the success Lee's army had achieved since the Seven Days. "[V]ictory after victory has crowned our arms and our gallant and victorious army [is] yet driving the enemy before them . . .," he wrote enthusiastically. "[M]ay we continue to drive them until not a vestige of that invading army tramp on that soil, ever again tread upon southern soil." Following the turbulent middle third of September, the bulk of McClellan's army *did not* mount an effort to tramp across Virginia's Potomac frontier. No major action erupted, and the armies entered a somnolent spell that prompted innumerable comments like John B. Jones's "All quiet in Northern Virginia" on October 7 and Cornelia McDonald's "No news from our army, and no further indication of a falling back" eighteen days later. Confederates relaxed after a protracted season of stirring military operations, content that Lee and his army would meet whatever challenge the Yankees might offer.[31]

Contemporary comparisons of Lee and his army with their counterparts in the Western Theater reveal another outcome of operations in the summer and autumn. Because Lee had won two major offensive victories in Virginia and, according to the dominant view, left a crippled Union army cringing in Maryland, relatively few Confederates judged his actions harshly. Braxton Bragg and Earl Van Dorn, architects of the retreat from Kentucky and the defeat at Corinth respectively, received less forgiving treatment. British traveler W. C. Corsan's journal suggests the extent of the double standard. Corsan described the military situation in the Confederacy upon his arrival in Richmond in November 1862, mentioning Jackson's presence at Winchester, Lee's at Culpeper, and McClellan's at Warrenton — without a word about the impact of the Maryland campaign. Poor Bragg did not fare as well. "Of course," stated Corsan matter-of-factly, "his conduct and plans were criticised severely."[32]

William Blackford typified this willingness to forgive Lee but not

Bragg. After the former's return to the Virginia side of the Potomac, Blackford praised his "splendid campaign around Richmond, in the Valley and in Maryland." But the similar withdrawal from Kentucky, against which no solid triumphs on Bragg's part could be juxtaposed, elicited a withering blast. "The evacuation of Kentucky by Bragg is un fait accompli," stated Blackford. "He brought out immense quantities of plunder of all kinds, but the result has been disastrous if not disgraceful to our arms." Lamenting Bragg's inability to deny Don Carlos Buell access to Louisville, Blackford voiced a sentiment that undoubtedly would have been widely seconded: "Oh, that we had another Lee and another Jackson to send out there." [33]

Jefferson Davis almost certainly took a more pessimistic view of the Maryland campaign than did the majority of his people. Robert Garlick Hill Kean, head of the Confederate Bureau of War and nephew-in-law of Secretary of War George Wythe Randolph, recorded a famous description of the president's mood: "He was very low down after the battle of Sharpsburg. . . . I remember the then Secretary of War told me that he said our maximum strength had been laid out, while the enemy was but beginning to put forth his." [34] George Washington Custis Lee, who served as the president's military aide, may have contributed to Davis's doubts. Having joined the army near Martinsburg in late September, Robert E. Lee's oldest son reported that officers told him "our troops were shaky from the day they went into Maryland, . . . that if even the few (comparatively) who were present had fought with their usual spirit at both Boonsboro, and Sharpsburg, the enemy would have been badly whipped. As it was, I believe from what I have heard, that they got the worst of it." Lee predicted that the army would make a better fight when resupplied with food and clothing and reinforced by the return of stragglers; however, "the worst of it" was that the enemy "can refit faster than we can." [35]

Davis unburdened himself to Robert E. Lee about pressures from behind the lines. Members of Congress, newspaper editors, and private citizens—none of whom, in Davis's view, had a proper understanding of the military situation—had clamored for an aggressive strategy. With Lee's troops arrayed along Virginia's northern frontier after Sharpsburg, many of these people called for the army to take up a defensive position closer to Richmond. "The feverish anxiety to invade the North," wrote Davis with scarcely concealed temper, "has been relieved by the counter irritant of apprehension for the safety of the Capital in the absence of the Army, so long criticized for a 'want of dash.'" Davis, who trusted that Lee would be unmoved by the demands of such amateur strategists, raised the prospect of reinforcements for the Army of Northern Virginia from Louisiana and elsewhere. Whatever his expectations for the future, Davis knew what Lee had wrought since June and sent his heartfelt expression of gratitude: "In the name of the Confederacy I thank you and the brave men of your Army for the deeds which have covered our flag with imperishable fame."[36]

The soldiers of that army knew better than anyone else what they had endured. Their letters and diaries evaluated the various components of the Maryland campaign, shed light on the physical condition and morale of the army, judged the quality of the army's leaders, and speculated about the likely short- and long-term direction of the war.

Men and officers alike described Sharpsburg as a cataclysmic battle that had pushed them to the breaking point, but virtually all their accounts stress that Lee's battered units held the field. The emphasis on maintaining ground might seem like a transparent effort to deflect attention away from the fact that the Army of Northern Virginia eventually retreated; however, for Civil War soldiers the ability to avoid being driven from a battlefield carried great psychological weight. As they would do after Gettysburg ten months hence, Lee's veterans took pride in overcoming disadvantages of ground, numbers, and matériel, and in inflicting horrendous casualties on the Federals. Many historians, including myself, have taken Lee to task for remaining on the battlefield at Sharpsburg through September 18 after nearly suffering disaster the previous day. To do so with his back against the river, and with only Boteler's Ford available as a possible route of escape, seemingly placed his army at risk without the potential of any real gain. But testimony from soldiers proud of holding the field in the face of a powerful enemy suggests that Lee might have known better than his critics in this instance.[37]

Five witnesses convey the tenor of innumerable Confederate reactions to the battle. "The fight Raged all day with great fury," wrote a private in the 13th Mississippi Infantry. "It was indeed a frighfull scene and looked as if we would be completely annihilated but we drove them back with great loss." This man admitted a heavy Confederate butcher's bill, but insisted it was "not[h]ing to compare with that of the enemy" and proudly stated that "We Slept on the Battle field last nigh[t]." An officer on Stonewall Jackson's staff told his uncle that at Sharpsburg "the greatest battle of this war was fought, at least the longest— We repulsed the enemy with heavy loss & he was too crippled to renew the attack the next day, tho we waited & invited him to do so." Sgt. Daniel Lane of the 2nd North Carolina Infantry survived the maelstrom of the Bloody Lane, confiding to his diary that night, "It was surely a hot day with us. . . . Our loss was heavy in wounded & near half of the company is missing. Our troops held part of the battle field at night & the enemy held a portion of it." On the 18th, Lane recorded that the Confederates "held their position all day"; the nonaggressive Federals, he guessed, "were satisfied with what they got yesterday."

A member of the 56th Virginia—who considered Sharpsburg "the grandest battle of the war, or indeed that was ever fought"—captured the ebb and flow of the fighting: "Sometimes the enemy drove us, and sometimes we drove the enemy. He made a desperate effort to dislodge us from our position, *but failed most signally.* Some of us count it a drawn battle. Others claim it as a great victory." After mentioning that Lee held the field for "a whole day" after the battle, this soldier strove for a literary touch in addressing casualties. "The loss of the enemy is immense," he noted. "His dead are scattered in the Antietam valley about as 'thick as leaves in Vallambrosa.'" A South Carolina enlisted man looked back to the Seven Days for a point of comparison. "We were in the hottest part of the fight under Jackson," wrote Taliaferro N. Simpson, "and for me to give an idea of the fierceness of the conflict, the roar of musketry, and the thunder of artillery is as utterly impossible as to describe a thousand storms in the region of Hades. The Malvern Hill fight was a circumstance." Although Federals "fought better than they ever did before," the Confederates repulsed every attack and pushed the enemy back on both flanks.[38]

Powerful Union artillery dominated several sectors of the battlefield at Sharpsburg, leading southern gunners to term the contest an "artillery hell" and prompting frequent comments in letters and diaries. Two Georgians in infantry regiments dwelled on the fact that the Federal long arm had occupied advantageous ground. "Their artillery was placed where we could not charge it, and it was used with terrible effect," Theodore Fogle of the 2nd Georgia explained to his parents; when Union guns could not sweep the field, however, "we just used up their infantry wherever it met us." The singularly named Lt. Ujanirtus Allen of the 21st Georgia Infantry echoed Fogle's thoughts and language. "The enemy had the best position in the last fight and made an artillery fight of it," he wrote. "He had some heavy batteries which controlled the right of the field. They were on the side of the mountain and we could do nothing with them." An artillerist made essentially the same points in a letter to the *Richmond Weekly Dispatch*. "But for the disposition of the enemy's artillery," he claimed, "I am satisfied we would have whipped him. . . . It was almost impossible to charge batteries posted upon such high hills." This gunner also fulminated about the "almost worthless" southern artillery ammunition. "The shells and spherical case," he said, "generally don't explode at all." Another gunner suggested that Lee retreated across the river "partly on account of batteries, which the enemy were erecting on the mountain (running perpendicular to our right flank) which would have swept the rear of our army." [39]

Although nearly all of Lee's soldiers took pride in not being driven from the field, they differed in assessing the consequences of the withdrawal to the south bank of the Potomac. Some were openly chastened by the retreat. Brig. Gen. Roswell S. Ripley, who had been wounded leading his brigade on the morning of the 17th, confided to P. G. T. Beauregard that he feared "we have lost in the moral effect on the north by our being obliged by circumstances to evacuate Maryland." A Georgia captain who judged the fighting at Sharpsburg a draw also was pessimistic about its aftermath: "I fear this Md. trip has rather injured us more than good done. Wee lost more than wee gained in it, I think." A gunner in the Fluvanna Artillery listed a number of positive aspects of the campaign, including the capture of Harpers Ferry and heavy Union losses at Sharpsburg, yet seemed thrown off balance by the retreat. Combat on the 17th "resulted unexpectedly to me and inauspiciously for the early ending of the war, in the withdrawing of our army from Maryland and, consequently a triumph for the enemy or rather an apparent triumph." [40]

A larger number of Confederates treated the recrossing of the river as no more than the last phase of a largely successful campaign. Lt. John Hampden Chamberlayne of the Purcell Artillery cataloged the bright spots of the operation—including Harpers Ferry, the slaughter of Yankees at Sharpsburg, and the rearguard action at Shepherdstown—before cautioning his sister: "Don't begin to suppose we were driven out of Maryland: no such thing; our campaign is almost unexampled for quickness & completeness of success. We have done much more than a sane man could expect." In an account published shortly after the end of the campaign, Chaplain Nicholas Davis of the Texas Brigade marshaled the same evidence as Chamberlayne to support his conclusion that Lee had carried out a "brilliant campaign of twelve days across the Potomac." A private in the 21st Georgia Infantry wasted no words in making the point that the army's hard work had changed the strategic picture in the Eastern Theater for the better: "Most all the Yankees is whiped out of Virginia," stated Edward Jones. "Went over in [Maryland] and had one fight and then we retreated back into Virginia." Another believer in brevity, James E. Keever of the 34th North Carolina Infantry, summed up action since the Seven Days in six short sentences: "We have been in ten battles and marched over one thousand miles. The first battle was at Cedar Run. The second at Manassas Junction, also three hard fightings on Bulls Run where the big fight was last year. The sixth battle was at Ox Hill, the seventh at Harpers Ferry and the eight in Marriland. We whip the enemy and drove them back every time with great slotter. Our loss was not half as many as the enemy." His tolerance for campaign narrative exhausted, Keever abruptly announced, "I will now quit the fighting subject and tell you of the crops." [41]

Walter Taylor of Lee's staff also considered the campaign an overall success. "I suppose it will be generally concluded that our march through—or rather into—Maryland & back was decidedly meteoric," he wrote while the army was near Martinsburg. "It was however by no means without happy results." The taking of Harpers Ferry alone "was sufficiently important to compensate for all the trouble experienced"; moreover, the fight at Sharpsburg left the enemy too battered to maintain the offensive and "taught us the value of our men, who can even when weary with constant marching & fighting & when on short rations, contend with and resist three times their own number." Taylor did not claim a victory on the 17th, but "if either had the advantage, it certainly was with us." With some badly needed rest and reinforcements, the army would be ready to fight again and "with God's help we will again be victorious." [42]

Doubts about the long-term influence of military events plagued some of the soldiers who proudly tallied an unbroken string of victories since the Seven Days. Elisha Franklin Paxton, Ujanirtus Allen, and Benjamin Franklin Jones expressed opinions typical of this group. Paxton saw operations between June and mid-September as one huge campaign that would go down in history as "the most astonishing expeditions of war, for the severity of the battles fought and the hardships endured by our soldiers." Should McClellan advance against Lee again, Paxton projected "a splendid victory for us." "Our victories, though, seem to settle nothing," he went on, "to bring us no nearer the end of the war. It is only so many killed and wounded, leaving the work of blood to go on with renewed vigor." Shortly after the army reached safety in Virginia, Lieutenant Allen assured his wife that the "anemy had been too roughly handled" to strike again at the Confederates. But he foresaw no early end to fighting: "We defeat them again and again but like the hordes of Goths and Vandals that laid waste to South Europe; still they come.... Our regiment has been under fire about twenty times and is not much larger than a company now." Jones had decided by late fall 1862 that the Confederacy would need assistance to vanquish the North. "I think that some other Nation will have it to settle this winter though we whip them every fight we get into," he observed, "but there is so many of them that it looks like that they are ready for another fight rite off." [43]

Soldiers who held various opinions about the retreat agreed that the army had not been able to bring off all the wounded from Sharpsburg. Just as holding ground carried immense psychological weight, so also did protecting disabled comrades. To their credit, Confederates forthrightly admitted their failure in this regard—though often in tandem with assurances that the army had exhibited valor at Sharpsburg. "[W]ee crost back on the virginia side of the potomac last fridy nite," wrote South Carolinian S. M. Crawford; "our forses faught the yankeys manful but wee had to leave some of our friends in Maryland." Jesse Steed McGee of the 7th South Carolina Infantry mirrored Crawford in substance (if not in facility at spelling): "We remained on the field untill the next night after the fight when we fell back across the River leaving behind several of our dead [and] wounded among the rest." Walter Battle of the 4th North Carolina Infantry, who had helped treat wounded men during the battle, probably found it especially difficult to leave some of them behind. "Many were wounded and left on the battlefield," he informed his mother, "and had to be left in the hands of the Yankees when we fell back this side of the Potomac." Another participant, whose account was published later in the war, described the retreat as "slow, orderly, and unmolested." But it could not be denied "that large numbers of dead and wounded were left behind to the tender mercies of the foe."[44]

Nor did anyone in the army deny that straggling on an immense scale bedeviled Lee in Maryland. From generals down through soldiers in the ranks, Confederates wrote about the extent of the problem, its impact on the battlefield, and the need to correct it. As in the civilian sphere, some veterans expressed empathy for men whose physical condition prevented their keeping up with Lee's fast-moving force. Others considered the stragglers unpatriotic slackers who willfully shirked their duty, calling for harsh penalties that would send a message to anyone who contemplated falling out of the ranks.

The physical condition of the army explained much of the straggling. Because evidence of this phenomenon is abundant and frequently cited, a few examples will suggest the degree to which Lee's men, many of whom were poorly fed and insufficiently clothed and shod, had been driven to the verge of collapse. As the army marched through Maryland, a member of the 15th Georgia Infantry observed "that a great many of our soldiers were barefoot." This man "had on a pair of shoes one No. 5 and the other No. 10," but neither he nor anyone else in the regiment had changed their clothes for the past forty-five days. "The men are very much exhausted and need rest imperatively," wrote a diarist in the 35th North Carolina Infantry shortly after Sharpsburg. A march the previous day from Martinsburg to Shepherdstown and back had left them "completely exhausted." On September 22, a Mississippian sketched a pathetic picture: "Our army is very much wornout and that is not all, it is almost starved out. Our Rations has been Beef and flour since we left Richmond and not more than half enough of that. Many times we have had Green Corn and apples issued to us and were glad to get that." A man in the 8th Georgia Infantry reported only ten men in his company on September 23. Several of those present lacked shoes, and "8 others are at Winchester with no prospect of getting any." If ordered to march, the men would "suffer terrible." In late September, a pair of privates in Georgia regiments provided tellingly terse comments. "The Army is in poor condition, half naked and barefooted," said one in the 4th Georgia Infantry. "My own clothes and shoes are in pieces and there is no chance of getting them replaced." The second man used only eight words to make his point: "Times is hard hear. Provision is scarce hear." [45]

Some soldiers tried to find something hopeful in their raggedness and hunger. Members of the 47th Alabama Infantry, for example, interpreted the extreme shortage of shoes and clothing as a sign that the war was about to end. "[T]he oficer has made out requicition for close for us," stated James P. Crowder, "tho we hav never got any yet and I dont think that we will ever get any. that is the reason why we think peace will bea made thay are not a fixing for winter." After detailing how dirty and hungry he and his comrades in the 53rd Georgia Infantry had been, William Stillwell sounded a positive note: "[A]fter summing up the whole matter, I think our independence ought to be worth a great deal, for it cost enough. But, thank God, men fighting on corn and baked apples was never subdued and never will be." [46]

Everyone understood that factors other than fatigue and material deprivation had contributed to the straggling. Thousands of men had left the ranks because they chose not to cross the Potomac, or simply because they had seen enough campaigning.[47] The absence of such men infuriated many of those who had risked their lives on the seemingly endless day of combat at Sharpsburg. A soldier wounded on the 17th vented feelings certainly shared by many others in calling for stringent measures to end straggling. "It is truly disgraceful to see the number of stragglers after a battle has been fought or even while it is raging furiously, and the day still doubtful," he wrote to the *Richmond Enquirer*, "while hundreds of both officers and privates would be startled and made to blush, could they see the long list of this class." Brig. Gen. William Dorsey Pender attacked stragglers even more stridently, calling them the most "filthy unprincipled set of villains" he had ever seen. "The officers are nearly as bad as the men," Pender insisted. "In one of my Regts. the other day when they thought they were going to get into a fight, six out [of] ten officers skulked out and did not come up until they thought all danger over." Half the brigade left ranks the same day. "Oh dear, oh dear, our army is coming to a pretty pass," concluded the shaken young brigadier. Capt. Alexander Cheves Haskell of Brig. Gen. Maxcy Gregg's staff chose less volatile language to make essentially the same point: "Our Army is small, but fights gloriously. . . . Great numbers of men have straggled off, until none but heroes are left." [48]

Many of Haskell's "heroes" could imagine a different outcome at Sharpsburg had stragglers shouldered their muskets on the firing lines. Sgt. Sanford W. Branch of the 8th Georgia Infantry described the Army of the Potomac as "too badly crippled to renew the contest" on the 18th. The Confederates were equally fought out, but "[i]f we had of had our 30 thousand stragglers engaged we would of been in Baltimore by this time." Two soldiers invoked higher authority on this topic. "General Lee said we would have routed the enemy at Sharpsburg, Maryland, if it had not been that our army straggled so," commented an artillerist. "I think there was about 20,000 of our army that straggled off and were not in the fight." A lieutenant from Georgia expressed the same idea: "Genl Lee says if evrybody else had fought like we did it would have been a great victory. He also says we had them whiped if our reinforcements had come time enough." A North Carolinian probably had stragglers in mind when he claimed, "If we had only been supported by the rest of our troops we would have carried the day before us for we broke their lines completely." [49]

The army remained in the lower Shenandoah Valley through the weeks following Sharpsburg, welcoming back thousands of stragglers and recovering wounded. During that period, a pervasive sentiment favored continued rest and refitting before reengaging the enemy. In early October, a Georgia private confessed ignorance about what lay ahead, but he avowed that for the present "one thing sure we need rest verry bad we have been going ever since we have been in Va sure and fought as hard as any body." Thomas J. Goree, who served on James Longstreet's staff, commented shortly thereafter that the soldiers were "enjoying the rest and quiet so much needed." With supplies of shoes and clothing arriving daily, Goree thought the army would "soon be in better fighting condition than at any time since the battles around Richmond." By mid-October, a second lieutenant in the 49th Georgia Infantry could enter an optimistic passage in his diary: "We have had a long rest, and the army has greatly increased both in numbers & health." Writing a week later, Reuben A. Pierson of the 9th Louisiana Infantry offered an even more upbeat assessment. "Our troops have been stationed in camp about five weeks resting and recruiting," he stated. "They are now as jovial as a set of college students and are in remarkable good health." [50]

Unlike comrades who welcomed a respite from campaigning, a significant minority of Confederates probably preferred a return to the strategic offensive. At Stonewall Jackson's headquarters, where aggressive thinking almost always held sway, staff officer Sandie Pendleton calculated on October 8 that 25,000 men had returned to the army. He hoped this enlarged force could "fight McClellan's army about Sharpsburg again," projecting not only a result "very different from that of the battle of September 17" but also rejuvenation of the army. "We have been idle now for more than three weeks, and our generals are not given to inaction," he opined with considerable understatement. "Activity and motion have gotten to be a necessity for us, as giving some food to the mind." An officer in the 5th South Carolina Infantry also deplored the army's inactivity in the region around Winchester. He found that a "state of idleness after having been so actively employed is very trying . . . soldiers and all would hail an order to march with tokens of delight." [51]

Virtually no one in the Army of Northern Virginia would have supported another campaign designed to liberate Maryland. Two uncomfortable weeks in that state had soured the soldiers, who, like the four men quoted below, took every opportunity to inveigh against its residents. Walter Taylor remarked about Marylanders who practiced the "disreputable & unmannerly habit of shooting at Confed. soldiers from windows." "Don't let any of your friends sing 'My Maryland,'" Taylor scribbled at the top of a letter to his sister, "not 'my Westn' Md anyhow." In response to a query from his brother about how he liked Maryland, Georgia infantryman William R. Montgomery responded, "Well it is the prettiest country I ever saw, but as for enjoyment I don't want to go any more & I think we had better let (Md) alone for she seems joined to her Idols ('Union')." A South Carolinian agreed with Montgomery's view, hoping that whatever movement lay ahead would not be "to Maryland for we are all tired of Maryland there are too many Unionist there for us, . . . the majority I think is against us." A Georgian evinced even less charitable feelings in a letter to the editor of a newspaper in Macon: "We do not like the idea of crossing the Potomac again, unless they allow us to pillage and inflict some retribution for the outrages of Federals in Virginia." [52]

No element of the Maryland campaign exceeded in importance its role in strengthening the bond between Lee and the men in his army. When he stepped into Joseph E. Johnston's place after Seven Pines, Lee had inspired mixed reactions among his soldiers. Some considered him too cautious, and others certainly saw him as a temporary stand-in until Johnston recovered from his wounds.[53] Between June and October 1862, Lee went a long way toward making the army his own, winning the trust and admiration of soldiers who rapidly came to expect dramatic movements and victories from their chief. Although Stonewall Jackson remained the Confederacy's preeminent military idol, Lee stepped firmly onto center stage as the fledgling nation's premier field commander. The troops saw Lee as the grand designer, Jackson as the brilliant lieutenant who executed his superior's plans. This is not to say that everyone in the army cast only rapturous looks toward army headquarters. Testimony about Lee from men who had straggled or deserted is hard to find, but by the end of September thousands of soldiers undoubtedly had cursed him for pressing them unmercifully on the march and in battle. The army's hemorrhaging in Maryland underscored the inability or unwillingness of as many as a third of the army to meet Lee's high standard of performance. By the end of the quiet period following Sharpsburg, however, most of the troops who had reflected on their accomplishments since the previous June looked to Lee as one whose intellect and daring would yield many future triumphs.

Statements from four soldiers underscore how far Lee had gone toward achieving his later stature as the Confederacy's primary national hero. Just after the army crossed the Potomac, one man wrote, "We have confidence in Genl. Lee in directing our operations, confident of the justness of our cause." An officer in the 3rd Georgia Infantry remarked that at Sharpsburg "Gen. Lee, as usual, displayed his splendid military talents in a great degree, and in his retreat across the Potomac completely foiled the Federal commander." "The army almost worship him," stated this Georgian, "and believe that with Lee, Jackson, and Longstreet at the head, nothing is impossible." Theodore Fogle, another Georgian, said roughly the same thing in fewer words: "I have every confidence in our generals and am perfectly willing to trust our cause and safety in their hands." Artillerist Ham Chamberlayne went much further, fixing Lee at the center of the Confederacy's war. "With Lee for our great archer," he wrote metaphorically, "though string after string be frayed and broken, and the bow, the nation itself, be bent & weakened, yet arrow after arrow goes home to the mark and the prize is won at last." Whenever Chamberlayne happened to see Lee, or even to think about him, "there looms up to me some king-of-men, superior by the head, a Gigantic figure, on whom rests the world."[54]

Unlike soldiers such as Chamberlayne, William Dorsey Pender and William Nelson Pendleton resisted lavishing unqualified praise on Lee. Enthusiastic as the Army of Northern Virginia camped at Frederick during the first week in September, Pender gushed that "Gen. Lee has shown great Generalship and the greatest boldness. There never was such a campaign, not even by Napoleon." Yet the wretched physical state of the army alarmed Pender, who argued that "Jackson would kill up any army the way he marches and the bad management in the subsistence Dept.—Gen. Lee is my man." Sharpsburg and the retreat to Shepherdstown dramatically influenced the North Carolina brigadier. He decided that the incursion into Maryland had been a mistake and objected when Lee elected to keep the army close to the Potomac River. "I had supposed we would have left here before this," he wrote from near Bunker Hill, "but strategy or Gen. Lee's great dislike to give up Md. prolongs our stay beyond what looks to us inferiors as useless." Also frustrated because he had no idea where the army would move next, Pender directed another gibe at Lee: "If the keeping of our own counsel goes to constitute a general, Lee possesses that to perfection."

Artillery chief Pendleton, who nearly had lost all of the army's reserve guns at Shepherdstown on September 19, chose to criticize Lee obliquely. He favored falling back from the Potomac, both to shorten the army's "immensely long line of communication" and because he believed the men "did not fight as well in Md as in Va." An implicit sigh of resignation accompanied Pendleton's next pair of sentences, which anticipated that Lee would remain along the Potomac: "Still wiser heads must determine that. I am willing as the old bishop said to 'defend Rome under the walls of Carthage.' "[55]

Closely related to the growing faith in Lee was a sense that the Army of Northern Virginia might carry an increasing share of the burden of winning Confederate nationhood. Bad news from Mississippi, Kentucky, and elsewhere west of the Appalachians engendered low expectations for southern forces in the Western Theater, a fact illustrated by three letters written on October 13, 1862. "I understand that General Brag got whipt in the west," commented James W. Lineberger of the 49th North Carolina Infantry, "but I dont think that we will be whipt on this side soon. . . . [I]f the yanks comes over they will knot find it sharpsberge in mariland for our boys is rested and is ancious for a fite again." Georgian Shepherd G. Pryor, who had called Sharpsburg a drawn battle and believed that if

McClellan pursued Lee "wee can whip them back again," rendered a gloomy verdict about Bragg's efforts. "I think the news of our army in the West is rather unfavorable," he stated. "The last fight, weev been whiped pretty badly. I hope the next news from there is more favorable."

Ham Chamberlayne alluded to reports from the West as "grave certainly, but, after all, such as might at any time be possible, such as we must always be ready for." Chamberlayne condescendingly suggested that the western news affected the common soldiers but little because "they never know the full bearings of such a thing." As for Lee's officers, they "seem to feel the news as they should do, that is it makes them cease idle dreams of furloughs or of peace, but I have yet to see any who are so unreasonable as to despond over it." [56]

As people across the Confederacy sought to understand what had happened in Maryland, Robert E. Lee revealed his own thoughts about the campaign in a series of letters to Jefferson Davis and others. Lee had marched north in an effort to maintain the strategic initiative gained during the period from the Seven Days through Second Manassas, as well as to push the military frontier even farther from the Virginia heartland on which his army relied for food and fodder. He hoped to maneuver in Maryland or southern Pennsylvania through the autumn, provisioning his men and animals and forestalling another Federal offensive against Richmond in 1862. He also joined Jefferson Davis in believing his army's presence might inspire Marylanders to rise in support of the Confederacy. Although Lee understood before leaving Virginia that his army lacked "much of the material of war," was "feeble in transportation," and contained thousands of men "poorly provided with clothing, and . . . destitute of shoes," he thought invasion his best option.[57]

The truncated stay north of the Potomac satisfied some of Lee's goals but left him frustrated about others. On the positive side, he had pulled the Army of the Potomac out of Virginia and, in the fighting at Sharpsburg, rendered it immobile for several weeks. On October 11, Lee informed Secretary of War Randolph that "Whatever may be General McClellan's ultimate intentions, I see no evidence as yet of any advance upon Richmond; and, notwithstanding the assertions in the Northern papers, I think this army is not yet sufficiently recuperated from its campaign in Maryland to make a vigorous forward move." While McClellan sat in the vicinity of Sharpsburg, Lee's men consumed provisions in the lower Shenandoah Valley that otherwise would be lost to the Federals. "If the enemy can be detained in our front for some weeks," predicted Lee, "it will give them but little time before winter to operate south of the Potomac." In the meantime, reinforcements were arriving from Richmond, and stragglers and the wounded returning to their units. On October 8, Secretary Randolph cheerfully noted "an increase of 20,000 men in eight days" and, citing returns from September 30, remarked that the army's "strength cannot now be much short of its standard when you left Richmond."[58]

Whatever the condition and intentions of the Federal army, Lee knew that the Army of Northern Virginia suffered from serious problems. Lack of supplies remained vexing, and he repeatedly pressed officials in Richmond to forward additional shoes, clothing, and other material as soon as possible.[59] Even more alarming was the continued absence of thousands of stragglers and deserters. The loss of so much manpower had helped convince Lee to retreat to Shepherdstown. During the first few days back in Virginia, he bluntly acknowledged the scope of the problem. He described the army on September 21 as "greatly paralyzed by the loss to its ranks of the numerous stragglers." Although he had "taken every means in my power from the beginning to correct this evil," it had grown worse since the army returned to Virginia. Lee ordered Jackson and Longstreet to see that their officers made "greater efforts . . . to correct this growing evil," and he suggested to Secretary Randolph that Congress give the president or the War Department authority to "degrade . . . from their positions" all officers found guilty of exhibiting "bad conduct in the presence of the enemy, leaving their posts in time of battle, and deserting their command or the army in the march or in camp." An unacceptable level of plundering accompanied the problem of absenteeism, casting into sharper relief the army's uncertain discipline.[60]

Maryland's reaction to the Confederate invasion also disappointed Lee. On September 8, he had issued a proclamation to its people announcing that the Army of Northern Virginia came among them "to assist you with the power of its arms in regaining the rights of which you have been despoiled. . . . This army will respect your choice whatever it may be, and while the Southern people will rejoice to welcome you to your natural position among them, they will only welcome you when you come of your own free will." Maryland's choice soon became all too clear. In terms of both gathering provisions and attracting recruits, the operation had to be reckoned a failure. "I regret that the stay of the army in Maryland was so short as to prevent our receiving the aid I had expected from that state," Lee told the secretary of war in late September. Summoning a measure of forced optimism, he went on to say that "Some few recruits joined us, and others are finding their way across the river to our lines." In a similar vein, Lee speculated that Lincoln's recent actions had suppressed civil liberty in Maryland to the degree that conservative Marylanders, "unless dead to the feelings of liberty, will rise and depose the party now in power." [61]

Lee's greatest disappointment stemmed from having to abandon the strategic initiative to McClellan. He had wished to operate in Maryland for several weeks, forcing the Federals to react to his movements, spreading fear and doubt through the northern government, and choosing the place and time to bring his opponent to battle. He might forage successfully after Sharpsburg from his position south of the Potomac, but he had taken a step backward toward the time when McClellan set the strategic agenda in the weeks leading up to the Seven Days.

No period of the war better illustrates Lee's pronounced preference to be the aggressor than the month following the retreat from Sharpsburg. Outnumbered, plagued by absenteeism, and severely short of supplies, he nevertheless chafed to regain the initiative. In a message to Jefferson Davis written on September 21 from the Confederate encampment on Opequon Creek, he expressed his continuing "desire to threaten a passage into Maryland, to occupy the enemy on this frontier, and, if my purpose cannot be accomplished, to draw them into the Valley, where I can attack them to advantage." Two days later, in language that told how grudgingly he had relinquished the offensive, Lee informed Davis that he retired from Maryland only because losses at Sharpsburg and the absence of deserters and stragglers had left him "unable to cope with advantage with the numerous host of the enemy." On the 25th, Lee wrote again to Davis, revealing that his intention at the time of the retreat had been "to recross the Potomac at Williamsport, and move upon Hagerstown." The army's condition had prevented such a movement, but Lee still believed that from "a military point of view, the best move . . . the army could make would be to advance upon Hagerstown, and endeavor to defeat the enemy at that point." He would do so immediately even with his "diminished numbers, did the army exhibit its former temper and condition." But morale was such that Lee feared the "hazard would be great and a reverse disastrous."[62]

Lee projected that many of the hard-won fruits of the past ten weeks could slip away if his army simply awaited another Federal offensive. Should Richmond be the object of such a Union advance, the Army of Northern Virginia might find itself on the Rappahannock or, perhaps, even near the battlegrounds of the Seven Days. A letter to Maj. Gen. Gustavus W. Smith, who held a command at Richmond, indicated how precarious Lee considered the strategic situation: "I fear, for want of sufficient force to oppose the large army being collected by General McClellan, the benefits derived from the operations of the campaign will be but temporary." Lee knew that Smith's small force at Richmond was vulnerable. "If I felt sure of its safety," he stated, "I could operate more boldly and advantageously."[63]

In the end, Lee settled for a series of maneuvers in the lower Valley, during which his soldiers destroyed sections of the Baltimore & Ohio Railroad and other lines. Walter Taylor attested to the difficulty with which Lee reconciled himself to the situation. "I believe my Chief was most anxious to recross the Potomac into Maryland," he observed in late September, "but was persuaded by his principal advisers that the condition of the army did not warrant such a move. This is conjecture on my part. I only know of his opinion & *guess* why he did not follow it." Taylor agreed with those who counseled against another lunge northward, believing that "it would have indeed been hazardous to reenter Maryland."[64]

Disappointments aside, Lee had learned that he led an army capable of astonishing feats. Just as the men had developed a deeper trust in him during the campaign from Richmond to Maryland, so too had he formed a high opinion of their bravery and tenacity. He expected no less than a superior performance. "[T]he army has had hard work to perform, long and laborious marches, and large odds to encounter in every conflict," he conceded, "but not greater than were endured by our revolutionary fathers, or than what any army must encounter to be victorious." The men who steadfastly faced the Federals at Sharpsburg, and whose conduct contrasted so strongly with that of the stragglers, met Lee's unforgiving standard: "There are brilliant examples of endurance and valor on the part of those who have had to bear the brunt in the battle and the labor in the field in consequence of this desertion of their comrades."[65]

As the army lay in camps near Winchester in early October, soldiers who had discharged their duty received formal congratulations from Lee. "In reviewing the achievements of the army during the present campaign," read General Orders No. 116, "the commanding general cannot withhold the expression of his admiration of the indomitable courage it has displayed in battle and its cheerful endurance of privation and hardship on the march." Lee tallied the army's many victories, including the Seven Days, Cedar Mountain, Second Manassas, Harpers Ferry, and Shepherdstown. At Sharpsburg they had fought a foe three times their number, repulsed all of his attacks, and during the "whole of the following day . . . stood prepared to resume the conflict on the same ground" before retiring "without molestation across the Potomac." History offered "few examples of greater fortitude and endurance than this army has exhibited." Having fed his men's egos, Lee gave notice that more hard work beckoned. "Much as you have done, much more remains to be accomplished," he warned. "The enemy again threatens with invasion, and to your tried valor and patriotism the country looks with confidence for deliverance and safety. Your past exploits give assurance that this confidence is not misplaced."[66]

Lee did not exaggerate how important his soldiers' activities would be to future Confederate morale. Between June and September 1862, the Army of Northern Virginia had earned spectacular victories that helped cancel the effects of defeats in other theaters. The retreat from Maryland, itself counterbalanced by the capture of Harpers Ferry and the tidy success at Shepherdstown, did not detract appreciably from laurels won at Richmond and Second Manassas. Similarly, the bitter contest at Sharpsburg, seen by most Confederates as a bloody drawn battle, confirmed the gallantry of Lee's soldiers. In the space of less than three months, the Confederate people had come to expect good news from the Army of Northern Virginia, investing ever more emotional capital in its leaders and soldiers. That investment led to a belief in possible victory that would be as important as any other factor in lengthening the life of the Confederacy.

NOTES

1. Jedediah Hotchkiss, *Make Me a Map of the Valley: The Civil War Journal of Stonewall Jackson's Topographer*, ed. Archie P. McDonald (Dallas, Tex.: Southern Methodist University Press, 1973), 83–84; Alexander D. Betts,

Experiences of a Confederate Chaplain, 1861–1865, ed. W. A. Betts (190[?];
reprint, [Sanford, N.C.]: n.p., n.d.), 16–17; letter signed "A. B. C.," September 24, 1862, in *Richmond Weekly Dispatch*, September 30, 1862.

2. Clement Eaton, *A History of the Southern Confederacy* (New York: Macmillan, 1954), 193; Robert Selph Henry, *The Story of the Confederacy*, rev. ed. (New York and Indianapolis: Bobbs-Merrill, 1936), 191; Clifford Dowdey, *The Land They Fought For: The Story of the South as the Confederacy, 1832–1865* (Garden City, N.Y.: Doubleday, 1955), 218. In *The Confederacy* (Chicago: University of Chicago Press, 1960), 80–81, Charles P. Roland added Earl Van Dorn's defeat at Corinth and Braxton Bragg's retreat from Kentucky, both in October, to Lee's withdrawal from Maryland to make a similar point about Confederate fortunes in the fall of 1862: "These reverses spread demoralization throughout the South and crippled the prestige of the administration. . . . Many Southerners began to doubt the ability of the Confederacy to win the war."

3. James M. McPherson, *Battle Cry of Freedom: The Civil War Era* (New York: Oxford University Press, 1988), 545; Brooks D. Simpson, *America's Civil War* (Wheeling, Ill.: Harlan Davidson, 1996), 86–87; Charles P. Roland, *An American Iliad: The Story of the Civil War* (Lexington: University Press of Kentucky, 1991), 83.

4. Gary W. Gallagher, "The Maryland Campaign in Perspective," in Gallagher, ed., *Antietam: Essays on the 1862 Maryland Campaign* (Kent, Ohio: Kent State University Press, 1989), 94.

5. The conclusions in this essay rest on testimony from officers and soldiers within Lee's army, government officials, and men and women behind the lines. Material from all major sections of the Confederacy is included, and every effort was made to find witnesses of various economic and social classes. Still, slaveholders are somewhat overrepresented, and the sample would not meet any social-scientific standard.

6. In *The Road to Appomattox* (Memphis, Tenn.: Memphis State College Press, 1956), 60–61, Bell I. Wiley argued that a revival of Confederate spirits in the summer and early fall of 1862 "began to lose force with the coming of winter" and continued downward until reaching a crisis in the summer of 1863. The testimony examined for this essay does not sustain Wiley's conclusions.

7. Edward A. Pollard, *Southern History of the War: The Second Year of the War* (1863; reprint, New York: Charles B. Richardson, 1865), 142–43.

8. *Charleston Mercury*, September 23, 1862; *Charleston Daily Courier*, September 24, 1862; *Richmond Dispatch*, September 23, 1862; *Richmond Enquirer*, September 23, 1862.

9. The *Charleston Mercury* departed from the majority of papers in running a column on September 25 that suggested Lee gambled too much in sending most of his army to capture Harpers Ferry: "With the lights before us, the taking of Harper's Ferry looks like a military mistake—risking a pound to gain a penny. Hill's corps, at Boonsboro' was so exhausted by McClellan's attack in force, that it must have been of little use afterwards. Had we kept our army together we might have sent McClellan back to Washington, and that would have been worth many Harper's Ferries."

10. *Richmond Weekly Dispatch,* September 26, 1862; *Charleston Daily Courier,* October 3, 1862; *(Macon) Georgia Journal & Messenger,* October 8, 1862, reprinting Alexander's piece from the *Savannah Republican.*

11. *Charleston Mercury,* September 23, 1862; *Richmond Dispatch,* September 23, 1862; *Richmond Enquirer,* September 23, 1862.

12. *Richmond Daily Enquirer,* September 24, 1862. See also the *Richmond Dispatch,* September 23, 1862, which argued that "the great object of the operations in Maryland was the capture of the Yankee army of the Valley. That object was triumphantly accomplished."

13. *Charleston Mercury,* September 29, 1862; *Atlanta Southern Confederacy,* October 30, 1862.

14. *Richmond Weekly Dispatch,* September 26, 1862 (piece dated September 22 from near Winchester); *(Macon) Georgia Journal & Messenger,* October 8, 1862, reprinting a piece from the *Savannah Republican; Richmond Dispatch,* September 30, 1862.

15. *Richmond Whig,* October 2, 1862; *Charleston Daily Courier,* October 4, 1862; *Richmond Dispatch,* October 13, 1862.

16. *Charleston Mercury,* October 15, 1862. For other expressions of disappointment at the failure to win Maryland to the Confederate cause, see the *(Macon) Georgia Journal & Messenger,* October 8, 1862, and the *Charleston Daily Courier,* October 4, 1862.

17. *Charleston Daily Courier,* October 4, 1862; *Richmond Whig,* October 2, 1862; *Richmond Enquirer,* October 14, 1862.

18. *Charleston Daily Courier,* October 4, 1862; *Richmond Dispatch,* September 23, 1862; *Richmond Daily Enquirer,* September 24, 1862.

19. *(Macon) Georgia Journal & Messenger,* October 8, 1862, reprinting Alexander's piece from the *Savannah Republican.*

20. Catherine Ann Devereux Edmondston, *"Journal of a Secesh Lady": The Diary of Catherine Ann Devereux Edmondston, 1860–1866,* ed. Beth Gilbert Crabtree and James W. Patton (Raleigh: North Carolina Division of Archives and History, 1979), 261, 267; Edmund Ruffin, *The Diary of Edmund Ruffin,* ed. William Kauffman Scarborough, 3 vols. (Baton Rouge:

Louisiana State University Press, 1972–89), 2:449 (entry for September 23, 1862); Charles C. Jones Jr. to Charles C. Jones, September 27, 1862, in Robert Manson Myers, ed., *The Children of Pride: A True Story of Georgia and the Civil War* (New Haven, Conn.: Yale University Press, 1972), 966–67.

21. Lucy Rebecca Buck, *Shadows on My Heart: The Civil War Diary of Lucy Rebecca Buck of Virginia*, ed. Elizabeth R. Baer (1940; revised reprint, Athens: University of Georgia Press, 1997), 151 (entry for September 19, 1862); Dolly Lunt Burge, *The Diary of Dolly Lunt Burge*, ed. James I. Robertson Jr. (Athens: University of Georgia Press, 1962), 82 (entry for September 29, 1862); Sarah Morgan, *The Civil War Diary of Sarah Morgan*, ed. Charles East (1913; revised reprint, Athens: University of Georgia Press, 1991), 293 (entry for October 4, 1862); Susan Leigh Blackford and Charles Minor Blackford, eds., *Memoirs of Life In and Out of the Army in Virginia during the War between the States*, 2 vols. (1894; reprint, Lynchburg, Va.: Warwick House, 1996), 1:217.

22. Fanny Hume, *The Fanny Hume Diary of 1862: A Year in Wartime Orange, Virginia*, ed. J. Randolph Grymes Jr. (Orange: Orange County Historical Society, 1994), 151 (entry for September 20, 1862); Faye Acton Axford, ed., *"To Lochaber Na Mair": Southerners View the Civil War* (Athens, Ala.: Athens Publishing Company, 1986), 93, Fielding diary entry for September 28, 1862; Amanda Virginia Edmonds, *Journals of Amanda Virginia Edmonds: Lass of the Mosby Confederacy, 1859–1867*, ed. Nancy Chappelear Baird (Stephens City, Va.: by the editor, 1984), 116 (entry for September 16, 1862); Anne S. Frobel, *The Civil War Diary of Anne S. Frobel of Winton Hill in Virginia*, ed. Mary H. Lancaster and Dallas M. Lancaster (Birmingham, Ala.: by the editors, 1986), 70.

23. Betty Herndon Maury, *The Civil War Diary of Betty Herndon Maury (June 3, 1861–February 18, 1863)*, ed. Robert A. Hodge (Fredericksburg, Va.: by the editor, 1985), 69–70; [Judith W. McGuire], *Diary of a Southern Refugee during the War* (1867; reprint, Lincoln: University of Nebraska Press, 1995), 157 (entry for September 25).

24. Elijah P. Petty, *Journey to Pleasant Hill: The Civil War Letters of Captain Elijah P. Petty, Walker's Texas Division, C.S.A.*, ed. Norman D. Brown (San Antonio: Institute of Texas Cultures, 1982), 87; Edwin H. Fay to his wife, September 26, 1862, in Edwin H. Fay, *This Infernal War: The Confederate Letters of Sgt. Edwin H. Fay*, ed. Bell Irvin Wiley (Austin: University of Texas Press, 1958), 162; Benjamin M. Seaton, *The Bugle Softly Blows: The Confederate Diary of Benjamin M. Seaton*, ed. Harold B. Simpson (Waco, Tex.: Texian Press, 1965), 23–24 (entry for September 29, 1862).

25. Blackford and Blackford, eds., *Memoirs of Life In and Out of the Army in Virginia*, 1:218 (William M. Blackford diary, October 14, 1862); John B. Jones, *A Rebel War Clerk's Diary, at the Confederate States Capital,* 2 vols. (1866; reprint, Alexandria, Va.: Time-Life Books, 1982), 1:172 (entry for October 17, 1862).

26. Jane Howison Beale, *The Journal of Jane Howison Beale of Fredericksburg, Virginia, 1850–1862,* ed. Barbara P. Willis (Fredericksburg: Historic Fredericksburg, Inc., 1979), 64 (entry for October 4, 1862); Ada W. Bacot, *A Confederate Nurse: The Diary of Ada W. Bacot, 1860–1863,* ed. Jean V. Berlin (Columbia: University of South Carolina Press, 1994), 149–50 (entry for September 21, 1862); Kate Stone, *Brokenburn: The Journal of Kate Stone, 1861–1868,* ed. John Q. Anderson (Baton Rouge: Louisiana State University Press, 1955), 146 (entry for October 2, 1862). For another example of anti-Maryland sentiment, see Susan Middleton to Harriett Middleton, September 20, 1862, in Isabella Middleton Leland, ed., "Middleton Correspondence, 1861–1865," *South Carolina Historical Magazine* 63 (July 1962): 172.

27. Charles C. Jones to Charles C. Jones Jr., October 2, 1862, in Myers, ed., *Children of Pride,* 972.

28. Benjamin Fleet to Alexander F. Fleet, October 12, 1862, in Betsy Fleet and John D. P. Fuller, eds., *Green Mount: A Virginia Plantation Family during the Civil War, Being the Journal of Benjamin Robert Fleet and Letters to His Family* (Lexington: University of Kentucky Press, 1962), 174; Edmondston, *Journal,* 277 (entry for October 18, 1862); Josiah Gorgas, *The Journals of Josiah Gorgas, 1857–1878,* ed. Sarah Woolfolk Wiggins (Tuscaloosa: University of Alabama Press, 1995), 53–54 (entries for October 4, 17, 1862).

29. Blackford and Blackford, eds., *Memoirs of Life In and Out of the Army,* 1:225 (William M. Blackford diary entry for October 13, 1862); Cornelia Peake McDonald, *A Woman's Civil War: A Diary, with Reminiscences of the War, from March 1862,* ed. Minrose C. Gwin (Madison: University of Wisconsin Press, 1992), 83 (entry for October 14, 1862); Frobel, *Diary,* 73 (entry for September 27, 1862).

30. Jones, *Diary,* 1:157, 161–62 (entries for September 27, October 2, 1862).

31. John W. Stone to Julia A. Wood, September 22, 1862, in Margaret Williams Bayne, ed., *The Wood Family of Fluvanna County, Virginia, 1795–1969* (Norfolk, Va.: privately printed, 1984), 187–88; Jones, *Diary,* 1:164; McDonald, *A Woman's Civil War,* 85.

32. W. C. Corsan, *Two Months in the Confederate States: An Englishman's Travels through the South*, ed. Benjamin H. Trask (Baton Rouge: Louisiana State University Press, 1996), 76–77.

33. Blackford and Blackford, eds., *Memoirs of Life In and Out of the Army*, 1:218, 225, 219 (entries for September 26, October 23, September 30). For a representative comment about Van Dorn's defeat at Corinth, see Susan Emeline Jeffords Caldwell to Lycurgus Washington Caldwell, October 10, 1862, in John K. Gott and John E. Divine, eds., *"My Heart Is So Rebellious": The Caldwell Letters, 1861–1865* (Warrenton, Va.: Fauquier National Bank, [circa 1992]), 157. "[O]f course you read of our defeat at Corinth—I was grieved to hear of it. Oh! that we could have peace to reign once again in our dear land and prosperity abound—the cloud seems to darken again over and around us."

34. Robert Garlick Hill Kean, *Inside the Confederate Government: The Diary of Robert Garlick Hill Kean*, ed. Edward Younger (New York: Oxford University Press, 1957), 86 (entry for June 27, 1863). Kean commented on Davis's post-Sharpsburg state of mind in the context of the president's pessimistic attitude in the early summer of 1863: "Judge [John A.] Campbell told me this morning that a member of the Cabinet and an intimate friend of the President told him that Mr. Davis *despairs* of success in our struggle. . . . He is liable to exultation and depression."

35. G. W. C. Lee to Jefferson Davis, September 25, 1862, in Jefferson Davis, *The Papers of Jefferson Davis*, ed. Lynda Lasswell Crist et al., 10 vols. to date (Baton Rouge: Louisiana State University Press, 1971–), 8:405–6.

36. Jefferson Davis to Robert E. Lee, September 28, 1862, in Davis, *Papers*, 8:408–9. On September 30, 1862, the *Charleston Mercury* leveled the latest in a series of blasts at what it perceived to be the president's overly defensive strategy: "Our readers are aware that, from the commencement of the existing war, we have condemned the inactive defensive policy of the Administration, and have advocated an active aggressive policy in carrying it on. . . . We are rejoiced now to find that the overwhelming majority of the popular branch of Congress approve of the policy we so early advocated, and which exposed us to some unmerited obloquy."

37. For my criticism of Lee's decision to hold the field on the 18th, see Gallagher, "Maryland Campaign in Perspective," 89.

38. John E. Fisher, ed., "The Travels of the 13th Mississippi Regiment: Excerpts from the Diary of Mike M. Hubert of Attala County (1861–1862)," *Journal of Mississippi History* 45 (November 1983): 309 (entries for September 17, 18, 1862); Edward Willis to Uncle, October 4, 1862, drawer 71, box 76 (microfilm), Georgia Department of Archives and History,

Atlanta; Daniel Lane, Diary, typescript provided by Robert E. L. Krick; letter from "Valley" (probably a member of the 56th Virginia Infantry), September 20, 1862, printed in *Richmond Daily Enquirer*, September 25, 1862; Taliaferro N. Simpson to Anna Talullah Simpson, September 24, 1862, in Guy R. Everson and Edward H. Simpson Jr., eds., *Far, Far from Home: The Wartime Letters of Dick and Tally Simpson, 3rd South Carolina Volunteers* (New York: Oxford University Press, 1994), 150. For other similar testimony, see Charles E. Denoon to his father, September 25, 1862, in Charles E. Denoon, *Charlie's Letters: The Civil War Letters of Charles E. Denoon*, ed. Richard T. Couture (Collingswood, N.J.: Civil War Historicals, 1989), 28, and James A. Graham to his father, September 29, 1862, in James A. Graham, *The James A. Graham Papers, 1861–1864*, ed. H. M. Wagstaff (Chapel Hill: University of North Carolina Press, 1928), 132.

39. Mills Lane, ed., *"Dear Mother: Don't grieve about me. If I get killed, I'll only be dead." Letters from Georgia Soldiers in the Civil War* (Savannah, Ga.: Beehive Press, 1977), 190; Ujanirtus Allen to his wife, September 23, 1862, in Ujanirtus Allen, *Campaigning with "Old Stonewall": Confederate Captain Ujanirtus Allen's Letters to His Wife*, ed. Randall Allen and Keith S. Bohannon (Baton Rouge: Louisiana State University Press, 1998), 165; letter from "A. B. C.," September 24, 1862, printed in *Richmond Weekly Dispatch*, September 30, 1862; Greenlee Davidson to his mother, September 19, 1862, in Greenlee Davidson, *Captain Greenlee Davidson, C.S.A.: Diary and Letters, 1851–1863*, ed. Charles W. Turner (Verona, Va.: McClure Press, 1975), 54.

40. Roswell S. Ripley to P. G. T. Beauregard, September 29, 1862, in Ripley's General and Staff Compiled Service Record, M331, roll 212, National Archives, Washington; Shepherd G. Pryor to his wife, September 23, 1862, in Shepherd G. Pryor, *A Post of Honor: The Pryor Letters, 1861–63; Letters from Capt. S. G. Pryor, Twelfth Georgia Regiment and His Wife, Penelope Tyson Pryor*, ed. Charles R. Adams Jr. (Fort Valley, Ga.: Garret Publications, 1989), 262; William B. Pettit to his wife, September 20, 1862, in Charles W. Turner, ed., *Civil War Letters of Arabella Speairs and William Beverly Pettit of Fluvanna County, Virginia, March 1862–March 1865*, 2 vols. (Roanoke, Va.: Virginia Lithography and Graphics, 1988), 1:54–55.

41. John Hampden Chamberlayne to Lucy Parke Chamberlayne, September 22, 1862, in John Hampden Chamberlayne, *Ham Chamberlayne— Virginian: Letters and Papers of an Artillery Officer in the War for Southern Independence, 1861–1865*, ed. C. G. Chamberlayne (Richmond, Va.: Dietz, 1932), 110–12; Nicholas A. Davis, *The Campaign from Texas to Maryland, with the Battle of Fredericksburg* (1863; reprint, Austin, Tex.: Steck Company, 1961), 93; Edward J. Jones to his brother, October 6, 1862, in Georgia

Division of the United Daughters of the Confederacy, *Confederate Reminiscences and Letters, 1861–1865*, 15 vols. to date (Atlanta: Georgia Division of the UDC, 1995–), 5:203; James E. Keever to Alexander Keever, October 2, 1862, in Elsie Keever, ed., *Keever Civil War Letters* (Lincolnton, N.C.: by the editor, 1989), 9.

42. Walter H. Taylor to Mary Louisa Taylor, September 21, 1862, in Walter H. Taylor, *Lee's Adjutant: The Wartime Letters of Colonel Walter H. Taylor, 1862–1865*, ed. R. Lockwood Tower (Columbia: University of South Carolina Press, 1995), 44–45.

43. Elisha F. Paxton to Elizabeth Paxton, October 12, 1862, in Elisha Franklin Paxton, *The Civil War Letters of General Frank "Bull" Paxton, CSA: A Lieutenant of Lee and Jackson*, ed. John Gallatin Paxton (Hillsboro, Tex.: Hill Jr. College Press, 1978), 58; Ujanirtus Allen to Susan Fuller Allen, September 21, 1862, in Allen, *Campaigning with "Old Stonewall,"* 164–65; Benjamin Franklin Jones to W. Sanford Jones, November 1, 1862, in Georgia Division UDC, *Confederate Reminiscences and Letters*, 5:204.

44. S. M. Crawford to his wife, October 22, 1862, in South Carolina Division of the United Daughters of the Confederacy, *Recollections and Reminiscences: 1861–1865 through World War I*, 10 vols. to date (n.p.: South Carolina Division, UDC, 1990–), 2:189; Jesse Steed McGee to My dear Mollie, September 24, 1862, in E. D. Sloan, ed., *McGee-Charles Family Papers (1852–1924)* (Greenville, S.C.: by the editor, [1996]), 58; Walter Battle to his mother, September 29, 1862, in Walter Raleigh Battle, "The Confederate Letters of Walter Raleigh Battle of Wilson, North Carolina," ed. Hugh Buck Johnston (Wilson, N.C.: typescript by the editor, circa 1977), unpaginated (letters arranged chronologically); [An English Combatant], *Battle-Fields of the South, from Bull Run to Fredericksburgh: With Sketches of Confederate Commanders and Gossip of the Camps* (1864; reprint, Alexandria, Va.: Time-Life Books, 1984), 492–93.

45. Tia Atwood, ed., *Prologue: Portrait of a Family* ([Enis, Tex.]: by the editor, 1980[?]), 105; William H. S. Burgwyn, *A Captain's War: The Letters and Diaries of William H. S. Burgwyn, 1861–1865*, ed. Herbert M. Schiller (Shippensburg, Pa.: White Mane, 1994), 20 (entries for September 20, 21, 1862); Fisher, ed., "Travels of the 13th Mississippi," 310; Sanford W. Branch to his mother, September 23, 30, 1862, in Mauriel Phillips Joslyn, ed., *Charlotte's Boys: Civil War Letters of the Branch Family of Savannah* (Berryville, Va.: Rockbridge Publishing Company, 1996), 132–33; Ansel Sterne to Dear Friend, September 28, 1862, in William H. Davidson, ed., *War Was the Place: A Centennial Collection of Confederate Letters* (n.p.: Chattahoochee Valley Historical Society, Bulletin 5 [November 1961]), 73–74; William J. Evers to

his wife, September 30, 1862, in Georgia Division UDC, *Confederate Reminiscences and Letters*, 6:207.

46. James P. Crowder to his mother, October 5, 1862, in Ray Mathis, ed., *In the Land of the Living: Wartime Letters by Confederates from the Chattahoochee Valley of Alabama and Georgia* (Troy, Ala.: Troy State University Press, 1981), 49; William Stillwell to his wife, September 18, 1862, in Lane, ed., *Dear Mother*, 185.

47. Daniel Harvey Hill, whose division defended the Sunken Road at Antietam, later wrote about the "demoralized condition of the army" during the Maryland campaign. "No one not with our Army at that time & not cognizant of its deplorable condition," he stated in a revealing letter to Robert Lewis Dabney on July 19, 1864, could understand how vulnerable Lee's force had been in mid-September. (The letter is in the Robert Lewis Dabney Papers, Special Collections, Union Theological Seminary, Richmond, Va.)

48. Letter from "A Private," September 20, 1862, printed in *Richmond Enquirer*, October 14, 1862; William Dorsey Pender to Fanny Pender, September 19, 1862, in William Dorsey Pender, *The General to His Lady: The Civil War Letters of William Dorsey Pender to Fanny Pender*, ed. William W. Hassler (Chapel Hill: University of North Carolina Press, 1965), 175; Alexander Cheves Haskell to his parents, September 23, 1862, in Louise Haskell Daly, ed., *Alexander Cheves Haskell: The Portrait of a Man* (1934; reprint, Wilmington, N.C.: Broadfoot, 1989), 84.

49. Sanford W. Branch to his mother, September 30, 1862, in Joslyn, ed., *Charlotte's Boys*, 133; Edgar Richardson to his mother, October 1, 1862, in Lane, ed., *Dear Mother*, 192; Ujanirtus Allen to Susan Fuller Allen, in Allen, *Campaigning with "Old Stonewall,"* 165; James A. Graham to his mother, September 21, 1862, in Graham, *Papers*, 132.

50. John W. Hodnett to Miss Mary Hodnett, October 1, 1862, in Davidson, ed., *War Was the Place*, 75; Thomas J. Goree to Sarah Williams Kittrell Goree, October 10, 1862, in Thomas J. Goree, *Longstreet's Aide: The Civil War Letters of Major Thomas J. Goree*, ed. Thomas W. Cutrer (Charlottesville: University Press of Virginia, 1995), 99; Draughton Stith Haynes, *The Field Diary of a Confederate Soldier, Draughton Stith Haynes, While Serving with the Army of Northern Virginia C.S.A.*, ed. William G. Haynes Jr. (Darien, Ga.: Ashantilly Press, 1963), 22 (entry for October 18, 1862); Reuben A. Pierson to his father, October 26, 1862, in Thomas W. Cutrer and T. Michael Parrish, eds., *Brothers in Gray: The Civil War Letters of the Pierson Family* (Baton Rouge: Louisiana State University Press, 1997), 130–31.

51. Alexander S. Pendleton to his mother, October 8, 1862, quoted in

William G. Bean, *Stonewall's Man: Sandie Pendleton* (Chapel Hill: University of North Carolina Press, 1959), 81; John William McLure to his wife, October 2, 1862, in Sarah Porter Carroll, ed., *Lifeline to Home for John William McLure, CSA, Union County, S.C.* (Greenville, S.C.: A Press, 1990), 108.

52. Walter H. Taylor to Mary Louisa Taylor, September 21, 1862, in Taylor, *Lee's Adjutant*, 45; William R. Montgomery to his brother, October 4, 1862, in William R. Montgomery, *Georgia Sharpshooter: The Civil War Diary and Letters of William Rhadamanthus Montgomery, 1839–1906*, ed. George Montgomery Jr. (Macon, Ga.: Mercer University Press, 1997), 72; Jesse S. McGee to My dear Mollie, September 24, 1862, in Sloan, ed., *McGee-Charles Family Papers*, 59; Letter from an unidentified officer in the 1st Georgia Regular Infantry, September 23, 1862, printed in *Macon (Ga.) Daily Telegraph*, October 1, 1862.

53. On Lee's reputation in 1862, see Gary W. Gallagher, "The Idol of His Soldiers and the Hope of His Country," in Gallagher, *Lee and His Generals in War and Memory* (Baton Rouge: Louisiana State University Press, 1998). For the argument that many soldiers considered Lee to be a stand-in for Johnston, see William Garrett Piston, "Lee's Tarnished Lieutenant: James Longstreet and His Image in American Society," 2 vols. (Ph.D. diss., University of South Carolina, 1982), 1:175–76.

54. John W. Harrison to his mother, September 9, 1862, Confederate Miscellany, IA, folder 3, Robert Woodruff Library, Emory University, Atlanta, Ga.; Letter signed "G," October 16, 1862, printed in *Athens (Ga.) Southern Banner*, December 3, 1862; Theodore Fogle to his parents, September 28, 1862, in Lane, ed., *Dear Mother*, 190; John Hampden Chamberlayne to his mother, September 22, 1862, and Chamberlayne to Lucy Parke Chamberlayne, October 13, 1862, in Chamberlayne, *Ham Chamberlayne*, 114, 125–26.

55. William Dorsey Pender to Fanny Pender, September 7, October 24, 1862, in Pender, *General to His Lady*, 173, 185; William Nelson Pendleton to My Darling Wife, September 28, 1862, William Nelson Pendleton Papers, Southern Historical Collection, Wilson Library, University of North Carolina, Chapel Hill. For other criticism of Lee, see Kean, *Inside the Confederate Government*, 91. On August 13, 1863, Kean compared Lee's conduct at Gettysburg with his conduct at Sharpsburg: "The fact stands broadly out that, as at Sharpsburg, the enemy were more vigorous than he calculated and were amongst his troops before he was aware of their near approach."

56. James W. Lineberger to his wife, in James Wellington Lineberger, *Letters of a Gaston Ranger: 2nd Lt. James Wellington Lineberger, Company H,*

49th North Carolina Regiment, Ransom's Brigade, C.S.A., ed. Hugh Douglas Pitts (Richmond, Va.: by the editor, 1991), 23; Shepherd G. Pryor to his wife, in Pryor, Post of Honor, 269; John Hampden Chamberlayne to Lucy Parke Chamberlayne, in Chamberlayne, Ham Chamberlayne, 125.

57. Lee's report of the Sharpsburg campaign, in Robert E. Lee, The Wartime Papers of R. E. Lee, ed. Clifford Dowdey and Louis H. Manarin (Boston: Little, Brown, 1961), 312–13. Dated August 19, 1863, Lee's report succinctly lays out his reasons for invading Maryland. See also William Allan, "Memoranda of Conversations with General Robert E. Lee," in Gary W. Gallagher, ed., Lee the Soldier (Lincoln: University of Nebraska Press, 1996), 13, for Lee's postwar summary of the Sharpsburg campaign.

58. R. E. Lee to George W. Randolph, October 11, 1862, and Randolph to Lee, October 8, 1862, in U.S. War Department, The War of the Rebellion: A Compilation of the Official Records of the Union and Confederate Armies, 127 vols., index, and atlas (Washington: GPO, 1880–1901), ser. 1, vol. 19, pt. 2:662–63, 656–57 (hereafter cited as OR; all references are to ser. 1).

59. For Lee's requests for supplies, see his letters to Jefferson Davis on September 21, to Quartermaster General A. C. Myers on September 21, to Secretary of War George W. Randolph on September 21, to Davis on September 23 and 28, to Randolph on September 29 and 30, and to Davis on September 30, in OR 19(1):142–43, (2):614, 622–23, 633, 637, 643–44.

60. R. E. Lee to Jefferson Davis, September 21, 1862; R. H. Chilton to Generals Longstreet and Jackson, September 22, 1862; Lee to George W. Randolph, September 23, 1862, in OR 19(1):143, (2):618, 622. William Dorsey Pender joined Lee in excoriating soldiers who plundered. He informed his wife on September 19 that his men had "lost all honor or decency, all sense of right or respect for property. I have had to strike many a one with my saber" (Pender, General to His Lady, 175).

61. Lee, Wartime Papers, 299–300 (text of the proclamation); Robert E. Lee to George W. Randolph, September 30, and Lee to Jefferson Davis, October 2, 1862, in OR 19(2):636–37, 644.

62. OR 19(1):142–43, (2):622, 626–27.

63. Robert E. Lee to Gustavus W. Smith, September 24, 1862, in OR 19(2):624–25.

64. Walter H. Taylor to Mary Louisa Taylor, September 28, 1862, in Taylor, Lee's Adjutant, 45–46. For typical descriptions of tearing up railroads, see Ujanirtus Allen to his wife, October 24, 1862, in Allen, Campaigning with "Old Stonewall," 176; Capt. H. W. Wingfield's diary entries for October 18–29, 1862, in W. W. Scott, ed., Two Confederate Items (Rich-

mond: Virginia State Library, 1927), 18; and Joseph Head to Luckie Head, October 29, 1862, in Georgia Division UDC, *Confederate Reminiscences and Letters*, 6:232.

65. Robert E. Lee to Jefferson Davis, September 21, 1862, in *OR* 19(1): 143.

66. General Orders No. 116, dated October 2, 1862, in *OR* 19(2):644–45.

| THE YANKS HAVE |
| HAD A TERRIBLE |
| WHIPPING |
| *Confederates Evaluate the* |
| *Battle of Fredericksburg* |
| |
| |

The literature on Fredericksburg devotes minimal attention to the ways in which Robert E. Lee's soldiers and Confederates elsewhere reacted to the battle. Those works that have addressed the topic, however briefly, typically stress one of two pictures. Perhaps taking their cue from Lee, some writers describe Confederates disappointed with a triumph that inflicted no lasting damage on the Army of the Potomac. The far more common view portrays joy over a victory that turned back another Union advance against Richmond, inflicted hideous casualties on the enemy, rocked northern civilian morale, and set the stage for more juggling within the northern army's high command. Testimony from the six-week period following the battle discloses significant shading between these two extremes. Although far from definitive as a canvass of Confederate responses to the fighting along the Rappahannock in December 1862, this evidence reveals clear patterns. Beyond shedding light on perceptions of Fredericksburg, it also raises questions about Confederate expectations and Lee's apparent inability to look beyond the battle's immediate military consequences—topics pertinent to historians interested in what strategy best suited the South's effort to win independence and the relative significance of offensive and defensive triumphs on the battlefield.[1]

Early Confederate writers tended to question the importance of

Fredericksburg. During the war, Edward A. Pollard, editor of the *Richmond Examiner* and a bitter critic of Jefferson Davis, developed a number of themes in his *Southern History of the War* that would appear in subsequent writings. "At the thrilling tidings of Fredericksburg the hopes of the South rose high that we were at last to realize some important and practical consequences from the prowess of our arms," he noted. Ambrose E. Burnside's battered army cowered along the river, vulnerable to a counterattack that might turn a tactical success into a decisive victory. But hopes lay dashed after news arrived of the Federal withdrawal across the Rappahannock: "It was the old lesson to the South of a barren victory. The story of Fredericksburg was incomplete and unsatisfactory; and there appeared no prospect but that a war waged at awful sacrifices was yet indefinitely to linger in the trail of bloody skirmishes." Lee could claim only "the negative advantage of having checked the enemy without destroying him, and the vulgar glory of our having killed and wounded several thousand men more than we had lost."[2]

Three years later, Pollard reiterated these points in his widely quoted *The Lost Cause*. He emphasized Burnside's "appalling extremity" after the repulse of his assaults on December 13, a soaring belief in Richmond that final victory was at hand, northern fears of "the same result," and cruel disappointment at "the astounding news" of Burnside's escape. "Various excuses have been made for Gen. Lee's omission to assume the offensive, and realize the proper result of his victory at Fredericksburg," stated Pollard. "These excuses have mostly originated in the generosity of friends and admirers." Lee himself admitted his error in supposing the Federals would resume their attacks on December 14–15 and maintaining his admirable defensive position rather than taking the offensive.[3]

Two accounts published in 1867 affirmed Pollard's assessment. In her narrative of life in wartime Richmond, Sallie Putnam employed very similar language. "Victory once more perched on the banner of the Confederates," she maintained, "and the utter rout of the army of Burnside was only prevented, perhaps, by the failure on the part of the 'rebels' to attack his forces on the next day, while they remained at Fredericksburg." Because the Federals managed to get across the Rappahannock without molestation, the Confederates "repeated the old story of a barren victory. A powerful check had been given to the enemy, but no more than a check." William P. Snow's collection of Confederate military biographies similarly stressed the absence of substantive gain. "Thus ended another terrific battle," he wrote, "wherein immense slaughter occurred, and no positive advantage was gained to either side." Although skeptical of the results, Snow displayed empathy for Lee. Observers outside the Army of Northern Virginia believed the Confederate chief had fumbled a Cannae-type opportunity to annihilate Burnside, but Snow insisted "they little knew the almost utter impossibility of such a task on either side."[4]

Near the end of the nineteenth century, Thomas C. DeLeon's analysis in *Four Years in Rebel Capitals* conformed closely to that of previous southern critics of the results at Fredericksburg. First reports of the fighting encouraged the notion that "this time *surely* the enemy would be pushed—this time he was indeed a prey! Broken and demoralized, with a deep river in his rear that he *must cross in pontoons*, the people felt that he could surely be destroyed before reaching his Stafford stronghold." But two days of grace allowed Burnside to extricate his "shattered and broken legions." "Great was the amaze, bitter the disappointment of the people," recalled DeLeon, "and the inquiry how and why this had been done, became universal." By 1890, when *Four Years in Rebel Capitals* appeared, few southern writers dared criticize Lee overtly, and DeLeon, undoubtedly aware of his critique's implications, added that Confederates "above every other feeling had now come to cherish a perfect and unquestioning faith in General Lee; and even while they wondered at a policy that invariably left a beaten army to recover, and only become stronger— still they questioned with a firm reliance that there *must* be some reason, invisible to them but good and potent still."[5]

Modern scholars have advanced equally negative conclusions about the impact of Fredericksburg. Douglas Southall Freeman accented Lee's unhappiness with the outcome. "He was deeply depressed that he had not been able to strike a decisive blow," observed the general's most famous biographer. Moreover, added Freeman, the "army and the country shared his chagrin."[6] Clifford Dowdey, Freeman's successor as the premier Virginia interpreter of the Army of Northern Virginia, conceded positive Confederate civilian reaction while averring that, from a southern perspective, the "battle had been glorious during its action but . . . nothing had been accomplished." Dowdey concluded that "Militarily the battle had no effect on the war." In his history of the Confederacy, Clement Eaton bluntly stated that Lee "lost a magnificent opportunity to counterattack the Federal army with the river at its back." Northern artillery along

Stafford Heights might have inflicted significant casualties, but "the Confederates could have come so close to them that the Federal guns would have been dangerous to their own troops." Eaton depended heavily on the prominent British military analyst J. F. C. Fuller, who claimed that in failing to counterattack Lee lost nothing less than "his one and only opportunity for ending the war."[7]

Although unfavorable appraisals of Confederate accomplishments at Fredericksburg have persisted for more than a century, they stand as counterpoint to the dominant interpretation of the battle as a major victory. Some works of the latter type err on the side of hyperbole: "The news from Fredericksburg was greeted with jubilation throughout the South," commented the author of a popular treatment of Fredericksburg. Ignoring Lee's well-known misgivings about the battle, this narrative quoted a correspondent for the *Charleston Mercury* who mistakenly described the general as "jubilant, almost off balance, and seemingly desirous of embracing everyone who calls on him." In a more reasoned discussion, Frank E. Vandiver suggested the Confederates "almost wrecked the reconstituted Army of the Potomac at Fredericksburg. . . . Costs to Lee were comparatively light and the fruits of victory were important: the Virginia front was stable once again."[8]

Several of the best general histories of the war highlight the disproportionate Union casualties and the firestorm of debate across the North after the battle, passing over Confederate reaction in silence. In *Battle Cry of Freedom,* James M. McPherson labeled Fredericksburg "one of the worst defeats of the war" for a Federal army. He then explored the impact on northern civilians repelled by the ghastly slaughter in front of Marye's Heights and on politicians bickering about why the rebels always seemed to best the Army of the Potomac. Allan Nevins dismissed the Federal "disaster" as the work of "an improvised general [who] had fought an improvised battle" before turning his attention to the "storm of sorrow and wrath which at once swept the North." James G. Randall and David Donald thought the battle, with its "series of forlorn, desperate Union charges against the withering musketry and artillery fire of the Confederates," sent civilian morale in the North plummeting toward nadir. Without a sentence on the Confederacy, they focused northward: "Sorrow caused by the death or mutilation of thousands of brave men turned into rage as the people wondered how so fine a fighting instrument as the Army of the Potomac had been used with such stupid futility." Nor did Bruce Catton pause to look at the impact of Fredericksburg on the Confederacy in his "Centennial History of the Civil War." Like McPherson, Nevins, and Randall and Donald, he proceeded from the battlefield to the crisis of politics and morale north of the Potomac.[9] This approach to Fredericksburg's aftermath probably implies no lack of interest in the Confederacy; rather, it seems likely that the authors assumed a favorable southern reaction to victory and saw no reason to dwell on it.

Literary evidence from the six weeks after Burnside's retreat across the Rappahannock illuminates a more complex pattern of Confederate responses than previously described by historians and other writers. Most newspapers adopted a positive stance. On December 16, before Burnside withdrew, the proadministration *Richmond Daily Dispatch* called Fredericksburg "the greatest battle ever fought on this continent." Lee's defeat of an imposing host of Yankees demonstrated that "no superiority of numbers or of preparation can avail them in a pitched battle with the forces of the Confederacy—a truth so patent, and so often exemplified, that we believe they are the only people on earth who venture to deny it." The *Daily Dispatch* proclaimed total victory when news of Burnside's retreat reached Richmond. The paper did allude to reports that many Confederate soldiers regretted the enemy's escape without further harm—but cited them as evidence of unflagging spirit in the ranks rather than as criticism of Lee. Throughout the rest of the month, the *Daily Dispatch* mentioned political unrest in the North, Radical Republican pressure to restructure Lincoln's cabinet, rumors of Burnside's demise, and disaffection in the Army of the Potomac as positive results of the victory. By New Year's Day, the editor detected so much confidence among his readers that he warned of the need for continued resolve. The Army of the Potomac surely would mount another "On to Richmond" campaign, and no one should "hope for peace until we have destroyed, dispersed, or worn out that army."[10]

Other newspapers joined in a happy chorus. The *Richmond Enquirer* told readers of "an interest and enthusiasm among our citizens, not less vivid than the intensist feeling concurrent with the memorable battles around Richmond" the previous summer. Boasting about an article in the *New York Herald* portraying a glum North, the *Enquirer* predicted that whether Burnside remained in control made no difference; his retention would demoralize the Yankee army, while his replacement by an officer acceptable to the Radicals would alienate northern conservatives. "We contend against large odds," allowed the *Charleston Daily Courier* on December 16, but "Generals of unsurpassed genius and talents," gallant soldiers who had won victories on many fields, and a righteous cause would win out. Influenced by pessimistic coverage of Fredericksburg in northern newspapers and an absence of Confederate defeats elsewhere, the *Daily Courier* raised the possibility of French intervention. The *Petersburg (Va.) Daily Express* singled out Abraham Lincoln, whose "vigorous efforts to keep up appearances" rang hollow: "The battle of Fredericksburg he knows has prodigiously shattered his Grand Army, and it will be the work of months to put it in a condition to resume offensive operations, even if it be capable of being thus renovated and reinvigorated, which is exceedingly questionable." [11]

Few papers matched the enthusiasm of the *Richmond Whig*, which sketched a Federal army so disheartened it refused to continue the fight after December 13. According to the *Whig*, a captured member of Burnside's staff and other prisoners had affirmed that the Union commander canceled assaults on the 14th and retreated because he doubted the valor of his men. Such an army posed little danger in the near term: "The campaign in Virginia, and we think in North Carolina, is ended for the winter, so far as the enemy are concerned. It has been to them a campaign of unbroken failure and disgrace. . . . Lee winds up the campaign in Virginia with a blow at Fredericksburg that makes the whole of Lincolndom reel like a drunken man." [12]

Newspapers in the hinterlands relied on letters from soldiers to help tell the story of the battle. These accounts spoke of heavy enemy casualties, dispirited Federals, and striking Confederate success. In the *Atlanta Southern Confederacy*, Dr. J. N. Simmons, writing from Richmond, assured readers of a "disastrous defeat" for the Yankees. Men and officers in Lee's army had wished for additional Union assaults; however, Burnside aborted a planned offensive on December 14 because Federal soldiers "refused to risk the fate of their dead comrades." A member of Joseph B. Kershaw's brigade penned an account printed in the *Sumter (S.C.) Tri-Weekly Watchman*. "I have often heard of the dead being piled in heaps," stated this witness after viewing the Union corpses below Marye's Heights, "but never before have scene it literally true." He pronounced the battle "a great victory" whose "moral effect will, I think, be as great if not greater than any battle we have fought." A soldier in the 38th Georgia of A. R. Lawton's brigade, who had fought at Seven Pines, Malvern Hill, and Sharpsburg, confused readers of the *Sandersville (Ga.) Central Georgian* by mixing images of George B. McClellan's retreat after Malvern Hill with those of the Union army on the Rappahannock: "Once more the 'Dixie Boys' as usual, have triumphed and driven Old Abe's horde of thieves to the shelter of their gunboats, under whose friendly protection they are to day hiding their cowardly carcasses." [13]

Another Georgian quoted in Athens's *Southern Banner* speculated wistfully about what might have been before closing triumphantly. The splendid Confederate position resulted in an unparalleled repulse for the enemy. Had Burnside pressed the offensive on either the 14th or 15th, Lee's men might have ended the war by destroying the Army of the Potomac. "As it is," wrote this captain in the 9th Georgia of George T. Anderson's brigade, "I think this battle has saved Richmond for the winter." More optimistic than ever despite the enemy's escape, he added that "*This army can never be whipped* by all the power of Yankeedom combined, and I now predict that the treaty of peace when made, be it soon or late, will find it still victorious." [14]

A minority of newspapers chose more muted language for their coverage. Pollard's *Richmond Examiner* posed questions about the victory that foreshadowed opinions in his later books. Rumors of a "demoralized and unmanageable" Federal army, a North in "the flames of revolution," and rioting in New York City that had claimed 1,500 lives circulated in Richmond on December 17 (the editor vouched for the accuracy of none of these reports), while intelligence from Lee's army indicated "unlimited rejoicings" among soldiers who regarded Burnside's retreat as acknowledgment of defeat. More insightful men, wishing for another opportunity to smite the Federals, received word of the enemy's withdrawal "with unfeigned sorrow." Lee and Longstreet presented a cheerful front, but "the stubborn fact exists the enemy had put the river between himself and the rebels he had rushed from Warrenton, to 'scatter like chaff,' and those who can not rejoice over the retreat put a cheerful face upon the matter." The other leading antiadministration paper, Charleston's *Mercury*, worried that Burnside might soon advance along some other avenue. That specter aside, the paper bravely added, "General Lee knows his business and that army has yet known no such word as fail." [15]

Opinions among civilians and soldiers outside the Army of Northern Virginia corresponded to coverage in the newspapers. Jefferson Davis spent most of December away from Richmond, returning after the New Year. On January 7, he responded to a serenade outside his home with high praise for Lee and his victory: "Our glorious Lee, the valued son, emulating the virtues of the heroic Lighthorse Harry, his father, has achieved a victory at Fredericksburg, and driven the enemy back from his last and greatest effort to get 'on to Richmond.'" That success, together with Union frustration at Vicksburg and the battle of Murfreesboro—then thought to be a comparable Confederate win—opened a tantalizing vista. "Out of this victory is to come that dissatisfaction in the North West," proclaimed Davis, "which will rive the power of that section; and thus we see in the future the dawn—first separation of the North West from the Eastern States, the discord among them which will paralyze the power of both,—then for us future peace and prosperity." [16]

Fuller news from Tennessee revealed Murfreesboro to be at best a bloody stand-off, leaving Davis to mull over the losses of 1862. Varina Davis recalled that the roster of defeats from Fort Donelson and Nashville through Island No. 10, Memphis, and Murfreesboro oppressed her husband. He shared none of the revived hope for European recognition evinced by many Confederates. Indeed, wrote Mrs. Davis, Lee's "victory at Fredericksburg was the one bright spot in all this dark picture." [17]

The outcome at Fredericksburg prompted some Confederates to speak about an end to the war. John B. Jones, whose diary makes him the most famous midlevel bureaucrat in the Confederacy, observed on December 19 that "Many people regard the disaster of Burnside as the harbinger of peace." The impact of Lee's victory—as well as the uncertain power of events to hold the public imagination—stand out in a passage from Jones's diary four days later: "The battle of Fredericksburg is still the topic, or the wonder, and it transpired more than nine days ago. It will have its page in history, and be read by school-boys a thousand days hence." William M. Blackford of Lynchburg, who willingly sent five sons into Confederate military service, thought he saw "indications of a cessation of hostilities, though many months may pass before peace is established." The cumulative effect of Lee's campaigns in 1862 especially impressed Blackford. "The defeats of the enemy in the Valley, in the Peninsular, in the Piedmont, the invasion of Maryland, the capture of Harper's Ferry and lastly the victory at Fredericksburg," he noted, "taken all together, are achievements which do not often crown one year." [18]

Ample additional testimony supports Jones's observation about Confederates taking heart at dimmed Union prospects. "[T]he Yanks have had a terrible whipping at Fredericksburg," exulted Amanda Virginia Edmonds from near Paris, Virginia. "The whole loss supposed to be forty or fifty thousand. Oh! I hope it is true." Two weeks later, Edmonds confided in her diary that the "months do not pass speedily enough for I feel it is that much nearer peace. War's alarm is that much nearer being calmed." In early January, some Confederates tied Fredericksburg to good news from other theaters. "The papers are very encouraging," went a typical comment. "We are beginning to hope for peace. We have had another victory at Vicksburg and one at Murfreesboro."[19]

Coverage in the northern press imparted confidence to persons conditioned to dispute accounts in enemy newspapers. "From their papers we learn that 'the whole nation is filled with grief and shame at the disaster before Fredericksburg,[']" Cornelia Peake McDonald of Winchester recorded on January 1, 1863. "Shouts of execration against them come up from one side, wails of despair from another, cries of vengeance against treacherous Europe, and a voice above all, as of one trying to pour oil on the troubled waters—crying cheerily, 'The Union is not lost yet.'" McDonald bragged that Yankees could "say in the words of the Hero of yore—'We have met the enemy, and we are theirs.'"[20] Edmund Ruffin, the inveterate old fire-eater who commented extensively on public events in his expansive diary, happily observed that "instead of being (as usual,) boasting," comments in northern papers "are in the tone of lamentation & gloom." Dependent on northern accounts, a loyal Confederate in Fairfax, Virginia, found that initial reports spoke of Union victory. By December 20, the tenor of coverage had changed markedly: "[T]he papers are filled with Burnside's defeat, they do not pretend to deny, or gloss it over [as] hitherto—"[21]

Georgian Mary Jones combined gratitude for victory at Fredericksburg with a heartfelt tribute to Lee. Federals probably outnumbered Confederates five or six to one, she estimated, yet despite their "deadly appliances of modern warfare" failed to overwhelm the defenders. "I have not the words to express the emotions I feel for this signal success," Jones informed her son, a colonel. She felt "thankful that in this great struggle the head of our army is a noble son of Virginia, and worthy of the intimate relation in which he stands connected with our immortal Washington. What confidence his

Confederates took heart from the North's bitter reaction to Ambrose E. Burnside's defeat at Fredericksburg. In this cartoon, an accusing Columbia asks Abraham Lincoln, General Burnside, and Secretary of War Edwin M. Stanton: "Where are my 15,000 sons—murdered at Fredericksburg?" (Author's collection)

wisdom, integrity, and valor and undoubted piety inspire!" Others echoed her faith in Lee, as when war clerk John B. Jones displayed no concern that Burnside would menace Richmond from another direction. Before the Union commander could do so, "Lee would be between him and the city, and if he could beat him on the Rappahannock he can beat him anywhere." [22]

Many Confederates perceived that the political impact of the battle outweighed its purely military effect. This should not obscure the fact that nearly everyone mentioned approvingly the grim harvest of Union attackers—some dwelled on grisly details more than others—and took delight in stories about poor morale in the Army of the Potomac. Yet few Confederates believed Federal casualties posed a long-range problem to the heavily populated North, and they had seen beaten Federals rebound before. Loss of civilian morale and political chaos among the Republicans, however, did threaten the Union war effort. Edmund Ruffin, who gloried in Burnside's repulse, asserted that "the most remarkable effects, & manifest acknowledgment of this disastrous defeat have been displayed at Washington. A private meeting (or caucus) of the members of the Senate was held, which requested the President to dismiss Seward, & to reconstruct his whole cabinet."[23]

From eastern North Carolina, Catherine Ann Devereux Edmondston surveyed an apparently chaotic North in her remarkable journal. "The news of Burnside's repulse and retreat from Fredericksburg has fallen like an avalanch upon the North," she wrote on December 21. "They have found out that Lincoln's 'jests' have but little comfort in them, that their Secretary of War is a *bungling idiot*," say that their President knows nothing of the state of feeling throughout the country & abuse their whole Cabinet, their Government, & their Generals in the most unmeasured terms."[24] Lucy Rebecca Buck reacted similarly to rumors of Burnside's removal, William H. Seward's resignation from Lincoln's cabinet, and quarrels between Salmon P. Chase and Edwin M. Stanton. "Glorious!" she exclaimed from her home at Front Royal, Virginia. "With division in their councils—disorganization of their army and dissatisfaction among the people I think their prospects of subjugating us a very poor one."[25]

What of the widespread unhappiness with Lee's victory described by Pollard and DeLeon? Did a substantial number of Confederates see their expectations raised to giddy heights by events on December 13, only to be smashed when Lee allowed Burnside to return quietly to the north bank of the Rappahannock? A few civilian sources seem to bear this out. One Louisiana woman conveyed a decidedly mixed impression of the battle in her diary entry of January 1, 1863. "We have repulsed the enemy twice between the Yazoo and Vicksburg," she affirmed. "Our victory at Fredericksburg was complete but barren of result, only it has depressed and surprised the North. Altogether we are getting the better of our foes." Inability to inflict greater harm on the Army of the Potomac must explain this use of "barren" regarding a battle that caused consternation in the North. At the Bureau of War, Robert Garlick Hill Kean also rendered a mixed verdict. He believed that "Burnside's official jacket was whipped off at Fredericksburg," but he questioned rumors of disruption in Lincoln's cabinet and accused Lee of reporting too few Confederate casualties. Upset earlier that Lee had permitted the enemy to cross the Rappahannock "almost without resistance," Kean likely considered the failure to attack the Federals while they remained on the south side of the river a mistake as well.[26]

Concern about a potential lost opportunity shows up more frequently among soldiers in the Army of Northern Virginia. The diary of artillerist Henry Robinson Berkeley furnishes an excellent example of mounting disillusionment. "When darkness came," Berkeley wrote on the evening of December 13, "we had the satisfaction of knowing the Yanks had been repulsed at every point with very heavy loss." In the absence of more Federal assaults on the 14th, Berkeley observed, "It seems to me that we ought to go down on the plain and drive them into the river, or at least try to do it." "I don't see why our army doesn't assail the Yanks down on the plain," he repeated on the 15th. "I fear they will get away from us." Dawn on the 16th confirmed the worst: "At light this morning we saw plainly that Gen. Burnside had withdrawn his entire army to the north side of the river and had given us the slip." An officer in the 10th Virginia, a regiment in Jackson's corps that experienced virtually no combat on December 13, thought a counterattack on the 13th "could have turned their repulse into an utter rout." Daylight ran out, however, "and in consequence of our not pursuing them they escaped with their cannon." Fredericksburg might have ended the war "could the power have been given our Generals, like Joshua of old, to have stayed the sun an hour or two in its course." Because the contest ended without further fighting, the armies would "soon again meet in battle on some other field and God grant us the victory." [27]

Some men ventured oblique criticism of Lee. "The Yanks made repeated attempts to advance but failed in every attempt being repulsed with heavy loss," a member of Joseph B. Kershaw's brigade related to his sister. Kershaw's soldiers had supported T. R. R. Cobb's infantry in the Sunken Road and thus witnessed the Federal assaults at their most futile. "The fight was kept up until night when it ceased," continued this man, "every person believing the next day would be the bloody day but in this everyone was deceived even our generals." Capt. Charles Minor Blackford informed his wife that after the bloody success of December 13, Confederates "expected the battle to be renewed the next day." On the night of the 15th, "the enemy quietly withdrew." Blackford praised Burnside's skill in accomplishing this—"for as far as I can see, it was done without the knowledge of our generals, and certainly without an effort to interrupt." "I take it General Lee knows better what should have been done than I do," he added with little enthusiasm, "or than the newspapers who criticize him for not attacking." In any event, Blackford thought the "war is over, at least for the winter."[28]

James T. McElvaney of the 35th Georgia informed his mother that "our victory is pronounced by Generals Lee & Jackson Complete." Part of Edward L. Thomas's brigade in A. P. Hill's division, the 35th suffered eighty-nine casualties on the 13th and "expected a harder fight on Sunday." Burnside's able retreat left McElvaney unconvinced that the Army of Northern Virginia's triumph was complete: "There is a great deal of speculation as to what the enemy will do or where he will turn up again," he stated. "I would be glad to see this war end but cant see where it will stop." A colonel in the Stonewall Brigade agreed that Fredericksburg augured no dramatic shift in the war. "We repulsed them all along the line with tremendous slaughter," wrote James K. Edmondson on December 17, yet the Federals had withdrawn safely and likely would cross the river again at Port Royal, some twenty miles below Fredericksburg. Edmondson expected "another heavy battle in a day or so." A South Carolinian in Kershaw's brigade predicted "another great battle in less than a month" because the "enemy have by no means retreated but apparently have fallen back to their former position." He passed along a rumor that Port Royal would be the next target, expressing confidence that "Gen. Lee is well prepared to meet them and states that if attacked he will defeat them with greater ease."[29]

Regret at losing the advantage of a superb defensive position probably animated at least as many men as the failure to launch counterattacks. A Georgian explained on December 18 that his comrades had anticipated Union assaults on the day following the battle: "It was universally supposed that this would be *the* terrible day and every soldier in our ranks wished for the attack to begin, for never before had we had such an advantageous position." But December 14 revealed that the enemy "had skedaddled" to safety. "It was a sad disappointment to our soldiers," he confessed. "If they had to fight, they desired to fight here." Another Georgian seconded this view, describing disbelief among Confederates when they grasped that Burnside had recrossed the Rappahannock. "I had no idea that they were so badly whipped," he wrote. "They can still be seen across the river. I do not think they will attack us again. All the better if they do. I think we can whip a million of them! This is one of the best positions in the world." William Beverley Pettit of the Fluvanna Artillery mentioned a "general regret that the enemy withdrew without renewing the fight, for all who viewed the battleground and the superior [strength] . . . of our position felt confident that we could whip them badly, no matter in what force they may attack."[30]

More than most of their subordinates and soldiers in the ranks, members of the high command believed the Federals had escaped too lightly. Robert E. Lee's response, which may have set the tone for many of his lieutenants, will be discussed at length below. "Stonewall" Jackson's desire to smite the enemy with some type of offensive counterstroke is well known. In his report, Jackson indicated that he ordered preparations for "an advance of our troops across the plain." But Federal artillery "so completely swept our front as to satisfy me that the proposed movement should be abandoned." Artillery chief William Nelson Pendleton identified Monday as the day "we looked for the great fight of the war. But lo! when dawn appeared no Yankees remained this side of the Rappahannock, except dead and wounded." Burnside had "used the dark, rainy night" to pull back to the protection of Stafford Heights, and the Federals now lay "out of our reach." Heros von Borcke, a Prussian officer serving on J. E. B. Stuart's staff, visited Lee's Hill shortly after the Confederates learned of Burnside's retreat. "[W]e found a great number of the generals assembled around our Commander-in-Chief," he recalled a few months after the battle, "all extremely chagrined that the Federals should have succeeded in so cleverly making their escape."[31]

Like their civilian counterparts, the bulk of Lee's soldiers placed the battle in a decidedly favorable light. Several threads run through their letters and diaries. The extent of Union casualties inspired lengthy comment—particularly the gruesome scene below Marye's Heights. The impact of the battle on morale in Burnside's army, disaffection behind the lines in the North, and improving prospects for peace also show up repeatedly in writings from the weeks after the battle. The spectacle of one huge army coming to grips with another in the amphitheatrical valley of the Rappahannock fascinated some observers. The battle seemed to many an omen of good days ahead—marred only by the sad ruin of the city of Fredericksburg and the desperate plight of its inhabitants.

"Jeb" Stuart touched on two of these themes in a pair of brief communications. "We were victorious yesterday," he telegraphed his wife on December 14. "Repulsing enemy's attack in main force with tremendous slaughter." Four days later he related to George Wash-

The scale of carnage below Marye's Heights impressed Confederate soldiers and civilians. Here Federal burial parties protected by a flag of truce gather the corpses of comrades slain by James Longstreet's infantry and artillery. (Author's collection)

ington Custis Lee that English observers with the army "who surveyed Solferino and all the battlefields of Italy say the pile of dead on the plains of Fredericksburg exceeds anything of the sort ever seen by them." The city itself lay in ruins—"It is the saddest sight I ever saw." A South Carolinian addressed the same topics in recounting his first sight of Fredericksburg after the battle. "The number of dead bodies were considerable that I ever saw," he stated somewhat clumsily. "Appparently men who were severely wounded and carried into houses and afterwards died. I also saw numbers of feet, legs, hands, and the like which had been shot and cut off." The town "was the most complete wreck" he ever saw. "Quite a number of houses were burnt down and those that were left standing was shot to pieces." Obviously troubled by the scene, this man knew his correspondent would "perceive my nerves are very much shattered." A captain in T. R. R. Cobb's brigade termed December 13 a "glorious day" because Confederates "slaughtered them by the thousands losing very few ourselves." Federal bodies *"literally* covered" the field outside Fredericksburg, which itself presented a "dreadful sight." The Federals presumably wrecked the town "just in mere wantoness." [32]

Evidence of demoralization in Burnside's ranks and among north-ern civilians buoyed the Confederates, who often linked it to hopes for final victory. During a truce on December 17, a quartermaster with the 13th Mississippi talked with Union officers who admitted they "suffered a serious defeat in the late battle and express them-selves as very tired of the war." [33] Philip H. Powers wrote home on Christmas Day: "[Y]ou will see from the papers how terribly whipped Burnside was and what a commotion it has produced in Yankeedom." "I think the sky brightens and our chances for peace improve," Powers continued, but "still the war may linger on another year, or even to the end of Lincoln's term." Maj. Eugene Blackford of the 5th Alabama conversed with a number of Federals during a truce on December 15. "They all seemed ashamed to look our men in the face," noted Blackford, and "without exception, men and offi-cers, professed themselves utterly sick of the war, and declared their desire to see it end in any way." A native Vermonter serving with the 51st Georgia drew broad conclusions from the victory. "They have retired without one achievement to cheer them or one hope," he wrote with evident satisfaction. "One nation is now shaded with dis-appointment and one is clo[th]ed with garments of joy.... A proud and haughty people are humbled and brought to a stand. A reckless politician and statesman has received another intimation of speedy ruin which will come embittered by the curses of two nations." [34]

One artillerist described Confederate pickets taunting their Fed-eral counterparts about the battle until the latter finally "acknowl-edged that we gave them a severe whipping." The Federals refused to admit anyone had resigned from Lincoln's cabinet, though the Confederates had it from "quite a good authority—an aid of Gen. Stewart." A trooper from the 13th Virginia Cavalry, also quoting Union pickets, pronounced the privates in the Army of the Poto-mac "willing to give us anything we ask" to achieve peace. With the rank and file of the enemy alienated from the northern cause, he be-lieved that "by spring our brightest hopes will be consummated." [35] William B. Bailey of the Louisiana Guard Artillery in Richard S. Ewell's division mentioned demoralization so serious among the enemy that "deserters are coming over to us daily in squads." "It is no use for the nigger Government to try to take Richmond, 'that can't be did,'" he exulted. "Our army can't be whipped, no matter how large a force the nigger government may send against us." A North Carolinian rejoiced that the Yankees failed "to destroy our nationality and every thing else that belonged to Southron institutions." Fredericksburg marked "the first clear back down they ever have made." [36]

A Virginian in D. H. Hill's division feared Lee's victory at Fredericksburg had been too decisive. The Army of the Potomac would be so quiet during the winter that units from the Army of Northern Virginia could be sent to defend the North Carolina coast. "It is surmised that Hill's Division will be sent off," he wrote unhappily. "We hope not, for we are not anxious to fight both winter and summer." Despite this worry, he ended his letter on a positive note: "I am now beginning to entertain hope of a speedy peace." If Bragg's victory at Murfreesboro turned out to be significant, Vicksburg held, and the coasts remained safe, "peace, I trust, will come with Spring." [37]

Not all general officers shared the outlook Heros von Borcke described among those atop Lee's Hill on December 16. James J. Archer, who commanded a brigade in A. P. Hill's Light Division, reflected on the events of December in letters to members of his family. "The prospects I think look bright for peace since [the] battle of Fredericksburg & since the democrats at the north have found their tongues," he told his brother. A victory in the West "would settle the matter." Retaining his optimism after word of Bragg's retreat reached Virginia, Archer admitted disappointment that success at Murfreesboro "was not greater," adding that Confederates had "amply shown all sober people at the North that they are engaged in a Vain attempt & I for one look for a speedy peace." Brig. Gen. Elisha Franklin Paxton of the Stonewall Brigade also forecast victory. "I feel, perhaps, too confident," he confessed to his wife. "Our independence was secured in the last campaign when we proved our capacity to beat the finest army they could bring in the field." War weariness in the North would prevent the North's fielding a larger army, and Confederate victory had become nothing more than a matter of time: "The war may be protracted, there is no telling how long; but we have shown our capacity to beat them, and we are better able to do it now than ever before." [38]

Apart from its effect on the military situation and northern morale, Fredericksburg left many Confederates with visual images of triumph on a grand scale. Capt. Shepherd Green Pryor of the 12th Georgia termed it "the grandest sight I ever saw in my life. Youv seen pictures of armies, but no artist could do that sight justice. . . . It was a grand sight after the fight to see the two armies within 1000 yards of each other, dead & wounded yankeys and horses lying over the field, & those dead & wounded all Federals." Pryor concluded rather cold-bloodedly that "Such sights as those are grand to those that are use[d] to seeing dead men." A staff officer who had not written to his mother in some months took time in April 1863 to recapture the drama and sweep of Fredericksburg. Certain she had read of Burnside's "ignominious defeat," he concentrated on the vista from the summit of Lee's Hill: "Never in my life do I expect to see such a magnificent sight again. From the crest of a hill where I was stationed with Lee, Longstreet, Pickett, Stuart, and others of our principal generals the whole scene of conflict was before our eyes, and at out feet, the glorious sun shining out as tho' bloodshed and slaughter were unknown on the beautiful earth; the screaming of shells and the singing of rifle bullets adding a fearful accompaniment to the continued booming of the heavy guns." [39] This same panorama inspired Lee's oft-quoted remark, "It is well that this is so terrible! we should grow too fond of it!" [40]

In contrast to the implications of Lee's famous quotation, the aftermath of the victorious spectacle on December 13 found him notably disgruntled. Bryan Grimes, a colonel in temporary command of Stephen Dodson Ramseur's North Carolina brigade, remembered the general's "deep chagrin and mortification" on learning definitively that the Federals were gone. [41] Lee had hoped for additional assaults against his confident and well-positioned army. "The attack on the 13th had been so easily repulsed, and by so small a part of our army," he explained in his official report, "that it was not supposed the enemy would limit his efforts to an attempt, which, in view of the magnitude of his preparations and the extent of his force, seemed to be comparatively insignificant." Believing the enemy would try more assaults, and mindful of his own strong position and the powerful Union artillery on Stafford Heights that would decimate any counterattack, Lee opted to remain in place. "[W]e were necessarily ignorant of the extent to which he [the enemy] had suffered," his report read, "and only became aware of it when, on the morning of the 16th, it was discovered that he had availed himself of the darkness of night, and the prevalence of a violent storm of wind and rain, to recross the river." [42] This language conveys disappointment as well as a measure of contempt for a foe who would slink away from a battlefield after what the Confederate chieftain considered less than an all-out effort.

From atop an eminence that would later come to be dubbed "Lee's Hill," the Con-federate commander and his principal subordinates watched a panorama of easy victory below. H. A. Ogden's postwar print included George E. Pickett, Stonewall Jackson, and James Longstreet (left to right) in a grouping with Lee. (Author's collection)

Lee's comments to his wife, Mary, three days after the battle an-ticipated the thrust of his report. "Yesterday evening I had my sus-picions that they might retire during the night, but could not be-lieve they would relinquish their purpose after all their boasting & preparations," he wrote, "& when I say that the latter is equal to the former, you will have some idea of its magnitude." The enemy now lay safely across the Rappahannock, having gone "as they came, in the night." Lee's concluding remarks underscored his unhappiness: "They suffered heavily as far as the battle went, but it did not go far enough to satisfy me. . . . The contest will have now to be renewed, but on what field I cannot say." Robert E. Lee Jr. probably misread his father when he met him several days after the battle. Years later, Lee recollected that he found the general "as calm and composed as if nothing unusual had happened, and he never referred to his great victory, except to deplore the loss of his brave officers and soldiers or the sufferings of the sick and wounded." This passage suggests the son inferred that modesty prevented his father from boasting of a grand victory; instead, the commander may have seen no reason to celebrate what he considered a meaningless success.[43]

In July 1863, Lee shared his negative views about Fredericksburg with Secretary of War James A. Seddon's brother John. Major Seddon subsequently talked with Henry Heth about the conversation, and Heth recalled Seddon's comments in a postwar letter. "At Fredericksburg we gained a battle," Lee said to the major, "inflicting very serious loss on the enemy in men and material; our people were greatly elated—I was much depressed." In Lee's opinion, the Confederates "had really accomplished nothing" at Fredericksburg: "[W]e had not gained a foot of ground, and I knew the enemy could easily replace the men he had lost; and the loss of material was, if any thing, rather beneficial to him, as it gave an opportunity to contractors to make money."[44] Fear of misguided Confederate elation also showed up in a letter from Lee to the secretary of war in January 1863. After imploring Seddon to increase the size of the Confederate armies, the general cautioned that the "success with which our efforts have been crowned, under the blessing of God, should not betray our people into the dangerous delusion that the armies now in the field are sufficient to bring this war to a successful and speedy termination."[45]

Lee must have found positive and negative newspaper coverage of Fredericksburg equally disturbing. Editors who accentuated Yankee losses, plunging morale in Burnside's army, northern political and civilian unrest, and heightened prospects for peace ran the risk of creating a mood in which the Confederate populace might relax its determination. More critical editors such as Pollard, by questioning Lee's failure to launch counterattacks, overlooked Burnside's cannon on Stafford Heights and other factors that likely would have doomed any aggressive Confederate movement. Their distortions could lead to a drop in morale among citizens like Sallie Putnam who worried that sacrifices on the battlefield went for naught.[46]

Lee's attitude toward Fredericksburg makes sense only if he viewed the battle in strictly military terms. It is true that the Army of Northern Virginia gained no territory and that Federal losses could be replaced easily. But repercussions within the Army of the Potomac and behind the lines in the North should have heartened Lee. As an assiduous reader of northern newspapers, he certainly knew about the battle's political ramifications and impact on Union morale. Why did he place at best only marginal value on the crises in Lincoln's cabinet and in the high command of Burnside's army? Why did reports of war weariness in the North not count for more?

The answer cannot be that Lee lacked an appreciation for factors beyond the battlefield. He frequently manifested a grasp of how military events could influence politics and civilian morale in ways beneficial to the Confederate cause. In September 1862, for example, he outlined nonmilitary goals for his army as it marched northward into Maryland. A year had passed "without advancing the objects which our enemies proposed to themselves in beginning the contest," he observed to Jefferson Davis. The time had come to offer peace to the North. If Lincoln's government rejected the offer, Northerners would see that "continuance of the war does not rest upon us, but that the party in power in the United States elect to prosecute it for purposes of their own." "The proposal of peace," concluded Lee, "would enable the people of the United States to determine at their coming elections whether they will support those who favor a prolongation of the war, or those who wish to bring it to a termination."[47] Although Lee did not state the obvious, the presence of the Army of Northern Virginia on Union soil during the fall of 1862 could affect the political process considerably.

Lee again alluded to the relationship between military activity and Union civilian morale in the spring of 1863. He detected growing doubt and weakening resolve among the enemy. Should the Confederates "baffle them in their various designs" during 1863, Lee thought "our success will be certain." In the fall "there will be a great change in public opinion at the North. The Republicans will be destroyed & I think the friends of peace will become so strong as that the next administration will go in on that basis."[48] Fredericksburg stood as a prime example of "baffling the enemy's designs" and causing consternation in the North; indeed, Lee's guarded optimism in

April 1863 must have stemmed at least in part from his last success along the Rappahannock.

Why then his public and private depreciation of Fredericksburg? Perhaps the answer lies in his concern about overconfidence expressed to Secretary of War Seddon. Whatever Fredericksburg's impact on the enemy, Lee knew the war would continue. He knew as well that fellow Confederates gave great weight to his statements. Any suggestion that his latest victory might mark a significant step toward independence could lull the public into a false sense of security. In a contest with an opponent who enjoyed vastly superior resources, such a response could be fatal.

Those who emphasize the aggressive part of Lee's military personality might suggest that he refused to view any battle in which his opponent dictated the action as positively as one in which he controlled the strategic or tactical flow. It cannot be denied that Lee's wartime correspondence bristles with allusions to striking offensive blows that could crush the enemy.[49] Yet during the talk with Major Seddon in which he claimed Fredericksburg availed the Confederacy nothing, Lee dismissed Chancellorsville as even less satisfactory. In the latter case, Lee seized the initiative from Joseph Hooker and used a series of assaults during three days of hard fighting to defeat the Army of the Potomac. His estimate of the campaign nonetheless remained harsh: "At Chancellorsville we gained another victory; our people were wild with delight—I, on the contrary, was more depressed than after Fredericksburg; our loss was severe, and again we had gained not an inch of ground and the enemy could not be pursued."[50]

In the end, there can be no definitive explanation for Lee's attitude. He chose to categorize Fredericksburg strictly in terms of ground gained or lost, and by that yardstick it paled in comparison to the Seven Days or Second Manassas campaigns—though those two operations caused scarcely more political or civilian unrest in the North.

This canvass of opinion relating to Fredericksburg might prove useful to historians interested in broader questions. A desire for decisive offensive victories left a substantial minority of Confederates, including some soldiers who might have become casualties had Lee counterattacked, only partially satisfied with the battle. Few of these individuals indulged in serious criticism of Lee, who, after all, had demonstrated his willingness to take great risks in pursuit of overwhelming victories in every stage of the campaigning from the Seven Days through Sharpsburg. But their expectations spawned harsher estimates of lesser generals such as Joseph E. Johnston, whose retreats on the Peninsula and later in North Georgia left many of his fellow Confederates exasperated. Anyone who maintains that Lee should have avoided the offensive wherever possible, or that the Confederate national strategy should have traded territory for time in a broad defensive effort, must reckon with the likely civilian reaction.

On the other hand, a majority of Confederates seem to have welcomed the victory and its obvious impact on morale in the most famous Federal army and among northern civilians. A fair number considered it a major step toward eventual Confederate independence. Would a string of Fredericksburgs have sustained the Confederates in their quest for nationhood? A more systematic, comparative examination of responses to various battles and campaigns would afford a clearer picture of this aspect of Confederate history.

The comments of many of Lee's soldiers indicate they welcomed a shift toward fighting on the defensive after five months of bloody operations. Does this suggest the army as a whole would have been content to fight a defensive war? The army repeatedly had demonstrated its élan in offensive combat, and it would do so again at Chancellorsville, Gettysburg, and during the 1864 Overland campaign. The ease with which they repulsed Burnside's army, however, made a profound impression. As one man put it, Fredericksburg "was but a frolic for our men, being the first time that they had ever had the pleasure of being entrenched and await[ing] the enemy." John B. Jones viewed the question more analytically. "I fear the flower of our chivalry mostly perished in storming batteries," he wrote. "It is true *prestige* was gained" in such endeavors, but Fredericksburg underscored the importance of advantageous ground. Jones hoped commanders might learn the lesson that "no necessity exists for so great an expenditure of life in the prosecution of this war. The disparity of numbers should be considered by our generals."[51] Jones did not offer advice on how to guarantee a regular supply of Federal officers who would order assaults against well-situated defenders. Nor does the testimony about Fredericksburg place soldier attitudes within a larger context. As with the civilian reaction, a comparative look at different campaigns would be instructive.

Students of the Civil War tend to place victories and defeats in pairs or groups for purposes of analysis. Examples of this tendency come readily to mind: The Seven Days and Second Manassas paved the way for Lee's first move across the Potomac and brought Europe to the verge of recognizing the Confederacy; Fredericksburg and Chancellorsville set the stage for a potentially crucial swing in the momentum of the war; Sharpsburg and Gettysburg blunted the two most promising Confederate offensives of the war; Gettysburg and Vicksburg signaled a major turning point. Although admittedly useful (not to mention irresistible), this device obscures important differences between the operations in each pairing. Examination of each campaign's impact on the respective populations would help historians construct a more sophisticated portrait of the nation at war. If Fredericksburg, a straightforward campaign logically subject to very little difference of interpretation by either side, yields a greater range of responses than expected, it seems reasonable that more complex operations might hold greater surprises.

NOTES

1. This essay rests on testimony from individuals across the Confederacy (only Arkansas and Florida lack representation), including soldiers of all ranks within the Army of Northern Virginia, soldiers in Confederate service elsewhere, politicians, civil servants, and men and women in a variety of private circumstances. It is possible that responses drawn from a far wider group of witnesses might yield different results.

2. Edward A. Pollard, *Southern History of the War: The Second Year of the War* (1863; reprint, New York: Charles B. Richardson, 1865), 195–96.

3. Edward A. Pollard, *The Lost Cause: A New Southern History of the War of the Confederates* (New York: E. B. Treat, 1866), 345–46.

4. Sallie Putnam, *In Richmond during the Confederacy* (1867; reprint, New York: Robert M. McBride Company, 1961), 198; William P. Snow, *Lee and His Generals* (1867; reprint, New York: Fairfax Press, 1982), 85.

5. Thomas C. DeLeon, *Four Years in Rebel Capitals: An Inside View of Life in the Southern Confederacy, from Birth to Death* (1890; reprint, [Alexandria, Va.]: Time-Life Books, 1983), 248.

6. Douglas Southall Freeman, *R. E. Lee: A Biography*, 4 vols. (New York: Scribner's, 1934–35), 2:473. In *Lee's Lieutenants: A Study in Command*, 3 vols. (New York: Scribner's, 1942–44), 2:383–84, Freeman offered a different perspective: "Although the Confederate commanders were chagrined that the enemy had escaped with no more punishment than that of a costly repulse, the South was jubilant." Freeman quoted from several newspapers in support of this view.

7. Clifford Dowdey, *The Land They Fought For: The Story of the South as the Confederacy, 1832–1865* (Garden City, N.Y.: Doubleday, 1955), 235; Clement Eaton, *A History of the Southern Confederacy* (New York: Macmillan, 1954), 196; J. F. C. Fuller, *Grant and Lee: A Study in Personality and Generalship* (1932; reprint, Bloomington: Indiana University Press, 1957), 174.

8. William K. Goolrick and the Editors of Time-Life Books, *Rebels Resurgent: Fredericksburg to Chancellorsville* (Alexandria, Va.: Time-Life Books, 1985), 92; Frank E. Vandiver, *Their Tattered Flags: The Epic of the Confederacy* (New York: Harper's Magazine Press, 1970), 168.

9. McPherson, *Battle Cry of Freedom: The Civil War Era* (New York: Oxford University Press, 1988), 572–75 (quotation on p. 572); Allan Nevins, *The War for the Union*, 4 vols. (New York: Scribner's, 1959–71), 2:350; James G. Randall and David Donald, *The Civil War and Reconstruction*, 2nd ed. (Lexington, Mass.: D. C. Heath, 1969), 225; Bruce Catton, *Never Call Retreat* (Garden City, N.Y.: Doubleday, 1965), 24–26.

10. *Richmond Daily Dispatch,* December 16 (first two quotations), 17, 19, 23, 1862; January 1, 1863 (third quotation).

11. *Richmond Enquirer,* December 16 (first quotation), 30, 1862; *Charleston Daily Courier,* December 16 (second and third quotations), 19, 24, 1862; *Petersburg (Va.) Daily Express,* December 29, 1862 (quoted in Beulah Gayle Green, comp., *Confederate Reporter 1861–64* [Austin, Tex.: Burrell Printing Company, 1962], 112). Lincoln's depression following Fredericksburg is well known. "If there is a worse place than Hell," he remarked, "I am in it." James M. McPherson, *Ordeal by Fire: The Civil War and Reconstruction,* 2nd ed. (New York: McGraw-Hill, 1992), 303.

12. *Richmond Whig,* December 19, 20, 1862.

13. *Atlanta Southern Confederacy,* December 27, 1862 (Simmons's letter dated December 20, 1862); *Sumter (S.C.) Tri-Weekly Watchman,* January 5, 1863 (soldier's letter dated December 17, 1862); *Sandersville (Ga.) Central Georgian,* January 14, 1862 (soldier's letter dated December 15, 1862).

14. *Athens Southern Banner,* January 7, 1863 (soldier's letter dated December 18, 1862).

15. *Richmond Examiner,* December 18, 1862; *Charleston Mercury,* December 15, 1862.

16. Jefferson Davis, *Jefferson Davis, Constitutionalist: His Letters, Papers and Speeches,* ed. Dunbar Rowland, 10 vols. (Jackson: Mississippi Department of Archives and History, 1923), 5:391–92.

17. Varina Davis, *Jefferson Davis: Ex-President of the Confederate States of America, A Memoir by his Wife,* 2 vols. (1890; reprint, Baltimore, Md.: Nautical & Aviation Publishing, 1990), 2:369.

18. John B. Jones, *A Rebel War Clerk's Diary at the Confederate States Capital*, 2 vols. (1866; reprint, [Alexandria, Va.]: Time-Life Books, 1982), 1:218; William M. Blackford diary, December 31, 1862, quoted in Susan Leigh Blackford and Charles Minor Blackford, eds., *Letters from Lee's Army, or Memoirs of Life In and Out of the Army in Virginia during the War between the States* (New York: Scribner's, 1947), 152–53. Many northern observers also saw Fredericksburg as an indication that peace might come soon. Joseph Medill of the *Chicago Tribune*—a friend of the Lincoln administration—articulated what many others thought when he wrote to Elihu Washburne on January 14, 1863, that "An armistice is bound to come during the year '63." Nevins, *War for the Union*, 2:351.

19. Amanda Virginia Edmonds, *Journals of Amanda Virginia Edmonds: Lass of the Mosby Confederacy, 1859–1867*, ed. Nancy Chappelear Baird (Stephens City, Va.: Commercial Press, 1984), 129–30; Lucy Breckinridge, *Lucy Breckinridge of Grove Hill: The Journal of a Virginia Girl, 1862–1864*, ed. Mary D. Robertson (Kent, Ohio: Kent State University Press, 1979), 93–94.

20. Cornelia Peake McDonald, *A Woman's Civil War: A Diary, with Reminiscences of the War, from March 1862*, ed. Minrose C. Gwin (Madison: University of Wisconsin Press, 1992), 108. *Harper's Weekly* agreed with McDonald that the northern people almost had reached a breaking point: "They have borne, silently and grimly, imbecility, treachery, failure, privation, loss of friends and means, almost every suffering which can afflict a brave people. But they cannot be expected to suffer that such massacres as this at Fredericksburg shall be repeated." Quoted in McPherson, *Ordeal by Fire*, 305.

21. Edmund Ruffin, *The Diary of Edmund Ruffin*, ed. William Kauffman Scarborough, 3 vols. (Baton Rouge: Louisiana State University Press, 1972–89), 2:518–19; Anne S. Frobel, *The Civil War Diary of Anne S. Frobel of Wilton Hill, Virginia*, ed. Mary H. and Dallas M. Lancaster (Florence, Ala.: Birmingham Printing and Publishing Company, 1986), 105–6.

22. Mary Jones to Col. Charles C. Jones Jr., December 19, 1862, quoted in Robert Manson Myers, ed., *The Children of Pride: A True Story of Georgia and the Civil War* (New Haven, Conn.: Yale University Press, 1972), 1001; Jones, *Diary*, 1:214 (entry for December 16, 1862). Some northern soldiers also praised Lee after Fredericksburg. A Georgian talked with Federal pickets who said, "[I]f they had such generals as Lee and Jackson they could crush the rebellion, but as it is they are satisfied they will never succeed." Anonymous to Dear Frank, December 30, 1862, quoted in Mills

Lane, ed., *"Dear Mother: Don't grieve about me. If I get killed, I'll only be dead."* *Letters from Georgia Soldiers in the Civil War* (Savannah, Ga.: Beehive Press, 1977), 210.

23. Ruffin, *Diary*, 2:518–19. Ruffin did not exaggerate conditions in the North. For example, Senator Charles Sumner of Massachusetts, a leading Radical Republican, wrote on December 21 that "There has been a terrible depression here & I recognise it throughout the country." Two weeks later, Sumner insisted on the removal of Lincoln's key advisers—though he confessed seeing "great difficulties in organizing a true & strong Cabinet." Charles Sumner to Henry W. Longfellow, December 21, 1862, and Charles Sumner to Orestes A. Brownson, January 4, 1863, in Charles Sumner, *The Selected Letters of Charles Sumner*, ed. Beverly Wilson Palmer, 2 vols. (Boston: Northeastern University Press, 1990), 2:133, 138.

24. Catherine Ann Devereux Edmondston, *"Journal of a Secesh Lady": The Diary of Catherine Ann Devereux Edmondston, 1860–1866*, ed. Beth Gilbert Crabtree and James W. Patton (Raleigh: North Carolina Division of Archives and History, 1979), 321. George Templeton Strong's diary confirms Edmondston's comments about Stanton. "It is generally held that Stanton forced Burnside to this movement against his earnest remonstrance and protest," wrote the New Yorker on December 18, 1862. "Perhaps Stanton didn't. Who knows? But there is universal bitter wrath against him throughout this community, a deeper feeling more intensely uttered than any I ever saw prevailing here. Lincoln comes in for a share of it." George Templeton Strong, *The Diary of George Templeton Strong: The Civil War, 1860–1865*, ed. Allan Nevins and Milton Halsey Thomas (New York: Macmillan, 1952), 281.

25. Lucy Rebecca Buck, *Sad Earth, Sweet Heaven: The Diary of Lucy Rebecca Buck during the War between the States, Front Royal, Virginia, December 25, 1861–April 15, 1865*, ed. William P. Buck (Birmingham, Ala.: Cornerstone Publisher, 1973), 157.

26. Kate Stone, *Brokenburn: The Journal of Kate Stone, 1861–1878*, ed. John Q. Anderson (Baton Rouge: Louisiana State University Press, 1955), 168; Robert Garlick Hill Kean, *Inside the Confederate Government: The Diary of Robert Garlick Hill Kean*, ed. Edward Younger (New York: Oxford University Press, 1957), 33, 35.

27. Henry Robinson Berkeley, *Four Years in the Confederate Artillery: The Diary of Private Henry Robinson Berkeley*, ed. William H. Runge (Chapel Hill: University of North Carolina Press [for the Virginia Historical Society], 1961), 37–38; Green B. Samuels to Kathleen Boone Samuels, December 18,

1862, quoted in Carries Esther Spencer, Bernard Samuels, and Walter Berry Samuels, eds., *A Civil War Marriage: Reminiscences and Letters* (Boyce, Va.: Carr, 1956), 150.

28. Edward E. Sill to Dear Sister, December 20, 1862, Edward E. Sill Papers, William R. Perkins Library, Duke University, Durham, N.C. (repository hereafter cited as DU); Blackford and Blackford, eds., *Letters from Lee's Army*, 146, 148. Blackford's remarks about Fredericksburg are undated, but he almost certainly wrote them before the end of December 1862.

29. James T. McElvaney to My Dear Mother, December 19, 1862. Typescript in the collections of Fredericksburg and Spotsylvania National Military Park (repository cited hereafter as FSNMP); James K. Edmondson to My darling wife, December 17, 1862, quoted in James K. Edmondson, *My Dear Emma: (War Letters of Col. James K. Edmondson, 1861–1865)*, ed. Charles W. Turner (Verona, Va.: McClure Press, 1978), 115; Charles Kerrison to Dear Uncle Edwin, December 18, 1862, Kerrison Family Papers, University of South Carolina, Columbia.

30. David Winn to his wife, December 18, 1862, quoted in Lane, ed., *Letters from Georgia Soldiers*, 201; S. W. Branch to his mother, December 17, 1862, quoted in ibid., 200; William Beverley Pettit to My Dear Wife, December 16, 1862, quoted in Charles W. Turner, ed., *Civil War Letters of Arabella Speairs and William Beverley Pettit of Fluvanna County, Virginia, March 1862–March 1865*, 2 vols. (Roanoke, Va.: Virginia Lithography and Graphics, 1988–89), 1:80.

31. U.S. War Department, *The War of the Rebellion: A Compilation of the Official Records of the Union and Confederate Armies*, 127 vols., index, and atlas (Washington: GPO, 1880–1901), ser. 1, vol. 21:634 (hereafter cited as *OR*; all references are to ser. 1); William Nelson Pendleton to [?], December 17, 1862, quoted in Susan P. Lee, *Memoirs of William Nelson Pendleton, D.D.* (1893; reprint, Harrisonburg, Va.: Sprinkle Publications, 1991), 247; Heros von Borcke, *Memoirs of the Confederate War for Independence*, 2 vols. (1866; reprint, New York: Peter Smith, 1938), 2:147.

32. James E. B. Stuart to Mrs. Stuart, December 14, 1862, and Stuart to G. W. C. Lee, December 18, 1862, quoted in James E. B. Stuart, *The Letters of General J. E. B. Stuart*, ed. Adele H. Mitchell (n.p.: Stuart-Mosby Historical Society, 1990), 284–85; Edward E. Sill to Dear Sister, December 20, 1862, Edward E. Sill Papers, DU; Benjamin Edward Stiles to dear Aunt, December 21, 1862, Mackay-Stiles Collection, MS no. 470, Southern Historical Collection, Wilson Library, University of North Carolina, Chapel Hill (repository hereafter cited as SHC).

33. William H. Hill Diary, December 17, 1862, Mississippi Department of Archives and History, Jackson. Testimony from Federal sources corroborates Confederate claims of demoralization in the Army of the Potomac. Henry Livermore Abbot of the 20th Massachusetts, a Democrat who supported bringing McClellan back to the army, stated that the "army isn't worth a brass farthing in the way of fighting now. . . . The strongest peace party is in the army. If the small fry at Washington want to hear treason talked, let them come out to the army." Henry Livermore Abbot to My Dear Carry, December 21, 1862, in Henry Livermore Abbot, *Fallen Leaves: The Civil War Letters of Major Henry Livermore Abbot*, ed. Robert Garth Scott (Kent, Ohio: Kent State University Press, 1991), 155. Writing the same day as Abbot, Artillerist Charles S. Wainwright tried to be more upbeat but still conveyed a depressing picture: "In the army the effect has been, as far as I can see, to take all life out of it: it is not really demoralized, but every bit of the enthusiasm which was so marked as we came down through Loudoun County is gone. Very little is said about Burnside, but neither officers nor men have the slightest confidence in him." Charles S. Wainwright, *A Diary of Battle: The Personal Journals of Colonel Charles S. Wainwright, 1861–1865*, ed. Allan Nevins (New York: Harcourt, Brace & World, 1962), 148–49.

34. Philip H. Powers to his wife, December 25, 1862, Lewis Leigh Collection, United States Army Military History Institute, Carlisle, Pa. (repository hereafter cited as USAMHI); L. Minor Blackford, *Mine Eyes Have Seen the Glory* (Cambridge, Mass.: Harvard University Press, 1954), 211–12; Milo Grow to [?], December 17, 1862, quoted in n.a., *Milo Grow's Letters from the Civil War* (Lake Seminole, Ga.: privately printed for the Grow family reunion, 1986), 7.

35. Henry Herbert Harris to Dear Sister, December 26, 1862, typescript at FSNMP; Irvin Cross Wills to his brother, January 1, 1863, quoted in n.a., *Three Rebels Write Home: Including the Letters of Edgar Allan Jackson (September 7, 1860–April 15, 1863), James Fenton Bryant (June 20, 1861–December 30, 1866), Irvin Cross Wills (April 9, 1862–July 29, 1863), and Miscellaneous Items* (Franklin, Va.: News Publishing Company, 1955), 81. A soldier in the Iron Brigade described similar conditions. "Soldier's are all discouraged," wrote Henry Matrau. "We think that this war is never going to be ended by fighting for the North & the South are to[o] evenly matched. No troops ever fought better than did our's the other day at Fredericksburg, but to no avail." Henry Matrau to his mother, December 22, 1862, in Henry Matrau, *Letters Home: Henry Matrau of the Iron Brigade*, ed. Marcia Reid-Green (Lincoln: University of Nebraska Press, 1993), 39.

36. William Britton Bailey to Dear Brother, December 17, 1862, HCWET-C—[?] Collection, USAMHI; John Andrew Ramsey to his cousin, December 17, 1862, John Andrew Ramsey Papers, MS no. 3534, SHC.

37. W. R. M. Slaughter to My Dear Sister, January 4, 1863, MSS 25L 1575B, Virginia Historical Society, Richmond (repository hereafter cited as VHS).

38. James J. Archer to R. H. Archer, January 2, 1863, and James J. Archer to My Dear Mother, January 12, 1863, quoted in C. A. Porter Hopkins, ed., "The James J. Archer Letters: Part I," *Maryland Historical Magazine* 56 (June 1961): 140–41; Elisha Franklin Paxton to his wife, January 17, 1863, quoted in Elisha Franklin Paxton, *The Civil War Letters of General Frank "Bull" Paxton: A Lieutenant of Lee and Jackson*, ed. John Gallatin Paxton (Hillsboro, Tex.: Hill Junior College Press, 1978), 71.

39. Shepherd Green Pryor to Penelope Tyson Pryor, December 23, 1862, quoted in Shepherd Green Pryor, *A Post Of Honor: The Pryor Letters, 1861–1863*, ed. Charles R. Adams Jr. (Fort Valley, Ga.: Garret Publications, 1989), 296; Francis W. Dawson to My dear Mother, April 23, 1863, quoted in Francis W. Dawson, *Reminiscences of Confederate Service, 1861–1865*, ed. Bell I. Wiley (1882; reprint, Baton Rouge: Louisiana State University Press, 1980), 192. H. A. Ogden's famous print of Lee at Fredericksburg portrays almost precisely the cast and scene described by Dawson.

40. John Esten Cooke, *A Life of Gen. Robert E. Lee* (New York: D. Appleton, 1871), 184. In *R. E. Lee*, 2:462, Douglas Southall Freeman cited Cooke's biography but changed the quotation to: "It is well that war is so terrible—we should grow too fond of it!" Freeman's more dramatic form of the statement is quoted far more often than Cooke's original version and has become one of the most famous of Lee's utterances. In *Military Memoirs of a Confederate: A Critical Narrative* (New York: Scribner's, 1907), 302, Edward Porter Alexander remarked that "it is told that, on one of the Federal repulses from Marye's Heights, Lee put his hand upon Longstreet's arm and said, 'It is well that war is so terrible, or we would grow too fond of it.'" Freeman considered Alexander's book the most valuable account of Lee's operations and may have taken his wording in *R. E. Lee*, which differs only in the deletion of "or" and the substitution of "should" for "would," from Alexander while citing Cooke's work because it first established the basic quotation. Longstreet's postwar writings made no mention of Lee's saying anything like this on December 13, 1862.

41. Bryan Grimes, *Extracts of Letters of Major-General Bryan Grimes, to His Wife, Written While in Active Service in the Army of Northern Virginia,*

comp. Pulaski Cowper (1883; reprint, Wilmington, N.C.: Broadfoot, 1986), 26–27.

42. *OR* 21:555.

43. R. E. Lee to Mrs. Lee, December 16, 1862, quoted in Robert E. Lee, *The Wartime Papers of R. E. Lee*, ed. Clifford Dowdey and Louis H. Manarin (Boston: Little, Brown, 1961), 365; Robert E. Lee Jr., *Recollections and Letters of General Robert E. Lee* (1904; reprint, Wilmington, N.C.: Broadfoot, 1988), 87.

44. Henry Heth, "Letter from Major-General Henry Heth, of A. P. Hill's Corps, A.N.V.," in J. William Jones et al., eds., *Southern Historical Society Papers*, 52 vols. (1877–1959; reprint with 3-vol. index, Wilmington, N.C.: Broadfoot, 1990–92), 4:153–54 (hereafter cited as *SHSP*). Lee made his comments about Fredericksburg in the context of a discussion of Confederate public opinion relating to Gettysburg.

45. R. E. Lee to James A. Seddon, January 10, 1863, in Lee, *Wartime Papers*, 388–89.

46. Questions about Lee's decision to remain on the defensive after the 13th persisted after the war. He paraphrased his official report in answering queries from William M. McDonald in April 1868: "The plain of Fredericksburg is completely commanded by the heights of Stafford. . . . To have advanced the whole army into the plain for the purpose of attacking General Burnside, would have been to have insured its destruction by the fire from the continued line of guns on the Stafford hills. It was considered more wise to meet the Federal army beyond the reach of their batteries than under their muzzles, and even to invite repeated renewal of their attacks. When convinced of their inutility, it was easy for them, under cover of a long, dark and tempestuous night, to cross the narrow river by means of their numerous bridges before we could ascertain their purpose." "Letter from General R. E. Lee," in *SHSP* 7:445–46.

47. R. E. Lee to Jefferson Davis, September 8, 1862, quoted in Lee, *Wartime Papers*, 301.

48. R. E. Lee to Mrs. Lee, April 19, 1863, quoted in ibid., 437–38.

49. For a systematic—and disapproving—analysis of Lee's penchant for the offensive, see chapter 4 of Alan T. Nolan, *Lee Considered: General Robert E. Lee and Civil War History* (Chapel Hill: University of North Carolina Press, 1991). For my more sympathetic interpretation, see Gary W. Gallagher, *Lee and His Generals in War and Memory* (Baton Rouge: Louisiana State University Press, 1998), 1–20. For convenient summaries of the arguments for and against Lee's greatness as a general, see Alan T. Nolan, "Historians' Perspectives on Lee," *Columbiad: A Quarterly Review of the War*

between the States 2 (Winter 1999): 27–45; and Gary W. Gallagher, "Reconsidering Lee's Revisionists," *Columbiad: A Quarterly Review of the War between the States* 4 (Spring 2000): 122–36.

50. Heth, "Letter from Major-General Heth," 154.

51. Anonymous letter to Dear Frank, September 30, 1862, quoted in Lane, ed., *Letters from Georgia Soldiers*, 208; Jones, *Diary*, 1:223.

LEE'S ARMY HAS NOT

LOST ANY OF ITS PRESTIGE

The Impact of Gettysburg

on the Army of

Northern Virginia & the

Confederate Home Front

A canvass of Confederate sentiment in the summer of 1863 suggests that many southerners did not view the battle of Gettysburg as a catastrophic defeat. Robert E. Lee's soldiers typically saw it as a temporary setback with few long-term consequences for their army. Although conceding its heavy toll in casualties, they considered neither their withdrawal from the battlefield nor the retreat from Pennsylvania as evidence that the Federals had won a decisive victory. On the home front, civilians generally drew a sharp distinction between Gettysburg and Vicksburg. The latter represented an unequivocal disaster in which the Confederacy lost an entire army, huge quantities of arms, and reliable access to the states of the Trans-Mississippi. Gettysburg presented a far more ambiguous result, and few observers believed that it anticipated eventual failure in the Eastern Theater. In a season marked by the loss of Vicksburg and Port Hudson, the opening of major Union naval operations against Charleston, and Braxton Bragg's inept maneuvering during the Tullahoma campaign, Lee's operations in Pennsylvania did not stand out as especially harmful to the Confederate cause.[1]

Yet Gettysburg and Vicksburg usually appear in the literature on the Civil War as twin calamities that marked a major turning point in the conflict. Emory Thomas struck a common note in his perceptive history of the Confederacy by observing that Gettysburg and Vicksburg, together with unsuccessful diplomatic initiatives in Europe, triggered among white southerners a "severe loss of confidence in themselves." Similarly, James M. McPherson noted in his influential history of the Civil War and Reconstruction that the "losses at Gettysburg and Vicksburg shook the Confederacy to its foundations."[2] Both Thomas and McPherson cited Josiah Gorgas to illustrate their point. "Events have succeeded one another with disastrous rapidity," wrote the Confederate chief of ordnance on July 28, 1863. "One brief month ago we were apparently at the point of success. Lee was in Pennsylvania, threatening Harrisburgh, and even Philadelphia. Vicksburgh seemed to laugh all Grant's efforts to scorn, & the Northern papers had reports of his raising the siege." Thirty days later, Lee had retreated from Pennsylvania, Vicksburg and Port Hudson had fallen, and irreplaceable men and matériel had been lost. "Yesterday we rode on the pinnacle of success — today absolute ruin seems to be our portion," stated an apparently shaken Gorgas. "The Confederacy totters to its destruction." Quoting Gorgas as a man "who best bespoke the mood" in the South, Thomas concluded that "evidence of Southern vincibility was very real in the summer of 1863."[3]

Before making the case that Gettysburg did not thrust most Confederates into depression, it is important to acknowledge that various witnesses did portray it and Vicksburg as comparably devastating reverses, questioned Lee's generalship, or believed the campaign weakened the morale and reduced the physical prowess of the Army of Northern Virginia. Representative of the latter group was diarist John B. Jones, who wrote on July 9, 1863, that the "fall of Vicksburg, alone, does not make this the darkest day of the war, as it is undoubtedly. The news from Lee's army is appalling." After prophesying on July 10 that if Lee returned to Virginia "a great revulsion of feeling" would sweep the Confederacy, Jones recorded on July 17 that "Gen. Lee has recrossed the Potomac! Thus the armies of the Confederate States are recoiling at all points, and a settled gloom is apparent on many weak faces." Robert Garlick Hill Kean of the Bureau of War reacted almost identically. "This week just ended has been one of unexampled disaster since the war began," he observed on July 12. In addition to Vicksburg and Bragg's withdrawal, "it turns out that the battle of Gettysburg was a virtual if not an actual defeat." A month later, Pierre Soulé, recently returned to the Confederacy after a brief imprisonment in the North, similarly remarked about the "sad reverse to our arms" at Gettysburg and the loss of Vicksburg and Port Hudson. "Never, since we entered upon this war," stated Soulé, "had so dreadful a blow been inflicted on our fortunes."[4]

Similarly gloomy opinions existed within the Army of Northern Virginia. "Our cause is, undoubtedly, at serious disadvantage just now," remarked William Nelson Pendleton, Lee's chief of artillery, on July 18. "The loss of Vicksburg is in itself not very injurious; but Grant's army being set free to co-operate with Rosecrans is a serious evil. Our failure at Gettysburg and these events on the Mississippi will give us a vast deal of trouble." On the same day that Pendleton wrote, one of Lee's soldiers despaired about the fall of Vicksburg and Federal threats along the coast of North Carolina. Sarcastically alluding to Lee's withdrawal across the Potomac as "what we call retreat under cover of night," this North Carolinian hoped the war would soon end. "The men are saying they will stop it next spring if nobody else can," he warned. "You understand of coarse that I think they intend fighting no longer. They are looking for those men who can whip 10 Yankees to show up. If they don't we will be whipped."[5]

Lee's performance elicited criticism from a variety of individuals. Robert G. H. Kean confided to his diary on July 26 that "Gettysburg has shaken my faith in Lee as a general." Calling the battle "worse in execution than in plan," Kean thought it "the worst disaster which has ever befallen our arms." Maj. Eugene Blackford of the 5th Alabama announced bitterly that his "blind confidence in Gen. Lee is utterly gone . . . to hurl his Army against an enemy entrenched on a mountain top, it exceeds my belief." In another harsh appraisal, Brig. Gen. Wade Hampton labeled the campaign a "complete failure" and deplored Lee's assaults against a position that "was the strongest I ever saw." Some soldiers cloaked criticisms in more gentle language, as when Alexander McNeil of Joseph B. Kershaw's brigade stated that "our wise Gen. Lee made a great mistake in making the attack."[6]

The staggering carnage at Gettysburg may have motivated thousands of men to slip away from their units on July 4. "The day after the last battle at Gettysburg," Lee informed Jefferson Davis on July 29, "on sending back the train with the wounded, it was reported that about 5,000 well men started back at night to overtake it." This message followed by two days one in which Lee told Davis of "many thousand men improperly absent from this army" and asked for a presidential proclamation of amnesty to lure them back. Lee himself issued an appeal to stragglers and deserters on July 26.[7] It is impossible to determine precise motivations for men who left the ranks (the need to attend to harvests may explain many of the absences), but the timing and scale of the problem in July and August imply a relationship between Gettysburg and the desertions.[8]

The impact of Gettysburg on the peace movement in North Carolina is more easily identified. William Woods Holden, editor of the *North Carolina Standard* of Raleigh and the state's leading proponent of a negotiated end to the conflict, had decided by mid-June 1863 that "the people of both sections are tired of war and desire peace." One of the editor's biographers notes that the "twin Confederate disasters at Gettysburg and Vicksburg," together with considerable local support for an earlier proposal to end the war, "convinced Holden that he should strike a bolder blow for peace." Throughout the summer and fall, Holden and his compatriots vociferously pressed their cause in North Carolina.[9]

Although the foregoing evidence suggests Gettysburg sent destructive tremors through Lee's army and across the South, a substantial body of testimony contradicts the idea that most Confederates classified Gettysburg as a debacle equivalent to Vicksburg, lost confidence in Lee, or believed that his army incurred irretrievable damage during the campaign. Inside the Army of Northern Virginia, soldiers stressed their tactical victory on the first day, the supreme gallantry of their assaults against powerful Federal positions, and the inability of the enemy to drive them from the field or administer a killing blow during the retreat. The following assessment relies almost exclusively on writings from the period July–August 1863 in seeking to convey a sense of how Confederates *at the time* chose to conceive of the campaign. It draws on a group of witnesses that includes soldiers from various states in Lee's army, their comrades in service outside the Army of Northern Virginia, and civilians in states across the Confederacy. As with the conclusions in the preceding two essays, those drawn from this sample must be tentative. Yet this testimony leaves no doubt that Confederate reaction to Gettysburg covered a wider spectrum than is commonly supposed.

Many newspapers initially cast Lee's raid in a positive light. Notable among these was the proadministration *Richmond Daily Dispatch*, which asserted on July 13 that the "Battle of Gettysburg was, on our part, a triumphant success—an overwhelming victory." That same day, the *Lynchburg Virginian* suggested Lee's maneuvering in

Pennsylvania had disrupted Union plans to advance against Richmond from the south. Moreover, the Army of Northern Virginia had fought "one of the bloodiest battles of the war, and inflicted upon the enemy injuries which, in all probability, exceed anything he has yet suffered in a pitched battle. Their own admissions respecting their appalling loss in officers, prove this." Pronouncing the Federals already "severely chastized," the *Virginian* predicted Lee's command would inflict further damage before recrossing the Potomac. Various newspaper accounts trumpeted, among other things, up to 40,000 Union prisoners, the Army of the Potomac in retreat toward Baltimore, and the deaths of prominent northern officers.[10]

Much of the southern press remained loath to label Lee's raid a failure analogous to Vicksburg even after his army returned to Virginia. The *Dispatch* spoke on July 18 of "both good and evil" results and was "disposed to think that the good more than balances the evil." Lee had not accomplished all that he wished, but his expedition had provided relief to war-ravaged northern Virginia, gathered enormous quantities of supplies, and above all "taught the Yankees that they, as well as we, are open to invasion." After mentioning the retreat from Pennsylvania, the fall of Vicksburg, and other reverses during the first two weeks of July, the *Charleston Daily Courier* "pass[ed] by the retrograde movement of Gen. Lee with the single observation that we feel no uneasiness concerning that great Captain and his invincible army." Three days later the *Daily Courier* disparaged the North's initial burst of joy over "the capture of Vicksburg, and the falling back of Lee." Further reflection had tempered northern celebration because it became clear that the Army of the Potomac lost the first phase of Gettysburg and held its ground thereafter only through "frightful sacrifice." Lee retired "from the field in perfect order and slowly . . . while his antagonist remained on his heights, appalled by the desperate valor of the Confederates." In a long piece on the impact of military reverses in the summer of 1863, the *Houston Tri-Weekly Telegraph* ignored Gettysburg entirely, devoting its attention exclusively to the loss of Vicksburg and Port Hudson.[11]

Some accounts took a harsher view of Gettysburg. The *Charleston Mercury*, which habitually found little to praise in the Davis government's management of the war, on July 30 declared it "impossible for an invasion to have been more foolish and disastrous"—a stance strikingly at odds with the paper's earlier calls for a Confederate offensive. Few editors opted to join the *Mercury* in painting the campaign in predominantly dark hues, though many printed reporter Peter W. Alexander's piece on the battle that questioned Lee's decision to follow the successes of July 1 with additional assaults the next day.[12]

Reports in newspapers and the Federal failure to deliver a crushing stroke against Lee's army led many civilians to see Gettysburg as less ruinous than Vicksburg. Writing on July 9, 1863, South Carolinian Emma Holmes termed Vicksburg "a terrible blow to our cause" that would "prolong the war indefinitely." But when early notices of a triumph in Pennsylvania gave way to descriptions of Lee's retreat, Holmes observed calmly, "It certainly does not appear to be the great victory at first announced, though a very great battle." "Lee has recrossed the Potomac, in admirable order, and the army in splendid trim and spirits without loss," she noted on July 17 in her last entry devoted to the Pennsylvania campaign. "His retreat from Gettysburg was strategic, to draw Meade's army from the high hills behind which they took refuge." Floride Clemson, a granddaughter of John C. Calhoun living in Maryland, did not "think the times ever looked so dark" as they did on July 17: Vicksburg and Port Hudson had fallen, and rumor said the Yankees had taken Charleston as well. As for Lee, he was "not conquored, but weakened." A physician serving with the military in Richmond pronounced both Vicksburg and Gettysburg "serious blows" but immediately clarified his relative assessment of the two: "The latter was not a defeat—an accident only prevented it from being the ruin of the Yankees." Although the "accident" went unidentified in this letter, the surgeon manifestly considered Vicksburg a more harmful reverse.[13]

Catherine Edmondston of North Carolina, whose voluminous diary is a grand storehouse of information about the war behind the lines, learned of Pemberton's capitulation from a "Dispatch which freezes the marrow in our bones." "I have no heart to write," she stated the next day. "Vicksburg has fallen! It is all true." Like Emma Holmes, Edmondston also experienced a rapid change of emotions regarding Lee's fate: "Glorious news" of a stunning victory arrived on July 9; just two days later came the first reports of a withdrawal. Certain by July 17 that Lee was back in Virginia "in safety & unmolested," she praised God but acknowledged "sore disappointment." By July 25, she could report, with open disdain for the Federals, that "Gen Lee's army said to be in fine condition—in Va Meade crossing the Potomac in '*pursuit*,' the North much exasperated against him for '*allowing Lee to escape*.'"[14]

The curmudgeonly Edmund Ruffin also distinguished between Gettysburg and Vicksburg. Events along the Mississippi constituted "a disaster primarily because it will free Grant's army to go elsewhere." Upset that first reports of a smashing success in Pennsylvania proved groundless, Ruffin nevertheless treated Lee's campaign as anything but a tragedy. The Confederates had driven the enemy back during the battle of Gettysburg and then, carrying an immense quantity of captured stores, executed a leisurely march back to the Potomac, where they held a line along the river for more than a week without disturbance. "All this does not indicate that Gen. Lee had suffered a defeat at Gettysburg, or that Meade had any idea that he had gained a victory, or was strong enough to assume an aggressive position," insisted Ruffin. Had Meade really won a victory on July 1–3 he would have "followed upon the rear of Lee's very slowly retreating army."[15]

Even more revealing was Governor Joseph E. Brown's public statement to the people of Georgia on July 17. Brown urged his constituents not to despair over the "late serious disasters to our arms, at Vicksburg and Port Hudson, together with Gen. Bragg's retreat with his army to our very borders." Nowhere did the governor mention Lee or Gettysburg, though thousands of Georgians served in the Army of Northern Virginia. It seems reasonable to infer that Brown placed the Pennsylvania campaign, which involved a retreat from enemy territory rather than from Confederate ground, in an entirely different category than operations along the Mississippi and in southeastern Tennessee.[16]

So also did Jefferson Davis. Unfailingly supportive of Lee in the weeks after Gettysburg, the president conveyed to his most trusted field commander profound disappointment with developments in the Western Theater. "I have felt more than ever before the want of your advice during the recent period of disaster," wrote Davis in late July. "You know how one army of the enemy has triumphed by attacking three of ours in detail, at Vicksburg, Port Hudson and Jackson." Less than a week had passed when Davis, clearly concerned about his home state, again raised the subject of troubles in the West: "I need your counsel but must strive to meet the requirements of the hour without distracting your attention at a time when it should be concentrated on the field before you." Lee previously had told Davis

Although most Confederates at the time of Gettysburg probably had not seen an accurate likeness of their most famous general, some undoubtedly had access to this sketch of Lee in the field by British artist Frank Vizetelly. It appeared in the Illustrated London News *on February 14, 1863, and in* Harper's Weekly *precisely one month later. (*Illustrated London News, *February 14, 1863)*

of his "regret for the fall of Vicksburg" and now responded that "reverses, even defeats" were inevitable and should be used to summon greater commitment from the people. If its citizenry's determination proved equal to the challenge, the Confederacy would triumph. Pleased with Lee's reply, Davis remarked "that after the first depression consequent upon our disasters in the West" it appeared "our people will exhibit that fortitude . . . needful to secure ultimate success." [17]

Numerous diaries and letters of Confederates outside Virginia described Lee as unbeaten and unbeatable in early 1864—a telling indication that they did not consider Gettysburg a serious defeat. In July 1863, before details about the Pennsylvania campaign reached her in the Trans-Mississippi, Kate Stone hoped "Lee the Invincible" would offset dire news from Vicksburg. Ten months and the retreat from Gettysburg wrought no change in her attitude toward Lee. "A great battle is rumored in Virginia," she wrote in May 1864, "Grant's first fight in his 'On to Richmond.' He is opposed by the Invincible Lee, and so we are satisfied we won the victory." That same May, Tennessean Belle Edmondson commented on the war in the East: "They say we have had a glorious victory in Virginia, but a dearly bought one—loss heavy on both sides—the Confederates Victorious as always under our brave Gen. Lee." An officer serving in Louisiana revealed kindred sentiments on May 27, 1864, in reacting to conflicting rumors of clashes between Lee and Grant. "I believe nothing one way or the other, until further word is received," stated Felix Pierre Poché. "But I continue to have complete faith in General Lee, who has never been known to suffer defeat, and who probably never will." [18]

Within Lee's army, soldiers such as Reuben A. Pierson of the 9th Louisiana analyzed Vicksburg and Gettysburg in very different ways. "I had nearly despaired of hearing from home," he wrote his father on July 19, 1863, from near Bunker Hill, "as we had already received the news of the fall of the Queen City Vicksburg." The surrender of Pemberton's army jolted Pierson out of a sense of growing optimism: "Before receiving the news of the sad misfortune I began to imagine that the dawn of peace had already commenced arising but now a dark pall is thrown over the scene and the lowering clouds of new troubles seem to be enveloping the bright rays of a few short weeks ago." Yet he remained confident of victory—due in large part to the prowess of the Army of Northern Virginia, which he saw as undiminished by the recent campaign. "We have just returned from an extensive tour into Pennsylvania," he reported almost casually. Thousands of prisoners, thousands of cattle and horses, and other valuable material had been taken from the enemy. Desperate fighting at Gettysburg yielded heavy losses and no clear winner—though Pierson estimated Union casualties at 30,000 to 50,000, far greater than the Confederate total. The Confederate army lay safely in Virginia "in fine health and spirits and if the yankees advance upon us we will give them a dread of the hardy boys of Gen. Lee's command."[19]

Trust in Lee remained high in the the Army of Northern Virginia. Five weeks after Gettysburg, Eli Pinson Landers of William T. Wofford's brigade asked his mother to give "the Vicksburg boys" his respects. "I know it is bad to fight under officers without confidence," he stated. "I wish they had such officers as we have got. . . . General Lee has the confidence of our whole army." Another Georgian, "once more in Dixie, safe and sound" on July 18, affirmed his readiness "for anything that may turn up, either to move forward, or backward, run or fight, or anything else Robert E. Lee wants me to do." Sgt. William Beverley Pettit of the Fluvanna Artillery scolded his wife on July 26 for being "too severe on General Lee and President Davis. They are without their peers, now upon this globe." Col. James Drayton Nance, who commanded a regiment in Lafayette McLaws's division, conceded serious troubles in the West but spoke glowingly of the situation in Virginia: "Our army is in good condition, and is constantly improving and increasing. There is more reason to expect now a victory at the next onset between Gen. Lee and Meade than there has been on other occasions."[20]

A pair of foreign observers highlighted the strong bond between Lee and his men in the immediate aftermath of the battle. On the afternoon of July 3, Lt. Col. Arthur James Lyon Fremantle, a colorful British officer temporarily attached to James Longstreet's headquarters, rode among Confederate soldiers along Seminary Ridge in the wake of the Pickett-Pettigrew assault. Fremantle marveled at the spirit of a group of gunners whom he engaged in conversation. Lee rode by as they spoke, prompting a flurry of comments: "When they observed General Lee they said, 'We've not lost confidence in the old man: this day's work won't do him no harm. "Uncle Robert" will get us into Washington yet; you bet he will!' &c." Capt. Justus Scheibert of the Prussian army found the army's spirit "so extraordinary that the weary troops received the old general with enthusiastic cheers, despite the retreat and deluded hopes. Sincere calls, such as 'Old Lee is still alive! Now all is well!' etc., expressed the true sentiments of the men." Nothing the Prussian had seen in the Confederacy "touched and moved me more than the faithfulness of these thoroughly drenched, muddy, and ragged warriors to their noble leader in the disappointment of defeat."[21]

Knowledge that they had not been driven from the field enabled Lee's soldiers to treat Gettysburg as no more than a bloody disappointment. Many of them emphasized the dramatic Confederate triumph on July 1, rationalizing the costly repulses on the second and third days as inevitable because of the enemy's strong positions. "The first day our arms met with complete success," William Aiken Kelly of the 1st South Carolina observed soon after the battle, "every point which we attacked was carried, and the loss of the enemy far exceeded ours." The next two days "were not so successful"—though Kelly would "not say we were defeated by the enemy." The Federals held ground of "the strongest kind" and enjoyed superior numbers. "Had they left their protection, I think we would have defeated them," he concluded. "As it is, I consider that we were victorious on the first day, and that the other two were drawn battles, for on the 4th, the time we fell back, it is reported that the enemy did the same."[22]

Reuben Pierson similarly spoke of whipping the Federals badly on July 1 and driving them from their outer works before failing "to carry the heights on which their batteries were planted." Like Kelly, he also mentioned a Union predilection for safe ground: "[T]hey know we are superior in valor to their men and therefore always seek some advantages of position." Pierson placed casualties during the campaign in perspective as well, conceding the loss of "many noble and gallant men" but suggesting that "we should have lost equally as many in a battle of Virginia and besides we would not have procured a single lot of supplies."[23]

A lieutenant in the 11th North Carolina of J. Johnston Pettigrew's brigade echoed Pierson in placing Gettysburg in a broader military context. Although characterizing the battle as a very bloody encounter that extracted an "awful cost" from his regiment, William B. Taylor saw Gettysburg as just part of a larger season of campaigning: "I suppose that there will be one more battle this summer or fall," he mused on July 29, 1863, from Culpeper, "and if we do have a fight here we will give them one of the worst thrashings they ever got." Taylor inferred that the desultory Federal pursuit following July 3 indicated the Army of the Potomac lacked the fortitude to defeat Lee's army.[24]

The absence of aggressive Federal tactics either at Gettysburg or thereafter elicited extensive comment from Lee's soldiers. Charles Minor Blackford conceded a technical defeat because the southern assaults "failed to carry the enemy's lines." But he quickly stressed that "we held our own, slept on the battle-field and remained there for twenty-four hours without molestation, showing that we had so punished the enemy that they were incapable of an advance." A private in the Amherst Artillery wrote in his diary on July 4, "The Yanks have not come down from the hills east of Gettysburg and have shown no desire to attack us at any time during the day." In several later entries, this gunner alluded to the complete absence of offensive moves from the enemy. Looking back over the previous five weeks on August 15, 1863, Edgeworth Bird, a quartermaster in Henry L. Benning's brigade, remarked that the "Battle of Gettysburg so disabled Meade, that he is unable to resume the offensive." The Federals fought well when shielded by "rock walls built on the mountain side and tops," Bird had stated previously, but their "army retreated at the same time our fellows fell back and did not attempt to follow up." [25]

The natural strength of the Union line impressed almost all the Confederates. Brig. Gen. Stephen Dodson Ramseur, whose aggressiveness in battle matched that of anyone in the army, stated that "the enemy occupied a Gibralter of a position." Colonel Nance averred that his men understood they were not more successful only because "the position, against which they were thrown, was well nigh *impregnable.*" A Georgian who wrote from a Union hospital after the battle concurred with Nance, relating that an appreciation of the enemy's advantage in ground and supplies rendered the repulse "not attall discouraging to our army." Edgeworth Bird told his wife how the Confederates "found the enemy posted in a terribly secure position," adding that the attempt to drive Federals from "the heights and mountains at Gettysburg was certainly very unfortunate." Characteristic of the way in which soldiers accepted the disappointments of the campaign yet denied losing the battle, Bird stated that Lee "had met no defeat, but certainly failed in his plans at Gettysburg, and at great loss." A surgeon in A. P. Hill's corps, Spencer Glasgow Welch,

Contemporary Confederate accounts frequently praised the bravery Lee's troops exhibited in attacking well-positioned Union defenders at Gettysburg. This wartime engraving, which appeared in Frank Leslie's illustrated Newspaper, *shows the assault by North Carolina and Louisiana troops from Jubal Early's division against East Cemetery Hill on the evening of July 2. (Author's collection)*

put the case succinctly: "We drove the Yankees three miles from the battlefield to a long range of hills, from which it was impossible to dislodge them."[26]

There was no loss of honor in failing to capture such positions. Dutifully reporting to his fiancée that "our glorious army was repulsed at Gettysburg," Dodson Ramseur admired how "our gallant troops stormed and restormed" the enemy lines, "sometimes successfully but finally we were compelled to withdraw from the unequal contest." Edgeworth Bird lauded the infantrymen who "performed heroic deeds, and died heroic deaths" in doomed efforts to dislodge the entrenched Federals. As the attackers "rushed up into the very jaws of death," noted an appreciative artillerist, "our men performed deeds of daring and heroism which covered them with glory." Col. David Wyatt Aiken of the 7th South Carolina wasted few words in illustrating the same point: Pickett's soldiers "made several brilliant charges, but failed in driving the enemy from their walls." [27]

No one captured the sense of honorable failure better than Fremantle, who addressed the subject on July 14, four days after he had left the Army of Northern Virginia and entered Union lines. Hearing talk among northerners of the "total demoralization" of the rebels, Fremantle ventured the opinion that "Lee's army has not lost any of its prestige at the battle of Gettysburg, in which it most gallantly stormed strong intrenchments defended by the whole army of the Potomac, which never ventured outside its works, or approached in force within half a mile of the Confederate artillery." [28]

Lee's official report of the campaign also touched on this subject. After describing the commanding ground held by the Federals, Lee lavished praise on the soldiers who tried to seize it. "The conduct of the troops was all that I could desire or expect," wrote the appreciative general, "and they deserve success so far as it can be deserved by heroic valor and fortitude." Their ultimate failure at Gettysburg in no way diminished his "admiration of their noble qualities" or his "confidence in their ability to cope successfully with the enemy." [29] Such words undoubtedly bolstered his men's feelings of worthy striving against impossible obstacles and helped cushion the disappointment of repulse.

If the Federals had been denied their wonderful defensive position, agreed many Confederates, the battle would have gone differently. "I think we were too confident . . . ," admitted Virginia artillerist William Watts Parker. "We had forgotten the power of the spade and the immense advantages which position may give." Parker claimed that not a single man wanted to retreat across the Potomac—they sought only an opportunity "to whip the Yankees any day on a *fair field.*" Brig. Gen. Clement A. Evans adopted an almost smug tone in a July 8 postmortem on the battle: "At some points the Yankees fought pretty stubborn but where ever we had a fair field we whipped & slaughtered them in great numbers." In a follow-up analysis two days later, the Georgian termed the enemy "uneasy— not confident of their ability to whip us." Events of July 1 indicated "how easily we can whip them on fair ground." Employing essentially the same language, an artillerist in Richard S. Ewell's corps stated that it was evident the Yankees would not leave their high ground to "advance upon us, where we might whip them, for there we would be on equal grounds." As judicious a man as Edward Porter Alexander, who had directed the First Corps artillery in the heaviest fighting on July 2–3, remarked that he thought Lee would seek another battle—"and we are all anxious for it, thinking that we had not a fair showing at Gettysburg." [30]

Another thread running through Confederate accounts was that want of supplies rather than the Federal army dictated Lee's decision to retreat. General Evans's diary for July 9 singled out the lack of regular rations as the army's "greatest difficulty." Were food not a problem, "the Campaign in Maryland and Pennsylvania could be prolonged indefinitely but this difficulty will force us back to Virginia sooner than all the Yankee army ever could." The day after the battle, a captain in Harry T. Hays's Louisiana brigade recorded that "Gen. Lee at this time gave the Federal General a fine opportunity of attacking him, but it was declined." Because Lee had ammunition for just two days and "was far distant from his depots of supply," he "was obliged to put himself on the defensive." Another Louisiana soldier remarked that at Gettysburg each "party seemed to hazard all upon the issue and we should have gained the day but for a want of cannon ammunition." A North Carolinian sketched a stalemate on the battlefield followed by withdrawal precipitated by logistical needs. After the Federals threw out skirmishers on July 4 and "pretended as if they intended to advance upon us," the two armies, both "*badly* crippled, retired in different directions." "If we had only remained 'till next day we could have claimed the victory," believed this officer. "But our supplies were exhausted, and a retrograde movement absolutely necessary." [31]

With typical astuteness, Porter Alexander examined the recent campaign in a letter to his father shortly after returning to Virginia. As Lee's former chief of ordnance and the premier Confederate artillerist, he was especially sensitive to the problem of procuring ammunition at great distances from secure bases of supply. Three days of severe fighting at Gettysburg had left the army "almost entirely out of ammunition," a circumstance that seemed inevitable in campaigns of this type. "I do not think we can ever successfully invade," thought Alexander, "the ammunition question alone being enough to prevent it." No amount of courage and tactical gain could overcome this deficiency because "our army is not large enough to stand the casualties even of a victory in the enemy's country." [32]

A comment from FitzGerald Ross suggests the focus on supplies may have been quite general in the ten days after the battle. An Englishman serving as an officer in the Austrian Hussars, Ross accompanied Lee's army into Pennsylvania and mingled with a number of generals and their staffs. He noted the reaction when word of Lee's decision to recross the Potomac filtered through the army as it lay near Hagerstown: "Many were disappointed at this decision, as it had been the general opinion that the army was only waiting for fresh supplies to recommence offensive operations." It is not clear whether Ross noticed this phenomenon just among the officers with whom he spent most of his time, or if it existed within the ranks as well.[33]

Whatever the answer to that question, Brig. Gen. Ambrose R. Wright, "Jeb" Stuart, and Sgt. Alexander Murdock of the 2nd North Carolina Infantry exemplified those about whom Ross wrote. "What our next movement will be I cannot tell," Wright stated while near Hagerstown on July 7, "but I think that as soon as we get our ammunition supplied, we shall march in the direction of Washington." Wright hoped that recent heavy rains had not disrupted the flow of supplies to the degree that withdrawal into Virginia would be Lee's only option. As for Stuart, he thought the Confederates had "the better of the fight at Gettysburg," retiring only because of their inability to hold the ground they captured and a lack of sufficient ammunition. Lee's maneuvering the Federals out of Virginia represented the "grandest piece of strategy ever heard of"; 10,000 reinforcements and "*plenty of ammunition*" after Gettysburg would have permitted the army to achieve decisive results. After a period to recuperate and gather strength, Stuart predicted a return to Pennsylvania—"it is the only path to peace." Sergeant Murdock attributed Lee's retreat to a "scarcity of ammunition and provisions." "I am now again in Virginia," he informed his nephew on July 19. "From present appearances though I do not think we will remain long here but will again take the back track. I think we will go again into Maryland if not into Pennsylvania. I hope we will as I did not want to come back at all. We are not whipped yet and I do not believe that it is in the power of the whole Yankee army to give us one."[34]

A sense that the northern populace had gotten off too easily also provoked some unhappiness about recrossing the Potomac. "I had rather have stayed [north of the river] if wee could have been successful," wrote Capt. S. G. Pryor of the 12th Georgia on July 16. "I hated the idea of falling back again. I wanted them to feel the war more, have it at their homes; the people where the army has been know something about it." LeRoy S. Edwards of the 12th Virginia, writing on July 7, expressed strong reservations about returning to the Confederacy. He preferred that "the people of this country should feel more in their homes of war and thereby more fully appreciate the condition of Virginia, and note our unwavering undying determination to prosecute to the last, the end we had in view when we first marched to arms." [35]

Less strident but still willing to carry the war northward again was William L. Barrier of the 1st North Carolina Cavalry. Guessing that Lee meant "to make Pennsylvania feel the effects of war before he recrosses the Potomac," Barrier empathized with the "badly frightened" Pennsylvania Dutch who "take their little bundles under their arms and leave their homes to the ravages of the army." "It looks hard to see so fine a country overrun by an army," wrote Barrier, "but I guess it is fair." [36]

These frequent allusions to maintaining their position after July 3, the enemy's impressive advantage in ground and timidity in the open field, and the critical shortage of ammunition and other supplies help to explain a widespread conviction among Lee's soldiers that the Federals had not demonstrated superiority on the field at Gettysburg. That conviction led in turn to a defiant affirmation of the Army of Northern Virginia's spirit. Four days after the battle, while the Confederates faced a doubtful future north of the Potomac, Ambrose Wright wrote that the army had reached Hagerstown "in good condition, (except a scarcity of artillery ammunition) and in fine spirits." Just after crossing to the south side of the Potomac, a member of the 24th Georgia exuded confidence in predicting it would take Meade a long time to drive the Confederates out of their new lines: "We have given him one whipping since we have been over here and if he fools with us we will give it to him again." On July 16, Charles Minor Blackford described a relaxed and confident air at Bunker Hill, where the soldiers were "washing and dressing up again and repairing the ravages of the campaign upon their scanty wardrobe." "They are in fine spirits," concluded Blackford, "and not the least depressed by the results of the invasion." As both "crippled up" armies rested in early August, Surgeon Welch anticipated no imminent Union movement. The army was "in splendid health and spirits," and the "Yankees dread us too much" to initiate any action. Maj. Gen. Lafayette McLaws, whose division had suffered very heavy casualties on July 2, similarly detected the army's "old spirit" in mid-August as it awaited Meade's next move in northern Virginia.[37]

Some men tied their comments to reports of wavering morale behind the lines. "There is a terrible band of veterans here yet," Edgeworth Bird assured his wife on July 19. In light of events in Mississippi and Tennessee and at Charleston, he proudly held up the Army of Northern Virginia as "the great hope of the South." Comments by soldiers returning from furloughs in August left Bird "astonished at the state of public feeling in Georgia." "They say Georgia is now almost whipped, and she has hardly ever had an armed heel on her soil," he wrote from the stern perspective of one who had seen war-ravaged Virginia. "The army here thinks it can whip its weight in wild cats and has no mistrusts or apprehension," he stated pointedly. "I hope there is no truth in these reports." Captain Pryor, who worried that civilians in Georgia had become despondent and willing to give up the cause, assured his wife that people on the home front "kneed not fear: the old veterans of Lee's army isent whiped, never has been, and I think [it] will be a long time before they are whiped." Capt. Green Berry Samuels, a Virginian in George H. Steuart's brigade, also implored his wife not to feel discouraged: "We still have a grand army to battle for us ... and by God's grace we will soon strike the enemy such a blow, that his hopes of subjugation will be as far off as before the fall of Vicksburg." Two weeks later Samuels ventured the hope that the army, which was "in fine health," would punish the Yankees "for the horrid barbarities inflicted upon the helpless citizens within their lines." [38]

Back in Richmond, Josiah Gorgas evidently heard such positive reports from Lee's army. His diary entries in August and early September reflect greater optimism than the oft-quoted passage of late July. All seemed quiet on Lee's front, he recorded on the 24th, "and his army appears to be nearly in its original good condition." Gorgas estimated shortly thereafter that six hundred men a day were swelling Lee's ranks. By September 6, the ordnance chief alluded to the army's "excellent condition" and speculated that Lee was considering taking the offensive and perhaps marching into Maryland.[39]

An appreciable minority of soldiers went beyond protestations of good morale to paint a positive picture of the entire campaign. Their criteria for determining success included damage to northern civilians, capture of animals and supplies, and Union losses at Gettysburg. A quartet of Georgians touched on each of these topics. "We had a nice time of it in Pennsylvania," observed Lt. Joseph Hilton of the 26th Georgia, "and have inflicted serious injury upon the corpulent Dutch farmers of that loyal state." Sidney J. Richardson of the 21st Georgia concentrated on four-legged acquisitions: "[W]e have taken a great many wagon horses, and beef cattle over here, it is one of the greatest raids this army ever made." The army had to fight in Pennsylvania, but Richardson believed there would have been combat in any case. On July 8, a soldier in Wofford's brigade alluded to hard marching and fighting since his last letter home: "[W]e gave them another good whipping. . . . The enemy admit a loss of 25,000 men." [40]

Clement Evans deplored the fact that the campaign "accomplished a good deal but still the army & the Public are both disappointed." Expectations were too high. For the Army of Northern Virginia to capture Washington, destroy the Army of the Potomac, and end the war in six weeks, as some evidently hoped, "was a physical impossibility." Such unreasonable goals cast a shadow over the army's solid gains. The Confederates took a thousand wagons, perhaps two thousand horses, many provisions, and "taught the Pennsylvanians what war is & left in their state a great battle field to contemplate, with a large town full of their thousands of wounded." More than that, Evans believed that the Confederates "can make the Yankee army behave very respectfully in Virginia for the balance of the Summer." [41]

What of Robert E. Lee? He knew better than anyone else the objectives of the campaign, the tactical story at Gettysburg, and the extent of Confederate casualties. A series of letters written within a month of the battle, primarily to Jefferson Davis and Mary Lee, underscore the fact that he did not consider the campaign a major disappointment with ominous implications for his army and the Confederacy. On the contrary, as Lee described it, the foray into Pennsylvania accomplished much of what he had set out to do.

It is important to keep in mind Lee's goals before discussing his response to the campaign.[42] He favored a movement into the North for strategic and logistical reasons. A continued stance along the Rappahannock River invited Joseph Hooker's Army of the Potomac to "force this army back within the entrenchments" of Richmond or to pin it down while Federals on the Peninsula approached the Confederate capital from the southeast. If Lee marched northward with a reinforced Army of Northern Virginia, however, he could pull Hooker after him, siphon Union troops "from the Southern coasts and give some respite in that quarter," and perhaps find an opening to strike an effective blow. On June 25, from opposite Williamsport, Maryland, he summarized for Jefferson Davis the minimum he hoped to achieve: "I think I can throw Genl Hooker's army across the Potomac and draw troops from the south, embarrassing their plan of campaign in a measure, if I can do nothing more and have to return."[43] In terms of logistics, a raid into Pennsylvania promised the dual benefits of providing a respite for the farmers of north-central Virginia and the Shenandoah Valley and affording Lee's army access to badly needed food and fodder in the North.[44]

Lee first informed President Davis of the failed assaults at Gettysburg in a message dated July 4, conjecturing that "the enemy suffered severely" while acknowledging "our own loss has not been light." Three days later, with the army at Hagerstown, a second letter to Davis isolated the strong Union defensive position and logistical difficulties as the principal reasons for the retreat. Lee also wrote to his wife Mary on July 7, assuring her that "Our noble men are cheerful & confident." He expanded on the topic of morale (and mentioned again Meade's "much shattered" force) on the 8th. "Though reduced in numbers by the hardships & battles through which it has passed since leaving the Rappahannock," he stated to Davis regarding his army, "its condition is good and its confidence unimpaired." Lee was "not in the least discouraged," and his faith "in the fortitude of this army" remained unshaken. Reiterating on the 10th and 11th that the army was in "good condition," Lee mentioned that ammunition had been replenished but that food was becoming a problem because of the swollen Potomac.[45]

On July 12, Lee wrote to both Davis and Mary. In obvious reference to inaccurate newspaper coverage, he told Mary that "our success at Gettysburg was not as great as reported." The army had "failed to drive the enemy from his position" and had withdrawn to the Potomac. He reported all quiet to Davis, adding that if the waters of the Potomac had not risen everything "would have been accomplished that could have been reasonably expected": the Army of the Potomac pushed north of the river, Federal troops drawn from the Virginia and Carolina coasts, and a summer offensive by the enemy thwarted. His next letter to Mary placed the raid in a quite favorable context. The army, he said, had returned "rather sooner than I had originally contemplated, but having accomplished what I purposed on leaving the Rappahannock, viz., relieving the Valley of the presence of the enemy & drawing his army north of the Potomac."[46]

About this time Lee met with Maj. John Seddon, brother of the Confederate secretary of war, who later related the details of the conversation to Henry Heth.[47] Though not direct evidence, these comments correspond closely with Lee's written statements in July 1863 and bear specifically on how he viewed Gettysburg. As Heth quoted Seddon, the general argued that the heavy loss at Gettysburg did not exceed what "it would have been from the series of battles I would have been compelled to fight had I remained in Virginia." According to Seddon's account of the meeting, Lee rose from his chair after making this comment, gestured forcefully, and said: "[S]ir, we did whip them at Gettysburg, and it will be seen for the next six months that *that army* will be as quiet as a sucking dove."[48]

Once back in the lower Shenandoah Valley, Lee reported to Davis that his men needed shoes and clothing but enjoyed "good health and spirits." He soon shifted the army to Culpeper, whence he wrote Mary that his men had "laboured hard, endured much & behaved nobly." Echoing Clement Evans, he asserted, with implicit self-criticism, that the army "ought not to have been expected to have performed impossibilities or to have fulfilled the anticipations of the thoughtless & unreasonable." More explicitly self-critical was a letter in which he confessed to his cousin Margaret Stuart that the "army did all it could. I fear I required of it impossibilities." His movement across the Potomac had pulled the Federals north of the river, he informed his cousin, where they might have stayed "if we only could have been strong enough." The army had behaved "nobly and cheerfully, and though it did not win a victory it conquered a success." With no hint that he believed his soldiers less than equal to the task, he observed: "We must now prepare for harder blows and harder work."[49]

When Jefferson Davis expressed concern on July 21 about the absence of information on casualties, Lee promised an official tally as soon as he received one. "[A]s far as I can judge," he went on to say, "the killed, wounded, and missing from the time we left the Rappahannock until our return will not fall short of twenty thousand." The number of wounded and missing would be especially large. Many of the former had to be left in Pennsylvania; the missing included thousands of stragglers (some of whom had begun to return to the army) in addition to prisoners and the "wounded unfit to be transported." As to the Federals, information derived from local citizens and Union prisoners indicated an Army of the Potomac "much reduced in numbers" that seemed "content to remain quiescent."[50]

Lee gave Davis his fullest assessment of Gettysburg in a letter of July 31. The president had sent a censorious clipping from the *Charleston Mercury*, which Lee labeled ill informed and contradictory. "No blame can be attached to the army for its failure to accomplish what was projected by me," wrote Lee, "nor should it be censured for the unreasonable expectations of the public." Taking full responsibility, Lee admitted to Davis, as he had to Margaret Stuart, that he probably "expected too much" of his men's "prowess & valour." But in his opinion the army achieved "a general success, though it did not win a victory." He had thought victory within reach while on the field and still believed that "if all things could have worked together it would have been accomplished." Had he known the final assaults on July 3 would fail, he would have followed another course—though what "the ultimate result would have been is not so clear to me." The army's loss had been "very heavy," but so had been the enemy's, whose impaired condition made possible Lee's safe retreat.[51]

Lee's comments shared basic themes with those of many of his officers and men. The Confederates had faced a well-positioned foe at Gettysburg, fought gallantly but without ultimate success, and lost heavily while inflicting such reciprocal damage the Federals shunned any counteroffensive. Withdrawn in part because of problems of supply, the army retained its high morale during the retreat and after it recrossed the Potomac. Lee's suggestion that the raid accomplished most of its objectives was a more positive reading than all save a handful of his men gave the campaign, but he knew better than they that the capture of Washington or the destruction of the Army of the Potomac never had been goals. The Federals seemed content to sit quietly as the summer passed; Richmond faced no immediate threat; and the army had procured animals and food while north of the Potomac. Thus Lee could speak of a "general success" despite a costly reverse in the campaign's showcase battle.[52]

While there is no reason to dismiss Lee's postcampaign analysis as dishonest, some might question his lenient criteria for judging success. On three points at least he could have admitted greater disappointment. First, he originally hoped to stay north until late summer or early fall to partake of northern bounty and keep the enemy off guard.[53] Second, he almost certainly had not envisioned retiring to the Rappahannock River line so quickly after he returned to Virginia (whenever that might have been). And finally, despite his many allusions to Union casualties, the enormity of Confederate losses must have chastened him more than he betrayed.

Indeed, a hint of hidden disappointment surfaced in early August when persistent criticism in newspapers such as the *Charleston Mercury* provoked Lee to tender his resignation. "I have seen and heard of expression of discontent in the public journals at the result of the expedition," wrote the general to Jefferson Davis. "I do not know how far this feeling extends in the army. My brother officers have been too kind to report it, and so far the troops have been too generous to exhibit it." But Lee acknowledged that some of his soldiers likely harbored doubts about him, and no matter how able an officer might be, "if he loses the confidence of his troops disaster must sooner or later ensue." For this reason, and because of his uncertain health, Lee requested that Davis "take measures to supply my place." The president wasted no time in assuring his "dear friend" that there was no one "more fit to command," and that isolated carping could not "detract from the achievements which will make you and your army the subject of history and object of the world's admiration for generations to come." With that comforting reassurance in hand, Lee dropped the subject.[54] A fair interpretation of this coda to the campaign might be that while Lee did not believe he had been defeated in Pennsylvania, he harbored a sense of lost opportunity that left him easily wounded by criticism.

If Lee emerged from Pennsylvania poised but with some ambivalence about the campaign, his mood conformed to that of most of his soldiers and their kinfolk at home. There was reason not to despair over the campaign. After all, the Federals in Virginia *were* almost "as quiet as a sucking dove" for the rest of 1863 and well into the spring of 1864. The army's cocky assurance that every battle would be a victory regardless of the odds received a jolt at Gettysburg, but the vast majority of Lee's soldiers remained in the ranks and looked to him with undiminished confidence. Although casualties had been hideous, the Army of Northern Virginia (as well as other Confederate armies) had absorbed brutal losses on other fields and recovered rather quickly. From a civilian perspective, the negative results of the Pennsylvania campaign seemed largely transitory when contrasted with the loss of Vicksburg and other dire news in June and July 1863.

Confederates across the South persisted in viewing Lee as an invincible commander whose army increasingly sustained the hopes of the entire nation. For them, as for most of the men in the Army of Northern Virginia, Gettysburg was not a harbinger of eventual ruin.[55]

NOTES

1. It is worthwhile to note that Gettysburg did not loom as large in 1863 as it does today. A number of factors explain why it eventually captured the popular imagination as *the* decisive turning point of the Civil War—among them Lincoln's decision to explore the meaning of the war in his remarks at Gettysburg in November 1863, the immense volume of Lost Cause writings that focused on Gettysburg in search of the key to Confederate defeat, the sheer scale of the battle, and the fact that it represented the deepest penetration into northern territory of any southern army. But in attempting to gauge the immediate impact of Gettysburg on the Confederacy, it is important to bear in mind that Lincoln's speech lay months ahead, that Lost Cause warriors would not emerge as a major force for a decade, and that no one knew Gettysburg would be the bloodiest engagement of the conflict and the geographical high-water mark of Confederate arms. In sum, the battle now perceived as the most famous military event in American history did not overshadow all other campaigns at the time.

2. Emory M. Thomas, *The Confederate Nation, 1861–1865* (New York: Harper & Row, 1979), 243–44; James M. McPherson, *Ordeal by Fire: The Civil War and Reconstruction,* 2nd ed. (New York: McGraw-Hill, 1992), 332.

3. Josiah Gorgas, *The Civil War Diary of General Josiah Gorgas,* ed. Frank E. Vandiver (University: University of Alabama Press, 1947), 55; Thomas, *Confederate Nation,* 244. For McPherson's use of Gorgas's diary, see *Ordeal by Fire,* 332, as well as his *Battle Cry of Freedom: The Civil War Era* (New York: Oxford University Press, 1988), 665.

4. John B. Jones, *A Rebel War Clerk's Diary at the Confederate States Capital,* 2 vols. (1866; reprint, Alexandria, Va.: Time-Life Books, 1982), 1:374, 381; Robert Garlick Hill Kean, *Inside the Confederate Government: The Diary of Robert Garlick Hill Kean,* ed. Edward Younger (New York: Oxford University Press, 1957), 79; Pierre Soulé to Edwin De Leon, August 12, 1863, in *Catalog 89,* Chapel Hill Rare Books (Carrboro, N.C., 1994), item 125.

5. Susan P. Lee, *Memoirs of William Nelson Pendleton, D.D.* (1893; reprint, Harrisonburg, Va.: Sprinkle Publications, 1991), 297; B. R. Kinney to W. H. Badgett, July 18, 1863, typescript, Fredericksburg and Spotsylvania National Military Park Library, Fredericksburg, Va.

6. Kean, *Inside the Confederate Government*, 84; Blackford's letter of July 18, 1863, to an unnamed recipient in L. Minor Blackford, *Mine Eyes Have Seen the Glory* (Cambridge, Mass.: Harvard University Press, 1954), 220–21; Wade Hampton to Joseph E. Johnston, July 30, 1863, quoted in Herman Hattaway and Archer Jones, *How the North Won: A Military History of the Civil War* (Urbana: University of Illinois Press, 1983), 414; Alexander McNeil to his wife, July 8, 1863, Alexander McNeil Letters, Kershaw's Brigade File, Gettysburg National Military Park Library, Gettysburg, Pennsylvania (repository hereafter cited as GNMP). Uneasiness about Lee's aggressive tactics surfaced during the battle itself. Capt. Joseph Graham, whose Charlotte Artillery supported James Johnston Pettigrew's infantry on July 3, described how the prospect of direct assaults against formidable Federal positions recalled raw images of past failures. Pettigrew's infantry "moved right through my Battery," wrote Graham in late July 1863, "and I feared then I could see a want of resolution in our men. And I heard many say, 'that is worse than Malvern Hill,' and 'I don't hardly think that position can be carried,' etc., etc., enough to make me apprehensive about the result." Joseph Graham to William Alexander Graham, July 30, 1863, in William Alexander Graham, *The Papers of William Alexander Graham*, vol. 5 (1857–63), ed. Max R. Williams and J. G. de Roulhac Hamilton (Raleigh: North Carolina Office of Archives and History, 1973), 514.

7. U.S. War Department, *The War of the Rebellion: A Compilation of the Official Records of the Union and Confederate Armies*, 127 vols., index, and atlas (Washington: GPO, 1880–1901), ser. 1, vol. 27, pt. 3:1048, 1041, 1040 (hereafter cited as *OR;* all references are to volumes in ser. 1). On the problem of desertion after Gettysburg, see Douglas Southall Freeman, *Lee's Lieutenants: A Study in Command*, 3 vols. (New York: Scribner's, 1942–44), 3:217–19, which offers a good brief discussion, and Richard Reid, "A Test Case of the 'Crying Evil': Desertion among North Carolina Troops during the Civil War," *North Carolina Historical Review* 58 (July 1981): 235–62, which challenges the conventional view that North Carolinians deserted in especially large numbers because of the antiwar activities in their home state of William Woods Holden.

8. Regiments that had lost key officers, incurred especially heavy losses at Gettysburg, or lacked good leadership in general faced special problems of morale. One such unit was the 23rd North Carolina of Alfred Iverson's brigade. Subjected to needless butchery through Iverson's criminal sloth on July 1, the 23rd limped through July with declining morale and thinned ranks. "[O]ur soiders are very near give up all hope of ever whiping the Yanks," wrote one member of the 23rd on July 17. Another remarked that

the regiment needed "recruits here verry bad. There is but 7 in our Company. Times are verry disheartening here at present." This man was nonetheless sad to learn of a call for more conscripts from North Carolina: "I dont think their is any their to spair." J. F. Coghill to "Pappy, Ma, and Mit," July 17, 1863, J. F. Coghill Papers, Southern Historical Collection, Wilson Library, University of North Carolina, Chapel Hill (repository hereafter cited as SHC); W. J. O. McDaniel to Mrs. Torrence, July 20, 1863, in Haskell Monroe, ed., "'The Road to Gettysburg'—The Diary and Letters of Leonidas Torrence of the Gaston Guards," *North Carolina Historical Review* 36 (October 1959): 516. The 23rd lost 282 of its 316 men at Gettysburg, a percentage of 89.2 that ranked second only to the 8th Virginia's 92.2 percent casualties. John W. Busey and David G. Martin, *Regimental Strengths and Losses at Gettysburg* (Hightstown, N.J.: Longstreet House, 1986), 298.

9. William C. Harris, *William Woods Holden: Firebrand of North Carolina Politics* (Baton Rouge: Louisiana State University Press, 1987), 131–32. For a good brief discussion of the peace movement in North Carolina, see chapter 18 of W. Buck Yearns and John G. Barrett, eds., *North Carolina Civil War Documentary* (Chapel Hill: University of North Carolina Press, 1980).

10. *Richmond Daily Dispatch*, July 13, 1863; *Lynchburg Virginian*, July 13, 1863. See the *Richmond Daily Dispatch*, July 8, 1863, for a comparison of Gettysburg to Hannibal's victory of annihilation over the Romans at Cannae. The best brief account of southern newspaper coverage of the battle is in J. Cutler Andrews, *The South Reports the Civil War* (Princeton, N.J.: Princeton University Press, 1970), 302–19.

11. *Richmond Daily Dispatch*, July 18, 1863; *Charleston Daily Courier*, July 14, 17, 1863; *Houston Tri-Weekly Telegraph*, August 17, 1863.

12. The *Mercury* is quoted in Freeman, *Lee's Lieutenants*, 3:168; a brief discussion of the impact of Alexander's account is in Andrews, *The South Reports the Civil War*, 316–17. Some civilians felt betrayed by what they saw as dishonest press accounts. On learning of Lee's repulse, for example, Virginian William M. Blackford railed against newspapers that had reported "a grand and crowning victory." Blackford, *Mine Eyes Have Seen the Glory*, 222.

13. Emma Holmes, *The Diary of Miss Emma Holmes, 1861–1866*, ed. John F. Marszalek (Baton Rouge: Louisiana State University Press, 1979), 281–83; Floride Clemson, *A Rebel Came Home: The Diary and Letters of Floride Clemson, 1863–1866*, ed. Ernest J. Lander Jr. and Charles M. McGee Jr., rev. ed. (Columbia: University of South Carolina Press, 1989), 37; William Alexander Thom to Pembroke Thom, August 31, 1863, in Catherine Thom

Bartlett, ed., *"My Dear Brother"*: *A Confederate Chronicle* (Richmond, Va.: Dietz Press, 1952), 106. In *Civil Wars: Women and the Crisis of Southern Nationalism* (Urbana: University of Illinois Press, 1989), 211, George C. Rable emphasizes the importance of newspapers in molding women's perceptions of Lee's campaign: Gettysburg should have completed a "process of demoralization" triggered by high casualties and the absence of prospects for peace, "but curiously it did not. In many parts of the Confederacy, wildly inaccurate accounts led women to believe for a month or more that Lee had soundly whipped the Federals and was marching on Philadelphia or Baltimore or Washington."

14. Catherine Ann Devereux Edmondston, *"Journal of a Secesh Lady"*: *The Diary of Catherine Ann Devereux Edmondston, 1860–1866*, ed. Beth Gilbert Crabtree and James W. Patton (Raleigh: North Carolina Division of Archives and History, 1979), 425–27, 434, 440.

15. Edmund Ruffin, *The Diary of Edmund Ruffin*, ed. William Kauffman Scarborough, 3 vols. (Baton Rouge: Louisiana State University Press, 1972–89), 3:54, 68–69.

16. "To the People of Georgia," *(Macon) Georgia Journal and Messenger*, July 22, 1863.

17. Jefferson Davis to R. E. Lee, July 28, August 2, 11, 1863, and Lee to Davis, July 16, August 8, 1863, in Dunbar Rowland, ed., *Jefferson Davis, Constitutionalist: His Life and Letters*, 10 vols. (Jackson: Mississippi Department of Archives and History, 1923), 5:579, 584–85, 588–89. In his postwar memoir, Davis observed of Lee's raid into Pennsylvania that the "wisdom of the strategy was justified by the result." Jefferson Davis, *The Rise and Fall of the Confederate Government*, 2 vols. (1881; reprint, New York: Yoseloff, 1958), 2:447. Some Confederates sought to shore up morale by looking beyond Gettysburg to find evidence of weakness behind the lines in the North. For example, Helen Struan Bernard, who lived near Port Royal, Virginia, speculated about the effect of the recent antidraft riots in New York City. "Don't you think the lovers of Peace may gather a ray of hope from the dreadful riots now taking place in the North?" she asked in a letter dated July 22, 1863. "We are so anxious for todays papers to read farther particulars of them. They seem almost a repetition of the fearful scenes of the French Revolution." Rebecca Campbell Light, ed., *War at Our Doors: The Civil War Diaries and Letters of the Bernard Sisters of Virginia* (Fredericksburg, Va.: American History Company, 1998), 78.

18. Kate Stone, *Brokenburn: The Journal of Kate Stone, 1861–1868*, ed. John Q. Anderson (Baton Rouge: Louisiana State University Press, 1955),

230, 284; Belle Edmondson, *A Lost Heroine of the Confederacy: The Diaries and Letters of Belle Edmondson*, ed. William Galbraith and Loretta Galbraith (Jackson: University Press of Mississippi, 1990), 126; Felix Pierre Poché, *A Louisiana Confederate: Diary of Felix Pierre Poché*, ed. Edwin C. Bearss (Natchitoches: Louisiana Studies Institute of Northwestern State University of Louisiana, 1972), 126.

19. R. A. Pierson to W. H. Pierson [his father], July 19, 1863, Pierson Family Papers, Tulane University, New Orleans, La.

20. Elizabeth Whitley Roberson, *Weep Not for Me Dear Mother* (Washington, N.C.: Venture Press, 1991), 112; Lt. Joseph Hilton to his cousin, July 18, 1863, Hilton Family Papers, MS no. 387, Georgia Historical Society, Savannah; Charles W. Turner, ed., *Civil War Letters of Arabella Speairs and William Beverley Pettit of Fluvanna County, Virginia, March 1862–March 1865*, 2 vols. (Roanoke, Va.: Virginia Lithography and Graphics, 1988–89), 1:140; James Drayton Nance to Mr. Brantly, August 16, 1863, James Drayton Nance Papers, South Caroliniana Library, University of South Carolina, Columbia.

21. Arthur J. L. Fremantle, *Three Months in the Southern States: April–June, 1863* (1863; reprint, Lincoln: University of Nebraska Press, 1991), 270–71; Justus Scheibert, *Seven Months in the Rebel States during the North American War, 1863*, ed. William Stanley Hoole (1868; reprint, Tuscaloosa, Ala.: Confederate Publishing Company, 1958), 119.

22. "From Our Army," a letter from William Aiken Kelly printed in the *Charleston Daily Courier*, July 22, 1863.

23. R. A. Pierson to M. C. Pierson [his sister], August 11, 1863, R. A. Pierson to [?], [circa July 15, 1863], Pierson Family Papers. The undated letter, which is a fragment, was written from Hagerstown, Maryland: "Our army has fallen back to Hagerstown, Md. six miles from the Potomac and we are now resting from the fatigue of our long trip."

24. William B. Taylor to his mother, July 29, 1863, in Greg Mast, "Six Lieutenants: Vignettes of North Carolinians in America's Greatest Battle," *Military Images* 13 (July–August 1991): 12–13.

25. Charles Minor Blackford to his wife, July 7, 1863, in Susan Leigh Blackford and Charles Minor Blackford, eds., *Letters from Lee's Army, or Memoirs of Life In and Out of the Army in Virginia during the War between the States* (New York: Scribner's, 1947), 189–90; Henry Robinson Berkeley, *Four Years in the Confederate Horse Artillery: The Diary of Private Henry Robinson Berkeley*, ed. William H. Runge (Chapel Hill: University of North Carolina Press [for the Virginia Historical Society], 1961), 52–54; Edgeworth Bird to Sallie Bird, August 15, July 7, 9, 1863, in John Rozier, ed., *The*

Granite Farm Letters: The Civil War Correspondence of Edgeworth and Sallie Bird (Athens: University of Georgia Press, 1988), 135, 115, 118.

26. Stephen Dodson Ramseur to Ellen Richmond, July 8, 1863, Stephen Dodson Ramseur Papers, SHC; James Drayton Nance to Mr. Brantly, August 16, 1863, South Caroliniana Library; William B. Sturtevant to Jimmy, July 27, 1863, Metal Case 3, S 785, Museum of the Confederacy, Richmond, Va.; Edgeworth Bird to Sallie Bird, July 7, 12, 1863, in Rozier, ed., *Granite Farm Letters*, 115, 122; Spencer Glasgow Welch to his wife, July 17, 1863, in Spencer Glasgow Welch, *A Confederate Surgeon's Letters to His Wife* (1911; reprint, Marietta, Ga.: Continental Book Company, 1954), 59.

27. Stephen Dodson Ramseur to Ellen Richmond, July 19, 8, 1863, Ramseur Papers, SHC; Edgeworth Bird to Sallie Bird, July 7, 1863, in Rozier, ed., *Granite Farm Letters*, 115; William Beverley Pettit to his wife, July 8, 1863, in Turner, ed., *Letters of Speairs and Pettit*, 1:132; David Wyatt Aiken to his wife, July 11, 1863, in Annette Tapert, ed., *The Brothers' War: Civil War Letters to Their Loved Ones from the Blue and Gray* (New York: Times Books, 1988), 162–63.

28. Fremantle, *Three Months in the Southern States*, 297.

29. *OR* 27(2):309. Lee's report was dated July 31, 1863.

30. William Watts Parker to the *Richmond Sentinel*, July 10, 1863 (printed in the *Sentinel* on July 27, 1863), quoted in Robert K. Krick, *Parker's Virginia Battery, C.S.A.*, rev. ed. (Wilmington, N.C.: Broadfoot, 1989), 190–91; Clement A. Evans to his wife, July 8, 10, 1863, in Robert Grier Stephens Jr., *Intrepid Warrior: Clement Anselm Evans, Confederate General from Georgia, Life, Letters, and Diaries of the War Years* (Dayton, Ohio: Morningside, 1992), 231, 235; William Beverley Pettit to his wife, July 8, 1863, in Turner, ed., *Letters of Speairs and Pettit*, 1:133; Edward Porter Alexander to his father, undated letter (written after July 13 while the army was encamped near Winchester), in Marion Alexander Boggs, ed., *The Alexander Letters, 1787–1900* (1910; reprint, Athens: University of Georgia Press, 1980), 251–52. For a discussion of attitudes among soldiers about the acceptability of fighting behind defensive works, see Gerald F. Linderman, *Embattled Courage: The Experience of Combat in the American Civil War* (New York: Free Press, 1987).

31. Stephens, *Intrepid Warrior*, 232; William J. Seymour, *The Civil War Memoirs of Captain William J. Seymour: Reminiscences of a Louisiana Tiger*, ed. Terry L. Jones (Baton Rouge: Louisiana State University Press, 1991), 79; R. A. Pierson to M. C. Pierson, August 11, 1863, Pierson Family Papers, Tulane University; Joseph Graham to William Alexander Graham, July 30, 1863, in Graham, *Papers of Graham*, 5:514.

32. E. Porter Alexander to his father, undated letter (written after July 13 while the army was encamped near Winchester), in Boggs, ed., *Alexander Letters*, 251–52.

33. FitzGerald Ross, *Cities and Camps of the Confederacy*, ed. Richard B. Harwell (Urbana: University of Illinois Press, 1958), 80. Ross's account of the Gettysburg campaign and its aftermath first appeared in *Blackwood's Edinburgh Magazine* in 1864 and 1865. For a discussion of Ross and the publication history of his travel memoir of the Confederacy, see Harwell's introduction to *Cities and Camps of the Confederacy*.

34. Ambrose R. Wright letter of July 7, 1863, printed in the *Augusta (Ga.) Daily Constitutionalist*, July 23, 1863; James E. B. Stuart to his wife, July 10, 13, 1863, in James E. B. Stuart, *The Letters of Major General James E. B. Stuart*, ed. Adele H. Mitchell (n.p.: Stuart-Mosby Historical Society, 1990), 327–28; Alexander Murdock to his nephew, July 19, 1863, transcript of letter offered for sale by Steven S. Raab Autographs, *Catalog No. 35* (Ardmore, Pa., November 2000), 12–13 (transcript kindly brought to my attention by Dr. Mike Stevens of Fredericksburg, Va.).

35. S. G. Pryor to Penelope, July 16, 1863, in Charles R. Adams Jr., ed., *A Post of Honor: The Pryor Letters, 1861–63. Letters from Capt. S. G. Pryor, Twelfth Georgia Regiment and His Wife, Penelope Tyson Pryor* (Fort Valley, Ga.: Garret Publications, 1989), 377–78; LeRoy S. Edwards to his father, July 7, 1863, in LeRoy S. Edwards, *Letters of LeRoy S. Edwards Written during the War between the States*, ed. Joan K. Walton and Terry A. Walton (n.p.: [1985]), Letter no. 31 (no page numbers in text).

36. William Lafayette Barrier to his father, July 14, 1863, in Beverly Barrier Troxler and Billy Dawn Barrier Auciello, eds., *Dear Father: Confederate Letters Never Before Published* (n.p.: privately published by the editors, 1989), 112–13.

37. Ambrose R. Wright letter of July 8, 1863, in *Augusta (Ga.) Daily Constitutionalist;* Allen C. Jordan to his parents, July 15, 1863, in Max E. White, ed., "The Thomas G. Jordan Family during the War between the States," *Georgia Historical Quarterly* 59 (Spring 1975): 136; Charles Minor Blackford to his wife, July 16, 1863, in Blackford and Blackford, eds., *Letters from Lee's Army*, 193; Spencer Glasgow Welch to his wife, August 10, 1863, in Welch, *Confederate Surgeon's Letters*, 73–74; Lafayette McLaws to his wife, August 14, 1863, Lafayette McLaws Papers, SHC.

38. Edgeworth Bird to Sallie Bird, July 19, August 28, 1863, in Rozier, ed., *Granite Farm Letters*, 125, 145; S. G. Pryor to Penelope Tyson Pryor, August 6, 1863, in Adams, ed., *Pryor Letters*, 385; Green Berry Samuels to

his wife, August 7, 21, 1863, in Carrie Esther Spencer et al., comps., *A Civil War Marriage in Virginia: Reminiscences and Letters* (Boyce, Va.: Carr, 1956), 190.

39. Gorgas, *Diary*, 59–61.

40. Joseph Hilton to his cousin, July 18, 1863, Hilton Family Papers, MS no. 387, Georgia Historical Society; Sidney J. Richardson to his parents, July 8, 1863, Civil War Miscellany, Personal Papers, Georgia Archives; John A. Barry to his father, July 8, 1863, J. A. Barry Letter, MS no. 3015, SHC.

41. Clement A. Evans to his wife, July 15, 1863, in Stephens, ed., *Intrepid Warrior*, 249.

42. Only Lee's statements prior to the battle are included here. For his retrospective discussions of why he moved north, see his official report in *OR* 27(2):312–26 (also printed in R. E. Lee, *The Wartime Papers of R. E. Lee*, ed. Clifford Dowdey and Louis H. Manarin [Boston: Little, Brown, 1961], 569–85), and transcription of conversation between R. E. Lee and William Allan, April 15, 1868, pp. 13–14, William Allan Papers, SHC.

43. R. E. Lee to Jefferson Davis, May 10, 30, June 25, 1863, and Lee to James A. Seddon, May 10, 30, June 8, 1863, in Lee, *Wartime Papers*, 482–83, 496, 498, 505.

44. An indication of Lee's attention to logistics may be found in a letter of June 23 to Jefferson Davis, wherein he reported that Pennsylvania already had yielded enough food to supply Richard Ewell's corps for the next week, while 1,700 barrels of flour lay stockpiled in Maryland for the remainder of the army. Ibid., 530.

45. R. E. Lee to Jefferson Davis, July 4, 7, 8, 10, 11, 1863, and Lee to Mary Lee, July 7, 1863, in ibid., 538–45. Lee's letter to Davis of July 7 went astray, and the general sent a copy to the president on the 16th.

46. R. E. Lee to Mary Lee, July 12, 15, 1863, and Lee to Jefferson Davis, July 12, 1863, in ibid., 547–48, 551–52.

47. Lee and Seddon probably spoke on July 15 or 16. On the 16th, Lee informed Secretary Seddon that he had "received the communication sent me by your brother. He will inform you of the arrival of the army at this point. It is a little foot sore, & is much in need of shoes for men & horses." Ibid., 553.

48. Henry Heth, "Letter from Major-General Henry Heth, of A. P. Hill's Corps, A.N.V.," in J. William Jones et al., eds., *Southern Historical Society Papers*, 52 vols. (1876–1959; reprint with 3-vol. index, Wilmington, N.C.: Broadfoot, 1990–92), 5:54–55.

49. R. E. Lee to Jefferson Davis, July 16, 1863; Lee to Mary Lee, July 26, 1863; and Lee to Margaret Stuart, July 26, 1863, in Lee, *Wartime Papers*, 552, 560–61.

50. Jefferson Davis to R. E. Lee, July 21, 1863, in Rowland, ed., *Jefferson Davis*, 5:573; Lee to Davis, July 29, 1863, in Lee, *Wartime Papers*, 563–64.

51. R. E. Lee to Jefferson Davis, July 31, 1863, in Lee, *Wartime Papers*, 564–65.

52. It is worth remembering that ten months passed between Gettysburg and the next true Union offensive in Virginia, which began under U. S. Grant's direction in early May 1864.

53. Lee remarked in 1868 that he went into Pennsylvania intending "to move about, to manoeuver & alarm the enemy, threaten their cities, hit any blows he might be able to do without risking a general battle, & then towards Fall return & recover nearer his base." Transcription of conversation between R. E. Lee and William Allan, April 15, 1868, p. 14, William Allan Papers, SHC.

54. R. E. Lee to Jefferson Davis, August 8, 1863, in Lee, *Wartime Papers*, 589–90; Davis to Lee, August 11, 1863, in Rowland, ed., *Jefferson Davis*, 5:588–90. For Lee's brief response to Davis's letter, dated August 22, see Lee, *Wartime Letters*, 593. Lee kept his plans for resignation to himself. After the war, Charles Venable of his staff told Jubal A. Early that no copy of the general's letter to Davis "was ever seen in camp—and I suppose Gen Lee destroyed Mr. Davis's letter to him." Lee's staff learned of their chief's action only when they saw Davis's reply (aides typically opened all official letters for Lee except those from Davis; the latter were opened whenever Lee was away). Once they saw the "drift of the opening sentences," they put the letter aside with Lee's private correspondence to await his return. Charles A. Venable to Jubal A. Early, January 23, 1876, Jubal A. Early Papers, Library of Congress, Washington, D.C.

55. Many civilians found inspiration in the model of steadfast soldiers. For example, Pierre Soulé, who harbored concern about the impact of Gettysburg and Vicksburg on the civilian population, took heart from what he perceived to be generally strong military morale. "Where the spirit lives that moves us to great resolves," he noted, "the fervid patriotism that stops at no sacrifice . . . is in the army. . . . As long as that spirit is not extinct, our subjugation is impossible." Soulé to De Leon, August 12, 1863, in *Catalog 89*, Chapel Hill Rare Books.

| OUR HEARTS |
| ARE FULL OF HOPE |
| *The Army of* |
| *Northern Virginia & the* |
| *Confederacy in the Spring* |
| *of 1864* |
| |

A strong sense of optimism pervaded the Army of Northern Virginia as its officers and men approached the spring campaign of 1864. Although they had endured a winter marked by sometimes severe shortages of food and matériel, their letters and diaries give evidence of unshakable trust in Robert E. Lee, assurance that Ulysses S. Grant would achieve no more success than had his many predecessors, and hope that a decisive triumph on the battlefield might undercut northern civilian morale and bring Confederate independence within a year. Testimony from this period also illuminates attitudes within the army toward civilian leaders, concern that commitment to the cause on the home front was wavering, and a widespread sense that God would order things for the best if white southerners held fast to their struggle for nationhood. Many of the soldiers employed language that suggests allegiance to the Confederate nation—rather than to their states or localities—motivated them to remain at their posts. Three years of bloody war had not eroded to a significant degree the army's morale; indeed, in many respects the Army of Northern Virginia in 1864 matched in confidence, if not in numbers, the force that had marched into Pennsylvania the preceding June.

Some attention to overall Confederate morale in the winter and spring of 1864 will help set the stage for a closer look at Lee's army. Bell I. Wiley suggested in *The Road to Appomattox* that defeats at

Gettysburg, Vicksburg, and Chattanooga precipitated a plunge in morale from which the Confederacy did not recover until mid-1864. Those military setbacks, together with suspension of the writ of habeas corpus in February 1864 and a new conscription bill that set age limits at seventeen and fifty, sapped the will of southern white people. According to Wiley, only Confederate success in defending Richmond and Atlanta through May and into June, along with "evidences of increasing peace sentiment in the North and prospects of good crops in the Confederacy, lifted the Southern spirit from the deep despondency that had enthralled it since Gettysburg and Vicksburg." More recent work also suggests poor Confederate morale in early 1864. For example, the authors of *Why the South Lost the Civil War* note that a number of historians point to a "loss of the will to fight" that plagued the Confederacy after July 1863.[1]

Writing much closer to the events, Edward A. Pollard sketched a very different temper across the Confederacy in his *Southern History of the War*. The defeats of 1863 receded during early 1864 as news of one victory after another heartened Confederates. Often slighted in modern accounts, these successes loomed larger at the time. Brig. Gen. Joseph Finegan turned back a small northern army at Olustee, Florida, on February 20, and troopers under Nathan Bedford Forrest triumphed over Federals at Okolona, Mississippi, on February 22 and captured (and then largely slaughtered) a mixed garrison of black soldiers and white unionists at Fort Pillow, Tennessee, on April 12. In the East, Judson Kilpatrick's cavalry raid against Richmond in early March achieved nothing militarily but raised Confederate hackles when papers carried by a Federal colonel, Ulric Dahlgren, purportedly outlined plans to assassinate Jefferson Davis. West of the Mississippi River, Nathaniel P. Banks's campaign along Louisiana's Red River ended in ignominious retreat after battles at Mansfield and Pleasant Hill on April 8–9, while on the North Carolina coast Confederates commanded by Robert F. Hoke captured Plymouth. "The spirit of the Southern Confederacy was scarcely ever more buoyant than in the month of May, 1864," concluded Pollard. "The confidence of its people in the ultimate accomplishment of their independence was so firm and universal, that any other conclusion was but seldom referred to in general conversation . . . and in Richmond and elsewhere the hope was freely indulged that the campaign of 1864 was to be the decisive of the war, and to crown the efforts of the South with peace and independence."[2]

*The engagement at Fort Pillow, Tennessee, April 12, 1864. Confederates cele-brated Nathan Bedford Forrest's capture of Fort Pillow as one of several victories in the winter and spring of 1864. Northern opinion labeled the slaughter of Fed-eral troops, shown in this contemporary illustration, an atrocity. (*Frank Leslie's Illustrated Newspaper, *May 7, 1864)*

Morale probably fell somewhere between the extremes presented by Wiley and Pollard. A chaplain who traveled through the Lower South in December 1863 and January 1864 railed against "the stay-at-homes" who cared about nothing but profit and property: "Money and their negroes appeared to be their gods, and for these they were not only willing to sacrifice their own children, who were now fight-ing the battles of their country, but even the country itself." Travers-ing much of the same area a bit later on a medical inspection tour, Confederate physician William Alexander formed far more positive impressions. "Our Va. people are as determined as ever, & hopeful even to buoyancy," he wrote in mid-April. "This is also the case, with few exceptions, of the other states." [3]

In every corner of the Confederacy, citizens debated the mer-its of legislation designed to shrink the supply of paper money, tighten conscription, and limit antiwar activities. In Georgia, Governor Joseph E. Brown and Vice-President-in-exile Alexander H. Stephens loudly disapproved of the central government's actions, winning support from disgruntled individuals who believed, as one man put it, that a "bloody war among the Southern people" might ensue if some of the acts were not repealed. North Carolinians unhappy with the war clustered around William Woods Holden and others who opposed Jefferson Davis's administration and advocated peace negotiations. A majority of Confederates almost certainly agreed with Robert Garlick Hill Kean of the War Bureau, who labeled Brown, Stephens, and "their set . . . the most pestilent demagogues in the land, more injurious than the North Carolina buffaloes because more able and influential." In South Carolina, a young woman spoke a common sentiment in her journal entry for March 16: "All the talk is about the unfortunate currency, and thousands and one taxes, tho few, very few complain."[4]

Newspapers generally conceded problems of morale, urged citizens to sacrifice, and maintained a hopeful stance concerning eventual Confederate victory. In January, the proadministration *Richmond Dispatch* applauded the example of the men under arms, the nation's women, and most farmers and country people (the last two groups, "with a few shameful exceptions, [were] hopeful and resolute") but excoriated "the denizens of the towns, the money makers — the men who fear that further resistance may be the means of cutting off all their profits." The *Charleston Daily Courier* similarly observed that "avarice should be accounted an eternal disgrace, cowardice an unpardonable sin." Both papers called for harmony among all Confederates, and the *Dispatch* attributed "a certain degree of despondency" among the people to faithless politicians and newspaper Jeremiads. The *Richmond Enquirer* alluded to hunger in the armies and joined the other papers in calling for sacrifice on the home front: "Give the army subsistence, and the army will give the people peace; withhold subsistence now, and the war is prolonged, its miseries increased, and final ruin may be the consequences. . . . [T]he people must sacrifice their comforts, and, if necessary, endure hardships and want in order that the army may perform the duty of defending the country."[5]

Editors used volatile images of enslaved white southerners to paint a stark portrait of the consequences of defeat. The *Dispatch* spoke of Federal plans "to rob us of all we have on earth, and reduce our whole population to the condition of beggars and slaves."

The question no longer was whether African slavery would survive but "whether you and your children shall be slaves," whether Confederates should become "hewers of wood and drawers of water for their Yankee masters." In an editorial calling for determined resistance no matter how long the war lasted, the *Charleston Daily Courier* cataloged Federal atrocities: "They have . . . driven helpless families out of their homes and burned their habitations, murdered their husbands in the presence of their wives, put to death gray headed men and nurslings, done violence to female virtue, destroyed farming utensils, and, in a word, committed every possible deed of baseness, cowardice and cruelty." Confronted with such an enemy, asked the *Daily Courier,* "Who would not rather die than consent to live again under the shadow of their hateful flag?"[6]

The string of victories from February through April, together with encouraging reports from Confederate armies and news of increasing gold prices in the North, prompted many editors to forecast victory during 1864. The *Atlanta Southern Confederacy* thought it plausible that "the present year will close the contest. . . . The crisis of the North is near at hand. In another half year, if the South meet no further reverse, the quotations for gold will have increased at a fearful rate, and financial perplexities and distresses will accomplish what our bayonets have left unfinished." The *Montgomery Advertiser* noted in late March that the "general symptoms of the Confederacy are good. Our veteran soldiers have re-enlisted for the War, and are in better discipline and spirits than at any time before. . . . The courage and confidence of the people at home keeps pace, in the main, with that of the army, and they look forward hopefully to a bright and glorious future." The *Richmond Enquirer* pointed out that "repeated calls and drafts indicate greater difficulty on the part of the enemy in procuring men than any encountered by the Confederate authorities," and predicted that a new round of southern victories would kill the North's "War spirit, and fully and completely develop the prospect of an early peace." In Charleston, the *Daily Courier* averred that never had "the spirit of soldiers and people been more in keeping with the character of the occasion than at the present time." There was no need for despondency, the *Daily Courier's* editor subsequently predicted, if all Confederates did their duty: "[D]ark clouds will shortly break and roll away and under the bright shining of the sun we will march on to glorious triumph."[7]

As they read their newspapers and followed the progress of their armies during the spring of 1864, most Confederate civilians likely indulged a cautious optimism. Many of them looked to God. Prayer had helped to deliver the spring's victories, remarked a woman in Georgia: "What gratitude should fill our hearts as Christians for all these evidences of divine mercy!" "I have never despaired of the final issue, but I have never before felt the dawn of hope so near," she wrote. "I trust it is not a presumptuous delusion!" In Tennessee, Belle Edmondson gave thanks in her diary for Fort Pillow and Mansfield: "Oh! how thankful we are for the bright days which are dawning." From Warrenton, Virginia, which often lay behind Union lines, Susan Emeline Jeffords Caldwell assured her husband in Richmond that rumors of wavering spirit among the town's women were false. "We are all loyal," she stated. "We must exist and are dependent on the wretches for many things but . . . keep *true* to the South amid all our sore trials." [8]

Judith W. McGuire, a refugee in Richmond, struck a common chord in combining trepidation about the future with a belief that with God's assistance the Confederacy would win out. On April 25, she reported the "country in great excitement" over Hoke's capturing Plymouth. Along with the victories in Florida, Louisiana, and elsewhere, this indicated that the "God of battles is helping us, or how could we thus succeed?" McGuire knew a large Union army under Grant soon would threaten Richmond, but "with the help of God, we hope to drive them back again. . . . I don't think that any one doubts our ability to do it; but the awful loss of life necessary upon the fight is what we dread." [9]

Ulysses S. Grant's transfer from the Western to the Eastern Theater convinced most Confederates that Virginia would witness the decisive fighting in 1864. "Grant is now the presiding genius," the *Georgia Messenger & Journal* of Macon observed somewhat sarcastically on March 30, "and at the council of war which he recently attended in Washington, it was arranged that the capture of Richmond should be the primary object of the Spring campaign." This paper betrayed no doubt about the outcome of such an effort because in Lee's army "the spirit of both officers and men points but to one result—success." The *Atlanta Southern Confederacy* agreed that southern forces were "ready at all points, and especially at Richmond" to block the efforts orchestrated by "good Ulysses." In Charleston, the *Daily Courier* printed a piece from the *New York Herald* naming Virginia as the primary Union target: "We dare say that General Grant has discovered that Richmond is the head of the rebellion," stated the *Herald*, "and that *a telling blow upon the head is the readiest way to finish it*." Residents of Richmond learned from the *Dispatch* that Lee's veterans were eager for the Army of the Potomac to make its final effort. Denying Grant's greatness as a general, the *Dispatch* insisted that his past "performances bear no comparison whatever to those of Gen. Lee."[10]

Comments from outside Virginia echoed those of these editors. A Virginian whose regiment had been posted to Florida reported all his comrades anxious to return to the Old Dominion, "to which point the vast armies of the enemy seem to [be] concentrating for a final death grapple." H. W. Barrow of the 21st North Carolina wrote from Kinston that he thought "the Yankees are going to try to capture Richmond again as Grant has been successful out west and thinks he can manage Genl. Lee and his army." Believing the summer's campaign would end the war, this man predicted that Grant would "find some difference between Genl Lee and old Pemberton."[11]

Lee's soldiers also saw their role in the upcoming campaigns as crucial, and their morale in April fully justified the trust of their fellow Confederates. A lieutenant in the 51st Georgia put it succinctly less than two weeks before the Federals crossed the Rapidan River: "My opinion is that before another month rolls off a great battle will be fought in this part of Virginia and I am confident of success." Many of his comrades thought a victory would win Confederate independence—though he believed the "war would terminate by some means other than fighting." Brig. Gen. Stephen Dodson Ramseur, whose four North Carolina regiments had figured prominently in the army's operations during 1863, summed up the prevailing attitude in a pair of letters to his wife Ellen. "We are getting ready for an arduous summer Campaign," he wrote in late April. "Our hearts are full of hope. . . . Oh! I do pray that we may be established as an independent people, a people known and recognized as God's Peculiar People!" A week later he assured Ellen that every man focused on the coming campaign, that the army was in splendid condition, and that "All things look bright and cheerful."[12]

This is not to say that the Army of Northern Virginia experienced no problems in the winter and spring of 1864. Shortages of food, concern about the plight of loved ones at home, and general war weariness troubled many soldiers. Ramseur himself had confided to his brother-in-law in January that rations of an eighth to a quarter of a pound of meat and one-and-an-eighth pounds of flour per day had dampened spirits considerably. "The army must be fed," he insisted, "even if people at home must go without it." A member of the Stonewall Brigade complained in mid-January that the men drew at most only one-quarter of a pound of meat a day and sometimes went without it altogether. The government's inability to provide adequate rations and its decision to stop allowing conscripted men to hire substitutes (which he interpreted as a desperate measure to bring men into the ranks) convinced this soldier that "the Confederacy is about to play out." Should the meat ration remain inadequate, he prophesied darkly, "I dont think that the men will bare with that way of doing much longer."[13]

Robert E. Lee's letters from this period leave no doubt that he considered inadequate food and fodder the major danger facing the army. "We are now issuing to the troops a fourth of a pound of salt meat & have only three days' supply at that rate," he told Jefferson Davis early in the new year. "I can learn of no supply of meat on the road to the army, & fear I shall be unable to retain it in the field." As late as April 12, the commanding general confessed to Davis "anxiety on the subject of provisions . . . so great that I cannot refrain from expressing it to Your Excellency. I cannot see how we can operate with our present supplies." In the absence of improvement, Lee could not rule out a retreat into North Carolina.[14]

As during the late summer and fall of 1862 and the summer after Gettysburg, desertions also plagued the army—though numbers never reached a critical level. Lee speculated to the secretary of war in mid-February that "the discipline of the army is suffering from our present scarcity of supplies." Thomas J. Goree of James Longstreet's staff deplored the fact that many members of the famed Texas Brigade, while detached from the army for service in Tennessee, had "got it into their head to go across the Mississippi" to seek duty closer to home. "Shame upon the men who have gone to Texas for easy service, and have deserted their brave comrades here," scolded Goree from East Tennessee. He hoped all would be returned to the brigade to face justice. A member of the 41st Virginia of William Mahone's brigade mentioned in mid-January "numerous cases of disertion in some of the Brigades on the Rapid Ann," and Lt. Burwell Thomas Cotton of the 34th North Carolina commented on April 30 that "Soldiers keep deserting. Some tried to leave our Regt. last night but they were caught before they went far. Shot two in our Brigade a few days ago." Many North Carolinians faced especially hard choices because their state nourished a strong peace movement led by William Woods Holden. Most Tarheels remained steadfast, however, as "Jeb" Stuart reminded his wife in early February. "North Carolina has done *nobly in this army,*" affirmed the cavalry chief. "Never allow her troops to be abused in your presence."[15]

Letters and diaries frequently expressed compassion for the deserters as well as a belief that their crime merited harsh punishment. Typical was LeRoy S. Edwards of the 12th Virginia, who called the death penalty for two deserters in the 16th Virginia a "*terrible* penalty that the law attaches to a *terrible* crime." A noncommissioned officer in the 44th North Carolina reported the executions of a man from his regiment and another from the 11th North Carolina: "[T]hey was shot for desertion[.] Running away from the army is not fine work." "We are soldiers," he added, "and we have to stay as long as there is any 'war.' " An Alabamian wrote movingly of the execution of two men from the 9th Alabama, terming it "dreadful to bring out a man in good health and in a moment plung his soul into ever lasting perdition." Yet the pair "well knew the fate of deserters," he added, "but they heeded not."[16]

Determination to see the war through to a successful conclusion animated the vast majority of Lee's soldiers. Thousands reenlisted for the duration of the conflict before the Confederate Congress mandated continued service with the Conscription Act of February 17, 1864. A soldier in the 22nd Georgia described his comrades as in high spirits, "and to prove it our Regiment have all re-enlisted for the war." They expected a hard fight during the spring and summer but had "no notion of ever being subjugated, and we will fight as long as we have any territory to fight on." Another Georgian, James M. Garrett, admitted "getting very tyred of this war" but declared himself "willing to stay here for three more years and live off of bread and water before I will submit to an abolition dynasty." A Mississippian responded negatively to his wife's plea that he seek a place in one of their state's local units. "I would like to be near home where I could see you and the children occasionally," he stated, "but after serving in the Confederate army Honorably for Three years I can't Riconcile it to my Pride of Honor to go Into the Malitia. . . . I am not by any means willing to yield to the federal government." A lieutenant in the 5th Virginia proudly announced to his parents that the regiment had reenlisted for the war, adding that the "troops were never in better sperits—the people to are being inspired by the same feelings and are in excellent sperits now." [17]

The example of men willing to commit themselves to a prolonged struggle did inspire civilians, as evidenced by testimony from witnesses such as Kate Cumming and Emma Holmes. "I have received a letter from an officer who is in Longstreet's corps," commented Cumming, a volunteer nurse in Mobile, Alabama: "The whole of that corps has re-enlisted for the war, no matter how long it may last. Our whole army has done the same." South Carolinian Holmes expressed delight that "The whole army is animated with the brightest & most determined spirit and almost everywhere the soldiers are re-enlisting unanimously, by companies, regiments or brigades for *the war*, (& one body added) even if it lasts 40 years." The *Richmond Enquirer* suggested in late January that the "prompt and patriotic action of the army in re-enlisting for the war . . . [helped infuse] new life and spirit into the people." [18]

Many soldiers suspected that their homefolk and some political leaders lacked the army's optimism and devotion to the cause. For Georgians and North Carolinians, the actions and statements of Joseph E. Brown, Alexander H. Stephens, and William Woods Holden often proved an embarrassment. A captain in the 45th Georgia read extracts in the Richmond newspapers of Brown's message pronouncing the currency and military bills unconstitutional. "I am sorry the Gov. gets at loggerheads with the administration," he remarked, "because I think now is the time . . . for perfect harmony to exist throughout the Confederacy; all dissensions or quarrels in our midst but serve to encourage the energies of the enemy." Rumors that Holden would seek to replace Zebulon B. Vance in the North Carolina governorship prompted one officer to fume, "Surely, Surely, North Carolina is not so low, so disloyal, as to bow to Holden as Gov— If so—then Good bye to the old State." [19]

Holden's crusade for a negotiated peace spread enough disaffection among North Carolinians that Vance visited Lee's army to deliver a series of rousing speeches in support of the war to regiments from the state. Lee, Jeb Stuart, Richard S. Ewell, A. P. Hill, and other notables attended Vance's address to Junius Daniel's brigade, and a huge crowd heard the governor when he spoke later to Dodson Ramseur's regiments. "He had the whole assembly in an uproar in less than two minutes after he arose," stated one of Ramseur's admiring soldiers. "I was in a good place to hear every word that he said, and I don't think I ever listened to a more able speech of any kind in my life." Several generals gave brief comments following Vance's two-hour oration, after which the governor stepped forward to relate "two or three anecdotes relative to the Yankee characters and then retired amidst deafening 'Rebel Yells.'" James Graham of the 27th North Carolina of John R. Cooke's brigade estimated that "a *large majority* of the soldiers" agreed with Vance's sentiments, noting as well that the governor "does not mention Holden at all in his speeches." Another Tarheel wrote his sister that Vance's address was "very highly appreciated by a good portion" of Alfred M. Scales's brigade but was chagrined to admit "there are some here who prefer Holden." [20]

Antipathy toward Vice President Stephens ran deeply through the ranks of the army. Col. James Conner of the 22nd North Carolina called Stephens's criticism of conscription and suspension of the writ of habeas corpus (offered in a speech delivered on March 16) "injudicious, illtimed, uncandid, and calculated to do much mischief." Alluding to Holden's pro-peace activities in North Carolina, Conner accused Stephens of attempting "to place Virginia side by side with the Holdenites." Artillerist William Meade Dame employed far harsher language: "I would like to see that scoundrel Alexander Stephens our dishonoured vice-president tarred and feathered and hung," he blustered; "miserable traitor he stayed away from Congress when the Laws were being passed and then disclaims against them." Dame added that he was pleased to see "the Georgia Soldiers denounce Gov Browns course 'in toto.'" Ordnance chief Josiah Gorgas, who kept a close eye on affairs in Lee's army from his post in Richmond, noted approvingly in late March that Stephens and Brown "excite much remark, and are looked upon with general disfavor." [21]

Evidence of wavering morale at home frustrated soldiers who prided themselves on their own firm allegiance to the Confederacy. News from North Carolina, which along with Georgia seemed to have a significant number of disgruntled civilians, prompted James A. Graham to rebuke residents of his home state. Four men had been executed recently—"a very sad sight"—because they had deserted after receiving letters from North Carolina. "Many a poor soldier has met with the same disgraceful death from the same cause. I wish the people at home," concluded Graham, "would keep in as good spirits as the soldiers in the army." South Carolinian Abram Hayne Young, a sergeant in Joseph B. Kershaw's brigade, poured out his feelings

Vice President Alexander H. Stephens alienated many soldiers in the Army of Northern Virginia during the winter of 1863–64. Like Joseph E. Brown of Georgia and W. W. Holden of North Carolina, Stephens seemed to lack the deep devotion to the Confederacy that kept Lee's men in the ranks despite great hardship. (Robert Underwood Johnson and Clarence Clough Buel, eds., Battles and Leaders of the Civil War, *4 vols. [New York: Century, 1887–88], 1:100)*

on this subject in a letter that made up in fervor what it lacked in polish. "[T]his Armey hear is in as good Spirits as eny other part of the Confederte Armey, and there is non hoo have boore more of the hardships, and are still willing to endure them rather than Submit to Such men as are Seeking to destroy us and all we have," he affirmed. "I dont write this to disharte you but rather to encorage You to bare it with fermnance. . . . If the men at home and in Congress would doo their part the men in the field is Sufishent if fead well." [22]

Col. Clement A. Evans of the 31st Georgia confided to his diary a belief that a system of furloughs Lee instituted in January had a double benefit: "The soldier becomes satisfied and returns cheerfully to duty, and the people at home catch somewhat of the soldier's spirit of cheerfulness while he is at home." Most of the gloom in the Confederacy could be found among civilians, thought Evans, and some soldiers were happy to get back to their units because "at home, long faces, dolorous groans, and fearful apprehensions meet them at every turn." Dodson Ramseur agreed with Evans that the presence at home of men on furlough might operate for the good among the "weak kneed gentry." Ted Barclay of the Stonewall Brigade manifested impatience with homefolk who complained to soldiers at home and at the front that the war had altered their lives in unwanted ways. "I trust as our army, who have to stand the hardships of the war, are thus determined and consecrated to the cause," he wrote his sister, "that those at home will cheerfully bear the little inconveniences which must necessarily result from such a state of affairs and at least speak words of encouragement to the soldiers and not endeavor to shake their confidence in the cause of religious and civil liberty." [23]

Many of Lee's soldiers employed language suggesting a loyalty to the Confederacy that transcended attachments to state or locality. A quintet of Georgians illustrate this phenomenon. A sergeant in the 45th Georgia confessed to his wife that he longed to be with her and their son but could not enjoy time at home while still able to do duty. "Others would be fighting for their Country and My Country and home while I would be skulking my duty," he explained, "and it would render me miserable. I am happier just as it is while the war lasts." Daniel Pope took the occasion of his twenty-fourth birthday to muse about the fact that he had spent the most pleasant portion of his life in the army — a circumstance sad to contemplate. "But when we consider the great duty we owe our country in the struggle for independence," continued Pope, "I cannot be but content with my fate, although it may be, indeed, a cruel one. I am determined to do anything and everything I can for my country." If he fell in battle, Pope hoped his wife would believe that he had contributed his part to a struggle that would ensure her and their son "the great boon of freedom."

Private Garrett of the 35th Georgia, who vowed to fight three more years and subsist on bread and water, "never thought of any thing else but that we will gain our independence." He added: "Oh how I long to see the sun of peace and the banner of liberty float . . . triumphantly over the green fields of the Sunny South." Francis Marion Howard of the 18th Georgia used comparable phrases to make the same point: "I am willing to fight as long as we can keep an army together. . . . I *do* hope to live to see the South gain her independence & be free of the tyranical yoke of abolitionists." Howard savored the thought of "telling the yankee wherever I may meet him that his people ware not able to subjugate the South." In a touching letter to his children, Isaac Domingos, a sergeant in the 51st Georgia, explained that he might fall "on the battle field fighting for my God and my country, liberty and our homes."[24]

Men in the army often seemed more willing than their counterparts at home to sacrifice a measure of freedom to achieve nationhood. In February, Col. James Conner lauded Congress for passing legislation to restrict the currency, raise taxes, and expand conscription. These constituted "three very important Acts," he believed, "and severe as they unquestionably are, I think they will do good." Conner subsequently described the suspension of habeas corpus as "wise, just, and necessary, unless we meant to give up the army." Lt. Josiah Blair Patterson of the 14th Georgia took a similar view, affirming that Georgians in the field—unlike "Villainous grumblers and croakers" behind the lines—would "spurn with contempt any term of settlement less than an independent nationality." Congress had acted correctly regarding conscription, the currency, and habeas corpus, he insisted—though these measures admittedly threatened the bulwarks of states' rights and individual privileges. Condemning the challenges to central authority mounted by Joseph E. Brown, Alexander H. Stephens, and others, Patterson claimed Confederates must "win and possess rights national state and individual before we vex our brain in settling discriminating lines of demarcation."[25]

Men such as Conner and Patterson followed the lead of Robert E. Lee, who from the opening of the conflict had called for the subordination of all private concerns to the goal of achieving national independence. Throughout the late winter and spring, the army's commander pressed officials in Richmond to tighten conscription. He deplored the actions of speculators and urged Quartermaster General Alexander R. Lawton to impress leather for shoes if necessary. Aware of the potentially divisive effects of large-scale seizure of goods from civilians, Lee nonetheless advocated authorizing the government "to impress when necessary a certain proportion of everything produced in the country. . . . If it requires all the meat in the country to support the army, it should be had, and I believe this could be accomplished by not only showing its necessity, but that all equally contributed, and that it was faithfully applied." Proper oversight of impressment agents would limit civilian complaints, Lee stated, as would assurances that all impressed goods reached the men in the field. In mid-April, Lee urged Secretary of War James A. Seddon to seize temporary control of the railroads to guarantee timely delivery of supplies to the army.[26]

A profound bond with Lee formed a vital ingredient in the recipe for high morale in the army. One veteran impressed Catherine Ann Devereux Edmondston with his great devotion to the general. "He says 'Marse Robert,' as the men all call him, can carry them anywhere," recorded Edmondston in her journal. "They think him as pure a patriot as Washington and a more able General," and "Marse Robert" is used by them "as a term of endearment and affection." A woman in Richmond, after speaking about Lee with groups of furloughed soldiers, commented that "It is delightful to see how they reverence him, and almost as much for his goodness as for his greatness."[27]

Pvt. William L. Wilson of the 12th Virginia Cavalry conveyed much the same impression of Lee in far fewer words. "We are not sorry the campaign approaches," observed Wilson to his mother in April. "No army ever had such a leader as General Lee." At army headquarters, Walter H. Taylor, the young adjutant whose wartime letters expressed occasional unhappiness about Lee's penchant for running the army with minimal staff, exhibited utter confidence in his chief's military capacity. Ulysses S. Grant's army recently had been reinforced by Ambrose E. Burnside's command; together, predicted Taylor on May 1, they would soon "get matters into shape for an attack." But Taylor assured his fiancée that she should not doubt the outcome: "If all our army is placed under G[enera]l Lee's control, I have no fear of the result."[28]

A memorable scene involving Lee and the soldiers of James Longstreet's First Corps highlighted the ties between the army commander and his men. Longstreet's two divisions had returned to Virginia in April after several months of service in Georgia and Ten-

Catherine Ann Devereux Edmondston, the wife of a planter in eastern North Carolina, kept a diary filled with trenchant observations about the Confederate war. Her comments underscored Lee's importance to Confederate soldiers and civilians. (Capital Area Preservation at Mordecai Historic Park, Raleigh, N.C.)

nessee, setting the stage for what artillerist Edward Porter Alexander later likened to "a military sacrament." On a clear and pleasant late April day, Lee rode across a broad field where Longstreet's veterans were arrayed. Music and an artillery salute heralded his appearance; and when the soldiers caught sight of him on Traveller for the first time since the preceding summer, "a wild and prolonged cheer, fraught with a feeling that thrilled all hearts, ran along the lines and rose to the heavens." Men tossed their hats skyward, color bearers shook their standards, and palpable emotion surged through the assemblage. Lee moved forward to acknowledge the greeting, triggering, according to one witness, "on all sides expressions such as: 'What a splendid figure!' 'What a noble face and head!' 'Our destiny is in his hands!' 'He is the best and greatest man on this continent!' " A soldier in the 15th South Carolina recorded that Lee and Longstreet "were enthusiastically cheered by [the troops] as long as they were in sight." Another proudly told his sister that "Yesterday we had a grand review by the Greatest of Generals: Gen'l R. E. Lee. . . . There was a grate many of the fair Sex out to see us. And after the review was over they all crowded around the old Gen'l to Shake handes with him. And some Said they had Shuck handes with the gratest general in the world." [29]

The arrival of the First Corps boosted confidence to another level among Lee's soldiers. Images bespeaking an organic conception of the army appeared in letters and diaries remarking on the event. One officer told Lt. Col. Franklin Gaillard of the 2nd South Carolina that he "felt as if the right arm of the army had been restored." Walter Taylor, who had longed for the presence of the First Corps for many weeks, recorded with unabashed delight that "A portion of *our family* has been returned to us. Old Pete Longstreet is with us and all seems propitious." A member of Cobb's Legion thought Longstreet's appearance foreshadowed hard fighting. "[W]e have more men here now than we ever have had before," said Francis Marion Whelchel, "and they all are in high spirits. . . . I dont have any fears but what we will give the yanks the worst whiping they ever have got if they do attemed to take Richmond." As for Longstreet's troops, Thomas Goree described "pretty general rejoicing" among them. Although Goree thought a campaign into Kentucky by the First Corps might have yielded excellent results, he wrote his mother that "we ag[ain] constitute a part of the greatest of all armies under the leadership of the greatest living chieftain, and if we can succeed in inflicting on

Grant a crushing defeat, it will do much towards bringing about a speedy peace."[30]

Goree's prediction of victory over Grant reflected a widespread impression that the North's champion would be no match for Lee. Some of the men took a sarcastic view of the new Federal commander. Activity in the Federal camps during late April led O. H. Steger of the 21st Virginia to observe drolly that the Federals seemed to be preparing for another campaign: "Mr. Grant I reckon is getting too popular for Lincoln and he wishes Gen Lee to take him down which I believe by the help of Providence will be done." F. Stanley Russell mocked Grant as that "*mighty* man of *valour*" charged with accomplishing a task that had sent George B. McClellan, Ambrose E. Burnside, and Joseph Hooker into oblivion. "[P]oor Grant," wrote Russell, "his doom is sealed; the glory of his former deeds will fast fade, in the failure of his latter undertakings." James Conner passed along to his mother a new nickname the Confederates had given their opponent: "The Yankees call him 'unconditional surrender Grant'; our men already have given him a name; 'Up the spout, Grant.'" A Georgian warned his parents in less clever, but equally confident, prose that a battle with the enemy would soon erupt. "[A]ll we want you to do is to be hopeful & continue to ask God for aid," he implored on behalf of his comrades, "& Gen Grant will go down like the rest of [the] yankey Gens, that have bin brought against this army."[31]

Conspicuous in his dismissal of Grant as a worthy opponent, Walter Taylor may have conveyed the tenor of attitudes at Lee's headquarters. Speculating in March about whether Grant would finally be the Union general in chief or merely commander of the Army of the Potomac, Lee's adjutant professed not to fear him in either case. Overrated because of his victories against the inept Pemberton, Grant enjoyed a much inflated reputation. "He will find, I trust, that General Lee is a very different man to deal with," stated Taylor with more than a tinge of condescension toward the efforts of Confederate forces in the Western Theater, "& if I mistake not will shortly come to grief if he attempts to repeat the tactics in Virginia which proved so successful in Mississippi."[32]

Some men tempered their optimism with thoughts about impending carnage and the odds they faced. "Grant is evidently collecting a heavy force in our front, and a few short weeks will probably startle the country with the thunders of the most terrible battle of the war," Green Berry Samuels informed his wife. Satisfied that the army would fight desperately to defend their homes and families, Samuels bravely suggested that "with a decided success this summer, the enemy must forego all hopes of subjugating us." Brig. Gen. Wade Hampton noticed strong morale among his troopers and hoped "confidently for success," but at the same suffered anxiety about "many thousand of the brave hearts, now eager for the strife," who would be dead at the conclusion of the next campaign. Yet more pessimistic was Henry Robinson Berkeley of the Amherst Artillery, who looked at a landscape covered with enemy tents on the Culpeper side of the Rapidan River on April 23 and exclaimed, "What a mighty host to keep back!" "Can we do it?" he pondered. "We will try. Who of us will be left when peace comes?"

Capt. Charles Minor Blackford, who served on Longstreet's staff, agreed with Samuels that "Grant is certainly collecting a large army against ours." A victory would break Union military strength, and Confederate officers and men were confident of triumph. "I am also," averred Blackford without much enthusiasm, "but sometimes I find my fears giving away to the force of numbers. . . . Grant can afford to have four men killed or wounded to kill or disable one of ours. That process will destroy us at last, by using up our material." The next ninety days would be decisive. "If we succeed," Blackford summed up with marginally more enthusiasm, "we will have peace in less than twelve months." [33]

Relatively few of Lee's soldiers seem to have shared Blackford's understanding of the respective strengths of the armies. Instead, a sense that the Federals lacked their usual preponderance of manpower fueled expectations of victory. Typifying this frame of mind, Chaplain James B. Sheeran of the 14th Louisiana believed Lee's "well disciplined army, approximating somewhat to the enemy in numbers . . . and with hearts glowing with the purest of patriotism and minds determined to conquer" would smite the Federals. Both Clement Evans and Walter Taylor placed Grant's strength at 75,000 to 80,000 men (a considerable underestimate) and concurred that, as Evans put it, "We will be fully able to cope with them." Second Corps cartographer Jedediah Hotchkiss quoted Lee himself as saying on April 11 that "the enemy had not as large a force as they had last year,—though it was said they were coming with a large force in every direction." Even a good look at the enemy's extensive camps failed to impress Maj. Tully Francis Parker of the 26th Mississippi.

From atop Clark's Mountain on May 4, he spied "many a Yank in our front, but from what I can see they don't have any advantage on us." The soldiers placed great trust in Lee and would fight desperately, he confirmed, predicting that if Grant advanced "he will certainly meet with a bad defeat." [34]

Numbers aside, the notion of a demoralized enemy took root on the Confederate side of the Rapidan. At Second Corps headquarters, Lt. Gen. Richard S. Ewell received encouraging intelligence about Federal morale: "They are said to be re-enlisting very rapidly, but after receiving the bounty, to be deserting as fast." A lieutenant in the 4th Virginia contrasted Lee's "noble army voluntarily reenlisting for the war" with "the Yankees offering enormous bounties and getting so few soldiers at that." Influenced by a "frenzy of despair at the prospect of their fast failing cause," believed this man, the Federals would mount one last gigantic campaign to salvage their war effort. Similarly, Clement Evans mentioned Federal deserters who spoke of their army as "demoralized & deserting in large droves." A Virginian in the Stonewall Brigade made a common inference that Confederate victories in Louisiana, North Carolina, and Tennessee had been "very discouraging to the enemy," who would get "pretty badly whipped" if they crossed the Rapidan to attack the Army of Northern Virginia.[35]

Shifting their lens from the Army of the Potomac to the northern home front, some Confederates detected a broader malaise. Political turmoil and rising gold prices ranked among the most often mentioned examples of looming crises that might undermine Union civilian morale. An artillery lieutenant read about a resolution in the United States Congress to expel Alexander Long of Ohio for making speeches in favor of peace—an indication that "opposition to the war is getting stronger and more fearless." A Confederate military victory could loose the tongues of antiwar men such as Long and Mayor Fernando Wood of New York City against Lincoln and his party. In mid-April, Surgeon Spencer Glasgow Welch of the 13th South Carolina—who thought northerners more susceptible than Confederates to discouragement because "[t]heir cause is not just"—celebrated the latest economic news from the North: "Gold is 179 in New York, but if we whip Grant we may send it up to 300 for them." [36]

At the Bureau of War in Richmond, diarist Robert G. H. Kean mirrored the attitude of many soldiers in Lee's army. Skyrocketing gold prices constituted just one of many "hopeful indications of a general breaking up in the United States, political as well as financial," he wrote on April 3. Angry disputes between Democrats and Republicans in Congress, Lincoln's "military usurpation," and jockeying for the presidential succession augured well for the Confederacy. Having laid out this background of potential chaos in northern society, Kean turned to the factor that would settle the fate of both nations: "Everything depends on the next battle in Virginia."[37]

Misconceptions about Federal numbers and morale joined pervasive confidence in Confederate prowess to inspire thoughts about another offensive across the Potomac. A captain in the 60th Georgia of John B. Gordon's brigade reported Lee's army fully ready to counter Grant's movements and then march northward. "[T]he men are now very anxious to move forward," he told a cousin. "They are also anxious that Genl. Lee should carry them in to Penn. again." Sergeant Fitzpatrick of the 45th Georgia expected the campaign to open in May with Lee attacking Grant and then proceeding on to Pennsylvania. A member of Micah Jenkins's brigade, with retribution in mind, set his sights a bit farther south: "Something tells me we shall be successful if we invade Md. once more," stated Stephen Elliott Welch. "War is a curse but I want the Yanks to realize its horrors in their own boundaries."[38]

Dodson Ramseur savored a scenario involving a raid across the Potomac that would send destructive tremors through northern society. Lee's army would "crush Meade—*before* crossing the Potomac," strike through Maryland into Pennsylvania, subsist for a while off the fat of the Pennsylvania countryside, then withdraw to Virginia to await the next Federal move. "In the mean time the Yankee debt will go on piling up," asserted the young brigadier, who firmly believed that northerners cared more about their purses than anything else. "Gold will mount higher. Yanks will consider 'the job' bigger than they expected in which all concerned are apt to be hurt. Old Abe will be defeated for Pres't—& the people will be ready & anxious to sustain the peace policy of the new Pres't."[39]

A belief that victory would be impossible without God's blessing underlay virtually all of the speculation about the spring campaign. The army experienced a surge of religious activity in the winter and spring of 1864 that came to be called the "Great Revival."

Brig. Gen. Stephen Dodson Ramseur (shown here as a major of artillery earlier in the war) voiced great optimism about the war in the spring of 1864. His comments reflected a common attitude among soldiers in the Army of Northern Virginia. (Robert Underwood Johnson and Clarence Clough Buel, eds., Battles and Leaders of the Civil War, *4 vols. [New York: Century, 1887–88], 4:242)*

In describing this phenomenon in one part of the army, a South Carolinian noted approvingly that "a deep religious feeling pervades McLaws' Division. In three brigades there is preaching every night, with prayer and inquiry meetings . . . during the day." One historian places the number of converts at roughly 7,000 and estimates that the revivals touched at least thirty-two of the army's thirty-eight brigades of infantry. The specter of death in battle, hardships endured by soldiers and civilians alike, and uncertainties about the future all contributed to a milieu ripe for religious examination.[40]

Diaries and letters from Lee's army offer little evidence of fear that God had deserted the Confederacy—though many soldiers interpreted the war as God's punishment for their sins. J. M. Miller of the 14th South Carolina used typical language in making this point: "Now I believe the war was brought on us for our sins and whenever the people repent aright the war will end." Miller evinced, however, no doubt that God would favor the Confederates over their enemies, commenting that in the next campaign Grant "will undoubtedly get whipped and I hope and believe the war will end." Virginian William L. Wilson echoed Miller's sentiments. "[T]hough in the past three years He has suffered us to be sorely tormented and aliens to occupy our lands and strangers our houses," he wrote of God's hand in the war, "He never brought us so far in that struggle to turn us over to the tender mercies of the enemy." Wilson joined many other soldiers in hoping that "many humble fervent petitions of Christians throughout the Confederacy" would promote final success.[41]

Others identified God's blessings on a just cause and the continued devotion of the southern white populace as the keys to victory. "[I]f God does add another to our list of victories," averred Walter Taylor, "we may confidently look for peace soon thereafter. This army is determined, always presupposing Heaven's help, to accomplish this." Lee's brilliance and the army's fine material condition should encourage hope, wrote Ted Barclay in early May. "But more than this, our cause we believe to be a just one and our God is certainly a just God, then why should we doubt." A third soldier could not "but think that if we are true to ourselves and do our whole duty that a just and almighty God will crown our efforts with success and peace." This man thought it wonderful that Confederates had begun to "rely solely on God and themselves for success—they have ceased to look to Europe, the outside world for support."[42]

John W. Watson of the 47th Virginia found the prospect of a summer's hard fighting discouraging. "But it wont do to be so low spirited," he added quickly. "I believ it is the best way to chear up, and trust in our great Captain who can give the victory to whom he sees propper to give it to." Lt. John W. Hosford of the 5th Florida would have agreed with Watson's implication that the Lord would decide victor and vanquished. He insisted that only God could extricate the Confederacy from its difficult trials. "I do not believe we have done our duty to Him," he confided to his sweetheart, "from no other source need we expect peace."[43]

Robert E. Lee joined many of his men in believing a strict devotion to duty and the Almighty's favor would yield Confederate success. As the army grimly confronted hunger during the lean, cold days of January, he issued a general order that evoked the Christian sacrifice of the Revolutionary War generation. "Continue to emulate in the future, as you have in the past, their valor in arms, their patient endurance of hardships, their high resolve to be free . . . ," he implored, "and be assured that the just God who crowned their efforts with success will, in His own good time, send down His blessings upon yours." Lee also subscribed to the idea that God would bless the side that most closely followed a Christian path. The failure of Dahlgren's raid against Richmond and subsequent revelations about assassination plots elicited a strong response. Lee spoke of the enemy's "unchristian & atrocious acts" and observed that Dahlgren's "plans were frustrated by a merciful Providence, his forces scattered, & he killed."[44]

Did the commanding general share the confidence of his officers and men as May 1864 drew near? Logistics vexed him greatly, as demonstrated by his persistent search for food, fodder, and other materials throughout late winter and spring. Rations and supplies of shoes and clothing improved with time, but Lee remained partially hamstrung by logistics in his effort to meet Federal offensives. Among other expedients, he dispersed portions of the army's cavalry and artillery to areas able to support their heavy demands for fodder. Always in favor of holding the strategic initiative, he suggested to Jefferson Davis and James Longstreet that Confederate attacks in the East or West (or in both theaters) could disrupt Grant's plans. "The great obstacle everywhere is scarcity of supplies," he told Longstreet. Shortages might force the Confederates to conform to Federal plans "and concentrate wherever they are going to attack us."[45]

On March 30, Lee informed Davis that the time approached when "I shall require all the troops belonging to this army." Six days later he had concluded that Virginia would be the target of Grant's largest effort and recommended that Longstreet's corps be summoned to Virginia. Braxton Bragg, installed as a bureaucrat in Richmond after his removal from command of the Army of Tennessee, heard from Lee on April 7. "I think every preparation should be made to meet the approaching storm, which will apparently burst in Virginia," read Lee's dispatch, "& unless its force can be diverted by an attack in the West, that troops should be collected to oppose it." Lee asked for the return of Robert F. Hoke's and Robert D. Johnston's brigades "& all the recruits that can be obtained," and he urged the collection of supplies in Richmond. Interruption of railroads that fed into Richmond, warned Lee, would compel him to withdraw from Virginia.[46]

Lee's almost desperate requests for reinforcements stemmed from his knowledge that the Army of the Potomac would number at least 100,000 when it moved southward. Even with Longstreet's two divisions the Army of Northern Virginia would muster fewer than 65,000 men. The nearby presence of Ambrose E. Burnside's Federal corps—the objective of which Lee could only guess—and the rumored arrival of the Federal Eleventh and Twelfth Corps further tilted the odds against the Confederate defenders. Thus Lee scarcely could have shared the pervasive illusion that the armies would contend on fairly equal numerical terms. (Why Walter Taylor, who certainly must have been privy to the reports on which Lee based his estimates, indulged such an optimistic view in this regard is a mystery.)[47]

Offensive thoughts and logistical doubts continued to dominate Lee's thinking through April. He told Bragg that the addition of Longstreet's troops and George E. Pickett's division (which had been detached from the First Corps after Gettysburg) would provide the manpower necessary to mount an offensive against Grant along the Rappahannock. In that way Lee could oblige the enemy to look to the safety of their capital and relinquish thoughts about menacing Richmond. But logistics tied his hands: "I cannot even draw to me the cavalry or artillery of the army, and the season has arrived when I may be attacked any day. The scarcity of our supplies gives me the greatest uneasiness." On May 4, Lee telegraphed Bragg that the Federals had struck tents and were en route to the Rapidan River's fords. "This army in motion toward Mine Run," he reported. "Can Pickett's division move toward Spotsylvania Court House?" Lee's request for Pickett's brigades underscored his continuing concern about numbers as the opening clash with Grant's host drew near. Any thoughts of a strategic offensive must have re-

ceded as he planned to block the Army of the Potomac's strike southward through the Wilderness.[48]

However troubled by his army's relative paucity of numbers and
Grant's possessing the strategic initiative, Lee knew he led veterans who had delivered victories on many difficult fields. His soldiers
strode toward battle on May 5 with an equally unshakable faith in
their commander and an expectation of success. South Carolinian
Alexander Cheves Haskell had caught the essence of their esprit in
a pair of sentences penned near the end of March: "While I observe
no boastfulness or effervescence in the courage of our men, the indications of spirit are of a better kind than I have ever seen them.
Plenty of enthusiasm, but of a subdued and concentrated sort, that
fully appreciates the dangers ahead and a determination to put an
end, if possible, to the fighting this year." [49] The ensuing conflagra-
tion in Spotsylvania's grim Wilderness would fully justify the men's
confidence in themselves and their chief—and would leave gaps in
their ranks never to be filled with soldiers their equal.

NOTES

1. Bell I. Wiley, *The Road to Appomattox* (Memphis, Tenn.: Memphis
State College Press, 1956), 67–68, 70; Richard E. Beringer et al., *Why the
South Lost the Civil War* (Athens: University of Georgia Press, 1986), 425.
In his influential study of the Georgia upcountry, Steven Hahn portrays a
Confederate populace hugely disaffected from its government by the be-
ginning of 1864 (Hahn, *The Roots of Southern Populism: Yeoman Farmers and
the Transformation of the Georgia Upcountry, 1850–1890* [New York: Oxford
University Press, 1983], especially chapter 3). Other recent works that
portray serious erosion of southern white commitment to the war by the
end of 1863 include Malcolm C. McMillan, *The Disintegration of a Confederate State: Three Governors and Alabama's Wartime Home Front, 1861–1865*
(Macon, Ga.: Mercer University Press, 1986); Wayne K. Durrill's study of
Washington County, North Carolina, titled *War of Another Kind: A Southern Community in the Great Rebellion* (New York: Oxford University Press,
1990); and David Williams, *Rich Man's War: Class, Caste, and Confederate Defeat in the Lower Chattahoochee Valley* (Athens: University of Georgia Press,
1999). Hahn, Durrill, and Williams emphasize class antagonism between
yeomen and planters as a major factor in undermining civilian morale. For
an argument that Confederate morale remained strong well into 1864, see
Gary W. Gallagher, *The Confederate War* (Cambridge, Mass.: Harvard University Press, 1997).

2. Edward A. Pollard, *Southern History of the War: The Last Year of the War* (New York: Charles B. Richardson, 1866), 13–14.

3. James B. Sheeran, *Confederate Chaplain: A War Journal of Rev. James B. Sheeran, c.ss.r. 14th Louisiana, C.S.A.*, ed. Joseph T. Durkin (Milwaukee: Bruce Publishing Company, 1960), 72 (entry for January 21, 1864); Dr. William Alexander Thom to J. Pembroke Thom, April 16, 1864, in Catherine Thom Bartlett, ed., *"My Dear Brother": A Confederate Chronicle* (Richmond, Va.: Dietz Press, 1952), 156.

4. Samuel D. Knight to Joseph E. Brown, February 22, 1864, in Mills Lane, ed., *Times That Prove People's Principles: Civil War in Georgia* (Savannah, Ga.: Beehive Press, 1993), 137; Robert Garlick Hill Kean, *Inside the Confederate Government: The Diary of Robert Garlick Hill Kean*, ed. Edward Younger (New York: Oxford University Press, 1957), 140 (entry for March 13, 1864); Pauline DeCaradeuc Heyward, *A Confederate Lady Comes of Age: The Journal of Pauline DeCaradeuc Heyward, 1863–1888*, ed. Mary D. Robertson (Columbia: University of South Carolina Press, 1992), 38. On Brown, Stephens, Holden, and the controversies in which they played crucial roles, see Joseph H. Parks, *Joseph E. Brown of Georgia* (Baton Rouge: Louisiana State University Press, 1977); Thomas E. Schott, *Alexander H. Stephens of Georgia: A Biography* (Baton Rouge: Louisiana State University Press, 1988); and William C. Harris, *William Woods Holden: Firebrand of North Carolina Politics* (Baton Rouge: Louisiana State University Press, 1987). For a selection of documents that help illuminate the situation in North Carolina, see W. Buck Yearns and John G. Barrett, eds., *North Carolina Civil War Documentary* (Chapel Hill: University of North Carolina Press, 1980).

5. *Richmond Dispatch*, January 9, 13, 1864; *Charleston Daily Courier*, January 14, 16, 1864; *Richmond Enquirer*, February 5, 1864.

6. *Richmond Dispatch*, March 24, 1864; *Charleston Daily Courier*, February 16, 1864.

7. *Atlanta Southern Confederacy*, March 31, 1864; article from the *Mobile Advertiser* quoted in the *Atlanta Southern Confederacy*, March 24, 1864; *Richmond Enquirer*, February 6, 1864; *Charleston Daily Courier*, February 26, April 2, 1864.

8. Mary Jones to Mary S. Mallard, April 30, 1864, in Robert Manson Myers, ed., *The Children of Pride: A True Story of Georgia and the Civil War* (New Haven, Conn.: Yale University Press, 1972), 1162–63; Belle Edmondson, *A Lost Heroine of the Confederacy: The Diaries and Letters of Belle Edmondson*, ed. William Galbraith and Loretta Galbraith (Jackson: University Press of Mississippi, 1990), 113, 124 (diary entries for April 14, May 6, 1864); Susan Emeline Jeffords Caldwell to Lycurgus Washington Caldwell,

April 22, 1864, in J. Michael Welton, ed., *"My Heart Is So Rebellious": The Caldwell Letters, 1861–1865* (Warrenton, Va.: Fauquier National Bank, n.d.), 218.

9. [Judith W. McGuire], *Diary of a Southern Refugee during the War* (1867; reprint, Salem, N.H.: Ayer Publishers, 1986), 269–70.

10. *(Macon) Georgia Journal & Messenger,* March 30, 1864; *Atlanta Southern Confederacy,* March 27, 1864; *Charleston Daily Courier,* April 11, 1864; *Richmond Dispatch,* April 13, 1864.

11. Alexander Frederick Fleet to Benjamin Fleet, April 11, 1864, in Betsy Fleet and John D. P. Fuller, eds., *Green Mount: A Virginia Plantation Family during the Civil War, Being the Journal of Benjamin Robert Fleet and Letters of His Family* (Lexington: University of Kentucky Press, 1962), 320; Henry W. Barrow to John W. Fries, April 9, 1864, in Marian H. Blair, ed., "Civil War Letters of Henry W. Barrow to John W. Fries," *North Carolina Historical Review* 34 (January 1957): 81–82.

12. W. Johnson J. Webb to Dear Parents, April 22, 1864, Lewis Leigh Collection, United States Army Military History Institute, Carlisle, Pa.; Stephen Dodson Ramseur to Ellen Richmond Ramseur, April 24, May 3, 1864, Stephen Dodson Ramseur Papers, Southern Historical Collection, Wilson Library, University of North Carolina, Chapel Hill (repository hereafter cited as SHC).

13. Stephen Dodson Ramseur to David Schenck, January 28, 1864, Ramseur Papers, SHC; D. J. Hileman to Miss Kate McCutchan, January 18, 1864, Daniel J. Hileman Letters, James G. Leyburn Library, Washington and Lee University, Lexington, Va.

14. R. E. Lee to Jefferson Davis, January 2, April 12, 1864, in R. E. Lee, *The Wartime Papers of R. E. Lee,* ed. Clifford Dowdey and Louis H. Manarin (Boston: Little, Brown, 1961), 647, 698.

15. R. E. Lee to James A. Seddon, February 16, 1864, in ibid., 672; Thomas J. Goree to Sarah Williams Kittrell Goree, February 8, 1864, in Thomas J. Goree, *Longstreet's Aide: The Civil War Letters of Major Thomas J. Goree,* ed. Thomas W. Cutrer (Charlottesville: University Press of Virginia, 1995), 117; Charles E. Denoon to [?], January 16, 1864, in Charles E. Denoon, *Charlie's Letters: The Civil War Correspondence of Charles E. Denoon,* ed. Richard T. Coutier (Collingswood, N.J.: C. W. Historicals, 1989), 92; Burwell Thomas Cotton to My Dear Sister, April 30, 1864, in Michael W. Taylor, ed., *The Cry Is War, War, War: The Civil War Correspondence of Lts. Burwell Thomas Cotton and George Job Huntley, 34th Regiment North Carolina Troops* (Dayton, Ohio: Morningside, 1994), 172; J. E. B. Stuart to Flora Stuart, February 8, 1864, in James E. B. Stuart, *The Letters of Major Gen-*

eral J. E. B. Stuart, ed. Adele H. Mitchell ([Richmond, Va.]: Stuart-Mosby Historical Society, 1990), 370–71.

16. LeRoy S. Edwards to [?], January 10, 1864, in LeRoy S. Edwards, *Letters of LeRoy S. Edwards, Written during the War between the States*, ed. Joan K. Walton and Terry A. Walton (n.p.: n.p., [1985]), letter no. 59 (unpaginated work with letters arranged chronologically); Benjamin H. Freeman to W. H. Freeman, February 19, 1864, in Benjamin H. Freeman, *The Confederate Letters of Benjamin H. Freeman*, ed. Stuart T. Wright (Hicksville, N.Y.: Exposition Press, 1974), 34; Thomas J. Barron to Ada, April 23, 1864, in Ray Mathis, ed., *In the Land of the Living: Wartime Letters by Confederates from the Chattahoochee Valley of Alabama and Georgia* (Troy, Ala.: Troy State University Press, 1981), 115.

17. "A Fire Side Defender" [probably William Judkins of the 22nd Georgia] to the Editor, February 17, 1864, *Rome (Ga.) Tri-Weekly Courier*, March 3, 1864; James Marion Garrett to Dear Mother, April 14, 1864, typescript, Fredericksburg and Spotsylvania National Military Park Library, Fredericksburg, Va. (repository hereafter cited as FSNMP); Tully F. Parker to My Dear Wife and Children, May 4, 1864, typescript, bound vol. 201, FSNMP; John Henry Stover Funk to his parents, March 5, 1864, typescript of original in private hands provided by Keith S. Bohannon.

18. Kate Cumming, *The Journal of a Confederate Nurse, 1862–1865*, ed. Richard Harwell (Savannah, Ga.: Beehive Press, 1975), 177; Emma Holmes, *The Diary of Miss Emma Holmes, 1861–1866*, ed. John F. Marszalek (Baton Rouge: Louisiana State University Press, 1979), 339; *Richmond Enquirer*, January 30, 1864.

19. Charles Augustus Conn to Mary A. Brantley, March 18, 1864, in T. Conn Bryan, ed., "Letters of Two Confederate Officers: William Thomas Conn and Charles Augustus Conn," *Georgia Historical Quarterly* 46 (June 1962): 194; Stephen Dodson Ramseur to David Schenck, February 16, 1864, Ramseur Papers, SHC.

20. Walter Raleigh Battle to My dear Mother, March 29, 1864, typescript, bound vol. 85, FSNMP; James A. Graham to My Dear Mother, April 2, 1864, in James A. Graham, *The James A. Graham Papers, 1861–1884*, ed. H. M. Wagstaff (Chapel Hill: University of North Carolina Press, 1928), 184; Burwell Thomas Cotton to My Dear Sister, April 16, 1864, in Taylor, ed., *The Cry Is War*, 170.

21. James Conner to My dear Mother, April 3, 1864, in James Conner, *Letters of General James Conner*, ed. Mary C. Moffet (Columbia, S.C.: State Company, Printers, 1933), 121; William Meade Dame to My own Dear Mother, April 29, 1864, typescript, FSNMP; Josiah Gorgas, *The Civil War*

Diary of General Josiah Gorgas, ed. Frank E. Vandiver (University: University of Alabama Press, 1947), 88 (entry for March 25).

22. James A. Graham to My Dear Mother, February 1, 1864, in Graham, *Papers*, 178; Abram Hayne Young to Dear Parents and Sisters, March 13, 1864, in Mary Wyche Burgess, ed., "Civil War Letters of Abram Hayne Young," *South Carolina Historical Magazine* 78 (January 1977): 63.

23. Clement A. Evans, *Intrepid Warrior: Clement Anselm Evans, Confederate General from Georgia, Life, Letters, and Diaries of the War Years*, ed. Robert Grier Stephens Jr. (Dayton, Ohio: Morningside, 1992), 341–42 (diary entry for January 18–28); Stephen Dodson Ramseur to David Schenck, February 16, 1864, Ramseur Papers, SHC; Ted Barclay to Dear Sister, March 21, 1864, in Ted Barclay, *Ted Barclay, Liberty Hall Volunteers: Letters from the Stonewall Brigade (1861–1864)*, ed. Charles W. Turner (Natural Bridge Station, Va.: Rockbridge Publishing Company, 1992), 134–35.

24. Marion Hill Fitzpatrick to Amanda Olive Elizabeth White Fitzpatrick, April 10, 1864, in Marion Hill Fitzpatrick, *Letters to Amanda, from Sergeant Major Marion Hill Fitzpatrick, Company K, 45th Georgia Regiment, Thomas' Brigade, Wilcox Division, Hill's Corps, CSA to His Wife Amanda Olive Elizabeth White Fitzpatrick, 1862–1865*, ed. Henry Mansel Hammock (Nashville: Champion Resources, 1982), 125; Daniel Pope to his wife, March 12, 1864, in Mills Lane, ed., *"Dear Mother: Don't grieve about me. If I get killed, I'll only be dead." Letters from Georgia Soldiers in the Civil War* (Savannah, Ga.: Beehive Press, 1977), 282–83; James M. Garrett to Dear Mother, April 14, 1864, typescript, FSNMP; Francis Marion Howard to Dear Brother, April 19, 1864, typescript, bound vol. 104, FSNMP; Isaac Domingos to My dear son Joseph & daughter, Tallulah, April 19, 1864, Confederate Miscellany, 1b, Special Collections, Emory University, Atlanta, Ga.

25. James Conner to My Dear Mother, February 19, April 3, 1864, in Conner, *Letters*, 115, 122; Josiah B. Patterson to My Dear Niece Lizzie, March 17, 1864, in Garland C. Bagley, *History of Forsyth County, Georgia* (Easley, S.C.: Southern Historical Press, 1985), 529–30.

26. R. E. Lee to Jefferson Davis, January 13, 19, 1864; Lee to Alexander R. Lawton, January 19, 1864; Lee to James L. Kemper, January 29, 1864; and Lee to James A. Seddon, April 12, 1864, in Lee, *Wartime Papers*, 650–51, 653, 654–55, 663 (quotation), 696.

27. Catherine Ann Devereux Edmondston, *"Journal of a Secesh Lady": The Diary of Catherine Ann Devereux Edmondston*, ed. Beth Gilbert Crabtree and James W. Patton (Raleigh: North Carolina Division of Archives and

History, 1979), 524 (entry for February 10); [McGuire], *Diary*, 256 (entry for March 20).

28. William Lyle Wilson to My Dearest Ma, April 19, 1864, in Festus P. Summers, ed., *A Borderland Confederate* (Pittsburgh: University of Pittsburgh Press, 1962), 78; Walter H. Taylor to Bettie Saunders, May 1, 1864, in Walter H. Taylor, *Lee's Adjutant: The Wartime Letters of Colonel Walter Herron Taylor, 1862–1865*, ed. R. Lockwood Tower (Columbia: University of South Carolina Press, 1995), 158. In a rare dissent from the consensus that Lee was the ablest Confederate general, F. Stanley Russell of the 13th Virginia described Joseph E. Johnston as "the acknowledged strategist of the South." F. Stanley Russell, *The Letters of F. Stanley Russell: The Movements of Company H, Thirteenth Virginia Regiment, Confederate States Army 1861–1864*, ed. Douglas Carroll (Baltimore: Paul M. Harrod, 1963), 58. For the unpersuasive argument that Lee's preeminence in the Confederate military pantheon was a postwar phenomenon, see Thomas L. Connelly, *The Marble Man: Robert E. Lee and His Image in American Society* (New York: Knopf, 1977).

29. Edward Porter Alexander, *Fighting for the Confederacy: The Personal Recollections of General Edward Porter Alexander*, ed. Gary W. Gallagher (Chapel Hill: University of North Carolina Press, 1989), 346; R. to the editor of *The Daily South Carolinian*, May 1, 1864, printed in the *Daily South Carolinian* (Columbia), May 10, 1864; David Crawford to Dear Mother, April 30, 1864, typescript, FSNMP; Abram Hayne Young to Ever Dear Sister, April 30, 1864, in Burgess, ed., "Letters of Abram Hayne Young," 70.

30. Franklin Gaillard to Dear Maria, April 24, 1864, Gaillard Papers no. 3790, SHC; Walter Taylor to Bettie Saunders, April 24, 1864, in Taylor, *Lee's Adjutant*, 155; Francis Marion Whelchel to Dear Sisters and Cousin Mary, April 26, 1864, typescript, FSNMP; Thomas J. Goree to Sarah Williams Kittrell Goree, April 26, 1864, in Goree, *Longstreet's Aide*, 122–23.

31. O. H. Steger to [?], April 23, 1864, typescript, FSNMP; F. Stanley Russell to Dear Papa, March 31, 1864, in Russell, *Letters*, 64–65; James Conner to My dear Mother, April 3, 1864, in Conner, *Letters*, 122; Charles O. Goodwyne to Dear Pa & Ma, March 10, 1864, typescript, FSNMP.

32. Walter H. Taylor to Bettie Saunders, March 20, 1864, in Taylor, *Lee's Adjutant*, 139.

33. Green Berry Samuels to Kathleen Boone Samuels, April 3, 1864, in Carrie Esther Spencer et al., eds., *A Civil War Marriage in Virginia: Reminiscences and Letters* (Boyce, Va.: Carr, 1956), 211; Wade Hampton to Mary Fisher Hampton, February 14, May 6, 1864, in Charles E. Cauthen,

ed., *Family Letters of the Three Wade Hamptons* (Columbia: University of South Carolina Press, 1953), 103–4; Henry Robinson Berkeley, *Four Years in the Confederate Artillery: The Diary of Private Henry Robinson Berkeley*, ed. William H. Runge (Chapel Hill: University of North Carolina Press [for the Virginia Historical Society], 1961), 72; Charles Minor Blackford to Mrs. Blackford, May 3, 1864, in Susan Leigh Blackford and Charles Minor Blackford, eds., *Letters from Lee's Army, or, Memoirs of Life In and Out of the Army in Virginia during the War between the States* (New York: Scribner's, 1947), 242–43.

34. Sheeran, *Confederate Chaplain*, 85 (diary entry for April 26); Clement A. Evans to Dear Darling, April 20, 1864, in Evans, *Intrepid Warrior*, 373; Walter H. Taylor to Bettie Saunders, May 1, 1864, in Taylor, *Lee's Adjutant*, 158; Jedediah Hotchkiss, *Make Me a Map of the Valley: The Civil War Journal of Stonewall Jackson's Topographer*, ed. Archie P. McDonald (Dallas, Tex.: Southern Methodist University Press, 1973), 198–99; Tully F. Parker to My Dear Wife and Children, May 4, 1864, typescript, FSNMP.

35. Richard S. Ewell to Benjamin S. Ewell, February 18, 1864, in Richard S. Ewell, *The Making of a Soldier: Letters of General R. S. Ewell*, ed. Percy Gatling Hamlin (Richmond, Va.: Whittet & Shepperson, 1935), 126; Ted Barclay to Dear Sister, February 22, March 21, 1864, in Barclay, *Ted Barclay*, 128; Clement A. Evans to My dearest Dearest, May 2, 1864, in Evans, *Intrepid Warrior*, 380; John Garibaldi to Dear Wife, April 22, 1864, typescript, bound vol. 172, FSNMP. This view of Federal morale also appeared in civilian letters and diaries. For example, Susan Emeline Jeffords Caldwell wrote in April that Grant "has a very large army but many are heartily sick of the war and say they do not intend to reenlist. Their time will be out in August and they are going home to stay—I hope they will be true to their word." Caldwell to Lycurgus Washington Caldwell, April 22, 1864, in Welton, ed., *Caldwell Letters*, 218.

36. William Beverley Pettit to Arabella Speairs Pettit, April 19, 1864, in Charles W. Turner, ed., *Civil War Letters of Arabella Speairs and William Beverley Pettit of Fluvanna County, Virginia, March 1862–March 1865*, 2 vols. (Roanoke, Va.: Virginia Lithography and Graphics, 1988–89), 2:25; Spencer Glasgow Welch to his wife, January 16, April 19, 1864, in Spencer Glasgow Welch, *A Confederate Surgeon's Letters to His Wife* (1911; reprint, Marietta, Ga.: Continental Book Company, 1954), 86, 90–91.

37. Kean, *Diary*, 443–44.

38. Benjamin F. Keller to My dear Cousin Annis, April 7, 1864, in *The Land and the People: Readings in Bulloch County History, Book 5* (Statesboro,

Ga.: Bulloch County Historical Society, 1986), 55; Marion Hill Fitzpatrick to Amanda Olive Elizabeth White Fitzpatrick, April 14, 1864, in Fitzpatrick, *Letters to Amanda*, 127; Stephen Elliott Welch to Dear Mother, February 14, 1864, in Stephen Elliott Welch, *Stephen Elliot Welch of the Hampton Legion*, ed. John Michael Priest (Shippensburg, Pa.: Burd Street Press, 1994), 24.

39. Stephen Dodson Ramseur to David Schenck, March 13, 1864, Ramseur Papers, SHC.

40. R. to editor of *The Daily South Carolinian*, May 1, 1864, printed in the *Daily South Carolinian* (Columbia), May 10, 1864; Gardiner H. Shattuck Jr., *A Shield and a Hiding Place: The Religious Life of the Civil War Armies* (Macon, Ga.: Mercer University Press, 1987), 99.

41. J. M. Miller to My dear Cousin, April 7, 1864, in [Dotsy Boineau et al., comps. and eds.], *Recollections and Reminiscences: 1861–1865 through World War I*, 10 vols. to date (n.p.: McNaughton & Gunn [for the South Carolina Division United Daughters of the Confederacy], 1990–), 5:374–75; William Lyne Wilson to My Dearest Mother, April 19, 1864, in Summers, ed., *Borderland Confederate*, 78. For the argument that religion played a crucial role in bringing Confederate defeat, see Beringer et al., *Why the South Lost*, especially chapters 12 and 14.

42. Walter H. Taylor to Bettie Saunders, April 10, 1864, in Taylor, *Lee's Adjutant*, 150; Ted Barclay to Dear Sister, May 2, 1864, in Barclay, *Ted Barclay*, 143–44; F. Stanley Russell to Dear papa, March 14, 1864, in Russell, *Letters*, 62.

43. John W. Watson to My Dear Wife, April 19, 1864, typescript, FSNMP; John W. Hosford to Miss Laura, April 1, 1864, in Knox Mellon Jr., ed., "A Florida Soldier in the Army of Northern Virginia: The Hosford Letters," *Florida Historical Quarterly* 46 (January 1968): 269–70.

44. General Orders No. 7, dated January 22, 1864, in Lee, *Wartime Papers*, 659.

45. R. E. Lee to Jefferson Davis, March 25, 1864, and Lee to James Longstreet, March 28, 1864, in ibid., 682–85.

46. R. E. Lee to Jefferson Davis, March 30, April 5, 1864, and Lee to Braxton Bragg, April 7, 1864, in ibid., 690–93.

47. R. E. Lee to Braxton Bragg, April 13, 1864, in ibid., 698.

48. R. E. Lee to Braxton Bragg, April 16, May 4, 1864, in ibid., 701, 718.

49. Alexander Cheves Haskell to [?], March 27, 1864, in Louise Haskell Daly, *Alexander Cheves Haskell: The Portrait of a Man* (1934; reprint, Wilmington, N.C.: Broadfoot, 1989), 123.

Part Two

LEE AS A
CONFEDERATE
GENERAL

Much of the literature on the Civil War portrays Robert E. Lee as a grand anachronism. In a conflict often characterized, whether accurately or not, as the first great modern war,[1] the Confederate commander frequently appears as a soldier of considerable martial gifts who harkened back to an earlier time. Lee is cast as a man who thought of the struggle in terms of protecting his own state rather advancing the cause of the entire Confederacy, forged a personal bond with his soldiers reminiscent of feudal relationships, focused on winning set-piece battles without taking in the broader political and social landscape of a modern war, and failed to understand the implications of new weaponry such as the rifle-musket. Historians and other writers have employed an array of images that tie Lee to a knightly tradition and an agrarian age, presenting him as a localist for whom kinship and ancestral place meant everything. This Lee functions as the perfect foil to Ulysses S. Grant and William Tecumseh Sherman, Union generals typically described as forward-looking officers who recognized the necessity of waging a modern war that engulfed entire societies, plotted their strategy accordingly, and changed the nature of the conflict. Two very different groups of authors have nourished the anachronistic image of Lee as an old-fashioned general: those who admire him and intend their chivalric portrayal to be positive, and those more hostile who describe a commander out of touch with much of the military reality of his time. There is irony in the fact that these two groups became unlikely accomplices in creating a fascinatingly flawed interpretive tradition.

Before making a case for Lee as a general well attuned to the realities of mid-nineteenth-century warfare, it is necessary to review some of the literature that portrays him as a throwback to an earlier epoch. These works divide conveniently into two types: those that describe Lee as a magnificent and admirable anachronism, and those that more critically insist he was unwilling or unable to adapt to the demands of a mid-nineteenth-century modern war.

Titles of the first type began to appear almost as soon as the war ended and have continued to be published ever since. Many of the early ones nestle comfortably within the Lost Cause literature. Former Confederates such as Jubal A. Early described Lee as an exemplar of the South's antebellum agrarian civilization, a devout Christian of great humanity whose patriarchal bond with his soldiers helped forge a military record to which all white southerners could look with pride. Early delighted in contrasting Lee and his band of underfed and poorly equipped Confederates with a modern Union juggernaut dependent on technology and backed by unlimited material resources. In a famous address delivered at Washington and Lee University on the anniversary of Lee's birth in 1872, Early spoke of the confrontation between his hero and Grant. "For nine long months was the unequal contest protracted by the genius of one man, aided by the valor of his little force," stated Early. Lee finally surrendered "the mere ghost of the Army of Northern Virginia, which had been gradually worn down by the combined agencies of numbers, steam-power, railroads, mechanism, and all the resources of physical science." Early decried those who would "surrender cherished traditions" and "adopt the spirit of progress from our enemies," imploring his audience to remember and honor the prewar civilization that had produced such a noble figure as Lee—a man descended from "the Cavalier [class] from tide-water" Virginia.[2]

Other former Confederates also specifically linked Lee to the idea of a cavalier tradition in Virginia. Persistent identification of the general with this class of Virginians supported the idea that he was a man out of step with the modern world of the 1860s. Among the authors who wrote of Lee in this way was John Esten Cooke, a successful novelist and nonfiction writer who had served on "Jeb" Stuart's staff. Cooke's *Wearing of the Gray*, a combination of fiction and reminiscence published in 1867, included a character named Corporal Shabrach who remarked of Lee: "No man in public affairs now, to my thinking at least, is so fine a representative and so truthful a type of the great Virginia race of old times." Shabrach never looked at Lee without being transported "back to the days when Washington, and [John] Randolph, and [Edmund] Pendleton, used to figure on the stage, and which my father told me all about in my youth. Long may the old hero live to lead us, and let no base hand ever dare to sully the glories of our well beloved General—the 'noblest Roman of them all,' the pink of chivalry and honor." More than thirty-five years after the publication of Cooke's book, former artillery officer Robert Stiles's frequently quoted memoir similarly alluded to "the character and career of our great Cavalier." "It is our patent of nobility," added Stiles, "that he is to-day regarded—the world over—as the representative of the soldiery of the South." [3]

Orators at the dedications of statues of Lee at Washington and Lee University in 1883 and on Richmond's Monument Avenue in 1891 invoked a more distant chivalric past. Speaking at General Lee's college, John Warwick Daniel, a veteran of Jubal Early's wartime staff, adopted a heavily romantic Lost Cause approach. "As we glance back through the smoke-drifts of his many campaigns and battles," observed Daniel of Lee, "his kind, considerate acts towards his officers and men gleam through them as brightly as their burnished weapons; and they formed a fellowship as noble as that which bound the Knights of the Round Table to Arthur, 'the blameless King.'" At the ceremony in Richmond, Archer Anderson described Lee as the "grave and courteous commander, heir of all the knightly graces of the cavaliers," adding: "Let this monument . . . stand as a memorial of personal honor that never brooked a stain, of knightly valor without thought of self, of far-reaching military genius unsoiled by ambition, of heroic constancy from which no cloud of misfortune could ever hide the path of duty!"

Anderson also spoke to those who might be troubled by the seemingly complex late-nineteenth-century world, offering Lee as one who held unwaveringly to the simple virtues of the past—"the pure and lofty man, in whom we see the perfect union of Christian virtue and old Roman manhood." All the wealth and success of the post–Civil War United States were "less a subject for pride than this one heroic man—this human product of our country and its institutions."

A somewhat romantic wartime portrait of Lee by Edward Caledon Bruce, who stated that it was "painted in Richmond and begun at Petersburg from life, in the fall of the winter of '64–'65. It was exhibited in the State Capitol in Feb'y. '65, where numbers of Confederate officers and soldiers saw it, and I was told that their judgment was highly favorable." The original has been lost (the Virginia Historical Society owns what appears to be a study of Lee's head and shoulders), and this cabinet photograph of the painting is published here for the first time. (Author's collection)

Many of Anderson's listeners doubtless inferred that he meant ante-bellum southern institutions, rather than their northern counter-parts, had shaped Lee so favorably.[4]

Northern writers also contributed to Lee's image as an arche-typal cavalier. None had more influence in this regard than Charles Francis Adams, whose family rivaled the Lees as a force in American history and who had fought against the Army of Northern Virginia as a junior officer during the Civil War. In a lecture titled "Shall Cromwell Have a Statue?" delivered to the Phi Beta Kappa frater-nity at the University of Chicago in 1902, Adams sketched Lee as a man whose local loyalties and personal attributes belonged to a time long vanished from early-twentieth-century America. Like Cooke and many others, Adams emphasized Lee's familial and emotional links to colonial and revolutionary Virginia: "Of him it might, and in justice must, be said, that he was more than the essence, he was the quintessence of Virginia." Adams averred that Lee "represented, individualized, all that was highest and best in the Southern mind and the Confederate cause,—the loyalty to State, the keen sense of honor and personal obligation, the slightly archaic, the almost patri-archal, love of dependent, family and home." For Adams, Lee stood for "a type which is gone,—hardly less extinct than that of the great English nobleman of the feudal times, or the ideal head of the Scotch clan of a later period." Bluntly stating that he and other northerners had fought with "the moral right, the spirit of nationality, the sacred cause of humanity even" on their side, Adams nevertheless concluded that Lee deserved an equestrian statue that would look from the nation's Capitol building across the Potomac toward Arlington.[5]

Images of Lee as a cavalier general remained common in the literature throughout the twentieth century. In a series of popu-lar books on the Confederacy, Lee, and the Army of Northern Vir-ginia published between the mid-1940s and the mid-1960s, Clifford Dowdey recalled his nineteenth-century Lost Cause predecessors in presenting Lee as a romantic warrior out of step with more mod-ern northern opponents. "In his carriage and manners, as well as in his classic features," wrote Dowdey, who inherited Douglas Southall Freeman's mantle as the most widely read interpreter of Lee and his army, "he reflected the generic aristocracy from which he had sprung. As a traditional aristocrat, he possessed those qualities of *noblesse oblige* which derived from the Old South of the legend, with none of the excesses and assertiveness of the new." Dowdey's handling of Lee during the Seven Days battles in 1862 was typical: "To him the gathered knights—becoming soldiers since the time of elegant and lighthearted privilege in the first encampments—gave their allegiance. To him the foot soldiers found the patriarch who extended from their familiar parochial scene into the strange, new world of the army." Like Jubal Early, Dowdey juxtaposed a human Lee against Grant and the massive industrial power of the North. The Overland campaign of 1864, claimed Dowdey, "was not a test between Grant, the young and confident hero of the North, and Lee, the aging idol of the South. It was a showdown between the might of a nation, concentrated in Virginia, and one tired and disappointed old man." [6]

Serious works on Lee influenced the general's treatment in publications aimed at a younger audience, which in turn conditioned untold readers who would become adult students of the conflict to think of Lee as an anachronism. For example, children in the 1950s could find in MacKinlay Kantor's *Lee and Grant at Appomattox* a memorable passage linking Lee to medieval and ancient soldiers. "[L]et your eyes brighten as they witness the grave magnificence of Lee—'Marse Robert,' as his troops called him affectionately," urged Kantor. "His face was handsome, refined, as stern and commanding as the features of a marble statue. His beard and hair were silver. You could imagine him in the wars of long ago, in polished armor. You could imagine him in the wars of Biblical times, proud in his chariot, facing the Philistines." In Kantor's prose, poor Grant seemed an unlikely candidate to don armor or smite Philistines. He pursued a more modern strategy of pouring soldiers into bloody combat until Lee's gallant defenders had been vanquished. Hodding Carter's *Robert E. Lee and the Road of Honor* also used chivalric images in affirming that "no man who saw him or who rode beside him or who trudged behind him has written or said that Robert E. Lee was ever anything but the kindly knight, the Christian soldier, and the gallant leader." [7]

Gene Smith's dual biography of Lee and Grant outdid even the children's literature in portraying Lee as a chivalrous knight. Writing for a popular audience in 1984, Smith subscribed to a view of American history put forward by Charles Beard several decades earlier. He called the Civil War a conflict that the "Industrial Revolution won. Yesterday gave way to Tomorrow. Feudal Europe transported to the New World bowed to modern America." Lee personified the agrarian southern civilization for Smith, who breathlessly labeled him "the Christian soldier, the Knight-crusader of ancient lineage at the head of his legions," and "the Sir Galahad of the Old South, of Old Virginia . . . the flower of the civilization that produced him, complete unto himself, the Chevalier Bayard of America, a knight without fear and without reproach." Steeped in a tradition that stretched from Cannae to Waterloo, Smith's Lee believed "that single battles decided campaigns and the fate of nations." The Virginian remained unaware that "the railroad and steamship, the telegraph and the industrial power of modern nations, the new ability to mass enormous armies and equip them—the Industrial Revolution—made the single battle no longer so telling." But Grant "knew, as Lee did not, that they were in a war between societies, not armies." Although Smith's reading of history would set many an academic historian's teeth on edge, his book reached an initial audience swelled by book-club adoptions and remains in print.[8]

A final pair of works will suffice to make the point that this interpretive strain continues to thrive. In the 1980s, Time-Life published a twenty-six-volume history of the Civil War that introduced Lee in a photographic essay filled with allusions to his chivalric roots. "One of his ancestors had fought beside William the Conqueror; another had campaigned through the Holy Land in the Third Crusade; yet another had been knighted by Queen Elizabeth," read the text. "Lee was brought up to be a gentleman soldier. As a grown man, he was widely considered the spiritual heir to George Washington, and some associates thought he consciously acted out the role. . . . In fact, Lee made no bones about his strong sense of *noblesse oblige.*" James I. Robertson Jr., among the most prominent late-twentieth-century Civil War scholars, similarly highlighted Lee's aristocratic background and demeanor in a text accompanying selected paintings of Lee and "Stonewall" Jackson by the popular artist Mort Künstler. "In retrospect, the life of Robert Edward Lee seems incredibly blameless," stated Robertson in a chapter titled "Virginia Aristocrat." "He has been hailed as 'the incarnation of the cavalier tradition so dear to the southern heart.'" Robertson followed the lead of many others in suggesting a feudal relationship between Lee and his followers: "Lee commanded men through respect and wonder rather than through iron-willed discipline and fear. His leadership was paternal instead of autocratic."[9]

All of these authors undoubtedly believed that their descriptions of Lee as a knightly leader served his reputation well. But in choosing to emphasize and embellish Lee's undeniable aristocratic background and attitudes, they created a figure seemingly lost in time. Their choice of images often suggests a man of the past who looked to the past—a feudal leader using his highly personal gifts to hold back the North's modern military machine. This Lee is an able soldier whose best efforts could not stave off absolute defeat. In the hands of the romanticists, that defeat flowed naturally from their understanding of Lee as an attractive anachronism inevitably bowing to a more modern foe.

A second body of work presents a very different portrait of Lee as an old-fashioned general. Influential historians J. F. C. Fuller, T. Harry Williams, Russell F. Weigley, Peter J. Parish, Thomas L. Connelly, and Alan T. Nolan—a more rigorously academic group than most of the authors who have emphasized Lee's chivalric traits —depicted a provincial, backward-looking soldier who failed to grasp the all-encompassing nature of the Civil War. Several arguments stand out in their studies: Lee was a localist who thought first of Virginia and often ignored the broader needs of the Confederacy; Lee consistently sought to win crushing battlefield victories without understanding that technology and the political character of modern conflicts between democratic societies conspired to render truly decisive victories a thing of the past; Lee focused strictly on narrow military questions without seeing the many ways in which events on the battlefield and the home front intersected; Lee failed to grasp the terrible killing power of rifled shoulder weapons, and consequently pursued the tactical offensive so often that he nearly exhausted the South's shallow pool of manpower and thus shortened the life of the Confederacy.

J. F. C. Fuller's *Grant and Lee: A Study in Personality and Generalship* anticipated much of what others in this group would write about Lee. In this widely cited book, first published in England in 1932 and later reprinted several times, Fuller pronounced Grant to be a modern soldier while yoking Lee to an earlier time. The generals "were representatives of two diverging epochs, Lee belonging to the old agricultural age and Grant to the new industrial." Whereas Grant turned "intellectual conceptions into co-ordinated actions," Lee, as if a feudal chieftain at the head of a band of clients, "merely continued to stamp his spirit on the hearts of his men." Grant's "outlook was general, embracing the whole theatre of war," but Lee, governed by his devotion to Virginia, suffered from localism that caused him to fixate "on a small corner of the entire theatre." Although waging a war in which the armies acted as extensions of two democratic peoples, Lee remained essentially removed from nonmilitary concerns. "[B]ecause he would think and work in a corner," commented Fuller, "taking no notice of the whole, taking no interest in forming policy or in the economic side of the war, he was ultimately cornered and his cause lost." As if to clinch his argument that Lee did not fit comfortably into the world of mid-nineteenth-century warfare, Fuller praised the degree to which Lee's "self-sacrificing idealism" inspired soldiers and officers in his army: "To find a comparison we must go back to the days of the saints." [10]

T. Harry Williams and Russell F. Weigley refined some of Fuller's themes. In an immensely influential essay titled "The Military Leadership of North and South," Williams fashioned a multifaceted critique of Lee as an old-fashioned officer of restricted vision. "For his preoccupation with the war in Virginia, Lee is not to be criticized," stated a patronizing Williams. "He was a product of his culture, and that culture, permeated in its every part by the spirit of localism, dictated that his outlook on war should be local." Williams went on to argue that Lee—"in many respects . . . not a modern-minded general"—did not understand the function of a staff, made only a primitive use of maps, seemed not to realize the importance of railroads in modern warfare, and, most tellingly, failed "to grasp the vital relationship between war and statecraft." Much like George B. McClellan, Lee viewed war as preeminently "a professional exercise" to be carried out in isolation from the influence of politics. Like Fuller, Williams trotted out Grant as a modern contrast to Lee. Grant understood the importance of public opinion and shaped his campaigns with that in mind. "It was this ability of Grant's to grasp the political nature of modern war," asserted Williams, "that marks him as the first of the great modern generals." The North also had William Tecumseh Sherman, who, unlike Lee, shared Grant's insight that military forces must "gain public opinion by winning victories that depress the enemy's morale." [11]

A Virginia frame of reference, mistaken belief in the possibility of Cannae-type victories, and disregard for the defensive power of the rifled musket largely define Lee's generalship in Russell F. Weigley's unsparing evaluation. In *The American Way of War*, a justly lauded work first published in 1973, Weigley stressed that Lee clung tenaciously to Napoleon's notion of the climactic battle, despite overwhelming evidence that rifled weapons had wrought immense changes on the battlefield. The Virginian's pursuit of such victories yielded famous triumphs in 1862 and 1863 but rendered the battered Army of Northern Virginia incapable of mounting additional "general offensives against its major adversary." Weigley called Lee "remarkably indifferent" to events beyond the Appalachian Mountains, a fact that discouraged "greater realism" in his thinking and planning. "Like Napoleon himself," concluded Weigley, Lee allowed "his passion for the strategy of annihilation and the climactic, decisive battle as its expression" to destroy "in the end not the enemy armies, but his own." A more perceptive Grant knew he could not destroy an enemy force armed with rifled weapons in a single grand battle; instead, he plotted a strategy that applied constant pressure to Confederate armies while also striking at the South's logistical capacity. He perceived that industrial and economic resources would loom large in settling the conflict, and his friend Sherman added a psychological dimension to the Union effort by targeting Confederate popular will. The two most famous northern generals thus looked resolutely toward future wars of popular nationalism, while Lee, just as resolutely, looked back toward wars where clever generals could settle the issue in one daring stroke.

In a general history of the Civil War published more than a quarter-century after *The American Way of War*, Weigley reaffirmed his belief that Lee was "the most Napoleonic general of the war. . . . His strategy was an offensive strategy, and his aim, through all the war as long as his strength was enough to let him entertain the possibility, was the destruction of the enemy army." Times had passed Lee by, however, rendering him a "Napoleon come to warfare too late, as the Federal rifles showed at Mechanicsville, Gaines's Mill, and Malvern Hill."[12]

Peter J. Parish, part of a long tradition of British historians interested in the American war, echoed his countryman Fuller's conclusions about Lee. In a much-praised textbook on the Civil War published in 1975, Parish spoke about Grant's and Sherman's "broad conception of the business of war in the 1860s, not merely in its geographical compass, but in its psychological impact, and its relation to non-military considerations." Free of shackles to past military thinking and examples, Grant and Sherman were "prepared to throw overboard conventional but outmoded methods of waging war"—a willingness that set them apart from Lee. Compared to the North's premier team, Lee and his prime lieutenant Stonewall Jackson won several brilliant victories but "gradually came to look old-fashioned and narrow by comparison." The celebrated Confederate duo were "the last great exponents of a dying school; they won the kind of battles which were not to decide this kind of war." Parish added his voice to those who insisted that Lee's parochialism hurt the Confederacy. Always Virginia's advocate in debates about allocation of men and material, Lee opposed anyone who called for greater attention to the Mississippi or Tennessee theaters. "He was the final embodiment and idealisation of the cause of states rights, rooted in the basic instinct to defend one's hearth and home," observed Parish. "His whole system of ideals and loyalties precluded him from the kind of broad strategic approach developed by Grant and Sherman."[13]

Thomas L. Connelly and Alan T. Nolan reiterated and extended earlier critiques of Lee's generalship in a pair of highly influential studies. Connelly's *The Marble Man: Robert E. Lee and His Image in American Society* and Nolan's *Lee Considered: General Robert E. Lee and Civil War History*, published in 1977 and 1991 respectively,[14] garnered favorable attention from historians who believed Lee had been spared the type of intense scrutiny to which Grant and other leading Civil War figures had been subjected. They also elicited some apoplectic responses from Lee's partisans—especially from those outside academia.[15] In terms of Lee's generalship, both books followed closely in J. F. C. Fuller's and T. Harry Williams's interpretive footsteps. Connelly and Nolan highlighted what they saw as evidence of Lee's localism, overreliance on outdated offensive strategy and tactics, and failure to comprehend that military leadership in a war between democracies necessarily involved attention to politics and civilian morale as well as to maneuvering armies to set up a successful battle. Both authors also joined Russell F. Weigley in concluding that Lee's devotion to the offensive, however successful at winning victories in 1862–63, piled up casualties in such profusion as virtually to guarantee Confederate defeat.

A few quotations will suggest the tenor of Connelly's and Nolan's arguments. Connelly fervently believed that Virginia was less important than the trans-Appalachian arena in the Confederate strategic picture, and he blasted what he considered backward-looking localism that blinded Lee to the big picture. In a close paraphrase of T. Harry Williams, Connelly observed that Lee had little appreciation of "the relationship between war and statecraft and saw his responsibility as a commander of an army and little more." That army defended his ancestral home: "His concept of the war effort was totally identified with Virginia, and he felt that other theaters were secondary to the eastern front." In an earlier article that rehearsed many of the points in *The Marble Man,* Connelly had suggested that Lee seemed to be unaware of "the closeness of political and military matters" and questioned whether he "possessed a sufficiently broad military mind to deal with over-all Confederate matters." Nolan devoted most of his attention to what he labeled Lee's irresponsible aggressiveness in a world dominated by the power of defenders armed with rifled muskets. Lee's skillful maneuvering and headlong assaults won spectacular victories comparable to those crafted by famous captains of the past, but they came at too high a price. "If one covets the haunting romance of the Lost Cause," wrote Nolan, "then the inflicting of casualties on the enemy, tactical victory in great battles, and audacity are enough." But if the criterion for judgment is whether Lee took in the full picture of his nation's struggle and waged war in a way calculated to achieve Confederate independence, "a very different assessment of Lee's martial qualities is required."[16]

Connelly and especially Nolan have inspired a gaggle of virtual clones, whose work hammers on the same points but adds nothing new in the way of interpretation or evidence. Often performing without an adequate evidential net, so to speak, these authors sometimes reach rather strident conclusions. For example, recent titles by Bevin Alexander, Edward H. Bonekemper III, and John D. McKenzie claim that Lee literally, as Alexander put it, "never understood the revolution that the Minié ball had brought to battle tactics." The literature that has spun off from Connelly and Nolan is worthy of mention primarily to illustrate that the tradition of portraying Lee as an old-fashioned officer unable to cope with a modern war retains vigor.[17]

Before one makes the case that Lee was not an old-fashioned general, it is important to note that a number of scholars have given him some credit for adopting a quite modern approach. Albert Castel offered in the scholarly journal *Civil War History* a spirited reply to Thomas L. Connelly's arguments, and Charles P. Roland similarly responded to Connelly and, more particularly, to Nolan, in his *Reflections on Lee: A Historian's Assessment.* Joseph L. Harsh in his recent study of Lee's influence on Confederate strategy in 1861–62 also reached generally favorable conclusions about Lee's abilities as a broad military planner, as did Joseph T. Glatthaar in his examination of important martial partnerships during the conflict. Yet none of these historians developed in detail the reasons that Lee properly should be called a modern general within the context of his mid-nineteenth-century world.[18]

The remainder of this essay will argue against representations of Lee as either a glorious or misguided anachronism. Lee understood very well the kind of war in which he was engaged and what it would take to win it. He consistently took a nationalist as opposed to a local view, discreetly using his influence to counter localist tendencies in key southern states. He paid considerable attention to politics and civilian morale in both the Union and the Confederacy, and pursued battlefield victories as a means to undermine northern national morale in a conflict that pitted the Confederacy against a foe with huge advantages of manpower and material resources. He crafted a strategy based on a careful, if sometimes flawed, reading of the military and political situation and ultimately saw his best efforts dissolve in absolute defeat. In short, Lee adapted well to the demands of a conflict that far exceeded in scope and complexity anything he or anyone else could have anticipated in the spring of 1861.

Lee's national viewpoint stands out vividly in his wartime correspondence. From the opening of the conflict until the final scenes at Appomattox, he urged Confederate soldiers, politicians, and civilians to set aside state and local prejudices in their struggle to establish a new Confederate nation. This stance is especially impressive from a man who described himself in an early postwar interview as "a firm and honest believer in the doctrine of State rights." [19]

Lee left the United States Army in April 1861 because of Virginia's actions; but once his state joined the incipient slaveholding republic and he donned a Confederate uniform, he operated as a nationalist. As David M. Potter observed more than thirty-five years ago in his pathbreaking essay on southern nationalism, individuals hold a variety of loyalties to family, religion, locality, state, region, and nation—any one of which can loom largest at different times according to circumstances. This certainly was the case with Lee, who spoke often of family and place and Virginia but for whom, during the Civil War, the needs of the Confederacy stood paramount. It is crucial to recognize that attachments to state and nation are not mutually exclusive, and Lee, whose correspondence prior to the war revealed loyalty to the South as well as to Virginia and the United States, should not be seen as a localist for whom Virginia meant everything. Indeed, just weeks after joining the Confederate army, he unabashedly celebrated his new nation's triumph at First Manassas: "I almost wept for joy," he wrote Joseph E. Johnston, "at the glorious victory achieved by our brave troops on the 21st."[20]

Lee articulated some of his views about the relative importance of state and national concerns in a letter to Secretary of State Andrew G. McGrath of South Carolina in late December 1861. Responding to McGrath's request for advice about how South Carolina should react to Federal military threats, Lee, who had been assigned command of a department encompassing the coastal regions of South Carolina, Georgia, and eastern Florida, remarked: "I think it only necessary to repeat more emphatically than perhaps I have been able to do in person the urgent necessity of bringing out the military strength of the State and putting it under the best and most permanent organization." Though the war was only eight months old, Lee took the long view, worrying about what would happen as soldiers who had enlisted for a year in April 1861 neared the end of their terms of service. "The troops, in my opinion, should be organized for the war," stated Lee. "We cannot stop short of its termination, be it long or short."

Enlistments for less than the duration of the war threatened the national war effort, believed Lee, who turned his attention specifically to the topic of subordinating state to nation. "The Confederate States have now but one great object in view, the successful issue of war and independence," he explained to McGrath. "Everything worth their possessing depends on that. Everything should yield to its accomplishment." This meant the states should surrender control over such things as naming officers in units bound for national service. The president and Congress should have that power regarding officers from all states because it would "add to the simplicity and economy of our military establishment" if all appointments conformed "to the same principle of organization." The scheme adopted by Congress and implemented in the army grew out of "the united wisdom of the State representatives." The states should adopt it as well. "Special corps and separate commands" on the state level, added Lee, "are frequent causes of embarrassment."[21]

Want of sufficient national purpose among South Carolinians troubled Lee during his stint along the South Atlantic coast. Five days after writing to McGrath, he sent a rather cranky letter to his son Custis. The latter had expressed pleasure at news of the *Trent* affair, which many in the South hoped would trigger a military show-down between the United States and Great Britain. Lee considered that highly unlikely, correctly predicting that the Lincoln adminis-tration would do what was necessary to avoid such a conflict. Beyond the crisis over the *Trent*, Lee commented about a tendency among Confederates to look outside their borders for salvation as a nation. "We must make up our minds to fight our battles ourselves," he in-sisted. "Expect to receive aid from no one. Make every necessary sacrifice of comfort, money & labour to bring the war to a successful issue & then we will succeed." Tired of speculation about when and if outside help would materialize, Lee lashed out at the reluctance of South Carolinians to throw themselves wholeheartedly into the national struggle: "I am dreadfully disappointed at the spirit here. They have all of a sudden realized the asperities of war, in what they must encounter, & do not seem to be prepared for it."[22]

Lee consistently showed himself willing to take steps that chal-lenged what many in the Confederacy believed were fundamental state or personal rights. This behavior controverts the arguments of historians who paint him as a man who conceived of the conflict as a limited affair that would confine him to serving Virginia's inter-ests alone. As evidenced in his letter to McGrath, Lee insisted al-most from the outset that military-age white males should be avail-able for open-ended national service. Increasingly concerned about manpower during the winter and spring of 1861–62, he instructed his aide Charles Marshall to "draft a bill for raising an army by the direct agency of the Confederate Government." Lee wanted legis-lation that would extend the service of those who previously had enlisted in good faith for twelve months, place all other white males between the ages of eighteen and thirty-five into Confederate ser-vice, and give Jefferson Davis the power "to call out such parts of the population rendered liable to service by the law, as he might deem proper, and at such times as he saw fit." Marshall aptly noted that "This measure completely reversed the previous military legislation of the South. . . . The efforts of the Government had hitherto been confined to inviting the support of the people. General Lee thought it could more surely rely upon their intelligent obedience, and that it might safely assume command where it had as yet only tried to per-suade." Marshall's careful language softened the import of what Lee sought: a Richmond government with the power and will to compel service from its citizenry.

Marshall also summarized Lee's ideas about the issue of balancing individual rights and state and national authority. Again, the general took a stalwart nationalist stance that departed radically from states' rights advocates who accused Jefferson Davis of usurping power in the name of waging an effective war. "He thought that every other consideration should be regarded as subordinate to the great end of the public safety," wrote Marshall, "and that since the whole duty of the nation would be war until independence should be secured, the whole nation should for the time be converted into an army, the producers to feed and the soldiers to fight." Late in 1861, Lee had used virtually identical language and arguments in a letter to Governor John Letcher of Virginia. The Confederacy needed all of its manpower for the entire course of the conflict, he contended, and national conscription offered the best option. "The great object of the Confederate States is to bring the war to a successful issue," he added. "Every consideration should yield to that; for without it we can hope to enjoy nothing we possess, and nothing that we do possess will be worth enjoying without it."[23]

The North sometimes seemed to Lee less reluctant to take the centralizing steps required to win a massive modern war. During the winter of 1863, he unburdened himself on this topic to his eldest son. "You see," Lee stated with grudging admiration, "the Federal Congress has put the whole power of their country into the hands of their President. Nine hundred millions of dollars & three millions of men. Nothing now can arrest the most desolating war that was ever practiced." How did the Confederate Congress respond to the specter of untrammeled war? "As far as I know," an exasperated Lee commented with awkward phrasing, it had done nothing but "concocted bills to excuse a certain class of men from taking active service, & to transfer another class in service, out of active service, where they hope never to do service."[24]

Lee repeatedly objected when local concerns menaced the process of keeping adequate manpower in the national armies. Governors demanding large numbers of troops to defend their states against secondary Union threats met with his firm disapproval. When Governor Henry T. Clark of North Carolina requested reinforcements to protect his state's coastline in the summer of 1862,

Lee lectured him about the need to focus on the national rather than the local picture. The Confederacy lacked the resources "to pursue the policy of concentrating our forces to protect important points and baffle the principal efforts of the enemy, and at the same time extend all the protection we desire to give every district." The greater threat, Lee explained, lay along the military frontier guarded by the Army of Northern Virginia. "The safety of the whole State of North Carolina, as well as of Virginia, depends in a measure upon the result of the enemy's efforts in this quarter." Failure in Virginia would open North Carolina to "far more injurious and destructive" Federal campaigning "than anything they have yet been called upon to suffer."[25] When examining Lee's statements about the importance of defending Virginia, it is vital to keep in mind that he viewed the Commonwealth not simply as his "home" state but also as the scene of pivotal operations with enormous implications for the entire Eastern Theater and the ultimate resolution of the war.

Lee believed that governors should take the lead in ensuring that all eligible men found their way into national service. "Let the State authorities take the matter in hand, and see that no man able to bear arms be allowed to evade his duty," he recommended to the secretary of war in January 1863. Later in the war, after Zebulon B. Vance of North Carolina had written to him about the defensive needs of the Old North State, Lee tactfully but firmly redirected the governor's attention to the national level: "The prospect of peace and independence depends very much upon the success of this campaign. I need not, therefore, inform Your Excellency of the importance of bringing and maintaining in the field all our available force. The life and safety of the people demand it."[26]

The practice of diverting men subject to the draft into local service far from the primary military fronts greatly upset Lee. He complained to Jefferson Davis in January 1864 that this "evil . . . is greater in South Carolina than in any other State, though it exists to some extent in all." South Carolina units in the Army of Northern Virginia had suffered serious attrition, yet replacements were hard to come by "principally, if not entirely, on account of the encouragement given to men to volunteer in regiments engaged in the defense of the Department of South Carolina, Georgia, and Florida, and the measures adopted in that department to retain conscripts." Lee urged that no new enrollees be assigned to units in the department "but that they be equally distributed among those in the armies in Virginia and Tennessee." If the Department of War lacked the power to enforce such a rule, Congress immediately should confer it.[27]

Lee even risked Jefferson Davis's disapprobation on a question relating to state influence. During the spring and early summer of 1862, the president supported reshuffling regiments so that brigades would contain soldiers from just one state. Lee preferred mixed-state brigades, though he conceded that the men likely would prefer Davis's plan, a factor that carried "much weight" with him. In early June, Lee reported that he had begun the process of reassigning regiments to satisfy Davis's wish. "I fear the result," he candidly admitted. "I would rather command a brigade composed of regts from different states. I think it could be better controuled, more emulation would be excited & there would be less combination against authority." Uncharacteristically, Lee tweaked the president by adding that he could "understand why officers looking to political preferment would prefer" Davis's plan.[28]

Black as well as white southerners figured in Lee's conception of how best to mount a national defense. His counsel in this respect often ran against the thinking of slaveholders seeking to exploit their slaves' labor for personal rather than national ends. In the autumn of 1864, Lee engaged in a correspondence with President Davis and Secretary of War Seddon on the subject of replacing white noncombatants in the armies with African American laborers. The desperate search for military manpower prompted Lee's observation to Davis that a "considerable number could be placed in the ranks by relieving all able-bodied white men employed as teamsters, cooks, mechanics, and laborers, and supplying their places with negroes. I think measures should be taken at once to substitute negroes for white in every place in the army, or connected with it, where the former can be used." If this step were not taken, Lee pointed out, the enemy would use the black men against the Confederacy. To Seddon, Lee strongly recommended putting 5,000 black laborers to work for thirty days building fortifications—even if it meant pulling them away from agricultural production. When Seddon assured Lee that he would look into the matter, the latter reiterated what he had written to Davis a few days earlier, that "all white laborers in Government employ whose work can be done by slaves or free negroes" should be reassigned to combat duty.[29]

More famously, Lee urged that slaves be freed if they would

fight in the Confederate army. Nothing better indicated his willingness to take potentially unpopular positions if necessary to advance the national cause. The question of arming African Americans prompted an acrimonious debate in the Confederacy from the autumn of 1864 through the spring of 1865, and Lee's public expression of approval tipped the balance in favor of those who supported the idea. Long before that debate, however, he discussed the likely impact of some form of emancipation with Jefferson Davis. In conversations at Washington College after the war, Lee twice alluded to the subject. He told William Allan, a former staff officer under Stonewall Jackson, that he had counseled "Mr. Davis often and early in the war that the slaves should be emancipated, that it was the only way to remove a weakness at home and to get sympathy abroad, and to divide our enemies, but Mr. Davis would not hear of it." Shortly after discussing this with Allan, Lee "spoke pretty freely of the policy of the war" with William Preston Johnston. Johnston recorded that Lee claimed "he knew the strength of the United States Government" and saw the need of "a proclamation of gradual emancipation and the use of the negroes as soldiers." Lee also reaffirmed his wartime attitude about the impact of local sentiment on the southern war effort, agreeing when Johnston mentioned "the difficulty of a 'Confederate Government' resisting a centralized one." [30]

When Lee publicly advocated arming slaves in early 1865, he did so as a desperate expedient that might prolong southern military resistance. He fully appreciated that such an action would disturb a southern social structure already at risk in the face of northern military successes. [31] He explained his reasoning in letters to Virginian Andrew Hunter and Congressman Ethelbert Barksdale of Mississippi. "Considering the relation of master and slave, controlled by humane laws and influenced by Christianity and an enlightened public sentiment, as the best that can exist between the white and black races while intermingled as at present in this country," he told Hunter, "I would deprecate any sudden disturbance of that relation unless it be necessary to avert a greater calamity to both." Such a calamity loomed because the Confederacy was running out of white soldiers. The Federals would continue to penetrate deeper into the Confederacy, liberating more slaves as they went. The enemy's "progress will thus add to his numbers, and at the same time destroy slavery in a manner most pernicious to the welfare of our people. . . . Whatever may be the effect of our employing negro troops, it cannot be as mischievous as this." Lee laid out the stark alternatives for Hunter: "[W]e must decide whether slavery shall be extinguished by our enemies and the slaves used against us, or use them ourselves at the risk of the effects which may be produced upon our social institutions." He recommended enrollment of slaves with a promise of immediate freedom to those who enlisted, liberation at the close of the conflict for the families of all who served faithfully, and a promise that all these people could continue to live in the South.

Cognizant of the extremely volatile nature of the issue, Lee nonetheless suggested even broader measures. Slaves could find freedom by simply running toward Union lines, he noted, so they should not be expected to sign on with the Confederacy without proper incentives. "The reasons that induce me to recommend the employment of negro troops at all render the effect of the measures I have suggested upon slavery immaterial," he informed Hunter, "and in my opinion the best means of securing the efficiency and fidelity of this auxiliary force would be to accompany the measure with a well-digested plan of gradual and general emancipation." Because Union victory would bring freedom to all slaves anyway, reasoned Lee, it made sense for the Confederates to preempt the issue and derive some good from their action. In his letter to Barksdale, Lee offered a conditional sop to states' righters by allowing that "the matter should be left, *as far as possible*, to the people and to the States" (emphasis added).[32]

A majority in the Confederate Congress eventually voted to enroll slaves in the army. But they refused to grant freedom to African Americans who served.[33] Lee almost certainly stood in advance of most of his fellow Confederates in his willingness to accept profound social change in the quest for independence. Far from looking back toward the traditional South, he looked forward to a Confederate nation that in many ways would little resemble the society into which he had been born.

Other evidence abounds concerning Lee's willingness to break with precedent in subordinating private and state interests to maintain an effective national defense. During the winter of 1864, he stated that all the material resources of the country should be marshaled. Sensitive to civilian unhappiness about impressment of crops and other supplies, Lee favored stringent efforts to treat citizens fairly. But he left no doubt about the bottom line: "I think the present law and orders on the subject should be so modified as to authorize the Government to impress when necessary a certain proportion of everything produced in the country. . . . It should be made equal and as light as possible, and every care taken to deprive the execution of the measure of all harshness." Government requirements might not be light, however, in which case civilians would have to sacrifice. "If it requires all the meat in the country to support the army, it should be had," said Lee, "and I believe this could be accomplished by not only showing its necessity, but that all equally contributed, and that it was faithfully applied." The following spring, Lee similarly advocated that Secretary of War Seddon interfere in the civilian sector. Problems of supply plagued the Army of Northern Virginia, and Lee wanted all obstacles to deliveries removed. "I earnestly recommend that no private interests be allowed to interfere with the use of all the facilities for transportation that we possess until the wants of the army are provided for," he wrote. "The railroads should be at once devoted exclusively to this purpose, even should it be found necessary to suspend all private travel for business or pleasure upon them for the present." [34]

Lee exhibited no more localism in his strategic thinking than in his efforts to move the Confederacy toward national mobilization. The argument that he either dismissed or did not understand the military landscape west of the Appalachians, as propounded by scholars such as J. F. C. Fuller, Thomas L. Connelly, and Alan T. Nolan, assumes that because he called for resources in Virginia he must have been myopic when it came to looking beyond his home state. In fact, Lee monitored the entire Confederate military effort, often commenting on events in other theaters in his correspondence (and doubtless in his unrecorded private consultations) with the president and others. He read both Confederate and northern newspapers sedulously, exchanged letters that touched on the military and political dimensions of the conflict with a range of people, and discussed the war with foreign visitors. Well informed and blessed with a powerful intellect, he took into account innumerable variables in assessing the Confederacy's strategic situation. Based on all he knew and surmised, Lee reasonably concluded that the Army of Northern Virginia operated in the most important theater, stood the best chance among all southern forces of advancing the Confederate cause, and thus should be supported to the greatest possible degree in terms of reinforcements and matériel.

The factors that led Lee to these conclusions can be enumerated quickly. He understood the centrality of Richmond—based not on a provincial attachment to his native state's capital but on the city's undeniable political, psychological, and industrial importance to the Confederacy. He watched the war in the West unfold as a nearly unbroken series of Confederate disasters. Forts Henry and Donelson, Pea Ridge, Shiloh, the loss of Nashville and New Orleans, the loss of Vicksburg and control of the Mississippi River, Chattanooga, Atlanta, and numerous smaller failures paraded across the pages of the newspapers he read and came up in conversation and correspondence. He knew as well as anyone that the quality of generalship in other theaters failed to match that in the Army of Northern Virginia. Too careful with his official opinions to state plainly that other Confederate generals lacked his own ability and might not use resources as effectively, he nevertheless occasionally betrayed his true opinion. One such instance came in May 1863, when leaders in Richmond debated whether to weaken Lee's army to reinforce John C. Pemberton's force at Vicksburg or Braxton Bragg's in Middle Tennessee. Lee opposed detaching George E. Pickett's division for service along the Mississippi, and in a letter to the secretary of war he raised the subject of "the uncertainty of its application" under Pemberton. Well might Lee worry about how his troops would be applied to the Confederate defense elsewhere, as Braxton Bragg's misuse of two divisions under James Longstreet demonstrated later in 1863.[35]

Lee also knew that such victories as the Seven Days, Second Manassas, and Chancellorsville prompted most of the Confederate people to rely on him and the Army of Northern Virginia to bolster their national morale. This could be a burden, as he suggested when writing after Gettysburg of the "unreasonable expectations of the public" concerning his army's campaigns.[36] By the summer of 1863, Lee and his army had outstripped Davis and the Confederate government as the principal national symbol of the Confederacy. Just as George Washington and the Continental Army had come to represent the colonial cause in the minds of their fellow rebels during the Revolution, so also did Lee and his men fill that role during their war for nationhood. Most northern politicians and other observers in Washington, northern newspapers with the largest circulations, political leaders in London and Paris, and the majority of northern people living in states whose men fought primarily with the Army of the Potomac also considered Lee and his army the principal rebel threat. Nothing underscores this phenomenon more dramatically than the impact of Lee's surrender at Appomattox. The soldiers who stacked weapons and flags in that Virginia village on April 12, 1865, represented but a fraction of the Confederacy's men under arms, yet virtually everyone, North and South, interpreted Appomattox as the end of the war. However historians may choose to interpret the relative importance of different theaters during the conflict, wartime evidence points strongly toward the conclusion that Lee was correct in believing he operated in the vital geographic area.[37]

Lee planned his campaigns with an awareness of their impact within the broader political and social framework of the war. Historians who have propounded the "chessmaster" notion of Lee as a general who could not see past the immediate goal of thrashing the enemy's armies overlook ample evidence to the contrary. Far from defining the contest as involving only generals and soldiers on the respective sides—a "professional exercise" as T. Harry Williams termed it—Lee knew that it pitted entire societies against one another and that the key to victory lay in destroying the will of the enemy's populace to maintain a costly struggle.

His correspondence from the spring and summer of 1863—portions of which are quoted above in my discussion of Lee's reaction to the battle of Fredericksburg—is instructive in this regard. In mid-April, with northern newspapers devoting considerable attention to Copperhead activities and with no evidence of significant Union military progress in any theater, Lee ventured a cautious optimism in a letter to his wife. "I do not think our enemies are so confident of success as they used to be," he remarked in a passage that touched on both home fronts. "If we can baffle them in their various designs this year & our people are true to our cause & not so devoted to themselves & their own aggrandisement, I think our success will be certain." Much hard work and suffering lay ahead, but Lee believed the Army of Northern Virginia could influence the northern home front. "If successful this year, next fall there will be a great change in public opinion at the North," he predicted. "The Republicans will be destroyed & I think the friends of peace will become so strong as that the next administration will go in on that basis. We have only therefore to resist manfully."[38]

Two months later, as the Army of Northern Virginia began its march toward Pennsylvania, Lee sent a letter to Jefferson Davis that similarly emphasized the centrality of the northern home front. He conceded to the North "the superiority claimed by them in numbers, resources, and all the means and appliances for carrying on the war." "Under these circumstances," he continued, "we should neglect no honorable means of dividing and weakening our enemies, that they may feel some of the difficulties experienced by ourselves." The best way to accomplish that object lay in encouraging the peace party in the North. Lee opposed drawing what he termed a "nice distinction between those who declare for peace unconditionally and those who advocate it as a means of restoring the Union, however much we may prefer the former." Navigating perilously close to the shoals of dishonorable conduct, Lee suggested that the Confederacy refrain from categorical demands for independence in fostering northern support for an end to the conflict. Friends of peace in the North needed the backing of fellow citizens devoted to the idea of reunion, and holding out "such a result as an inducement is essential to the success of their party." With the need to satisfy the vast unionist majority in mind, Lee offered Davis pragmatic advice: "Should the belief that peace will bring back the Union become general, the war would no longer be supported, and that, after all, is what we are interested in bringing about." If a majority in the North decided to propose peace, the Confederacy's leadership could address terms with confidence that "the desire of our people for a distinct and independent national existence will prove as steadfast under the influence of peaceful measures as it has shown itself in the midst of war." [39]

What Lee certainly understood but did not mention in writing Davis was the role his military campaigns had played in encouraging peace sentiment in the North. The ten months between the Army of Northern Virginia's victories at the Seven Days and Chancellorsville had witnessed an erosion of northern optimism and enthusiasm for the war, and military reverses in Virginia also had helped persuade Abraham Lincoln to press for emancipation as a measure that would assist the Union effort. Emancipation in turn had further alienated untold northern Democrats.

Lee had addressed the connection between military events and northern civilian morale the preceding September during his advance into Maryland. As he pointed out to Davis, "For more than a year both sections of the country have been devastated by hostilities which have brought sorrow and suffering upon thousands of homes, without advancing the objects which our enemies proposed to themselves in beginning the contest." The time had come to propose peace on the basis of Confederate independence. "[M]ade when it is in our power to inflict injury upon our adversary," reasoned Lee with his army's northward movement in mind, such a proposal "would show conclusively to the world that our sole object is the establishment of our independence, and the attainment of honorable peace." Should the Lincoln government reject the proposal, northerners would know that full responsibility for continuance of the war rested with the Republicans rather than with the Confederacy. Voters would go to the polls in November 1862 "to determine . . . whether they will support those who favor a prolongation of the war, or those who wish to bring it to a termination, which can but be productive of good to both parties without affecting the honor of either." [40]

Although Lee and Davis undoubtedly disagreed on some military and political questions, they developed an excellent working partnership that compares favorably with the oft-praised relationship between Lincoln and Grant. Lee emulated his idol Washington's example during the American Revolution in rigorously deferring to Davis and civilian authority, despite the presence of considerable late-war Confederate sentiment that would have supported his elevation to what might be called a benevolent feudal dictatorship. In this regard, Lee adhered to a decidedly modern democratic standard that required ultimate civilian control. As a team, Lee and Davis strongly supported national policies that would harness the Confederacy's human and material resources. Davis knew Lee's victories acted as a catalyst that boosted Confederate civilian morale, granting his commander wide latitude in planning and executing operations in the Eastern Theater and soliciting his advice about other military questions. The president expressed his admiration for Lee's achievements when, in the wake of Gettysburg, he predicted that the Army of Northern Virginia and its chief would "become the subject of history and object of the world's admiration for generations to come." William C. Davis has neatly summarized the impact of the Lee-Davis partnership: "[T]hese two very different men, who in another time or under different circumstances probably would not — could not — have been friends, achieved a synergy that helped to keep the Confederacy afloat in the East far longer than could have been expected with any of the other full-rank generals of the South in command." [41]

Historians who criticize Lee as being old-fashioned because he pursued offensive tactical victories almost invariably give him scant

Jefferson Davis. As ardent Confederate nationalists, Lee and Davis agreed that an effective prosecution of the war must take precedence over all other concerns. Stephen R. Mallory, Davis's secretary of the navy throughout the war, observed that the president saw Lee as "standing alone among the confederate soldiers in military capacity. . . . [A]ll others were, in comparison to him, beginners." (National Archives)

credit for linking such battles to civilian morale. Yet no one knew better than he that the Union possessed ample resources to win a protracted conflict if the northern people remained resolute. As he told his son Custis in early 1863, nothing could "arrest" the enemy's power "except a revolution among their people" that would erode Union commitment to prosecuting the war. And only "systematic" Confederate military success would effect such a revolution. Nor did any officer on either side have a better grasp of how quickly civilian spirits rose and fell in reaction to reports from the battle fronts. He learned from his attention to newspapers, for example, that his victory at the Seven Days profoundly affected Confederate attitudes about the likelihood of success in their fight for nationhood—just as Lincoln learned, as he put it in a letter to a French diplomat, that the "moral effect was the worst of the affair before Richmond" in June–July 1862.[42]

From first to last, Lee never doubted that Confederate success or failure would depend on civilian will. Asked by Secretary of War John C. Breckinridge for his views about the condition of the Confederacy late in the war, he responded: "Everything in my opinion has depended and still depends upon the disposition and feelings of the people." He always hoped his operations would undermine northern resolve, while concomitantly fretting about their impact on Confederate sentiment. He worried that southern civilian morale soared too high after Fredericksburg and Chancellorsville, describing the public as "greatly elated" after the former and "wild with delight" after the latter. Still concerned about the effects of Fredericksburg nearly a month after the battle, he shared his thoughts with the secretary of war: "The success with which our efforts have been crowned, under the blessing of God, should not betray our people into the dangerous delusion that the armies now in the field are sufficient to bring this war to a successful and speedy conclusion." Whether looking north or south of the Potomac, the point is that Lee always had in mind the ways in which his strategic decisions might shape civilian morale.[43]

In settling on a strategy, he was convinced that a predominantly defensive posture would allow the enemy to muster and apply his strength at leisure. In this vein, he wrote to Secretary of War Seddon in the wake of Chancellorsville: "As far as I can judge, there is nothing to be gained by this army remaining quietly on the defensive, which it must do unless it can be re-enforced." Lee proposed an offensive movement designed to draw Joseph Hooker's Army of the Potomac away from its strong position along the Rappahannock River, perhaps opening the way for a successful tactical offensive. If the Confederates failed to take the initiative, the Union army would "take its own time to prepare and strengthen itself to renew its advance upon Richmond, and force this army back within the entrenchments of that city. . . . I think it is worth a trial to prevent such a catastrophe."[44]

Few possibilities alarmed Lee as much being pinned down in a siege. Events at Fort Donelson, Vicksburg, and elsewhere (including, probably, Vera Cruz during the war with Mexico) had taught him that sieges invariably favored the aggressor. He sought to use the strategic offensive to keep the Federals off balance, find opportunities to bring them to battle under favorable circumstances, and inflict defeats that would bolster morale in the South and weaken it in the North. This admittedly risky strategy was predicated on his ability to craft enough victories to persuade the North to abandon the war. Undeniably costly in terms of casualties, it nevertheless produced battlefield successes in 1862 and 1863 that worked wonders in inspiriting the Confederate people (who almost never accused Lee of wasting lives unnecessarily). Equally important, these victories also inspired the men in Lee's army, the large majority of whom remained steadfastly at their posts until very late in the conflict. In the short term, a white South that favored precisely the type of aggressive strategy that Lee pursued elevated him to an unrivaled position as a national hero. Over the longer haul, Confederates behind the lines maintained a faith in him and his soldiers that prompted them to continue their resistance despite gathering signs of impending doom.[45]

Obsessed with counting casualties and quick to argue that Lee did not understand the relationship between his strategy and the Confederacy's best interests, a number of historians have revealed a poor understanding of what bolstered southern national morale. With the unerring precision of hindsight, these critics have emphasized the utterly obvious facts that Lee suffered heavy casualties and eventually lost the war—before moving on to argue that he must have developed a flawed strategy. In fact, Lee conducted campaigns based on his sound evaluation of each side's resources and his reading of the tempers of the respective populations. He sometimes erred in his judgments, as when he asked too much of his exhausted army on

September 16–18 at Sharpsburg or ordered the assaults at Gettysburg on July 3, but those errors and his eventual failure should not obscure his fundamentally sound approach to applying the Confederacy's resources under the most daunting of military and political circumstances.[46]

Although many modern historians subscribe to the idea that defensive strategy and tactics in Virginia would have saved men and served the Confederacy well, the war's reality teaches another lesson. Predominantly defensive operations usually ended in southern military disasters that tested civilian resolve. Albert Sidney Johnston's Kentucky campaign, Braxton Bragg's defense of Middle Tennessee after the battle of Murfreesboro, John C. Pemberton's operations at Vicksburg, Joseph E. Johnston's withdrawal toward Atlanta, and the siege of Petersburg and Richmond in 1864–65 represent just five examples of this phenomenon—the last of which precipitated events that quickly led to the end of the war. Moreover, had Joseph Johnston not been wounded at the battle of Seven Pines on May 31, 1862, his defensive campaign on the Peninsula almost certainly would have resulted in a siege and the loss of Richmond during the summer of 1862. Lee's victory at Fredericksburg stands out as a conspicuous exception to this pattern but should not seduce anyone into believing it offered a model that could have brought Confederate independence.[47]

Criticism that Lee failed to grasp the tactical implications of evolving weaponry can be dismissed quickly. The notion that he, a gifted engineer with substantial experience on Mexican battlefields dominated by smoothbores and Civil War battlefields dominated by rifles, did not comprehend the power of rifled shoulder arms is simply ludicrous. Lee and Grant, Sherman, McClellan, Joseph E. Johnston, and every other army commander in the Civil War, whether deemed "modern" or "old-fashioned" by historians, agreed that defenders with rifled weapons posed a daunting challenge to any assault. The addition of earthworks as the war progressed further magnified the defender's advantage. Yet all of these men, reacting to various military and political factors, launched frontal assaults at one time or another.

There are elements of Lee's military leadership and personality that seem to support those who claim he functioned as a somewhat romantic traditionalist in a modern war won by the hard-bitten realists Grant and Sherman. For example, Lee's public and private correspondence bristles with strong statements against the idea of making unbridled war against civilians. A much-quoted instance came during the Gettysburg campaign, when he issued an order congratulating his soldiers for respecting private property and reminding them that "the duties exacted of us by civilization and Christianity are not less obligatory in the country of the enemy than in our own." Lee contrasted his men's behavior in Pennsylvania with what he termed "the barbarous outrages upon the unarmed and defenseless and the wanton destruction of private property, that have marked the course of the enemy in our own country." Yet it is worth noting that he considered orderly foraging to support his army an acceptable policy and that the Army of Northern Virginia engaged freely in such activity while in Pennsylvania.[48]

Lee also was unwilling to take harsh measures against Union soldiers captured in the line of duty. He called for restraint when a clamor arose in some quarters to execute Federals captured during Col. Ulric Dahlgren's raid against Richmond in February–March 1864. Papers found on Dahlgren's body after he was killed outside the city outlined a plan to burn Richmond and assassinate Jefferson Davis and other Confederate political leaders. Outraged southerners, including a number of prominent leaders such as Braxton Bragg, Josiah Gorgas, and Secretary of War Seddon, favored executing some or all of the prisoners. Lee favored publication of the papers Dahlgren had carried, so that "our people & the world may know the character of the war our enemies wage against us, & the unchristian & atrocious acts they plot and perpetrate." But he opposed executions, explaining to Seddon that the prisoners may not have known about Dahlgren's plans. "I think it better to do right," he stated, "even if we suffer in so doing, than to incur the reproach of our consciences & posterity."[49]

To the unwary, Lee's leadership also might seem more familial than professionally military. His men referred to him as "Marse Robert" or "old grand pa" or in similarly affectionate ways.[50] This phenomenon undoubtedly influenced Charles Francis Adams to compare Lee to feudal noblemen or Scottish heads of clans, who would have relied on personal ties and honor rather than on a rigorous application of military rules. The many descriptions of Lee as a patriarchal leader also probably derive in part from the way in which the soldiers described and reacted to him. Yet Lee's own behavior leaves no doubt that he set a firm soldierly example, expected his subordinates to do likewise, and favored stringent measures to ensure discipline and effective performance on the march and in battle. Nothing better illustrates this than his willingness to execute deserters. The aftermath of Gettysburg affords a useful example. Confronted with mounting absences, Lee tried a period of amnesty to attract those who had left the ranks. But he soon reverted to his usual policy when dealing with those who failed to do their duty. "I would now respectfully submit to your Excellency," he wrote Jefferson Davis, "the opinion that all has been done which forebearance and mercy call for and that nothing will remedy this great evil which so much endangers our cause except the rigid enforcement of the death penalty in future in cases of conviction." [51]

Should Robert E. Lee be considered an old-fashioned general whose temperament and ideas marked him as an anachronism in a nineteenth-century modern war? If willingness to wage unconstrained war against civilians and their property is the controlling criterion, the answer must be yes. For unlike Ulysses S. Grant, William Tecumseh Sherman, and Philip H. Sheridan, who carried out wide-scale campaigns of logistical destruction in Virginia, Georgia, the Carolinas, and elsewhere, Lee would not cross that line.[52] But civilians and their possessions had been savaged by countless military leaders from ancient times forward, including eighteenth- and nineteenth-century European and American officers who fought against Native Americans. Making war on civilians is thus a poor basis on which to render a judgment. A far better test is whether Lee fully understood the implications of a massive conflict between mid-nineteenth-century democratic societies. By this standard he certainly qualifies as a modern warrior. He knew the war would require extensive national mobilization at the expense of state or local concerns. He saw the direct connection between military events and civilian morale, plotting a strategy designed to erode northern popular will before it exhausted inferior Confederate resources. His efforts fell short of ultimate triumph, an outcome influential historians across several generations incorrectly have attributed to an anachronistic approach to the conflict. These critics and the many admirers who described Lee as a chivalric leader combined to create a grossly distorted image. Far from being a knightly throwback who sought to apply old lessons to a new situation, Lee was an able practitioner of modern mid-nineteenth-century warfare.

NOTES

1. Historians are fond of debating whether the Civil War was a modern "total" war or a more limited nineteenth-century conflict. See, for example, Robert A. Daughty, Ira D. Gruber, et al., *The American Civil War: The Emergence of Total Warfare* (Lexington, Mass.: D. C. Heath, 1996); Mark Grimsley, *The Hard Hand of War: Union Military Policy toward Southern Civilians, 1861–1865* (Cambridge: Cambridge University Press, 1995); James M. McPherson, "Lincoln and the Strategy of Unconditional Surrender," in Gabor S. Boritt, ed., *Lincoln, the War President: The Gettysburg Lectures* (New York: Oxford University Press, 1992); Mark A. Neely Jr., "Was the Civil War a Total War?," *Civil War History* 37 (March 1991): 5–28; Charles Royster, *The Destructive War: William Tecumseh Sherman, Stonewall Jackson, and the Americans* (New York: Knopf, 1991); and Daniel E. Sutherland, *The Emergence of Total War* (Fort Worth: Ryan Place Publishers, 1996).

2. Jubal A. Early, *The Campaigns of Gen. Robert E. Lee: An Address by Lieut. General Jubal A. Early, before Washington and Lee University, January 19th, 1872* (Baltimore: John Murphy, 1872), 38, 40, 44–45.

3. John Esten Cooke, *Wearing of the Gray, Being Personal Portraits, Scenes, and Adventures of the War* (1867; reprint, Baton Rouge: Louisiana State University Press, 1997), 355, 359–60; Robert Stiles, *Four Years under Marse Robert* (1903; reprint, Dayton, Ohio: Morningside, 1977), 22. Postwar writers who described Lee as a chivalric figure built on a tradition begun during the conflict. For example, the *Richmond Dispatch* of May 1, 1861, offered this description of Lee: "[N]o man is superior in all that constitutes the soldier and the gentleman—no man more worthy to head our forces and lead our army. . . . His reputation, his acknowledged ability, his chivalric character, his probity, honor, and—may we add to his eternal praise—his Christian life and conduct make his very name a 'tower of strength.' "

4. John Warwick Daniel, *Ceremonies Connected with the Inauguration of the Mausoleum and the Unveiling of the Recumbent Figure of General Robert Edward Lee, at Washington and Lee University, Lexington, Va., June 28, 1883. Oration of John W. Daniel, LL.D. Historical Sketch of the Lee Memorial Association* (Richmond: West, Johnson, 1883), 71; Archer Anderson, *Robert Edward Lee: An Address Delivered at the Dedication of the Monument to General Robert Edward Lee at Richmond, Virginia, May 29, 1890* (Richmond: William Ellis Jones, Printer, 1890), 31, 44–45.

5. Charles Francis Adams, *Three Phi Beta Kappa Addresses* (Boston:

Houghton Mifflin, 1907), 81, 96–97. Adams developed many of the same themes in his famous speech at Washington and Lee University on the 100th anniversary of Lee's birthday, published as *Lee's Centennial: An Address by Charles Francis Adams Delivered at Lexington, Virginia, Saturday, January 19, 1907, on the Invitation of the President and Faculty of Washington and Lee University* (n.p.: n.p., [1907]).

6. Clifford Dowdey, *The Land They Fought For: The Story of the South as the Confederacy, 1832–1865* (Garden City, N.Y.: Doubleday, 1955), 99, 196, 317. For reiteration of the theme of Lee as an aristocratic warrior, see also Dowdey's other books: *Death of a Nation: The Story of Lee and His Men at Gettysburg* (New York: Knopf, 1958); *Lee's Last Campaign: The Story of Lee and His Men against Grant—1864* (Boston: Little, Brown, 1960); *The Seven Days: The Emergence of Lee* (Boston: Little, Brown, 1964); and *Lee* (Boston: Little, Brown, 1965). All of these titles except *The Land They Fought For* have been reprinted by university presses. See also Fletcher Pratt's *Ordeal by Fire: An Informal History of the Civil War* (1935; rev. ed., New York: William Sloane, 1948), 177, for a description of Lee as a "knightly and gracious" soldier.

7. MacKinlay Kantor, *Lee and Grant at Appomattox* (New York: Random House, 1950), 32–33; Hodding Carter, *Robert E. Lee and the Road of Honor* (New York: Random House, 1955), 105. Both of these books appeared in the popular Landmark series. For other children's literature that employed knightly imagery in describing Lee, see Jonathan Daniels, *Robert E. Lee* (Boston: Houghton Mifflin, 1960); Stanley F. Horn, *The Boy's Life of Robert E. Lee* (New York: Harper & Brothers, 1935); and Iris Vinton, *The Story of Robert E. Lee* (New York: Grosset & Dunlap, 1952).

8. Gene Smith, *Lee and Grant: A Dual Biography* (New York: McGraw-Hill, 1984), ix–x, 182, 210.

9. Editors of Time-Life Books, *Lee Takes Command* (Alexandria, Va.: Time-Life, 1984), 8; James I. Robertson Jr., *Jackson and Lee: Legends in Gray. The Paintings of Mort Künstler* (Nashville, Tenn.: Rutledge Hill, 1995), 17, 30.

10. J. F. C. Fuller, *Grant and Lee: A Study in Personality and Generalship* (1932; reprint, Bloomington: Indiana University Press, 1957), 242, 244, 252, 257–58, 280.

11. T. Harry Williams, "The Military Leadership of North and South," in David Donald, ed., *Why the North Won the Civil War* (Baton Rouge: Louisiana State University Press, 1960), 40–41, 44–45. Williams noted that almost all other Confederate generals shared Lee's localism and inability to conceive of war as an exercise that involved all of society.

12. Russell F. Weigley, *The American Way of War: A History of United States Military Strategy and Policy* (New York: Macmillan, 1973), 108, 102, 125–27, 141–43, 145–46, 149–51; Weigley, *A Great Civil War: A Military and Political History, 1861–1865* (Bloomington: Indiana University Press, 2000), 134.

13. Peter J. Parish, *The American Civil War* (New York: Holmes & Meier, 1975), 581–82.

14. Knopf published Connelly's book, and the University of North Carolina Press Nolan's.

15. For a brief review of the critical response to both books, see Gary W. Gallagher, ed., *Lee the Soldier* (Lincoln: University of Nebraska Press, 1995), xii–xiii.

16. Connelly, *Marble Man*, 200–202; Thomas L. Connelly, "Robert E. Lee and the Western Confederacy," *Civil War History* 15 (June 1969): 129–30; Nolan, *Lee Considered*, 69, 106.

17. Bevin Alexander, *Robert E. Lee's Civil War* (Holbrook, Mass.: Adams Media, 1998), xi; Edward H. Bonekemper III, *How Robert E. Lee Lost the Civil War* (Fredericksburg, Va.: Sergeant Kirkland's Press, 1997), 200–201; John D. McKenzie, *Uncertain Glory: Lee's Generalship Re-examined* (New York: Hippocrene Books, 1997), 358. See also Michael A. Palmer, *Lee Moves North: Robert E. Lee on the Offensive* (New York: John Wiley, 1998). In "Historians' Perspectives on Lee," *Columbiad* 2 (Winter 1999): 28, Alan T. Nolan remarked that "during the 1990s a change has occurred regarding how historians look at Lee. Writers no longer simply reiterate the canons of the Lee tradition; instead, they question and frequently reject perceived truths." Nolan's article praised the work of Bonekemper, McKenzie, and Palmer and noted that Alexander's book "virtually summarizes" the thesis in *Lee Considered* (ibid., 31–39, 41–43). For another title that repeats many of Nolan's arguments, see Thomas B. Buell, *The Warrior Generals: Combat Leadership in the Civil War* (New York: Crown, 1997). Buell, who stressed Lee's aristocratic roots, concluded that the Virginian "was committed to preserving the status quo, his vision was locked firmly in the past, and he sacrificed his army to protect the privileges of the oligarchy to which he belonged. Lee's fundamental strategy was fighting for the sake of fighting, . . . and in the end he destroyed his state trying to save it" (pp. xxx–xxxi).

18. Albert Castel, "The Historian and the General: Thomas L. Connelly versus Robert E. Lee," *Civil War History* 16 (March 1970): 50–63 (reprinted in Castel, *Winning and Losing in the Civil War: Essays and Stories* [Columbia: University of South Carolina Press, 1996], 63–78); Charles P. Roland, *Reflections on Lee: A Historian's Assessment* (Mechanicsburg, Pa.:

Stackpole, 1995), especially pp. 83–102; Joseph P. Harsh, *Confederate Tide Rising: Robert E. Lee and the Making of Southern Strategy, 1861–1862* (Kent, Ohio: Kent State University Press, 1998); and Joseph T. Glatthaar, *Partners in Command: The Relationships between Leaders in the Civil War* (New York: Free Press, 1994), chapter 2. See also Roland's essay "The Generalship of Robert E. Lee," in Grady McWhiney, ed., *Grant, Lee, Lincoln and the Radicals: Essays on Civil War Leadership* (n.p.: Northwestern University Press, 1964). Roland's and Castel's essays also may be found in Gallagher, ed., *Lee the Soldier*, 159–88, 209–24. The most detailed favorable interpretation of Lee's generalship remains Douglas Southall Freeman, *R. E. Lee: A Biography*, 4 vols. (New York: Scribner's, 1934–35), especially chapter 11 of volume 4.

19. April 24, 1865, interview with Lee by Thomas M. Cook, printed in the *New York Herald*, April 29, 1865. Cook, who admitted that he paraphrased Lee's comments, also reported that the general believed the Constitutional Convention of 1787 left the issue of states' rights unresolved. It would have been better if the question could have been settled peacefully, but, remarked Lee, "If the South is forced to submission in this contest, it of course can only be looked upon as the triumph of federal power over State rights, and the forced annihilation of the latter."

20. Potter's essay, "The Historian's Use of Nationalism and Vice Versa," first appeared in Alexander V. Riasonovsky and Barnes Riznik, eds., *Generalizations in Historical Writing* (Philadelphia: University of Pennsylvania Press, 1963), and was reprinted in Potter, *The South and the Sectional Conflict* (Baton Rouge: Louisiana State University Press, 1968). For expressions of loyalty to Virginia, the South, and the United States, see Lee's letter (probably to his son Custis) written from Fort Mason, Texas, on January 23, 1861, in J. William Jones, *Life and Letters of Robert Edward Lee: Soldier and Man* (1906; reprint, Harrisonburg, Va.: Sprinkle Publications, 1986), 120–21. The quotation is from R. E. Lee to Joseph E. Johnston, July 24, 1861, "Letters of Confederate Generals," no. 11576, Special Collections, Alderman Library, University of Virginia, Charlottesville.

21. Lee to Andrew G. McGrath, December 24, 1861, in U.S. War Department, *The War of the Rebellion: A Compilation of the Official Records of the Union and Confederate Armies*, 127 vols., index, and atlas (Washington: GPO, 1880–1901), ser. 1, vol. 6:350 (hereafter cited as *OR*; all references are to ser. 1 unless otherwise noted).

22. Lee to George Washington Custis Lee, December 29, 1861, in R. E. Lee, *The Wartime Papers of R. E. Lee*, ed. Clifford Dowdey and Louis H. Manarin (Boston: Little, Brown, 1961), 98.

23. Charles Marshall, *An Aide-de-Camp of Lee: Being the Papers of Colonel Charles Marshall, Sometime Aide-de-Camp, Military Secretary, and Assistant Adjutant General on the Staff of Robert E. Lee, 1862–1865*, ed. Sir Frederick Maurice (Boston: Little Brown, 1927), 30–32; Lee to John Letcher, December 21, 1861, in J. William Jones et al., eds., *Southern Historical Society Papers*, 52 vols. (1876–1959; reprint with 3-vol. index, Wilmington, N.C.: Broadfoot, 1990–92), 1:462 (hereafter cited as *SHSP*).

24. Lee to George Washington Custis Lee, February 28, 1863, in Lee, *Wartime Papers*, 411.

25. Lee to Henry T. Clark, August 8, 1862, in Lee, *Wartime Papers*, 249.

26. Lee to James A. Seddon, January 10, 1863, in Lee, *Wartime Papers*, 390; Lee to Zebulon B. Vance, September 10, 1864, in *OR* 42(2):1242.

27. Lee to Jefferson Davis, January 19, 1864, in Lee, *Wartime Papers*, 654–55. For other letters urging the utmost effort in bringing manpower into Confederate service, see Lee to Jefferson Davis, September 9, 1864, and Lee to Braxton Bragg, September 10, 1864, in Robert E. Lee, *Lee's Dispatches: Unpublished Letters of General Robert E. Lee, C.S.A., to Jefferson Davis and the War Department of the Confederate States of America, 1862–1865*, ed. Douglas Southall Freeman and Grady McWhiney (1915; rev. ed., New York: Putnam's, 1957), 293, 297; Lee to James A. Seddon, January 10, 1863, in Lee, *Wartime Papers*, 390; Lee's Special Orders No. 5, April 11, 1862, in *OR* 51(2):534; Lee to James A. Seddon, August 23, 1864, and Lee to Braxton Bragg, September 26, 1864, in *OR* 42(2):1199–1200, 1292.

28. Lee to Jefferson Davis, June 7, 1862, in Lee, *Lee's Dispatches*, 11.

29. Lee to Jefferson Davis, September 2, 1864, and Lee to James A. Seddon, September 17, 20, 1864, in *OR* 42(2):1228, 1256, 1260–61. Word of Lee's recommendations to Davis and Seddon filtered down to clerk John Beauchamp Jones in the War Department. "Gen. Lee has called for 2,000 negroes (to be impressed) to work on the Petersburg fortifications," wrote Jones in his diary on September 5, 1864. "Gen. Lee has been here two days, giving his advice, which I hope may be taken." John B. Jones, *A Rebel War Clerk's Diary at the Confederate States Capital*, 2 vols. (1866; reprint, Alexandria, Va.: Time-Life Books, 1982), 2:277.

30. William Allan, "Memoranda of Conversations with General Robert E. Lee," in Gallagher, ed., *Lee the Soldier*, 12; William Preston Johnston, "Memoranda of Conversations with General R. E. Lee," in ibid., 30. The conversations with Allan and Johnston took place on March 10 and May 7, 1868, respectively.

31. Lincoln's Emancipation Proclamation convinced Lee that the

South's entire social system was at stake in the war. He attacked the proclamation as a "savage and brutal policy . . . which leaves us no alternative but success or degradation worse than death, if we would save the honor of our families from pollution, our social system from destruction." Lee to James A. Seddon, January 10, 1863, in Lee, *Wartime Papers*, 390.

32. Lee to Andrew Hunter, January 11, 1865, in *OR*, ser. 4, 3:1012–13; Lee to Ethelbert Barksdale, February 18, 1865, in James D. McCabe Jr., *Life and Campaigns of General Robert E. Lee* (Atlanta: National Publishing Company, 1866), 574–75. The letter to Hunter was not made public immediately; that to Barksdale was released to the newspapers, and it proved very influential with the public and members of Congress. Lee had made substantially the same arguments in private correspondence with William Porcher Miles of South Carolina in the autumn of 1864. See Robert F. Durden, *The Gray and the Black: The Confederate Debate on Emancipation* (Baton Rouge: Louisiana State University Press, 1972), 135–36.

33. On the topic of enrolling slaves in the Confederate army, see Durden, *The Gray and the Black*, chapter 7 of which emphasizes the importance of Lee's opinion in the public debate.

34. Lee to James L. Kemper, January 29, 1864, and Lee to James A. Seddon, April 12, 1864, in Lee, *Wartime Papers*, 663, 696. For another example of Lee's recommending action that he knew would create hardship and unhappiness among civilians, see his letter to Jefferson Davis on November 25, 1862, in Lee, *Wartime Papers*, 345.

35. Lee's letter to Secretary of War Seddon, dated May 10, 1863, is in Lee, *Wartime Papers*, 482.

36. Lee to Jefferson Davis, July 31, 1863, in ibid., 565.

37. For more detailed arguments about the wartime (as opposed to the retrospective) preeminence of Lee and his army, see chapters 2–3 of Gary W. Gallagher, *The Confederate War* (Cambridge, Mass.: Harvard University Press, 1997), and chapter 1 of Gallagher, *Lee and His Generals in War and Memory* (Baton Rouge: Louisiana State University Press, 1998). See also Richard M. McMurry, *Two Great Rebel Armies: An Essay in Confederate Military History* (Chapel Hill: University of North Carolina Press, 1989), especially chapter 9. McMurry argued that the war was decided in the Western Theater, where Union armies won an almost unbroken string of victories between early 1862 and the spring of 1865. But he also noted that the Confederates lacked the resources and military leaders to hold both the West and the East: "Perhaps their only real chance for victory was to follow Lee's advice, trade space for time in the West—which is basically

the way the war was fought there anyway—and concentrate their strength in Virginia and seek to gain their independence by an overwhelming victory over the Army of the Potomac and the capture of Washington, D.C. Such a strategy would have employed their best army under their best general at the point where conditions were most favorable to them and where their enemy was at his weakest. If the Confederates could not have won their independence under such circumstances, they could not have won it anywhere under any possible conditions" (p. 155).

38. Lee to Mary Anna Custis Lee, April 19, 1863, in Lee, *Wartime Papers*, 437–38.

39. Lee to Jefferson Davis, June 10, 1863, in *OR* 27(3):881–82. See also Lee to Jefferson Davis, June 15, 1863, in Lee, *Wartime Papers*, 530, in which the general stated: "It is plain to my understanding that everything that will tend to repress the war feeling in the Federal States will inure to our benefit. I do not know that we can do anything to promote the pacific feeling, but our course ought to be shaped as not to discourage it."

40. Lee to Jefferson Davis, September 8, 1862, in Lee, *Wartime Papers*, 301.

41. Jefferson Davis to Lee, August 11, 1863, in Dunbar Rowland, ed., *Jefferson Davis, Constitutionalist: His Life and Letters*, 10 vols. (Jackson: Mississippi Department of Archives and History, 1923), 5:589; William C. Davis, "Lee and Jefferson Davis," in Gallagher, ed., *Lee the Soldier*, 304. For examples of support for a Lee dictatorship, see Gallagher, *Confederate War*, 88. See also Steven E. Woodworth's *Davis and Lee at War* (Lawrence: University Press of Kansas, 1995) for a detailed argument that Lee and Davis held fundamentally different views about strategic questions. Woodworth made a number of interesting points, but his analysis obscured the crucial fact that Lee and Davis agreed about how best to handle the most pressing issues facing the Confederacy.

42. Abraham Lincoln to Agénor-Etienne de Gasparin, August 4, 1862, in Abraham Lincoln, *The Collected Works of Abraham Lincoln*, ed. Roy P. Basler, 9 vols. (New Brunswick, N.J.: Rutgers University Press, 1953–55), 5:355.

43. Lee to John C. Breckinridge, March 9, 1865, in Lee, *Wartime Papers*, 913; "Letter from Major-General Henry Heth, of A. P. Hill's Corps, A.N.V.," in *SHSP* 4:153–54; Lee to James A. Seddon, January 10, 1863, in Lee, *Wartime Papers*, 388–89.

44. Lee to James A. Seddon, June 8, 1863, in *OR* 27(3):868–69.

45. For a fuller discussion of Lee's generalship as well suited to the needs of the Confederate people, see Gary W. Gallagher, "'Upon Their

Success Hang Momentous Interests': Generals," in Gabor S. Boritt, ed., *Why the Confederacy Lost* (New York: Oxford University Press, 1992), 94–108, and chapter 1 of Gallagher, *Lee and His Generals in War and Memory.*

46. George A. Bruce, a Union veteran whose historical writings in the early twentieth century touched on many points Alan T. Nolan and other critics of Lee later would emphasize, recognized that Lee conceived of his battles as a means of striking at civilian morale in the North. "In the short period of one year and seven days," wrote Bruce of Lee's initial period at the helm of the Army of Northern Virginia, "he fought six of the greatest battles of the war. In history there is no record that equals it. . . . If the people of the North were weak, volatile, lacking in purpose and resolution, he might well expect that, after such quick and powerful demonstrations, with trembling knees we would come suing for peace and ready to acknowledge the South their independence. On no other supposition were his methods justifiable." Bruce concluded that Lee's "powers of insight," however formidable in estimating the talents and movements of opponents such as George B. McClellan, "did not enable him to penetrate to the mind and purpose of a people." Although conceding that Lee did not fight battles under the mistaken impression that the war would be decided by confrontations between professional soldiers without reference to the home fronts, Bruce concluded that his generalship was deeply flawed. The Confederate commander should have emulated George Washington, who "looked at the war as a whole, estimated correctly all the advantages and disadvantages on either side, what would be the relative strength of forces, and adopted a method of warfare, generally defensive, but sometimes offensive when the chances were enough in his favor." George A. Bruce, "The Strategy of the Civil War," in Military Historical Society of Massachusetts, *Papers*, 14 vols. (1895–1918; reprint with new index volume, Wilmington, N.C.: Broadfoot, 1989–90), 13:467–69. The portion of Bruce's essay specifically on Lee was reprinted as "Lee and the Strategy of the Civil War" in Gallagher, *Lee the Soldier*, 111–38.

47. For a fuller discussion of this point, see Gallagher, *Confederate War*, 127–40.

48. General Orders No. 73, Headquarters, Army of Northern Virginia, June 27, 1863, in *OR* 27(3):943.

49. Duane Schultz, *The Dahlgren Affair: Terror and Conspiracy in the Civil War* (New York: Norton, 1998), 159; Lee to James A. Seddon, March 6, 1864, in Lee, *Wartime Papers*, 678.

50. For a reference to Lee as "old grand pa," see J. H. Reinhardt in the *Athens (Ga.) Southern Watchman*, August 5, 1863.

51. Lee to Jefferson Davis, August 17, 1863, in Lee, *Wartime Papers*, 123–24.

52. No senior military commanders on either side proved willing to attack civilians and their property with the unchecked brutality of Confederate and Union guerrilla leaders such as William Clarke Quantrill, "Bloody Bill" Anderson, and James H. Lane. In that regard, no ranking general practiced a twentieth-century-style "total war."

I HAVE TO
MAKE THE BEST
OF WHAT
I HAVE

Lee at Spotsylvania

The Spotsylvania campaign marked a crossroads for Robert E. Lee in his handling of senior subordinates in the Army of Northern Virginia. From an ominous beginning on May 8, when Third Corps chief A. P. Hill collapsed physically, to a disappointing coda at the Harris farm on May 19, when Richard S. Ewell waged an ineffective fight with his battered Second Corps, Lee confronted problems that taxed his abilities as both military administrator and combat leader. Consummate skill as a field commander enabled him to juggle personnel while staving off Ulysses S. Grant's powerful offensive blows, but only at the cost of taking an increasing burden on his already overtaxed shoulders. As the armies marched southward from Spotsylvania on May 21, Lee knew he lacked corps commanders on whom he could rely with the confidence he once had exhibited in "Stonewall" Jackson and James Longstreet.

Lee's actions at Spotsylvania shed considerable light on his style of generalship. He possessed unusual gifts as a military politician, an attribute much in evidence as he addressed crises arising at the level of corps leadership. His behavior at Spotsylvania and in its immediate aftermath also offers a revealing test of two commonly held assumptions about his generalship. Was he too much of a gentleman to make hard decisions concerning personnel? And did he follow a hands-off style in directing corps commanders that sometimes compromised his strategic and tactical plans?

Lee's conduct of the Overland campaign has generated a good deal of analysis. Most historians have praised his broad management of the operations, including his effort at Spotsylvania.[1] It is beyond the scope of this essay to critique Lee's tactical and strategic decisions at Spotsylvania, but a few words about his handling of the "Mule Shoe" salient in Ewell's sector of the battlefield are in order because it was controversial and illuminates a key element of his leadership. A pair of questions arise from any consideration of Lee and the Mule Shoe. First, why did he allow the hastily drawn line to remain in such a vulnerable configuration? And, second, aware that artillery would provide firepower essential to defending the salient, why did he order southern guns to be withdrawn on the night of May 11?

Edward Porter Alexander, whose perceptive critiques of Lee's campaigns are without equal among writings by participants, commented after the war about the Mule Shoe. "[B]y all the rules of military science," wrote Alexander, "we must pronounce these lines a great mistake although they were consented to, if they were not adopted by Gen. Lee's chief engineer Gen. M. L. Smith, who was a West Pointer & an ex-officer of the U.S. Engineers . . . & recently distinguished in the defence of Vicksburg." Lee probably accepted Smith's opinion that the salient could be defended if Ewell deployed his infantry behind well-prepared breastworks and supported it by adequate artillery. But Jedediah Hotchkiss later suggested that Lee, although acquiescing in the placement of the works, harbored significant doubts: "On the morning of [May] the 9th, Lee rode along the line that had been occupied, but was not favorably impressed with it."[2]

Lee's misgivings loom larger when considering his orders to withdraw artillery from the salient on the night of May 11. At 4:30 P.M. on that day, W. H. F. "Rooney" Lee, the commander's son and a major general of cavalry, reported a worrisome Federal march. "There is evidently a general move going on," stated the young cavalryman. "Their trains are moving down the Fredericksburg road, and their columns are in motion." Lee inferred from his son's information that Grant might be shifting away from Spotsylvania. If placed somewhere outside the wooded salient, he reasoned, the guns supporting Ewell's infantry could be moved rapidly toward the next point of danger. Winfield Scott Hancock's massive assault against the northern curve of the salient on the morning of May 12 succeeded in part because Confederate infantry fought without supporting artillery.[3]

Lee willingly took full responsibility for the consequences of his decisions concerning the Mule Shoe. Whatever his private thoughts about culpability, he publicly trained the spotlight directly on himself. William W. Old, a member of Edward "Allegheny" Johnson's staff who witnessed the debacle in the salient, recounted a discussion between Lee and Ewell on this point. "After the disaster of the 12th," wrote Old, "General Lee said to General Ewell, in my presence, that he had been misled in regard to the enemy in our front, by his scouts, and that the fatal mistake was in removing the artillery on our line." The army commander also approved an official report from William Nelson Pendleton, his chief of artillery, that attributed to Lee the decision to remove the artillery and alluded to "the unfortunate withdrawal of our guns" as a principal cause of the Union breakthrough. Lee's unhesitating assumption of responsibility for events in the Mule Shoe dramatically underscored his habit of leading by example — an element of his generalship that promoted trust and loyalty among his subordinates.[4]

May 1864 brought the third great watershed in the development of the Army of Northern Virginia's high command. The first had come in the wake of the Seven Days, when Lee reorganized the army into right and left wings commanded by Longstreet and Jackson respectively. During this period, division commanders Theophilus H. Holmes, Benjamin Huger, W. H. C. Whiting, and John Bankhead Magruder — all of whom had been Longstreet's and Jackson's peers — left the eastern army. When Congress approved the grade of lieutenant general in the autumn of 1862, Longstreet and Jackson were promoted to that rank and their commands designated the First and Second Corps. The structure that divided the army's strength between Longstreet and Jackson functioned effectively for nearly a year, a period that witnessed a string of notable victories from Second Manassas through Chancellorsville. During this period, Lee granted wide discretion to Longstreet and Jackson — the only practical arrangement by which the commander of a large army distributed over a wide area could exercise effective control — and the practice yielded excellent results.

Jackson's death in early May 1863 prompted Lee to reorganize a second time, reducing the size of the two existing corps and creating a new Third Corps. Longstreet retained the First Corps, Richard S. Ewell succeeded Jackson in command of the revamped Second, and A. P. Hill took charge of the Third. The triumvirate of Longstreet, Ewell, and Hill served as Lee's corps commanders for roughly a year, from the Gettysburg campaign through the battle of the Wilderness. Under this organization, Lee initially employed the same method of dealing with his corps leaders that he had used with Longstreet and Jackson, but episodes at Gettysburg and during the autumn of 1863 raised doubts in his mind about Ewell's and Hill's competence in their new positions.[5]

Events on May 6–7, 1864, triggered a third major reshuffling and inaugurated eleven months of relative flux among Lee's corps commanders.[6] Lee had begun the Overland campaign with problems at the corps level that reached crisis stage on the eve of fighting at Spotsylvania. The first harsh blow came at the battle of the Wilderness on May 6 when James Longstreet suffered a crippling wound while riding along the Plank Road. Although Longstreet had sulked at Gettysburg and failed ignominiously as an independent commander in East Tennessee during the fall and winter of 1863–64, his return with the First Corps to the Army of Northern Virginia in the spring of 1864 undoubtedly had cheered Lee. Justifiable concern that Longstreet's pouting behavior at Gettysburg might reappear probably gave way to relief at having his proven lieutenant back. Walter Taylor of Lee's staff likely mirrored his chief's feelings when he wrote in late April, "A portion of *our family* has been returned to us. Old Pete Longstreet is with us and all seems propitious." Longstreet's superior performance in blunting Hancock's assaults on the morning of the 6th and then mounting a telling counterattack highlighted his value to Lee. On hearing that his "Old War Horse" had been wounded, Lee manifested visible distress. Francis W. Dawson of Longstreet's staff described "the sadness in [Lee's] face, and the almost despairing movement of his hands, when he was told that Longstreet had fallen."[7]

Longstreet's loss proved doubly pernicious because both A. P. Hill and Richard S. Ewell had fallen short of Lee's expectations. Hill had been the obvious choice for promotion to lieutenant general after Jackson's death. Long the head of the Light Division, which counted as many bayonets in its ranks as most Federal infantry corps, Hill had earned Lee's respect in the summer and fall

James Longstreet's difficult days at Gettysburg and in East Tennessee lay ahead of him when this engraving appeared in the Southern Illustrated News. *His conduct at the outset of the Overland campaign recalled his glory days with the Army of Northern Virginia in 1862, and his wounds on May 6, 1864, deprived Lee of the only proven Confederate corps commander. (*Southern Illustrated News, *February 21, 1863)*

of 1862. Lee had confided to Jefferson Davis in October 1862 that except for Jackson and Longstreet, "I consider A. P. Hill the best commander with me. He fights troops well, and takes good care of them." Ten days after Jackson's death, Lee reiterated his belief that Hill "upon the whole, is the best soldier of his grade with me," and recommended his advancement to command the new Third Corps.[8]

Unfortunately for Lee, Hill never equaled at the corps level his previous record. On July 1 at Gettysburg, he allowed Henry Heth to stumble into battle with one Third Corps division (though Hill scrupulously kept Lee informed of his actions that day), then nearly disappeared during the next two tumultuous days of fighting. Lee's decision on July 3 to give Longstreet control over thousands of Hill's soldiers for the Pickett-Pettigrew assault implied a lack of confidence in Hill as well as demonstrating an awareness that "Little Powell" was suffering one of his numerous bouts of illness.[9] Lee's confidence almost certainly eroded further after the fiasco in October 1863 at Bristoe Station, where Hill rashly launched unsupported and costly assaults. Following the battle, Hill and Lee shared a tense ride over the field. According to Jedediah Hotchkiss, "Lee met Hill with stern rebuke for his imprudence, then sadly directed him to gather his wounded and bury his dead." Armistead L. Long of Lee's staff recalled that Hill, "mortified by his mishap, endeavored to explain the causes of his failure." Lee rode along in silence before answering "with sad gravity": "Well, well, general, bury these poor men and let us say no more about it."[10]

The battle of the Wilderness brought scant evidence that Hill had grown as a corps commander. Following heavy fighting on May 5, he chose to leave the divisions of Henry Heth and Cadmus M. Wilcox in vulnerable disarray astride the Orange Plank Road. Hill had been informed that James Longstreet's divisions would relieve his corps at about 1:00 A.M. on May 6 and elected to permit his tired men a night's rest rather than having them entrench. Federal attacks just after daylight on the 6th smashed the two divisions and threatened to divide Lee's army. Longstreet's soldiers arrived literally at the decisive moment to stave off disaster.

Both of Hill's division leaders wrote about the uneasy night of May 5–6. Heth claimed in his memoirs that he repeatedly requested Hill's permission to straighten his lines and dig in, provoking his superior, who once again had fallen ill, at length to lose his temper: "D[amn] it Heth, I don't want to hear any more about it; the men shall not be disturbed." Heth also stated that he and Wilcox went together to Hill's headquarters, although nothing from the latter's pen confirmed such a joint visit. Wilcox's official wartime account did note that he "reported to the Lieut. Gen. commanding and gave him a resume of affairs, and was informed that the Division would be relieved at day break by Gen. Longstreet's troops." After the war Wilcox described seeking out Lee that night to express concern about the condition of his lines. Before the division chief could explain the reason for his visit to army headquarters, Lee told him that Longstreet's corps and Richard H. Anderson's division of Hill's corps were nearby, and that "the two divisions that have been so actively engaged will be relieved before day." In light of Lee's comments, Wilcox ventured no suggestion about improving his division's position. But his postwar comments included the observation that "failure to rearrange his line" contributed to the calamitous Confederate rout on the morning of May 6. A correspondent for the *London Herald*, whose account appeared shortly after the battle, confirmed that Lee's assurances had not laid to rest Wilcox's doubts. According to this journalist, a still uneasy Wilcox "looked anxiously throughout the night for the coming of the divisions of Anderson and Field, and disappointed in the delay of their arrival, began at daybreak to cover his front by an abatis of felled trees." [11]

Most historians have accepted Heth's especially damning testimony as evidence that Hill erred in taking no precautions during the night of May 5–6. Whatever his division commanders and Lee thought, these scholars have argued, normal vigilance dictated that Hill prepare for the possibility that Longstreet might reach the field later than anticipated. A few historians have defended Hill by placing responsibility either above or below him in the chain of command. [12]

What did Lee think? A message to the secretary of war dated 8:00 P.M. on May 6 employed the blandest of language: "Early this morning as the divisions of General Hill, engaged yesterday, were being relieved, the enemy advanced and created some confusion." Elsewhere, Lee's wartime correspondence is silent on the subject; however, in postwar conversations with William Preston Johnston, who had served during the war as an aide-de-camp to Jefferson Davis, Lee implicitly criticized Hill. He observed that when Hancock attacked, Hill's "men received a blow that injured their morale." Lee stated that he "always felt afraid when going to attack after that"—a serious disappointment for a soldier with his strong predilection for the offensive. The depth of his distress at the spectacle of Hill's veterans sprinting away from the fighting, which obviously remained vivid during his conversation with Johnston six years later, had stood out starkly on the morning of May 6. "My God! Gen. McGowan," he had shouted to one of Hill's brigadiers, "is this splendid brigade of yours running like a flock of geese?" [13]

Ill health probably compromised Hill's effort to rally Heth's and Wilcox's broken divisions. For the second time in as many major battles since he became a lieutenant general, he collapsed physically at a critical juncture. On May 8, Special Orders No. 123 announced that "Lieut. Gen. A. P. Hill is relieved from duty on account of sickness." Jubal A. Early transferred from his division in the Second Corps as a temporary replacement at Third Corps headquarters. [14]

Hill's incapacity persisted throughout the fighting around Spotsylvania Court House. Charles S. Venable of Lee's staff charitably noted in the 1870s that "General Hill, though unable to sit up, in these days of Spotsylvania would have himself drawn up in his ambulance immediately in rear of the lines. Such was his anxiety to be near his troops." In a similar vein, a second witness noted that during the entire Overland campaign Hill "was dragged from field to field, yet unwilling to be absent from the post of duty and danger." His brothers implored Hill's physicians to insist that he take a rest away from the army, but the lieutenant general refused. On May 12, Hill ordered his ambulance almost to the firing line, whence he offered "the aid of his personality to Gen. Early" (Early's reaction to this assistance went unrecorded). [15]

On the 18th, Hill tried to resume command but lost his temper in Lee's presence. Furious that Brig. Gen. Ambrose R. Wright had mishandled his troops during an attack at Myer's Hill on the Confederate right, Hill vowed to convene a court of inquiry. "These men are not an army," Lee told the sputtering Hill, "they are citizens defending their country." Wright was not a professional soldier but a civilian fighting for his people's independence. "I have to make the best of what I have and lose much time in making dispositions," explained Lee, adding that Hill surely understood this. If Hill humiliated Wright by calling for an official inquiry, he might offend the people of Georgia. "Besides," asked Lee pointedly, "whom would you put in his place? You'll have to do what I do: When a man makes a mistake, I call him to my tent, talk to him, and use the authority of my position to make him do the right thing the next time." Hill's most

This rather wild-eyed depiction of A. P. Hill greeted readers of the Southern Illustrated News *in late March 1863. Then a successful division commander, Hill proved unable to make a smooth transition to corps command. Lee learned during the Overland campaign that he could count on neither Hill's health nor his competency. (*Southern Illustrated News, *March 28, 1863)*

recent biographer concluded that this episode convinced Lee that the Third Corps chief, who had been very ill as recently as May 16, "was not mentally up to the task" of resuming field command.[16]

A week later while back in charge of his corps at Jericho Mills on the North Anna, Hill learned to his discomfort that Lee also tried to persuade corps commanders who had attended West Point to "do the right thing." After a wasteful assault by Cadmus Wilcox's division against the Federal Fifth Corps on May 23, Lee contemplated the hundreds of casualties while examining the ground early the next morning. Jedediah Hotchkiss later wrote that Lee "sharply rebuked his lieutenant" for the action, closing with a stinging rhetorical question: "Why did you not do as Jackson would have done—thrown your whole force upon those people and driven them back?" Douglas Southall Freeman, who attributed Lee's hurtful words to ill humor arising from an "intestinal ailment," characterized the episode as perhaps "the stiffest rebuke ever administered to any of his general officers during the war." In his biography of Hill, James I. Robertson Jr. echoed Freeman's assessment: "Lee's outburst was more an expression of his own weakened condition than a judgment of what Hill did or did not do."[17]

Lee's dressing down of Hill at the North Anna also might have reflected exasperation with a corps commander who had exhibited rash behavior on two battlefields within eight months. That behavior, together with Hill's unfortunate habit of falling ill at times when Lee most needed stalwart corps leadership, likely persuaded him that his subordinate simply lacked the qualities requisite to succeed in his current position. Because no obvious replacement lay at hand, Lee kept Hill at his post. Just as corps commanders would have to do what they could with nonprofessional soldiers such as Ambrose Wright, Lee had "to make the best" of what he had in the way of potential lieutenant generals.

With Longstreet lost for the foreseeable future and Hill consistently unreliable, Lee might have turned to Richard S. Ewell, the third of the triumvirate that had headed corps since before Gettysburg. Unfortunately, Lee already had determined to ease Ewell out of his post on the grounds of incompetence. He had known Ewell far less well than Hill as a Confederate officer before both were promoted to lieutenant general after Chancellorsville. Only during the Seven Days had Ewell served directly under Lee's eye; in the 1862 Valley campaign and during the preliminary stages of the Second

Manassas campaign, he had been part of Jackson's semi-independent forces. Wounded at Groveton on August 28, 1862, Ewell lost a leg and endured a long convalescence. Lee believed him sufficiently recovered to resume field command in May 1863. Aware that the soldiers and officers of the Second Corps respected Ewell, he also might have heard rumors that Jackson, while lying near death at Guiney's Station, had remarked that "Old Bald Head" should be his successor.[18] On May 20, he recommended Ewell as Jackson's replacement in the Second Corps. Lee described the nominee to Davis as "an honest, brave soldier, who has always done his duty well"—tepid praise when compared to his touting of Hill in the same letter.[19]

Lee confessed after the war that he had experienced doubts from the outset about Ewell's capacity for corps command. In talks with William Allan, who had served as Ewell's chief of ordnance in the Second Corps, Lee indicated that on the basis of prewar familiarity with Ewell "he had long known his faults as a military leader—his quick alternations from elation to despondency his want of decision &c." At the time of Ewell's appointment to corps command, Lee hoped the forty-seven-year-old Virginian had gotten over his tendency to vacillate and "talked long & earnestly" with him on this subject. Ewell's subsequent conduct at Gettysburg generated considerable debate, especially his failure to attack Cemetery Hill and East Cemetery Hill late on the afternoon of July 1. Critics often have relied too heavily on postwar narratives that minimize the obstacles Ewell faced that day, but there is no doubt that Lee considered his performance less than distinguished. He complained to Allan of the "*imperfect, halting way in which his corps commanders* (especially Ewell) *fought the battle.*" Even Ewell's conduct during June 1863—a period for which most historians have given him high marks—disappointed Lee. At Second Winchester, Ewell first sent encouraging messages about his prospects for trapping the Federal defenders, then "suddenly sent a dispatch stating that upon closer inspection he found the works too strong to be attacked, and asking his (Lee's) instructions!" Such indecision from an officer on the ground deeply troubled Lee.[20]

The winter of 1863–64 added questions about Ewell's health to Lee's worries about his competence. Complications with the stump of his amputated leg caused Ewell to take sick leave more than once. In January, Ewell insisted to the secretary of war that he was strong enough to return to the field and sent a copy of his letter to Lee.

Lee somewhat tersely expressed pleasure that Ewell believed he had recovered but emphasized that a lieutenant should not expect his army commander "to take upon myself to decide in this matter. You are the proper person, on consultation with your medical advisers." Lee continued bluntly: "I do not know how much ought to be attributed to long absence from the field, general debility, or the result of your injury, but I was in constant fear during the last campaign that you would sink under your duties or destroy yourself." Turning his eye toward the spring campaigning, Lee closed with words that left no room for misunderstanding: "I last spring asked for your appointment provided you were able to take the field. You now know from experience what you have to undergo, and can best judge of your ability to endure it. I fear we cannot anticipate less labor than formerly." Ewell's own chief of staff had expressed similar concerns the preceding fall. In November, Sandie Pendleton somewhat cruelly complained about "our superannuated chieftain, worn out as he is by the prostration incident, in a man of his age, upon the amputation and doting so foolishly on his unattractive wife." [21]

The battle of the Wilderness deepened Lee's unhappiness with Ewell. As with his actions on July 1 at Gettysburg, Ewell's decision to delay an assault against the Federal right flank on May 6 inspired lively debate in which his critics too often have quoted John B. Gordon's self-serving reminiscences. Again, as at Gettysburg, there can be no doubt that Lee found his subordinate wanting. Lee told William Allan that he had "urged Ewell to make the flank attack, made later in the day by Gordon, several times before it was done. He (Lee) intended it to be a full attack in flank, & intended to support it with all Ewell's corps and others if necessary, and to rout the enemy." Lee surmised that Jubal Early persuaded Ewell to defer the assault, but he clearly held Ewell, as corps commander, rather than Early ultimately responsible. The belated attack, Lee concluded, commenced "too late in the day, and . . . was not supported with sufficient force to accomplish anything decisive." [22]

Events at Spotsylvania on May 12 and during the following week sealed Ewell's fate with the Army of Northern Virginia. From Lee's perspective, Ewell twice exhibited thoroughly unsatisfactory behavior. The first instance occurred on the morning of May 12, as both Ewell and Lee sought to direct reinforcements toward the broken Confederate line at the apex of the Mule Shoe. Lee's later acceptance of responsibility for what happened on the 12th should not obscure his initial unhappiness with the position of the Second Corps. During an inspection of the salient on May 9, he had observed, "This is a wretched line. I do not see how it can be held." Ewell shared that opinion but thought his corps should remain where it already had dug in. If relinquished, argued Ewell, the high ground in the salient could be used by Federal artillerists to threaten other parts of the Confederate position. Assurances from his engineers that sufficient artillery would make the line safe persuaded a reluctant Lee to go along with Ewell. On the night of May 11, Lee first ordered Ewell to pull his entire corps out of the Mule Shoe in anticipation of shifting it to thwart Grant's next movement. Ewell, however, persuaded him to remove only the guns and allow the infantry a good night's sleep in their somewhat sheltered lines.[23]

The stressful morning of the 12th likely summoned thoughts of Lee's initial estimate of Ewell as a man given to dramatic fluctuations of emotion. William J. Seymour of Harry Hays's Louisiana brigade described the "strong contrast in the demeanor" of Ewell and Lee during the initial phase of the effort to restore the Confederate line. "Gen. Ewell was greatly excited and, in a towering passion, hurled a terrible volley of oaths at the stragglers from the front, stigmatizing them as cowards, etc.," wrote Seymour. "Gen. Lee was calm, collected and dignified, he quietly exhorted the men not to forget their manhood and their duty, but to return to the field and strike one more blow for the glorious cause in which they were enlisted." Seymour closed with a slight to Ewell: "It is hardly necessary to say that Gen. Lee's course was by far the more effective of the two." Another witness similarly wrote that Lee "in the calmest and kindest manner" sought to rally the soldiers whereas an agitated Ewell bellowed: "Yes, G[o]d d[am]n you, run, run; the Yankees will catch you; that's right; go as fast as you can." This man emphasized that the soldiers "Gen. Lee addressed at once halted and returned . . . [and] all that Gen. Ewell so angrily reproached continued their flight to the rear."[24]

Lee agreed with the adverse judgments about Ewell's ineffectiveness during this critical moment. Eyewitness Walter A. Montgomery of the 12th North Carolina sketched a memorable confrontation between the two generals. "General Ewell, who was on the spot, personally engaged in trying to rally the men, lost his head, and with loud curses was using his sword on the backs of some of the flying soldiers," remembered Montgomery. "Just then General Lee rode up

*Richard S. Ewell wears a troubled look in this crude image published just after the battle of Gettysburg. Lee already had doubts about Ewell's ability as a corps chief by that time, and events at Spotsylvania convinced the Confederate commander to ease him out of the army. (*Southern Illustrated News, *July 4, 1863)*

and said: 'General Ewell, you must restrain yourself; how can you expect to control these men if you have lost control of yourself? If you cannot repress your excitement, you had better retire.'" For Lee, who prized self-control above almost all other virtues, Ewell had crossed a line. He later spoke of Ewell's "being perfectly prostrated by the misfortune of the morning, and too much overwhelmed to be efficient." [25]

The second incident involving Ewell's self-control occurred on May 19. Instructed on the evening of the 18th to locate the Federal right flank, Ewell received permission to conduct a reconnaissance-in-force with his corps (which numbered just 6,000 men after the hard fighting of the previous two weeks). On the 19th, his soldiers slogged along roads made nearly impassable by heavy rains over the preceding days. Fighting flared late in the afternoon at the Harris farm, northeast of Spotsylvania Court House near the Fredericksburg Road. Following an indecisive engagement, Ewell, who had taken a hard fall when his horse was killed, experienced some difficulty in extricating his soldiers. A newspaper correspondent reported shortly after the battle that because some Second Corps troops behaved poorly Ewell "did not press his advantages, nor bring off some forty-five wagons which he captured. . . . [H]e returned late at night to his former position, leaving his dead and a portion of his wounded behind." William Allan's postwar memoir succinctly summed up the day's action: "Ewell moved out to the front across the—river & tried Meade's right, had a severe fight and was glad to get back at night fall. I rode that march. The roads bad, wood & swamps. . . . Ewell had his horse killed this afternoon & at one time lost his head in the severity of the fight." [26]

William Allan's notes of Lee's postwar comments include a very harsh appraisal of Ewell on May 19. Ewell "lost all presence of mind, and Lee found him prostrate on the ground, and declaring he cd not get Rodes div. out. (Rodes being very heavily engaged with the enemy.) He (Lee) told him to order Rodes back and that if he could not get him out, he (Lee) could." It is possible that Ewell's fall from his horse may have prompted Lee's comment about finding him "prostrate on the ground." It seems at least as likely, however, that Lee used the phrase not to mean Ewell lay literally collapsed on the ground but that, to quote the *Oxford English Dictionary*, he was "laid low in mind or spirit; submissive; overcome; overthrown; powerless." [27]

Whatever the truth about Ewell's actions on the 19th, Lee decided to remove him from command of the Second Corps. The availability of Jubal Early, in whom Lee had great confidence, made this decision possible. A welcome pretext came late in May when Ewell fell ill. Lee replaced him on May 29 with Early, who had left his temporary post at Third Corps headquarters after A. P. Hill recovered from his latest malady. Informed by Lee that he could "retire from the field that he may have the benefit of rest and medical treatment," Ewell responded that he would be fit for duty in two days and—guessing Lee's real intention—"sent a certificate of Staff Surgeon [Hunter H.] McGuire to the same effect." Determined not to step aside quietly, Ewell reported for duty on the 31st. As he explained, he "remained over a week with the army, wishing to place the question of health beyond a doubt, but the change of commanders was made permanent, and on June 14 I was placed in command of the Defenses of Richmond." He followed up on June 1 with another note affirming his good health.[28]

Lee's official explanation stressed concern for Ewell's physical condition as the reason for his removal. In early June, he wrote about Ewell to Adj. and Insp. Gen. Samuel Cooper: "Although now restored to his usual health, I think the labor and exposure to which he would be inevitably exposed would at this time again incapacitate him for field service. The general, who has all the feelings of a good soldier, differs from me in this opinion," admitted Lee, "and is not only willing but anxious to resume his command. I, however, think in the present emergency it would jeopardize his life, and should his strength fail, it would prove disadvantageous to the service." In the midst of this sad drama, recalled Lee after the war, Maj. Gen. Robert E. Rodes, who led a division in the Second Corps, "*protested against E[well]'s being again placed in command.*" But friends of Ewell also went to work to counter such sentiments. An anonymous letter reached army headquarters urging Ewell's reinstatement on the grounds of Lee's long friendship with him, and others let Lee know that Ewell "thought hardly of his treatment." In retrospect, Lee affirmed that he was "very reluctant to displace him, but felt compelled to do so."[29]

Ewell eventually forced his chief to tell him the truth. After first pleading his case with Jefferson Davis, he went to see Lee on the morning of June 8. His wife Lizinka reported on the meeting in a long letter written that night to Ewell's brother Benjamin. Ewell told Lizinka that he assured Lee of his physical strength and asked if Early seemed preferable for other reasons. Lee replied that he chose Early solely because of the health issue. Ewell confessed to Lee his great anxiety during the days he had been denied restoration to command, to which Lee responded, "It is due Early and the Corps that he

receive the appointment just as Anderson has." Somewhat patheti-
cally, Ewell said he would "go somewhere to be out of the way." "You
are not in the way," answered Lee without giving any ground, "but
you had better take care of yourself." Lee offered a version of the
meeting that suggests Ewell shielded his wife from its most unpleas-
ant moments. When the Second Corps was about to depart for the
Shenandoah Valley under Early, stated Lee in 1868 referring to the
meeting of June 8, Ewell asked to be reinstated as its commander.
Lee "tried to put him off by sickness, but when E. insisted, he told
him plainly he could not send him in command."[30]

Most observers at the time and subsequent historians accepted
Lee's official explanation, which made for the smoothest possible
resolution of a vexing problem.[31] Members of Ewell's inner circle
better understood what had happened. Second Corps ordnance chief
William Allan later recalled that "every body was uncomfortable . . .
yet we all felt that his removal was inevitable & indeed was proper."
Campbell Brown, Ewell's stepson and staff officer, did not share this
attitude and seethed at what he considered a gross injustice. The
previous November, when Ewell's physical problems had obliged
Lee to replace him temporarily with Early, one of Early's staff officers noted that Ewell believed "there had been a conspiracy to get
rid of him." Remaining at corps headquarters after Early took over
in May 1864, Brown fueled Ewell's suspicion that "Old Jube" and
perhaps others had conspired to influence Lee. On June 13, Brown
informed his stepfather that "Old Early did not ask me how you were,
but I made my speech so that he will hear it." Brown vowed to avoid
Early as much as possible, adding bitterly: "He looks at me like a
sheep-stealing dog, out of the corner of his eye." For his part, Early
sought to reassure Ewell in a conciliatory letter that gave no hint
of his long-standing ambition for promotion: "I wish to say to you
General that in the arrangement which has been made by which I
am given the temporary command of the Corps I have had no agency
directly or indirectly either by procurement or suggestion. . . . I as-
sure you, General, I should regret excessively if any misunderstanding between ourselves should result."[32] Ewell undoubtedly declined
to accept Early's letter at face value. The two never communicated
after early June 1864.

Ewell's reassignment constituted the final act in a three-week
drama that had fractured the army's high command. In addition to
the problems besetting each of his infantry corps, Lee faced the cruel

loss of "Jeb" Stuart, who had led the Cavalry Corps with distinction until mortally wounded on May 11 at Yellow Tavern. Longstreet's wounding and Hill's and Ewell's various shortcomings presented the most vexing problems, and Lee displayed an array of skills in dealing with them. The ramifications of assigning Early to head the Third Corps on May 8 offer an excellent case in point. Lee had long since marked Jubal Early as a man capable of larger responsibility, and Hill's illness presented Old Jube with a trial run in corps command.[33] Early's departure from his division provided a similar opportunity for John Brown Gordon, a capable brigadier whom Lee wished to advance. Because Harry Hays ranked Gordon among Early's brigadiers, Lee shifted Hays's Louisiana brigade to Edward Johnson's division, where it was consolidated with the depleted Louisiana regiments formerly commanded by Leroy Stafford. Hays's removal not only cleared the way for Gordon to move up, but it also supplied adequate leadership for the Louisianians who had lost Stafford to a mortal wound during the first day's fight in the Wilderness. The loss of Hays's command left Early's division one brigade short: "In order to equalize your divisions," Lee wrote Ewell, "you will . . . transfer R. D. Johnston's brigade, or some other of Rodes's [five] brigades, whose command is junior to General Gordon, to General Early's division, so that General Gordon may take command of the latter."[34]

This shuffling underscored Lee's grasp of the command resources in his army, as well as his ability to focus on organization in the midst of taxing strategic and tactical circumstances. The process left each of the Second Corps divisions with four brigades, placed Early and Gordon where Lee wanted them, and neatly sidestepped potential acrimony about date of rank.

The lecture to A. P. Hill on May 18, during which Lee schooled his lieutenant about how to handle subordinates, revealed another facet of his leadership. Sensitive to the special problems of running an army whose officers predominantly were volunteers representing proud states of a republic, he understood the need to balance military and political needs and to gauge how decisions relating to command would affect morale behind the lines. Lee's grasp of the special needs of citizen soldiers eluded many—if not most—of his West Point–trained peers, and helped to explain the unparalleled bond he forged with his officers and men. His decision to name Richard H. Anderson as Longstreet's temporary successor, for example, likely stemmed at least in part from a belief that Longstreet's soldiers would welcome the South Carolinian (whose division had been in the First Corps before being transferred to the Third in May 1863). Lee surely had greater respect for Jubal Early's soldierly qualities, but First Corps staff officer Moxley Sorrel, speaking about the relative merits of Early and Anderson on the morning of May 7, addressed the matter of reaction with the corps. He conceded that Early probably was the ablest available man but thought he would "be objectionable to both officers and men" in the First Corps. Of Anderson, in contrast, Sorrel stated: "We *know him* and shall be satisfied with him." Sorrel believed Lee would select the best soldier; Lee took a broader view.[35]

Spotsylvania also demonstrated that Lee could exhibit a hard side concerning subordinates. This element of his generalship often has been obscured by contemporaries and historians who pronounced him too much of a gentleman to make difficult personnel decisions. British observer A. J. L. Fremantle stated in his famous diary that Lee's "only faults, so far as I can learn, arise from his excessive amiability." Walter H. Taylor, who spent more time with Lee than any other officer during the war, noted in his widely cited first memoir: "If it shall be the verdict of posterity that General Lee in any respect fell short of perfection as a military leader, it may perhaps be claimed . . . that he was too careful of the personal feelings of his subordinate commanders, too fearful of wounding their pride, and too solicitous for their reputation." Taylor believed this tendency prompted Lee to retain in command men "of whose fitness for their position he was not convinced, and often led him, either avowedly or tacitly, to assume responsibility for mishaps clearly attributable to the inefficiency, neglect, or carelessness, of others." Jefferson Davis similarly wrote that Lee's "habitual avoidance of any seeming harshness, which caused him sometimes, instead of giving a command, to make a suggestion, was probably a defect." [36]

Many historians have seconded Taylor's and Davis's thoughts. Two examples will convey the tenor of their analysis. Most influential has been Douglas Southall Freeman, who echoed Fremantle's language when he wrote of the deep "defect of Lee's excessive amiability." In a chapter weighing Lee's strong and weak points as a soldier, Freeman concluded that "His consideration for others, the virtue of the gentleman, had been his vice as a soldier." British historian J. F. C. Fuller delivered a less gentle verdict in claiming that it was Lee's "inexhaustible tact which ruined his army." [37]

Perhaps inevitably, a psychological dimension has been added to this long-standing interpretation. A psychiatrist and journalist recently coauthored an article that claimed to locate in Lee's boyhood the reason for his later habit of never confronting anyone. They maintained (without benefit of substantial historical evidence) that the young Lee grew up watching his father's "likely abuse of alcohol, his intense pain, volatile temperament, and narcissistic character disorder; and the inevitable eruption of abuse in such circumstances." Having seen "Light-Horse Harry" Lee shame his mother repeatedly, "Robert E. Lee would grow up, not to repeat the act of shaming, but to take the only other alternative—never to shame anyone at almost any cost." This trait carried over into his style of command. "Shame witnessed and shame felt were the source of his inability to control his subordinates," wrote these authors in a strikingly unsupported generalization. "Lee could not confront his wayward lieutenants for fear of shaming them. He was determined never, if at all possible, to let them feel humiliated as he had painfully watched his mother be mortified."[38]

Even a cursory look at the Spotsylvania campaign and its immediate aftermath should dispel the idea that Lee habitually shied away from confrontations with his lieutenants. He spoke plainly to both Hill and Ewell when he thought it necessary. With Hill, the exchange at the North Anna on May 23 could have left no doubt about Lee's displeasure; neither could his insistence that Ewell gain control of himself in the Mule Shoe on May 12 have been misinterpreted by his raging lieutenant. Lee's unhappiness with Ewell on the 19th and later refusal to reinstate him as commander of the Second Corps similarly indicated a willingness to take a stand. It no doubt pained Lee in early June to have to tell Ewell, about whom he "expressed the kindest of personal feelings,"[39] precisely why he would not return him to his old corps. For the good of the army and Ewell's reputation, Lee publicly hewed to the rationale based on physical condition, but to his old acquaintance in person he admitted doubts about his capacity to command.

This is not to say Lee relished such unhappy episodes. He dealt with failures among subordinates in a variety of ways and almost always sought to discipline or transfer officers with the least possible acrimony. Reassignment of such men as Benjamin Huger, Theophilus H. Holmes, and Daniel Harvey Hill left scarcely a ripple within the Army of Northern Virginia—a testament to Lee's ability to avoid the poisonous infighting that wracked the high command of the Army of Tennessee. But did he seek accommodation even if it hurt the army? Certainly Richard S. Ewell would say he did not.[40]

Closely related to the idea that Lee shunned confrontations is the argument that he allowed his corps commanders too much latitude. According to Justus Scheibert, a Prussian observer who campaigned with the Army of Northern Virginia at Chancellorsville and Gettysburg, Lee explained: "I strive to make my plans as good as my human skill allows, but on the day of battle I lay the fate of my army in the hands of God; it is my generals' turn to perform their duty." Citing Scheibert, Douglas Southall Freeman described this as a "mistaken theory of the function of the high command," adding that it may have resulted from Lee's gentlemanly concern for others. Conceding that this method might work on the wooded battlefields of Virginia, Freeman thought it returned disastrous dividends at Gettysburg on July 2–3.[41]

Down to the time Lee spoke with Scheibert, his method had worked beautifully with Jackson and Longstreet executing their commander's broad orders. When Hill and Ewell failed to operate equally well under a light rein at Gettysburg and—in Lee's opinion—in the Wilderness, he took a more active role. In other words, he adapted his style of command to suit changing personnel.

At Spotsylvania, this showed especially at the tactical level. On May 6 at the Wilderness, Lee had withdrawn from danger at the Widow Tapp farm once Longstreet arrived because he trusted his senior corps chief's ability to manage the fighting along the Plank Road. Just six days later, when Lee prolonged his involvement in the Mule Shoe—amid a crisis no greater than the one his army had confronted at dawn on May 6—he betrayed doubts that Ewell could orchestrate the Confederate defense. Ewell's erratic behavior on the 12th doubtless contributed to Lee's decision to remain under fire longer than was prudent. In effect, he functioned as both corps commander and army commander for much of that trying day, a circumstance that would have been unthinkable on battlefields where he had trusted Jackson and Longstreet to oversee their troops. Nor did A. P. Hill likely inspire much greater confidence in this respect. He had proved unable to rally his shattered troops on May 6 and had exercised little control over the action at the North Anna on May 23. As for Richard H. Anderson, Lee took special care to direct his movements with the First Corps.[42]

Events along the North Anna on May 24–26 revealed the crippling legacy of Spotsylvania. Ulysses S. Grant carelessly placed his army in an extremely vulnerable position, with three large bodies of troops separated by the curving river. Here was the tactical opening Lee had awaited since the opening of the Overland campaign. According to his physician Lafayette Guild, "Genl. Lee all though sick had not from the 5th to the 25th had two hours consecutive sleep." The commanding general succumbed to a severe intestinal malady on the 24th. For two days he tried to work through the pain, unwilling to entrust a tactical offensive to any of his corps commanders. Anderson had done well enough at Spotsylvania under close supervision but had yet to demonstrate that he could do more. Hill's latest failure lay only one day in the past, and Ewell's recent record fell below even that of Hill. A year earlier, Lee unhesitatingly would have directed Jackson or Longstreet to smite the exposed enemy; later in 1864, he probably would have called on Jubal Early. No such alternative existed on the 24th and 25th, rendering him unable to do more than deplore his misfortune. "We must strike them a blow—," Charles Venable quoted the prostrate Lee saying from his tent, "we must never let them pass us again—we must strike them a blow!" Perhaps unintentionally, Venable obliquely damned the lieutenant generals on whom the stricken army commander believed he could not rely: "But though he still had reports of the operations in the field constantly brought to him, and gave orders to his officers, Lee confined to his tent was not Lee on the battlefield." [43] Had Lee believed a disciplined and effective presence prevailed at any corps headquarters, one of those orders would have instructed a lieutenant general to strike the blow he desired.

A month after fighting ended at Spotsylvania, the armies settled into siege lines at Richmond and Petersburg. The relatively static nature of the last nine months of the war in eastern Virginia reduced the likelihood that poor corps leadership would initiate a strategic or tactical crisis. The brightest opportunities came to Jubal Early, whom Lee deployed to the Shenandoah Valley with the Second Corps in June 1864. Early achieved heartening success during his first eight weeks of detached duty before suffering utter defeat in a trio of battles between September 19 and October 19. Neither Longstreet, who returned to the First Corps before his wounds from the Wilderness had healed properly, nor Hill, whose infirmities continued until his death in early April 1865, added any laurels

*Despite his crumbling high command, Lee effectively countered Ulysses S. Grant's movements during the Overland campaign. This northern cartoon, which reflected wishful thinking rather than a sound reading of events, shows Grant administering a whipping to his famous opponent. (*Harper's Weekly, *June 11, 1864)*

to his earlier record. Richard Anderson presided quietly over a one-division demi-corps for much of the last period of the conflict, and youthful John B. Gordon, who succeeded Early as head of the Second Corps, made the most of limited opportunities to demonstrate promise in 1865.

Ironically, the siege Lee had dreaded from the moment Grant crossed the Rapidan River cushioned the effect of his disintegrating high command. The post-Spotsylvania version of the Army of Northern Virginia likely would have experienced major lapses of corps leadership if engaged in a war of maneuver comparable to that it had waged with Jackson and Longstreet at the height of their powers in 1862–63. Because Lee and his army sustained their nation's morale throughout the last year of the war, battlefield defeats arising from those lapses probably would have shortened the life of the Confederacy.

NOTES

1. Even critics of Lee's overall generalship during the Civil War usually have given him high marks for the Overland campaign. For example, Alan T. Nolan, who argued that Lee's strategic and tactical aggressiveness in 1862–63 hurt the Confederacy by rapidly depleting its manpower, praised his conduct of the Overland campaign. Nolan, *Lee Considered: General Robert E. Lee and Civil War History* (Chapel Hill: University of North Carolina Press, 1991), 100–101. Similarly, Grady McWhiney and Perry D. Jamieson, who also criticized Lee's penchant for the offensive, wrote glowingly about his "brilliant defensive campaign against Grant in 1864." McWhiney and Jamieson, *Attack and Die: Civil War Military Tactics and the Southern Heritage* (University: University of Alabama Press, 1982), 164.

2. Edward Porter Alexander, *Fighting for the Confederacy: The Personal Recollections of General Edward Porter Alexander*, ed. Gary W. Gallagher (Chapel Hill: University of North Carolina Press, 1989), 372; Douglas Southall Freeman, *R. E. Lee: A Biography*, 4 vols. (New York: Scribner's, 1934–35), 3:315; Jedediah Hotchkiss, *Virginia*, being vol. 4 of Clement A. Evans, ed., *Confederate Military History*, 12 vols. (Atlanta: Confederate Publishing Company, 1899), 447.

3. U.S. War Department, *The War of the Rebellion: A Compilation of the Official Records of the Union and Confederate Armies*, 127 vols., index, and atlas (Washington: GPO, 1880–1901), ser. 1, vol. 51, pt. 2:916–17, 36(1):1044 (hereafter cited as *OR*; all references are to ser. 1).

4. William W. Old, "Trees Whittled Down at Horseshoe," in J. William Jones et al., eds., *Southern Historical Society Papers*, 52 vols. (1877–1959; reprint with 3-vol. index, Wilmington, N.C.: Broadfoot, 1990–92), 33:24 (hereafter cited as *SHSP*); *OR* 36(1):1044.

5. For details of the various reorganizations, see Douglas Southall Freeman, *Lee's Lieutenants: A Study in Command*, 3 vols. (New York: Scribner's, 1942–44), 1:605–19, 670–75, 2:236–68, 683–714.

6. During the period May 7, 1864, to April 9, 1865, Richard S. Ewell, Jubal A. Early, and John Brown Gordon commanded the Second Corps; A. P. Hill and Early the Third; and James Longstreet and Richard H. Anderson the First. Lee also created a two-division corps for Richard H. Anderson in October 1864 (sometimes referred to as the Fourth Corps and other times as Anderson's Corps; this command was reduced to one division in late 1864). Thus, while Jackson and Longstreet provided continuity

at corps (and wing) headquarters for nearly a year between July 1862 and May 1863, corps leadership changed comparatively rapidly during the last phase of the war. On Anderson's corps, see Joseph Cantey Elliott, *Lieutenant General Richard Heron Anderson: Lee's Noble Soldier* (Dayton, Ohio: Morningside, 1985), 121–26, and *OR* 42(3):1280–86.

7. Walter H. Taylor to Bettie Saunders, April 24, 1864, in Walter H. Taylor, *Lee's Adjutant: The Wartime Letters of Colonel Walter Herron Taylor, 1862–1865*, ed. R. Lockwood Tower (Columbia: University of South Carolina Press, 1995), 155; Francis W. Dawson, *Reminiscences of Confederate Service, 1861–1865*, ed. Bell I. Wiley (1882; reprint, Baton Rouge: Louisiana State University Press, 1980), 116.

8. R. E. Lee to Jefferson Davis, October 2, 1862, in *OR* 19(2):643; Lee to Davis, May 20, 1863, in *OR* 25(2):810.

9. On Hill's performance at Gettysburg, see Gary W. Gallagher, "Confederate Corps Leadership on the First Day at Gettysburg: A. P. Hill and Richard S. Ewell in a Difficult Debut," in Gallagher, ed., *The First Day at Gettysburg: Essays on Confederate and Union Leadership* (Kent, Ohio: Kent State University Press, 1992).

10. Hotchkiss, *Virginia*, 426; A. L. Long, *Memoirs of Robert E. Lee: His Military and Personal History, Embracing a Large Amount of Information Hitherto Unpublished* (Philadelphia: J. M. Stoddart, 1886), 311.

11. Henry Heth, *The Memoirs of Henry Heth*, ed. James L. Morrison Jr. (Westport, Conn.: Greenwood Press, 1974), 184; Cadmus M. Wilcox's report for the period May 4–December 7, 1864, typescript, bound vol. 178, Fredericksburg and Spotsylvania National Military Park Library, Fredericksburg, Va.; Cadmus M. Wilcox, "Lee and Grant in the Wilderness," in [Alexander K. McClure], ed., *The Annals of the War Written by Leading Participants North and South* (1879; reprint, Dayton, Ohio: Morningside, 1988), 495; article by a correspondent for the *London Herald* dated May 18, 1864, reprinted in W. S. Dunlop, *Lee's Sharpshooters; or, the Forefront of Battle* (1899; reprint, Dayton, Ohio: Morningside, 1982), 400–401.

12. For accounts critical of Hill, see Freeman, *Lee's Lieutenants*, 3:353–55; Gordon C. Rhea, *The Battle of the Wilderness, May 5–6, 1864* (Baton Rouge: Louisiana State University Press, 1994), 276–82; and Gary W. Gallagher, "The Army of Northern Virginia in May 1864: A Crisis of High Command," *Civil War History* 36 (June 1990): 115. For a defense of Hill, see Peter S. Carmichael, "Escaping the Shadow of Gettysburg: Richard S. Ewell and Ambrose Powell Hill at the Wilderness," in Gary W. Gallagher, ed., *The Wilderness Campaign* (Chapel Hill: University of North Carolina Press, 1997).

13. *OR* 36(1):1028; William Preston Johnston, "Memoranda of Conversations with General R. E. Lee," in Gary W. Gallagher, ed., *Lee the Soldier* (Lincoln: University of Nebraska Press, 1996), 29; Edward Porter Alexander, *Military Memoirs of a Confederate: A Critical Narrative* (New York: Scribner's, 1907), 503.

14. *OR* 36(2):974–75. Scholars have offered different explanations for Hill's recurring illnesses. William W. Hassler's *A. P. Hill: Lee's Forgotten General* (Richmond, Va.: Garrett & Massie, 1957), 237–38, suggested that he "suffered from chronic malaria." James I. Robertson Jr., in *General A. P. Hill: The Story of a Confederate Warrior* (New York: Random House, 1987), 11–12, 250, attributed the general's problems to complications related to chronic prostatitis arising from a case of gonorrhea contracted while a cadet at West Point, a conclusion shared by Jack P. Welsh in *Medical Histories of Confederate Generals* (Kent, Ohio: Kent State University Press, 1995), 100. Douglas Southall Freeman, in *Lee's Lieutenants*, 3:442, postulated that "a psychosomatic malady" struck Hill down in the Wilderness. Russell P. Green, a physician, argued that Hill "suffered from depression." Green, "A. P. Hill's Manic Depression: 'Bury These Poor Men, and Let's Say No More about It,'" *Virginia Country's Civil War* (Middleburg, Va.: Country Publishers, 1986), 4:65–69.

15. Charles S. Venable, "The Campaign from the Wilderness to Petersburg," in *SHSP* 14:532; "Sketch of Gen. A. P. Hill," in *Land We Love* 2 (February 1867): 287–88; Robertson, *A. P. Hill*, 270.

16. Freeman, *Lee*, 3:330–31; Robertson, *A. P. Hill*, 272. Freeman's source for this anecdote was a letter dated June 25, 1920, from Col. William H. Palmer, who had served on Hill's staff and "on whose memory Lee's words were indelibly imprinted." Freeman also noted that another individual "had the same story from Colonel Palmer and made a detailed memorandum of it, which he generously gave the writer." Palmer stated that the episode took place on May 18; Freeman cited a telegraphic message from Lee to Jefferson Davis on the night of May 15 that "makes it almost certain that the incident occurred on the 15th" (p. 331, n. 12). In this instance, Freeman was confused; the incident involving Hill and Wright at Myer's Hill could not have taken place on May 15. Testimony from members of Wright's brigade indicates that their commander was ill on May 14–15 and that Lt. Col. M. R. Hall commanded the brigade in his absence (unsigned letter dated May 18, 1864, in *Macon Daily Telegraph*, May 31, 1864; James P. Verdery [Co. I, 48th Georgia Infantry] to Sister, May 17, 1864 [excerpts from both letters supplied to the author by Keith S. Bohannon of East Ridge, Tenn.]). Hill also was temporarily out of command because

of illness on the 15th. Finally, although the Confederates had launched a successful assault at Myer's Hill on May 14, they mounted no attack there the next day. On the 18th, there was a small southern assault in the vicinity of Myer's Hill, which the Federals repulsed easily. Wright's brigade held a position in that part of the Confederate line on the 18th, and both Wright and Hill could have been present (Hill resumed command of his corps on the 21st and might have been back in the field on the 18th as an observer). In sum, the nature of the action at Myer's Hill on the 18th and the likelihood that both Wright and Hill were present support Palmer's account.

17. Hotchkiss, *Virginia*, 460; Freeman, *Lee's Lieutenants*, 3:496–97; Robertson, *A. P. Hill*, 276.

18. On rumors of Jackson's supposed deathbed statement about Ewell, see William Dorsey Pender to Fanny Pender, May 14, 1863, in Pender, *The General to His Lady: The Civil War Letters of William Dorsey Pender to Fanny Pender*, ed. William W. Hassler (Chapel Hill: University of North Carolina Press, 1965), 237. "Do not believe all you see about the last words of Jackson," stated Pender, who had served as a brigadier under A. P. Hill, "for some designing person is trying to injure Gen. Hill by saying that he frequently said that he wanted Ewell to have his Corps."

19. Robert E. Lee to Jefferson Davis, May 20, 1863, in *OR* 25(2):810.

20. William Allan, "Memoranda of Conversations with General Robert E. Lee," in Gallagher, ed., *Lee the Soldier*, 11, 14.

21. Robert E. Lee to Richard S. Ewell, January 18, 1864, in *OR* 33:1095–96; W. G. Bean, *Stonewall's Man: Sandie Pendleton* (Chapel Hill: University of North Carolina Press, 1959), 151.

22. Allan, "Memoranda of Conversations with Lee," 11. Gordon's influential account is in his *Reminiscences of the Civil War* (New York: Scribner's, 1903), 243–61. For an able defense of Ewell, see Carmichael, "Ewell and Hill at the Wilderness."

23. Donald Pfanz, *Richard S. Ewell: A Soldier's Life* (Chapel Hill: University of North Carolina Press, 1998), 378, 382–83.

24. William J. Seymour, *The Civil War Memoirs of Captain William J. Seymour: Reminiscences of a Louisiana Tiger*, ed. Terry L. Jones (Baton Rouge: Louisiana State University Press, 1991), 125; *Columbus (Ga.) Daily Sun*, December 22, 1865.

25. Walter A. Montgomery, *The Days of Old and the Years That Are Past* (Raleigh, N.C.: n.p., n.d.), 28; Allan, "Memoranda of Conversations with Lee," 11.

26. *OR* 36(1):1073; Pfanz, *Ewell*, 392–93; *Richmond Daily Dispatch*, May 25, 1864; typescript (prepared by R. E. L. Krick) of William Allan mem-

oir, May–June 1864, folder 11, William Allan Papers, Southern Historical Collection, Wilson Library, University of North Carolina, Chapel Hill (repository hereafter cited as SHC).

27. Allan, "Memoranda of Conversations with Lee," 11. Donald C. Pfanz, Ewell's most careful biographer, described the evidence in Allan's memorandum as "damning testimony, to be sure" but added that Lee was not on the scene. "If Ewell did, in fact, lose his head during the fight," states Pfanz, "no credible evidence of it has yet come to light." Pfanz, *Ewell*, 393. The passage in Allan's memoir cited in the preceding note (and probably written after the ordnance officer's conversations with Lee) does mention one instance of loss of control.

28. *OR* 36(3):846, (1):1074, (3):863.

29. Robert E. Lee to Samuel Cooper, in Robert E. Lee, *The Wartime Papers of R. E. Lee*, ed. Clifford Dowdey and Louis H. Manarin (Boston: Little, Brown, 1961), 776; Allan, "Memoranda of Conversations with Lee," 11–12.

30. Lizinka C. Ewell to Benjamin Ewell, June 8, 1864, in Richard S. Ewell, *The Making of a Soldier: Letters of General R. S. Ewell*, ed. Percy Gatling Hamlin (Richmond, Va.: Whittet & Shepperson, 1935), 127–30; Allan, "Memoranda of Conversations with Lee," 11.

31. See, for example, Walter H. Taylor, *General Lee: His Campaigns in Virginia 1861–1865, with Personal Reminiscences* (1906; reprint, Dayton, Ohio: Morningside, 1975), 249; Alexander, *Military Memoirs*, 534; and Shelby Foote, *The Civil War: A Narrative, Red River to Appomattox* (New York: Random House, 1974), 277.

32. Everard H. Smith, ed., "The Civil War Diary of Peter W. Hairston, Volunteer Aide to Major General Jubal A. Early, November 7–December 4, 1863," *North Carolina Historical Review* 67 (January 1990): 76 (entry for November 16); William Allan memoir, William Allan Papers, SHC; Campbell Brown to Richard S. Ewell, June 13, 1864, and Jubal A. Early to Richard S. Ewell, June 5, 1864, box 1, folder 11, Polk, Brown, Ewell Papers, no. 605, SHC.

33. For more than eighteen months, Lee's assignments of responsibility to Early had demonstrated his confidence in the latter's potential for advancement. As a brigadier during the fall of 1862, Early often had commanded Ewell's division. Lee also had selected him over senior major generals to hold the Confederate position at Fredericksburg during the Chancellorsville campaign, and during the fall and winter of 1863–64 Early had stood in for the ailing Ewell at Second Corps headquarters.

34. *OR* 51(2):902–3, 36(2):974–75.

35. G. Moxley Sorrel, *Recollections of a Confederate Staff Officer* (1905; reprint, Jackson, Tenn.: McCowat-Mercer Press, 1959), 238–39. Lee's belief that Early might soon replace Ewell or the frail Hill also likely entered into his decision to name Anderson as Longstreet's replacement.

36. Arthur James Lyon Fremantle, *Three Months in the Southern States: April–June, 1863* (1863; reprint, Lincoln: University of Nebraska Press, 1991), 249; Walter Taylor, *Four Years with General Lee* (1877; reprint, Bloomington: Indiana University Press, 1962), 146–47; Jefferson Davis, "Robert E. Lee," in *SHSP* 17:371.

37. Freeman, *Lee*, 4:168; J. F. C. Fuller, *Grant and Lee: A Study in Personality and Generalship* (1932; reprint, Bloomington: Indiana University Press, 1957), 119.

38. J. Anderson Thomson Jr. and Carlos Michael Santos, "The Mystery in the Coffin: Another View of Lee's Visit to His Father's Grave," *Virginia Magazine of History and Biography* 103 (January 1995): 87–88, 93–94.

39. Allan, "Memoranda of Conversations with Lee," 12.

40. For discussions of Lee's skill at removing unwanted officers from his army, see Freeman, *Lee's Lieutenants*, 1:605–32, and Robert K. Krick, "The Army of Northern Virginia in September 1862: Its Circumstances, Its Opportunities, and Why It Should Not Have Been at Sharpsburg," in Gary W. Gallagher, ed., *Antietam: Essays on the 1862 Maryland Campaign* (Kent, Ohio: Kent State University Press, 1989), 196–97.

41. Freeman, *Lee*, 2:347, 4:168–69.

42. Freeman discussed Lee's oversight of Anderson in *Lee's Lieutenants*, 3:509.

43. William McWillie notebooks (typescript supplied by Robert K. Krick), Mississippi Department of Archives and History, Jackson; Venable, "Wilderness to Petersburg," 535. In *Lee*, 3:358, Freeman offered Ewell's health as the reason Lee believed he could not call on the Second Corps. He also mentioned P. G. T. Beauregard, who commanded below Richmond at Bermuda Hundred, as a potential candidate whose "hands were full" with his own duties.

| FIGHTING THE |
| BATTLES OF SECOND |
| FREDERICKSBURG & |
| SALEM CHURCH |
| *Lee & Jubal A. Early* |
| *at Chancellorsville* |
| |

Jubal A. Early had been living in Canada for more than two years when he composed a letter to Robert E. Lee in late November 1868. Begging Lee's indulgence for the intrusion, Early devoted most of this long missive to his role during the Chancellorsville campaign. "I think your official report, which I never saw until I came to this country, does not do full justice to my command," stated Early in carefully chosen words, "but that was my fault in not furnishing you the means of doing so." His report forwarded to Lee at the time had been far too brief, he conceded, a sketch "merely intended to aid you in giving the [War] department a brief account of the operations in advance of the official reports." Early had expected in his final report "to show . . . what my command had actually done," but the army's subsequent movement into Pennsylvania and other events had prevented his preparing a fuller account. While in Canada, Early had written a detailed narrative of his part in the campaign, a copy of which he now sent to Lee in the hope it would set the record straight and assist the general in writing a history of the Army of Northern Virginia. "The most that is left to us is the history of our struggle, and I think that ought to be accurately written," observed Early in language that foreshadowed his later activities as the preeminent Lost Cause controversialist.

"We lost nearly everything but honor, and that should be religiously guarded."[1] Early's postwar sensitivity about Chancellorsville mirrored his attitude immediately after the battle. The campaign marked Lee's first assignment of him to semi-independent command, and from the beginning "Old Jube" sought to place his actions in the best possible light. An examination of Early's conduct during the operation, his subsequent debates with William Barksdale, and his reaction to postwar writings concerning Second Fredericksburg and Salem Church is useful on several levels. It shows how Lee readily granted wide discretion to trusted subordinates but stepped in when he perceived a lack of skill or decisiveness (in this case on the part of Lafayette McLaws, who outranked Early at Salem Church and performed very poorly). Lee's deft handling of Early's dispute with Barksdale after the battle demonstrates how he disciplined lieutenants to control destructive backbiting. Most obviously, the essay sheds light on Early's characteristics as a soldier and provides a useful context for comparing him with more senior officers such as McLaws. The independence, decisiveness, and complex relationship with his troops so manifest during the 1864 Valley Campaign can be detected in the fighting along the Rappahannock River in 1863. Finally, Early's close attention to the treatment of Chancellorsville in official reports and later writings reveals how well he understood that the printed record—rather than the deeds themselves—shapes long-term understanding of historical events.

Early seemed an unlikely candidate for a leading role at Chancellorsville. Although he entered the campaign as the army's junior major general, he could claim considerable accomplishment as a brigade commander as well as success, while still a brigadier, leading the wounded Richard S. Ewell's division during the last part of the Maryland campaign and at the battle of Fredericksburg. Highly ambitious and quick to criticize officers who had advanced more quickly, Early openly sought promotion during late 1862. Both Lee and "Stonewall" Jackson recommended him for a major generalcy that fall, the latter remarking that Early "manages his men well in camp and also in action." Promotion came in January 1863, eliciting a typically acidic reaction from the new major general. "I know you will think that I am so much tickled with my promotion that I have given up grumbling," Early commented to Ewell, "but the truth is that it comes after so many have been made over me, that it looks very much like they were picking up the scraps now, & the greatest gratification I have in the matter is that others acknowledge the justice of my promotion."[2]

Despite Early's enviable record as a brigadier, senior division commanders such as A. P. Hill, Lafayette McLaws, and Richard H. Anderson seemed better choices to carry out critical elements of Lee's plan to thwart Joseph Hooker. But Lee discerned in Early, whom he affectionately called "My Bad Old Man,"[3] a capacity for command without close supervision and entrusted him with responsibilities during the campaign second only to those he placed in Jackson's hands. Chancellorsville anticipated the deployment of Early and the Second Corps to the Shenandoah Valley in June 1864, affording unmistakable evidence of Lee's belief that Early could function effectively when separated from the main army. Among all the corps commanders in the Army of Northern Virginia, only Jackson and Early received assignments that bespoke Lee's confidence in their ability to succeed under such circumstances.[4] Robert Stiles addressed this phenomenon in his postwar memoirs: "[Early's] native intellect, his mental training, his sagacity, his resource, his self-reliant, self-directing strength, were all very great, and the commanding general reposed the utmost confidence in him. This he indicated by selecting him so frequently for independent command, and to fill the most critical, difficult, and I had almost said hopeless, positions, in the execution of his own great plans; as for example, when he left him at Fredericksburg with nine thousand men to neutralize Sedgwick with thirty thousand."[5]

Early's generalship in opposing John Sedgwick raised questions in 1863 that have persisted in modern literature. Charged with watching Lee's eastern flank, he failed to hold the lines behind which the Army of Northern Virginia had vanquished Ambrose E. Burnside's Federals the previous December in the battle of Fredericksburg. He thus presided over a disappointing element in the larger Confederate success at Chancellorsville. Were his deployments faulty? Did he respond effectively to a succession of Federal threats on May 2–3? What role did he play in the lethargic Confederate effort at Salem Church on May 3–4? In short, did his performance justify Lee's confidence that he was the man to hold the Rappahannock River opposite Fredericksburg while the bulk of the army marched west to confront Joseph Hooker?

Maj. Gen. Jubal A. Early. (Francis Trevelyan Miller, ed., The Photographic History of the Civil War, *10 vols. [New York: Review of Reviews, 1911],* 10:245)

The campaign opened for Early just past daylight on a mist- and fog-enshrouded April 29, 1863, with word that Federal infantry had crossed the Rappahannock River on pontoons below Fredericksburg near the mouth of Deep Run. He immediately moved his division, a portion of which had been picketing that stretch of the river, into position along the Richmond, Fredericksburg & Potomac Railroad between Hamilton's Crossing on the right and Deep Run on the left. Three regiments moved east to the Richmond Stage Road as skirmishers. Soon came news of another Federal pontoon bridge farther downstream at "Smithfield," home of the Pratt family. Alerted by Maj. Samuel Hale of Early's staff, Brig. Gen. Harry Hays hurried his brigade of five Louisiana regiments toward the river. The 6th Louisiana relieved the 13th Georgia of Brig. Gen. John B. Gordon's brigade in rifle pits near the Rappahannock, holding the Federals at bay for more than an hour. By then, thousands of northern soldiers were on the Confederate side of the river at Deep Run, and a division was across at the lower site by late morning. Jedediah Hotchkiss heard reports of musketry and cannon fire from Early's part of the field at 6:30 or 7:00 A.M., adding that "We fired some artillery at them, soon after they came over, and did some damage to them." [6]

In an account of the artillery action to which Hotchkiss referred, a gunner from the Rockbridge Artillery described a meeting between Early and Lee on Prospect Hill. "The enemy's infantry having formed on our side near the river, under Gen. Early's order, we opened on them, and they soon retired under the bank," recalled David E. Moore many years after the war. "Soon after the firing commenced Gen Lee came up and said 'Gen. Early what are you making all this racket about?' Gen. Early replied 'the Yankees have crossed the river again' and Gen Lee said '[O]h the troublesome fellows.' This was the beginning of the artillery firing preceding the Battle of Chancellorsville." [7] Moore's reconstructed dialogue may be apocryphal, but it seems likely that Lee must have approved of Early's prompt response to the Federal crossings.

For the remainder of April 29 and into the next day, the Confederate commander watched Union movements on both sides of the Rappahannock, pondered intelligence from his cavalry about Federals marching upriver, and eventually decided that Hooker's main blow would come from the west. "It was, therefore, determined to leave sufficient troops to hold our lines," explained Lee, employing his usual passive voice, "and with the main body of the army to give battle to the approaching column." Most of the Confederate soldiers would take the roads westward toward Chancellorsville before the sun rose on May 1. To Jubal Early fell the task of holding the enemy in check along the long river front at Fredericksburg. [8]

How did Lee define "sufficient force" to oppose an enemy estimated at 30,000 men or more? Early would have approximately 7,500 men in the four brigades of his own division, comprising

Hays's Louisianians, Gordon's five Georgia regiments, Brig. Gen. Robert F. Hoke's four regiments and one battalion of North Carolinians, and William "Extra Billy" Smith's four Virginia regiments, together with the four batteries of Colonel R. Snowden Andrews's artillery battalion. Also placed under his command were 1,500 Mississippians in the four regiments of Brig. Gen. William Barksdale's brigade from McLaws's division, three companies of the Washington Artillery, and part of the army's general artillery reserve under Brig. Gen. William Nelson Pendleton. After careful study of his division's field returns and other documents after the war, Early estimated his strength to have been 9,000 infantry and forty-five guns. His figure for the infantry probably was accurate, though he perhaps underestimated the number of guns.[9] Whatever the total, many Confederates gazing at the obviously superior strength of their foe thought it too small. Looking back on the battle after the war, an officer in Smith's brigade somewhat bitterly assessed what Lee had expected of Early: "Our division occupied a line of battle of sufficient length to require forty thousand troops and as was always the case Gen. Early was selected to lead a forlorn hope."[10]

Early received specific instructions from his chief on the morning of May 1. Before departing to join the troops who would confront Hooker, "General Lee instructed me to watch the enemy and try to hold him; to conceal the weakness of my force, and if compelled to yield before overpowering numbers, to fall back towards Guiney's depot where our supplies were, protecting them and the railroad." Should Sedgwick withdraw all or a significant part of his strength, Early was to "join the main body of the army . . . leaving at Fredericksburg only such force as might be necessary to protect the town against any force the enemy might leave behind." These instructions allowed Early considerable discretion, though Lee suggested that a bombardment by long-range artillery on May 2 might provoke the Federals into revealing their strength.[11]

Early was familiar with the terrain he would defend. Essentially duplicating the line 75,000 men in the Army of Northern Virginia had held the preceding December, Early's position stretched more than six miles from Hamilton's Crossing on the Richmond, Fredericksburg & Potomac Railroad to Taylor's Hill on the Rappahannock River. Deep Run divided the field into northern and southern zones; Hazel Run wound eastward to join the Rappahannock just south of

Fredericksburg. Howison's Hill rose a mile and a half west of the mouth of Deep Run, the first of a string of excellent defensive positions that included, in order from south to north, Lee's Hill, Willis's Hill, Marye's Heights, Cemetery Hill, Stansbury's Hill, and Taylor's Hill. On December 13, 1862, the Federals had achieved their only breakthrough between Deep Run and Hamilton's Crossing; Early had played a key role in restoring that broken Confederate line. The bloody repulses for which First Fredericksburg became infamous in the Federal army occurred at the foot of Willis's Hill and Marye's Heights.

The immediate situation and memories of First Fredericksburg influenced Early's positioning of men and guns. His division held the ground between Deep Run and Hamilton's Crossing, where thousands of Federals had entrenched west of the Rappahannock at the pontoon sites. Barksdale's regiments with supporting artillery stretched between Lee's Hill and the Plank Road just north of Marye's Heights; this had been the strongest part of the Confederate line in December, and as yet no Federals had crossed the river at Fredericksburg. Artillery and skirmishers alone protected the area between Lee's Hill and Deep Run, while the line north of the Plank Road lay vacant. Pendleton concurred with Early's allocation of guns to the various parts of the line. Although far from ideal in terms of the number of men available along the extensive line, Early's dispositions made sense in the context of the existing Federal threat and the experience of the preceding December.[12]

May 1 passed quietly at Fredericksburg. Federal units mounted weak demonstrations in the course of the day, but no firing broke the silence along the river. The enemy remained entrenched at their bridgeheads and in obvious strength on the east side of the Rappahannock.[13] To the west, Lee and Jackson met Hooker's advancing columns on the edge of the Wilderness, seized the initiative, and ended the day near the crossroads at Chancellorsville.

Dawn on Saturday, May 2, revealed another uneventful scene. Pendleton arrived at Early's headquarters shortly after sunrise. Early informed the artillerist that "by General Lee's order, you would, within half an hour, feel the enemy by opening on him your long-range guns" and that he intended to start two brigades toward Lee if the Federals failed to respond aggressively to the fire.[14] Soon Confederate guns pounded the crossing points. Later in the morning, Pendleton and Barksdale reported Federals concentrating near

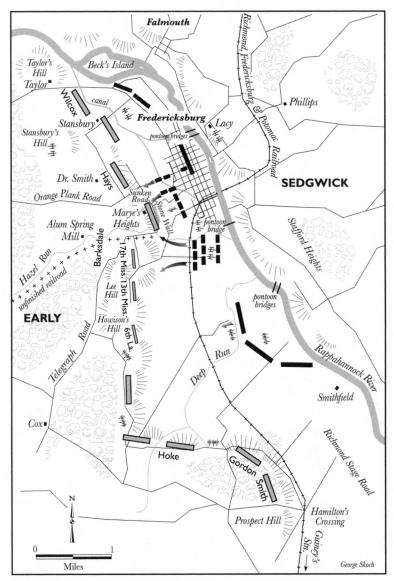

Battlefield at Second Fredericksburg, May 3, 1863

Falmouth and suggested it might be premature to send reinforcements to Lee. Early joined them on Lee's Hill, whence he hoped to discern what Union activity across the river portended. "[A]t about 11 o'clock A.M.," Early later wrote, "Colonel R. H. Chilton, of General Lee's staff, came to me with a verbal order to move immediately up towards Chancellorsville with my whole force, except a brigade of infantry and a part of Pendleton's reserve artillery." Those left behind would hold the enemy as long as possible, then retire in the direction of Spotsylvania Court House.[15]

Early protested that such a movement would be detected immediately, inviting a Federal assault against the remaining defenders. Pendleton added his own objections. Chilton "repeated his orders with great distinctness in the presence of General Pendleton," observed Early after the war, "and in reply to questions from us, said that there could be no mistake in his orders." In the midst of this tense conversation, Early learned that the enemy had abandoned their bridgehead at Smithfield but retained the one at the mouth of Deep Run. The Federals at Falmouth might be preparing to march toward Hooker, he conceded to Chilton, but thousands of them still menaced Fredericksburg. Moreover, he believed, "we were then keeping away from the army, opposed to General Lee, a much larger body of troops than my force could engage or neutralize if united to the army near Chancellorsville." Chilton ended the discussion by observing that Lee had considered all the points raised by Early and Pendleton, "but he was satisfied the great battle had to be fought upon the left, and had determined to get all the available force there." That settled the matter. Full of misgivings but a loyal subordinate, Early immediately issued orders that would leave Hays's brigade and one of Barksdale's regiments at Fredericksburg while the rest of the soldiers marched to reinforce Lee. Pendleton would remain behind to oversee the removal of most of the guns.[16]

Because of the need to mask the movement, it took several hours to set the division in motion. The head of the column was approaching the Plank Road just before dark when Early received a note from Lee indicating that Chilton had misrepresented his wishes: Early was to withdraw from Fredericksburg only if he could do so safely.[17] In language vindicating Early's own military judgment, Lee also granted his lieutenant the latitude to remain in place if he believed he could tie down a large number of Federals, which would "do as much or perhaps more service than by joining him." Certain the enemy at Fredericksburg had discovered his withdrawal, Early decided to press on. His lead units had progressed about a mile west on the Plank Road when a courier from Barksdale brought word that Federals had advanced in force against Hays and Pendleton. An artillerist who overheard this message delivered to Early recalled that "General Pendleton said if he did not come to his relief he would lose all the artillery." Barksdale already had turned back with his regiments, as had John B. Gordon, who offered to assist Barksdale without orders from Early. A divided command would accomplish little, reasoned Early, and he "determined to return at once to my former position," sending Major Hale to apprise Lee of his decision and another messenger to Barksdale. "We regained our former lines without trouble about ten or eleven o'clock at night," wrote Early about the conclusion of a stressful countermarch. "Barksdale occupied his old position and Hays returned during the night to the right of my line." While the Confederates were hurrying back to Fredericksburg, thought Early, Sedgwick "might have smashed every thing to pieces, but for his excessive caution." [18]

May 3 unfolded as a series of crises. William Barksdale appeared at Early's headquarters before sunrise to report Federals crossing the river at Fredericksburg. The previous evening Barksdale had complained about Early's inattention to his part of the line, remarking that it was hard to "sleep with a million of armed Yankees all around him." [19] Early dispatched Hays's brigade to bolster Barksdale, giving the latter authority for its placement. Daylight revealed that Sedgwick had shifted his entire force to the west side of the river. The Federals manifestly contemplated a major blow—but where? Although musketry and cannon fire had broken out to the north, Early still believed his right, where Federals were visible in the largest number, to be the most vulnerable. The valley of Deep Run also lay open to attack. He considered Barksdale's position the "strongest in natural and artificial defences & . . . better guarded by artillery" than any other part of the line. Col. Benjamin G. Humphreys of the 21st Mississippi, whose soldiers manned the trenches on Marye's Heights and had helped repulse two feeble Union assaults before 7:00 A.M. on May 3, agreed that initial Federal dispositions "seemed to justify the suspicians of Gen. Early, that the real attack would be made at Hamilton Station, and that the attack at Marye's Hill was only a feint and a feeler." [20]

The Confederates blunted a Federal demonstration against Deep Run shortly after sunrise, after which "heavy bodies of infantry were seen passing up towards Fredericksburg." Confederates opposite the town believed a major attack soon would be directed at them. Four of Hays's regiments went into line on Barksdale's left, north of the Plank Road, while the 6th Louisiana extended his right to Howison's Hill. Cadmus M. Wilcox, whose brigade had been covering Banks's

Ford, arrived at Taylor's Hill and promised further assistance should Barksdale require it. Early heard about the failed assaults against Marye's Heights from Barksdale and Pendleton but worried that the Federals moving toward Fredericksburg might presage a more serious effort in that quarter. The brigades of Hoke, Gordon, and Smith, in that order left to right, maintained positions between Deep Run and Hamilton's Crossing. Watching the battlefield from a point on Hoke's line, Early sent Lt. William G. Calloway of his staff to Lee's Hill to warn Barksdale and Pendleton of the Federal shift upriver and to "ascertain how they were getting on." When the aide failed to return expeditiously, Early rode toward Lee's Hill himself.[21]

Three riders met him en route to Lee's Hill. The first announced that Federals had been reported on Marye's Hill; the second, a courier from Pendleton, reported that northern attacks had been repulsed. Within minutes of hearing the cheering news from Pendleton, Early saw Calloway spurring toward him. His aide had just left Lee's Hill, where Barksdale and Pendleton had expressed confidence in their ability to hold off the enemy. But shortly after leaving the generals, Calloway had seen "that the enemy certainly had carried the heights."[22] Early eventually would learn that Sedgwick had sent columns against Stansbury's Hill, Lee's Hill, and Marye's Heights and that the Federals, at first repulsed at all points, had carried Barksdale's center by massing overwhelming strength opposite the 18th Mississippi and three companies of the 21st Mississippi holding the Sunken Road. Eight pieces of artillery and a significant number of prisoners fell into Federal hands.[23]

There would be time later to digest the particulars; for now, Sedgwick's success had compromised the entire Confederate line and Early acted quickly to limit the damage. He ordered Gordon to hasten forward from his position on the extreme right, then made his way to the Telegraph Road, where he rallied some guns that, together with elements of Barksdale's command and the 6th Louisiana, slowed the enemy's progress. Early directed a fighting withdrawal along the Telegraph Road, instructing Barksdale to make a stand at the Cox house, some two miles in the rear of Lee's Hill. There the men of Gordon's and Hays's brigades, supported by artillery, would join the Mississippians. Satisfied that the line at Cox's house could hold, Early rode to his right, where he directed Smith and Hoke to move their brigades and Andrews his battalion of artillery into positions closer to Barksdale. "We quickly and with good order formed a line of battle at right angles with our former one," stated a soldier in the 38th Georgia of Gordon's brigade, "and by the time that it was formed it was late at night." Early returned to the Cox house briefly before riding across Hazel Run to observe the Federals, who at first were moving slowly westward and eventually halted along the Plank Road.[24]

As he returned from his reconnaissance of Sedgwick's column, Early met Maj. Ellison L. Costin of Lafayette McLaws's staff at Hazel Run. Lt. Andrew L. Pitzer of Early's staff, present on Lee's Hill when Marye's Heights fell, had ridden immediately to apprise Lee of the situation, and the commanding general had dispatched McLaws to help stop Sedgwick. Early had fulfilled his primary mission of holding Sedgwick in check while Lee dealt with the main Union force, but now the eastern component of Hooker's army required greater attention. That afternoon elements of McLaws's division joined Cadmus Wilcox's brigade, which had disputed the Federal advance westward from Fredericksburg for several hours, to turn Sedgwick back near Salem Church. Costin conveyed Lee's wish that Early and McLaws cooperate to attack Sedgwick,[25] but only an hour of daylight remained, too little time for Smith's and Hoke's troops to get in position. Early immediately sent a note to McLaws informing him that he would gather his forces that night and attack the Federals early the next morning with the goal of driving them from Lee's Hill and Marye's Heights, cutting them off from Fredericksburg, and pressing their left flank north of the Plank Road. In the course of the advance, he would extend his left to touch McLaws's right. "I asked General McLaws' cooperation in this plan," Early wrote in his memoirs. "During the night, I received a note from him assenting to my plan and containing General Lee's approval of it also."[26]

McLaws confirmed in his official report and in a postwar narrative that Early proposed to retake the high ground on May 4 and that Lee approved the plan, but neither account mentions Early's request that McLaws cooperate in a more general assault. Yet in a message to McLaws dated midnight on May 3, Lee supported Early's plan "if it is practicable" and expressed a desire that if possible McLaws press the Federals "so as to prevent their concentrating on General Early."[27]

Expecting opposition from Federals on Lee's Hill and Marye's Heights, Early planned to employ his full force. Gordon's brigade would advance along the Telegraph Road with Barksdale's and Smith's behind it as a second line; the brigades of Hays and Hoke would cross to the north bank of Hazel Run and then move east along that stream. The initial assaults would cut the Federal connection to Fredericksburg, after which Early expected Gordon and Smith to move north toward the Rappahannock and west along the Plank Road while Hays and Hoke, shifting their focus to the north, would attack toward the Plank Road while extending their left to unite with McLaws's right flank. Barksdale's brigade would hold Marye's Heights and Lee's Hill against any Federal move from the east.[28] The goal was to force Sedgwick out of his strong position, which approximated a huge U with its flanks anchored on the Rappahannock near Banks's Ford and Taylor's Hill and its middle bulging across the Plank Road with its center north of the Downman house.

Early positioned Gordon's brigade at first light before accompanying Hoke's and Hays's brigades to their starting point north of Hazel Run. Expecting to accompany Gordon's men, he returned to find that the Georgian already had begun his movement. Surprised by Gordon's departure, Early ordered Barksdale and Smith to follow at once. Gordon's advance went beautifully, encountering no Federals on Lee's Hill and clearing Marye's Heights and Cemetery Hill with a rapid and nearly bloodless dash against Federals posted along the Plank Road west of the Marye House. "[F]or two miles we saw not a Yankee," wrote Adj. William C. Mathews of the 38th Georgia, "but on ascending a hill near the old plank road we got a sight of them in line of battle behind the road that afforded some protection to them. . . . [B]efore we could get near the road the Yankees were going like a parcel of sheep through the woods, having wounded but three in our regiment." Another of Gordon's men remarked that "the yankees made the poorest stand in this fight I ever saw. . . . I never saw yankees Skeedadle so in all my life." [29] Early directed Smith's brigade across Hazel Run to support Gordon and sent Barksdale's brigade, which Early later claimed had halted without orders a mile behind Lee's Hill, to occupy the Sunken Road below Marye's Heights and then push into Fredericksburg to capture a train of Federal wagons. Irritated at the time that Barksdale made no aggressive move toward the wagons, Early later discovered that a division of Federal troops occupied the town.[30]

Early had isolated Sedgwick from Fredericksburg and anxiously listened for the sounds of firing on McLaws's front. Gordon and

Smith were north of the Plank Road opposite Federals who had dug in facing east and southeast. Thinking Sedgwick's left might lack proper artillery support, Early ordered Smith to "feel the enemy on the heights on the Plank Road, above Fredericksburg." Heavy artillery from Taylor's Hill greeted Smith's soldiers, and Early instructed them to withdraw.[31] It was shortly after 8:00 A.M., and Early had made an excellent start on the plan sketched the previous night. More success would come only with McLaws's assistance, so Early sent Lieutenant Pitzer to ask the Georgian to open his attack. The messenger assured McLaws that Hoke's and Hays's brigades could be moved rapidly into position to connect on his right and that once the battle shifted toward the west Early would commit Gordon and Smith as well. In his report, McLaws stated that "General Early sent me word by his staff officer that, if I would attack in front, he would advance two brigades and strike at the flank and rear of the enemy. I agreed to advance, provided he would first attack, and did advance my right (Kershaw and Wofford) to co-operate with him; but finding my force was insufficient for a front attack, I withdrew to my line of the evening previous, General Early not attacking, as I could hear." In fact, none of McLaws's men took any aggressive action. McLaws did inform Lee of Early's request "and my objections to it and asked for additional forces." Receiving word that the balance of Richard H. Anderson's division was on its way from Chancellorsville, McLaws "directed that no attack should be made until General Anderson arrived." [32]

Pitzer related all of this to Early, whose cue to join a general attack against Sedgwick would be three cannons fired rapidly in succession. Soon Hoke settled into position southeast of the Downman house with Hays on his right near Alum Spring Mill. Anderson's brigades arrived at Salem Church before noon, as did Lee himself, who probably believed his presence necessary to prod McLaws into action.[33] Early's troops were ready by that time, but several hours dragged by as Anderson's brigades deployed between McLaws and Early. Edward Porter Alexander, whose artillery battalion stood ready to support the Confederate offensive, recalled Lee's ill humor at the delay. Based on Lee's conversations with him and with others within his earshot, Alexander mentioned three possible causes of the general's pique: "1st. That a great deal of valuable time had been already uselessly lost by somebody, some how, no particulars being given. 2nd. Nobody knew exactly how or where the enemy's line of

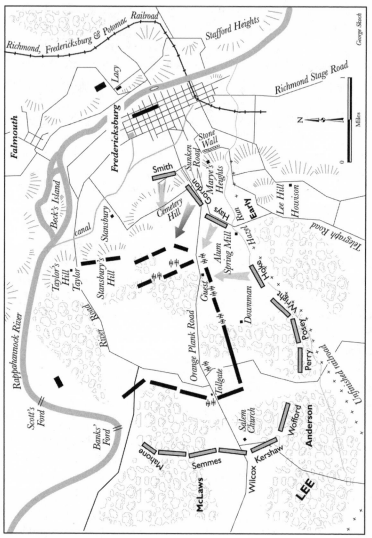

George Skoch

Battlefields at Second Fredericksburg and Salem Church, May 3–4, 1863

battle ran & it was somebody's duty to know. 3rd. That it now de-
volved on him personally to use up a lot more time to find out all
about the enemy before we could move a peg."³⁴

Lee presently joined Early along Hoke's line to discuss the impending attack. The Confederate commander found at least one of
his major generals prepared to take action. Early explained that he
planned for Hoke and Hays to advance to the Plank Road, where they
would pivot to the west, with Hays continuing the assault along the
north and Hoke the south side of that thoroughfare. Gordon would
strike toward the Taylor house, turning Sedgwick's left flank, while
"Extra Billy" Smith's brigade remained in reserve as potential reinforcements. If McLaws and Anderson applied concomitant pressure, Sedgwick's line surely must give way. Lee approved the plan,
directed Early to commence as soon as he heard the three-gun signal, then returned to Anderson's sector at about 2:00 P.M.³⁵

Capt. Richard Watson York of the 6th North Carolina in Hoke's
brigade later asserted that Lee's appearance reinvigorated many of
Early's soldiers. Because of the "marching and countermarching" of
the preceding two days, the "men and officers became thoroughly
demoralized. They had lost confidence in every body." The Federal
position looked strong, and rumors circulated that "Gen. Early was
drunk and was going to order a charge which would be disastrous."
Although York knew the rumor "was utterly false," the unit never
had seemed so "utterly and generally demoralised—I confess I, myself, to some extent participated." As soon as the men detected Lee's
presence, "every man instinctively commenced getting ready. The
word soon went down the line 'All is right, Uncle Robert is here. We
will whip them.'"³⁶

Following Lee's departure, another four hours crawled by before
the three signal guns announced the opening of the attack. Whether
inspired by Lee or not, Hoke's soldiers and those of Harry Hays exhibited admirable energy. Hoke's men moved across the plateau between the Downman property and Hazel Run, descended into the
creek bottom, then climbed the opposite ridge toward the Plank
Road. Hays's brigade kept pace to the right, while Gordon's regiments made progress toward Taylor's Hill. The advance of Hoke's
North Carolinians and Hays's Louisianians—the same soldiers who
two months hence would struggle up East Cemetery Hill at Gettysburg in another memorable assault—exhilarated Early, who
watched from a point near the Telegraph Road opposite Alum

Spring Mill and later termed it "a splendid sight."[37] Federal artillery near the Guest House had retired in the face of the attack, and the enemy's infantry also gave ground. Just as the brigades seemed poised to achieve significant success, Hoke received a crippling wound. Col. Isaac E. Avery assumed command but knew nothing of Early's instructions, and the brigade floundered across the Plank Road, drifting rightward into the path of Hays's men. Confusion resulted in woods north of the road as officers struggled in vain to regain momentum amid increasing darkness. An officer in Hays's brigade insisted that some of the North Carolinians fired into the rear of the Louisiana troops, while Federals poured musketry into their front.[38]

Early had spurred across Hazel Run toward the Plank Road when it seemed his brigades would sweep the enemy from the field. He arrived to find the disorganized men of Hays's brigade withdrawing from the woods. Reorganizing them and Hoke's survivors on open ground below the Guest house, Early also summoned two regiments from Smith's command. By the time they appeared and the other brigades reformed, "it had become too dark to make any further advance." Nightfall also stopped Gordon, who had reached a position near the Taylor house after driving the enemy back a good distance. After dark, Early met with Lee at the Downman house, receiving instructions to leave Gordon and Hoke perpendicular to the Plank Road facing west and shifting Smith and Hays eastward to go into line on either side of Barksdale's brigade.[39]

That night Sedgwick recrossed the Rappahannock, frustrating Lee's hope of defeating him decisively. Early shared Lee's disappointment with the result. The brigades of Hoke, Hays, and Gordon "fought the main action" on May 4, Early subsequently asserted, adding that only "two of Anderson's brigades, Posey's and Wright's, became engaged at all." Not until he was re-forming Hays's and Hoke's brigades had he seen "some of Anderson's men coming up and it was then near dark." "Had Anderson attacked with vigor, and McLaws come down," Early concluded, "there would have been no escape for Sedgwick."[40]

Although somewhat unfair to Anderson's men, Early's assessment generally was accurate. McLaws had spent May 4 as a bystander. His muddled report stated that late in the day "Distant firing in the direction of Fredericksburg was heard, indicating that the attack had commenced on the extreme right. Night now came

*Maj. Gen. Lafayette McLaws, who looks thinner and better groomed in this en-graving than in wartime photographs. At Salem Church on May 4, 1863, Lee lost patience with McLaws, whose lethargic behavior contrasted sharply with Jubal Early's aggressive demeanor. (*Southern Illustrated News, *April 4, 1863)*

rapidly on, and nothing could be observed of our operations." Even more revealing about his utter confusion during the last day's fighting, McLaws's postwar narrative devotes only a single sentence to May 4: "In response [to my message] Gen. Lee came in person with Gen. Anderson's Division and under his direction, as he states in his orders I have quoted, Sedgwick's command was driven over the river." This inept performance did not go unnoticed. While preparing a major speech about Chancellorsville in the late 1870s, Fitzhugh Lee was baffled by McLaws's behavior on May 4. "I am not going to find fault with anybody—because I know the difference between *hind*sight & *fore* sight—," Lee wrote Early, "but between you & I, what was the matter with McLaws in connection with the attack on Sedgwick on Tuesday 4th May!" Between the lines of Robert E. Lee's report, anyone could read implicit criticism of McLaws: "The speedy approach of darkness prevented General McLaws from perceiving the success of the attack until the enemy began to recross the river a short distance below Banks' Ford." [41]

The fighting on May 4 closed a week during which Jubal Early stepped into the circle of Lee's primary lieutenants. Newspaper coverage told him what later historical treatment confirmed: The action at Fredericksburg and Salem Church always would remain in the imposing shadow of Lee and Jackson's masterpiece in the Wilderness. [42] Crowded out of the headlines by dramatic details of Jackson's flank attack and Hooker's withdrawal from Chancellorsville, events at Fredericksburg and Salem Church also struck many as unfortunate brushstrokes on an otherwise perfect canvas. Artillerist William Ransom Johnson Pegram, who had fought brilliantly with the Confederate guns at Hazel Grove on May 3, speculated eight days later that "the greatest victory of the war" would have been even more resounding had Early "managed better below at Fredericksburg." On May 3, a gunner with Early's division expressed disgust with the Federal capture of Marye's Heights: "It is thought gross mismanagement somewhere has caused this loss," he wrote, adding that the "surprise was shameful." Silent about whether he blamed Early or Barksdale, this man placed his hope in Lee and Jackson, who according to rumor had whipped the enemy at Chancellorsville and "can very easily wipe out those now on this side of Fredericksburg." [43]

Whatever the consensus on the army's grapevine, Early knew he had the good opinion of his commander. Lee had selected him for an important post with wide discretion, approved his plans on May 3 for an offensive against Sedgwick at Salem Church, and, after seeking him out on May 4, once again sustained his judgment about how best to attack the enemy. Habitually economical with official praise for subordinates, Lee included a sentence in his report certain to gratify Old Jube: "Major General Early performed the important and responsible duty intrusted to him in a manner which reflected credit upon himself and his command."[44]

Early's conduct fully merited Lee's approbation. He had presided over the defense of an extensive line with relatively very few men. He met the initial Federal crossings with dispatch, and although questioned then and later, his placement of the bulk of his soldiers south of Deep Run was prudent in light of both the Federal deployment and the Confederate experience at First Fredericksburg. Had he massed more troops along the ridges north of Lee's Hill, the area from Deep Run to Hamilton's Crossing would have offered Sedgwick a more tempting target than did Barksdale's position on May 3. His decision to turn back to Fredericksburg after reaching the Plank Road on May 2 bespoke a grasp of the value of concentrated strength. When Barksdale requested assistance on May 3, Early immediately sent Hays's brigade. In the chaotic aftermath of the Confederate retreat from the hills west of Fredericksburg, Early supplied vigorous personal leadership along the Telegraph Road, maneuvered his brigades into strong positions, and then turned his attention to recapturing the initiative the next day. No evidence of panic accompanied any of his actions through May 3, and on the final day's battle his aggressiveness stood out among the three major generals on the field.

Some critics have argued that without Cadmus Wilcox's stout service on the afternoon of May 3 none of Early's efforts would have mattered. He also displayed a somewhat ungenerous spirit toward Barksdale and his men. But on balance Early justified his chief's confidence in him and staked a claim to larger responsibility in the future. The soldierly qualities he exhibited while in direct contact with Lee during the campaign helped bring him independent command in the Shenandoah Valley the following summer.[45]

A controversy with Barksdale in the wake of the campaign highlighted Early's sensitivity to criticism as well as his complete deference to Lee. In a letter to the editors of the *Richmond Enquirer* dated May 11, 1863, Early complained about "correspondents ignorant of the real facts, or writing in the interests of particular commands," who had offered flawed accounts of the capture of Marye's Heights. He bridled at the suggestion that he had failed to support the Mississippians defending the heights, calling attention to his transfer of Hays's brigade in prompt response to Barksdale's request for help.

Three regiments of Wilcox's brigade added additional strength to the northern end of the line. "This left only three brigades on the long and comparatively weak line from the heights in rear of Fredericksburg to the mouth of the Massaponax to confront the heavy columns of the enemy on this side at the mouth of Deep Run," remarked Early, "while there were two brigades and three regiments of another to defend the strong and comparatively short line in rear of and above Fredericksburg." Moreover, Barksdale benefited from the strongest natural position and the best artillery support along a seven-mile Confederate line for which Early had no reserves.

Professing to cast no censure on Barksdale's unit, Early chose language certain to provoke a response: "I will state that my division did not lose Marye's Hill, but one of my brigades (Gordon's, formerly Lawton's,) recaptured it before 9 o'clock on the next morning, and three of my brigades (Hays's, Hoke's, and Gordon's,) bore the brunt of the fight when the enemy was driven back across the River, Barksdale's brigade and Smith's, of my own division, having been left to keep the enemy in check from the direction of Fredericksburg." He had done all in his power to "avert the disaster, and to correct and retrieve it" and was "willing to abide by the judgment of the commanding General upon my own conduct and that of my division." [46]

Barksdale answered with barely controlled anger on May 13.[47] Resenting the "gratuitous and unfounded" insinuation that members of his brigade had complained to the press, Barksdale had been unaware that Early's "conduct in the late engagements around Fredericksburg had been made the subject of newspaper censure until I saw it announced over his own signature." Barksdale correctly pointed out that when he asked for help on the morning of May 3, his brigade covered a front "of not less than three miles" from Taylor's Hill to Howison's Hill rather than the " 'short line in rear of and to the left of Fredericksburg,' as stated by Gen. Early." Describing in detail his deployment and the course of the battle, he concluded that "It will thus be seen that Marye's hill was defended by one small regiment, three companies and four pieces of artillery, and not by the entire brigade. A more heroic struggle was never made by a mere handful of men against overwhelming odds." Early's letter produced the impression that Gordon's brigade drove the Federals from a position the Mississippians had failed to hold the day before. "I would scorn," stated Barksdale, "to detract from the well-earned reputation of this brigade and its gallant commander; but the truth is, the enemy had abandoned Marye's heights, and Gen. Gordon took possession without opposition."

Early responded to Barksdale's letter the same day he read it in the *Enquirer*.[48] Surprised at Barksdale's reaction to a letter intended only to deny the rumor that the Mississippians had fought without adequate support on May 3, Early reminded Barksdale that "shortly after the capture of Marye's hill by the enemy, he had stated to me that he had previously felt no uneasiness about the safety of his position, as he deemed it impregnable, but had felt a good deal of anxiety about my position on the right, which had been threatened all morning by a column of the enemy moving up Deep Run." Early loftily observed that he would shun a controversy that "accords neither with my taste nor sense of military propriety," contenting himself with correcting Barksdale's claims "that the enemy had abandoned Marye's hill on the 4th, and that it was taken possession of without opposition." Barksdale could not have known the situation on the hill because he and his brigade were "in the rear, and out of sight" of the action. Federals arrayed behind the Plank Road had resisted Gordon's advance, with assistance from a pair of nearby brigades on high ground near the upper mill on Hazel Run. With these comments, Early would "abstain from all further notice of this matter."

Barksdale's final volley appeared in mid-June. Flatly denying Early's version of their conversation after the fall of the heights, he insisted that from Lee's Hill he saw no threat along Deep Run to Early's right and neither felt nor expressed "solicitude as to his position." A mass of Federals evident in Fredericksburg did inspire doubts about the safety of his own line. As for Gordon's actions on the 4th, "I have the amplest testimony in my possession to establish it, that Marye's Hill had been abandoned, and that whatever engagement Gen. Gordon may have had with the enemy on Monday morning, was beyond the plank road, and to the left of Marye's hill." Barksdale published simultaneously a letter dated May 14, 1863, in which Early requested a detailed report of his operations so that Early could "do full justice to your brigade." "I am satisfied that the carrying [of] Marye's hill could not well have been avoided," stated this letter. "The whole line was exposed for want of reserves, and the enemy made his most determined and desperate effort against

William Barksdale in a late-antebellum photograph (there is no likeness of him from the war years). Barksdale's full wig appears to perch precariously above his high forehead. (National Archives)

the part defended by your brigade. . . . [A]ll of our troops, including yours, did their duty under the trying circumstances in which they were placed." [49]

Was there a winner in this episode? Early *had* supported Barksdale on May 3 and justly resented implications to the contrary, but the tone of his letters surely left readers with a sense that Barksdale and his men may have behaved less gallantly than the soldiers of Gordon, Hays, and Hoke. He also misrepresented the length of Barksdale's line and the number of men available at the crucial point. As for Gordon's "fight" on Marye's Heights on May 4, Early's own report, written several days before his first letter to the editors, stated that "Gordon succeeded in capturing Marye's Hill with ease." The problem may have been one of semantics: Federals along the Plank Road certainly did oppose Gordon, but they were not on the part of Marye's Heights associated with the fighting on December 13, 1862, and May 3, 1863. In the absence of corroborating evidence on one side or the other, it is impossible to say which of the men dissembled about the conversation after the Federals captured the heights.

Because Early instigated the exchange and was the senior officer, it reflected most negatively on him. A correspondent for the *Richmond Daily Dispatch* whose reporting initially had upset Early mocked the general and reprimanded him for tarnishing the victory: "I see that the *late* Gen. Early—Gen. Jubal—has shown his 'strategy' by poking his nose into a hornet's nest. It is no time for Confederates to quarrel." A friendlier piece in the *Enquirer* lauded the accomplishments of Early, Barksdale, and all their soldiers before scolding that "This is no time for bickerings and newspaper controversies among our braves in the field."[50]

A born controversialist (despite his second letter's profession of distaste for such jousting), Early probably would have answered Barksdale's second letter had Lee not intervened. Always eager to quiet friction among his often-disputatious subordinates, the commanding general reprimanded Early for airing grievances in public. "You gave me a mild rebuke for that," Early reminded Lee after the war, "and I never repeated the offence, not even when I was so unjustly assailed in regard to my valley campaign." No evidence reveals whether Barksdale received a similar rebuke from Lee.[51]

In the postwar years, Early paid close attention to writings about the Confederate experience. Believing his own operations were imperfectly understood, he published a memoir of his 1864 Valley campaign.[52] He sent Lee a copy of this book in the fall of 1866, asking if the general minded his expanding the account to embrace the earlier period of the conflict. "I have no objection to the publication of the narrative of your operations before leaving the Army of N. Va.," replied Lee. "I would recommend however that while giving the facts which you think necessary for your own vindication, that you omit all epithets or remarks calculated to excite bitterness or animosity between different sections of the Country." Widely known as a sarcastic man given to extreme statements, Early nonetheless approached his recollections with the instincts of a scholar. He asked a former aide to gather his military papers and send them to Canada. "I desire to write an account of my whole experiences and observations during the war," explained Early, "and I desire to obtain all the documents in regard to my command which I can." Among the items he mentioned as especially important were reports and other items relating to the Chancellorsville campaign.[53]

Early sent Lee the portion of his narrative covering Second Fredericksburg and Salem Church in late 1868.[54] In his cover letter, he explained at length how Gordon had met resistance on Marye's Heights on May 4. "General Barksdale felt a little sore about the loss of the heights," he added, "which he need not have done, and seemed to think it necessary, in order to defend his brigade, to depreciate the services of my division." Early hoped Lee would agree that the narrative was fair to all concerned in this phase of the battle. As for Salem Church, he disputed Richard Anderson's official report, which spoke of Early's and Anderson's brigades encountering only slight resistance on May 4. Hays and Hoke and Gordon had met fierce fire, losing heavily and inflicting severe loss on the enemy: "My pioneer party, buried, next day, more than 200 of the enemy picked up on the ground on which my brigades had fought."[55]

Early's narrative and comments to Lee defended the honor of his division against explicit and implied criticisms in earlier published accounts. He probably had seen Benjamin G. Humphreys's piece on Second Fredericksburg in the *Land We Love*, wherein the author scoffed at the notion that Gordon "recaptured" Marye's Heights: "[I]f 'recaptured' at all, it was by the ladies of Fredericksburg (God bless them,) who were found there quietly searching for wounded Mississippians, by . . . [members of Barksdale's brigade] in advance of Gordon's brigade of Early's division." He certainly had read Edward A. Pollard's four massive volumes on the Confederate war, the second of which spoke of "two remarkable misfortunes" that diminished Lee's victory at Chancellorsville. "The breaking of our lines at Fredericksburg" caused Lee to break off pursuit of Hooker at Chancellorsville, averred Pollard, and the failure to trap Sedgwick at Salem Church "robbed us of a complete success." Such passages undoubtedly infuriated Early, who lamented the fact that newspaper accounts and "Pollard's abominable books furnish the main source of information" about "the operations of Confederate armies."[56]

Early thought more highly of William Allan and Jedediah Hotchkiss's book on Chancellorsville, published in New York in 1867, but considered it deficient on Second Fredericksburg and Salem Church. "The description of the fighting at Fredericksburg is in accordance with the published reports, and it is not inaccurate," Early commented to Hotchkiss, "but it is not as full or minute as it might have been, had there been the material for writing a fuller account." Blame for the dearth of information lay with Early, who had failed to write a long report. "I now regret it very much," he admitted, "as it has prevented Allan's description from being perfect."[57]

Less than eight months after writing Hotchkiss, Early sent his own narrative of the campaign to Lee. He presumably considered it as close to "perfect" as possible but chose not to publish it during his lifetime. Why would he withhold an account that answered, in restrained and meticulous fashion, every question about his performance along the Rappahannock in April and May 1863? His return to the United States shortly after writing Lee disrupted his routine in the short term, and the need to earn a living as a lawyer left him pressed for time over the next few years. After the mid-1870s, however, a handsome annual income from the Louisiana Lottery freed him to pursue whatever he chose. Yet the narrative lay buried amid his voluminous personal papers.

The editors of *Century Magazine* offered Early a prominent national forum in 1884. Asking him to contribute his reminiscences of the Chancellorsville campaign for their war series, they emphasized their preference for colorful anecdotal material over an "official report" style. Early sniffed at the notion of writing for effect rather than seeking accuracy based on the records. He also disdained the practice of accepting money for military reminiscences (he had donated the meager proceeds from his earlier memoir to a variety of groups and individuals). In declining the invitation, he mentioned "that I had discovered that the practice of paying for articles in regard to the war had produced an immense deal of lying, as when such articles were paid for according to their length, their authors, to eke out their pay, had drawn on their imagination for their facts." Clarence Clough Buel tried to recruit Early again in 1887 when the Century Company decided to publish *Battles and Leaders of the Civil War*. The books would find a large audience, predicted Buel accurately, and would be used by ordinary people and historians in the future. Despite his concern about history's judgment, Early declined to write a new piece. He gave permission for Century to print extracts from his official papers, however, and two excerpts from his *Memoir of the Last Year of the War* appeared in *Battles and Leaders*.[58]

Perhaps Early resisted publishing the portion of his reminiscences dealing with Chancellorsville because he wanted to present the story whole. In her "Editor's Note" to his posthumous *War Memoirs*, his niece observed that he worked on the manuscript "to the end of his life." Another clue lies in a letter from the mid-1880s. "I begin to despair of ever having a true history of the war written," he confessed to William H. Payne. "If I were to attempt one, and were to express my honest opinions, I would at once be called a crank." Did he contemplate inserting more inflammatory material into his narrative, restrained by Lee's injunction to refrain from sectional controversy? He told Payne that nine-tenths of everything written about Grant was untrue and closed with a bitter passage capturing years of frustration with what others had written about the conflict: "I begin to believe . . . that the Muse of history is nothing but a 'lying-bitch.'"[59] With his death in Lynchburg less than a decade later, all control over assessments of Early's performance during the Chancellorsville campaign passed into the hands of that fickle muse.

NOTES

1. Jubal A. Early to R. E. Lee, November 20, 1868, box 25, folder titled "Introductory Chapter (Notes & Pages of a Rough Draft) I," John Warwick Daniel Papers, Alderman Library, University of Virginia, Charlottesville (collection hereafter cited as Daniel Papers, UVA).

2. U.S. War Department, *The War of the Rebellion: A Compilation of the Official Records of the Union and Confederate Armies*, 127 vols., index, and atlas (Washington: GPO, 1880–1901), ser. 1, vol. 19, pt. 2:682 (hereafter cited as *OR*; all references are to ser. 1); T. J. Jackson to Samuel Cooper, November 21, 1862, box 1, T. J. Jackson File, SHSP, Eleanor S. Brockenbrough Library, Museum of the Confederacy, Richmond, Va.; *OR* 21:1099; Jubal A. Early to Richard S. Ewell, James A. Walker Compiled Service Record, microfilm roll 257, National Archives, Washington, D.C.

3. For a wartime reference to Lee's bestowing this nickname on Early, see the letter by "Phax" published in the *Mobile Advertiser*, September 15, 1864.

4. Although James Longstreet exercised independent command at Suffolk in the spring of 1863, the strategic circumstances were far less compelling than those confronting Jackson and Early during their semi-independent commands.

5. Robert Stiles, *Four Years under Marse Robert* (1903; reprint, Dayton, Ohio: Morningside, 1977), 188–89.

6. Jubal Anderson Early, *Lieutenant General Jubal Anderson Early, C.S.A.: Autobiographical Sketch and Narrative of the War between the States* (1912; reprint, Wilmington, N.C.: Broadfoot, 1989), 193–94 (hereafter cited as Early, *Memoirs*); *OR* 25(1):1000; William J. Seymour, *The Civil War Memoirs of Captain William J. Seymour: Reminiscences of a Louisiana Tiger,* ed. Terry L. Jones (Baton Rouge: Louisiana State University Press, 1991), 48; Jedediah Hotchkiss, *Make Me a Map of the Valley: The Civil War Journal of Stonewall Jackson's Topographer,* ed. Archie P. McDonald (Dallas, Tex.: Southern Methodist University Press, 1973), 135.

7. David E. Moore to John Warwick Daniel, [1907?], box 22, folder titled "Chancellorsville 1907," Daniel Papers, UVA. Moore did not include this anecdote in his *Story of a Cannoneer under Stonewall Jackson, in Which Is Told the Part Taken by the Rockbridge Artillery in the Army of Northern Virginia* (1907; reprint, Alexandria, Va.: Time-Life Books, 1981).

8. *OR* 25(1):796–97.

9. Early, *Memoirs,* 198. Early took the strength for his division from the April 20, 1863, trimonthly field return, which he had in his possession in Canada but which does not appear in the *Official Records.* John Bigelow Jr.'s careful *The Campaign of Chancellorsville: A Strategic and Tactical Study* (New Haven, Conn.: Yale University Press, 1910), 268 n. 2, credits Early with fifty-six guns.

10. Samuel D. Buck, *With the Old Confeds: Actual Experiences of a Captain in the Line* (Baltimore: H. E. Houck, 1925), 77.

11. Early, *Memoirs,* 197; *OR* 25(1):811, (2):765.

12. Early, *Memoirs,* 198–99; William Barksdale to the Editors of the *Enquirer,* May 13, 1863, printed in *Richmond Semi-Weekly Enquirer,* May 19, 1863, and in *Richmond Daily Dispatch,* May 21, 1863; *OR* 25(1):810–11.

13. Early, *Memoirs,* 199.

14. *OR* 25(1):811. Although he was chief of artillery for the army, Pendleton submitted his report through Early as overall commander on the Fredericksburg line.

15. Early, *Memoirs,* 200; *OR* 25(1):811–12, 1001. Pendleton's report also placed the time of the meeting with Chilton at about 11:00 A.M.

16. Early, *Memoirs,* 201–2; *OR* 25(1):812.

17. No explanation for Chilton's mistake ever was offered. Lee's report stated simply that on May 2 he repeated his orders to Early of May 1, "but by a misapprehension on the part of the officer conveying it, General Early was directed to move unconditionally. . . . [T]he mistake in the transmis-

sion of the order being corrected, General Early returned to his original position." Ibid., 800.

18. Early, *Memoirs*, 203–4; Jonathan Thomas Scharf, *The Personal Memoirs of Jonathan Thomas Scharf of the First Maryland Artillery*, ed. Tom Kelley (Baltimore: Butternut & Blue, 1992 [Scharf wrote his memoirs during the war]), 67; *OR* 25(1):813–14; Jubal A. Early to Jedediah Hotchkiss, March 24, 1868, Mss2H7973b2, Jedediah Hotchkiss Papers, Virginia Historical Society, Richmond (repository hereafter cited as VHS).

19. Benjamin G. Humphreys, "Recollections of Fredericksburg, from the Morning of the 29th of April to the 6th of May, 1863," *Land We Love* 3 (October 1867): 448; an abridged version of this article appeared in J. William Jones et al., eds., *Southern Historical Society Papers*, 52 vols. (1876–1959; reprint with 3-vol. index, Wilmington, N.C.: Broadfoot, 1990–92), 14:415–28 (hereafter cited as *SHSP*). The Confederates learned later that the Federals Barksdale reported to Early had marched upriver from the vicinity of Deep Run rather than crossing at Fredericksburg; a pontoon was not in place opposite the Lacy House at Fredericksburg until later in the morning.

20. Early, *Memoirs*, 204–5; Jubal A. Early to Editors of the *Enquirer*, May 11, 1863, printed in *Richmond Daily Dispatch*, May 13, 1863; Humphreys, "Recollections of Fredericksburg," 450.

21. Early, *Memoirs*, 206, 209; *OR* 25(1):840, 856.

22. Early, *Memoirs*, 209.

23. For excellent accounts of this fighting, see Humphreys, "Recollections of Fredericksburg"; Ernest B. Furgurson, *Chancellorsville 1863: The Souls of the Brave* (New York: Knopf, 1992), 258–66; and Douglas Southall Freeman, *Lee's Lieutenants: A Study in Command*, 3 vols. (New York: Scribner's, 1942–44), 2:613–18.

24. Early, *Memoirs*, 209–11; William C. Mathews to Dear Father, May 8, 1863, printed in the *Sandersville (Ga.) Central Georgian*, June 3, 1863.

25. Lee sent a note to Early, dated 7:00 P.M. on May 3, that asked him to join McLaws in the type of attack described by Costin. See *OR* 25(2):769–70.

26. Early, *Memoirs*, 220; *OR* 25(2):220, (1):1001.

27. *OR* (1):827; Lafayette McLaws, "The Battle of Chancellorsville[:] The Most Remarkable One of the War," 25, undated typescript, folder 31, Lafayette McLaws Papers, no. 472, Southern Historical Collection, Wilson Library, University of North Carolina, Chapel Hill; *OR* 25(2):770.

28. Early, *Memoirs*, 221–22.

29. Ibid., 223–24; William C. Mathews to Dear Father, May 8, 1863, printed in the *Sandersville (Ga.) Central Georgian,* June 3, 1863; George M. Bandy to William Strain and family, May 15, 1863, in James Parker et al., comps., *The Strain Family* (Toccoa, Ga.: Commercial Printing Company, 1985), 223.

30. Jubal A. Early to R. E. Lee, November 20, 1868, Daniel Papers, UVA; Early, *Memoirs,* 224–25.

31. *OR* 25(1):1002–3; Early, *Memoirs,* 225–26. Several dozen members of the 58th Virginia and a few from the 13th who refused to brave Federal fire to rejoin their comrades became prisoners; the 58th also lost its colors, which Early refused to allow the regiment to replace until it captured a Federal flag.

32. Early, *Memoirs,* 226–27; *OR* 25(1):1001–2, 827; McLaws, "Battle of Chancellorsville," 26.

33. In *R. E. Lee: A Biography,* 4 vols. (New York: Scribner's, 1934–35), 2:550, Douglas Southall Freeman's discussion of Lee's decision to supervise the battle on his right includes speculation that "Perhaps he was the more readily prompted to do this by his knowledge of McLaws, who as senior of the three division commanders would assume command. Lafayette McLaws was a professional soldier, careful of details and not lacking in soldierly qualities, but there was nothing daring, brilliant, or aggressive in his character."

34. Edward Porter Alexander, *Fighting for the Confederacy: The Personal Recollections of General Edward Porter Alexander,* ed. Gary W. Gallagher (Chapel Hill: University of North Carolina Press, 1989), 213.

35. Early, *Memoirs,* 227–28; Freeman, *R. E. Lee,* 2:554.

36. Richard Watson York to George Washington Custis Lee, November 28, 1872 (copy made available by Robert K. Krick), Fredericksburg and Spotsylvania National Military Park, Fredericksburg, Va.

37. After the war, Maj. David French Boyd, the commissary officer in Hays's brigade, told a colorful story of Early on the afternoon of May 4: "He and Lee were standing on a little eminence, to see the effect of the charge over that wide, open plateau, swept as it was by cannon in front and by the heavy batteries on the north side of the Rappahannock; and when Harry Hays burst through two lines of the Federal army as if they were but paper walls, old Jubal in his enthusiasm and joy, forgetting the august presence of Lee, threw his old white hat with black ploom on the ground, exclaiming; 'Those damned Louisiana fellows may steal as much as they please now!'" David French Boyd, *Reminiscences of the War in Virginia,* ed. T. Michael Par-

rish (Austin, Tex.: Jenkins Publishing Company, 1989), 34; Boyd's reminiscences first appeared in the *New Orleans Times-Democrat* on January 31 and February 7, 1897. Although Terry L. Jones, *Lee's Tigers: The Louisiana Infantry in the Army of Northern Virginia* (Baton Rouge: Louisiana State University Press, 1987), 155, and Furgurson, *Chancellorsville 1863*, 297, as well as other works, cite this appealing anecdote, there is no other evidence that Lee and Early were together during the final assaults on May 4.

38. Early, *Memoirs*, 229–30; Seymour, *Memoirs*, 55.

39. Early, *Memoirs*, 232–33; *OR* 25(1):1002.

40. Jubal A. Early to Jedediah Hotchkiss, March 24, 1868, VHS; Jubal A. Early to R. E. Lee, November 20, 1868, Daniel Papers, UVA. See also Early, *Memoirs*, 230–31.

41. *OR* 25(1):828, 802; McLaws, "Battle of Chancellorsville," 26; Fitzhugh Lee to Jubal A. Early, July 31, 1879, Jubal A. Early Papers, Library of Congress, Washington, D.C. Lee's address is in *SHSP* 7:545–85. Confederate artillerist David Gregg McIntosh argued that Early should have attacked Sedgwick's left at Salem Church on May 3, suggesting that his failure to do so may have influenced McLaws's actions on May 4: "It would be uncharitable at this day to impute to McLaws any feeling of pique because of Early's failure.... But his conduct is inconsistent with the fine reputation he bore in the Army of Northern Virginia as one of its most tried and experienced division commanders." David Gregg McIntosh, "The Campaign of Chancellorsville," in *SHSP* 40:96–97.

42. For this essay, a canvass of the *Richmond Semi-Weekly Enquirer, Richmond Daily Dispatch,* and *Richmond Sentinel* between May 5 and June 1 revealed far greater attention to Chancellorsville than to Second Fredericksburg and Salem Church.

43. William Ransom Johnson Pegram to Mary Pegram, May 11, 1863, in James I. Robertson Jr., " 'The Boy Artillerist': Letters of William Ransom Johnson Pegram, C.S.A.," *Virginia Magazine of History and Biography* 98 (April 1990): 238; William B. Pettit to Arabella Speairs Pettit, May 3, 1863, in Charles W. Turner, ed., *Civil War Letters of Arabella Speairs and William Beverley Pettit of Fluvanna County, Virginia, March 1862–March 1865* (Roanoke, Va.: Virginia Lithography and Graphics, 1988), 106–7.

44. *OR* 25(1):803.

45. For a somewhat uneven analysis of Early's performance at Chancellorsville, see Freeman, *Lee's Lieutenants*, 2:653–54.

46. Jubal A. Early to the Editors of the *Enquirer*, May 11, 1863, printed in *Richmond Daily Dispatch*, May 13, 1863. The original letter, which dif-

fers in minor ways from the printed version quoted in this essay and which Barksdale read, is in the Early Papers, LC.

47. William Barksdale to the Editors of the *Enquirer,* May 13, 1863, printed in *Richmond Semi-Weekly Enquirer,* May 19, 1863. The *Daily Dispatch* ran Barksdale's letter on May 21.

48. Jubal A. Early to the Editors of the *Enquirer,* May 19, 1863, printed in the *Richmond Semi-Weekly Enquirer,* May 27, 1863. The original, which differs in minor ways from the printed version, is in the Early Papers, LC.

49. William Barksdale to the Editors of the *Enquirer,* May 31, 1863, and Jubal A. Early to William Barksdale, May 14, 1863, printed in the *Richmond Daily Enquirer,* June 15, 1863.

50. *Richmond Daily Dispatch,* May 15, 1863; *Richmond Semi-Weekly Enquirer,* May 15, 1863.

51. Jubal A. Early to R. E. Lee, November 20, 1868, Daniel Papers, UVA.

52. The first edition of Early's *A Memoir of the Last Year of the War for Independence, in the Confederate States of America, Containing an Account of the Operations of His Commands in the Years 1864 and 1865* appeared from the Toronto printer Lovell & Gibson in 1866; subsequent editions were published in Lynchburg, Mobile, and New Orleans.

53. R. E. Lee to Jubal A. Early, October 15, 1866, George H. and Katherine M. Davis Collection, Manuscripts Section, Howard-Tilton Library, Tulane University, New Orleans; Jubal A. Early to John Warwick Daniel, February 17, 1867, John Warwick Daniel Papers, Perkins Library, Duke University, Durham, N.C.

54. Jubal A. Early to R. E. Lee, November 20, 1868, Daniel Papers, UVA. The manuscript Lee received probably was nearly identical to chapter 20 in Early, *Memoirs.*

55. Jubal A. Early to R. E. Lee, November 20, 1868, Daniel Papers, UVA.

56. Humphreys, "Recollections of Fredericksburg," 445; Edward A. Pollard, *Southern History of the War: The Second Year of the War* (1863; New York: Charles B. Richardson, 1865), 262–63; Jubal A. Early to Jedediah Hotchkiss, March 24, 1868, VHS.

57. William Allan and Jedediah Hotchkiss, *The Battle-Fields of Virginia: Chancellorsville; Embracing the Operations of the Army of Northern Virginia, from the First Battle of Fredericksburg to the Death of Lieutenant-General Jackson* (New York: D. Van Nostrand, 1867). For Early's comments about the book, see Jubal A. Early to Jedediah Hotchkiss, March 24, 1868, VHS.

58. Editors to Jubal A. Early, April 23, 1884, May 7, 1884; Robert Underwood Johnson to Jubal A. Early, May 12, 1884; and Clarence Clough

Buel to Jubal A. Early, April 12, 1887, Early Papers, LC. Jubal A. Early to William H. Payne, August 4, 1885, Hunton Family Papers, Mss1/H9267/a/7, VHS. The excerpts appear in Robert Underwood Johnson and Clarence Clough Buel, eds., *Battles and Leaders of the Civil War*, 4 vols. (New York: Century Company, 1887–88), 4:492–99, 522–30.

59. Jubal A. Early to William H. Payne, August 4, 1885, VHS.

Part Three

LEE & HIS ARMY IN THE LOST CAUSE

┌─────────────────────────────┐
│ SHAPING PUBLIC   │
│   │
│ MEMORY OF THE   │
│   │
│ CIVIL WAR   │
│   │
│ *Robert E. Lee,*   │
│   │
│ *Jubal A. Early, &*   │
│   │
│ *Douglas Southall Freeman* │
│   │
└─────────────────────────────┘

Former Confederate general Jubal A. Early and historian Douglas Southall Freeman heavily influenced the way in which Americans have understood the Confederacy and the Civil War. Ardent Virginians and admirers of Robert E. Lee, Early and Freeman had much to do with creating the ironic situation in which the rebel commander—rather than Ulysses S. Grant, William Tecumseh Sherman, or some other Union war hero—stands alongside Abraham Lincoln as one of the two most prominent figures of the conflict. Thomas L. Connelly, Alan T. Nolan, and other scholars have assessed Early's and Freeman's impact on the literature and on popular perceptions. These historians typically have functioned as rather harsh critics of the two Virginians, insisting that they exaggerated Lee's prowess and wartime reputation, overstated the importance of his operations within the Confederate war effort, and placed too much emphasis on northern numbers as a factor in Union victory. In effect, runs a common argument, the work of Early and other Lost Cause writers, extended and strengthened by Freeman's scholarly publications in the 1930s and 1940s, self-consciously created an inaccurate version of Confederate history and an explanation for its defeat that gained wide acceptance following the conflict and unfortunately has remained remarkably durable.[1]

These historians raise a number of important questions. Was Lee's heroic image a postwar creation? Did Early and Freeman exaggerate Lee's military influence? Did northern human and material resources play the major role in defeating the Confederacy? And, finally, why do Early's and Freeman's principal interpretive points still have force in the literature? Any attempt to answer these questions leads to a more important one; namely, is it possible that arguments put forward for the purpose of managing the memory of the Confederacy's war might be rooted in fact? And if so, how can that be acknowledged without giving the appearance of also accepting the romance and apology characteristic of the larger Lost Cause interpretive tradition that cloaked the Confederacy in constitutional principle and denied the centrality of slavery to secession and the war? This essay cannot pretend to offer definitive answers to all these questions, but it can, perhaps, point the way toward a reconsideration of some Lost Cause claims.

Robert E. Lee played a major role in shaping postwar perceptions of the Confederate experience. Contradicting the popular image of a conciliatory statesman who harbored little animosity toward the North and sought only to get beyond the war, this aspect of his career has received less recognition than it deserves. In *Ghosts of the Confederacy,* for example, Gaines Foster accords brief attention to this topic, observing that after Lee's death "several of the more ardent and unreconciled Confederate historians had good reason to believe they were following the lead of their commander." In fact, Lee worked hard to have his views placed on the public record. He explicitly and repeatedly stated that Federal numbers explained the North's triumph, insisting that white southerners should attempt to educate the world about Confederate valor and steadfastness. Lee's postwar comments mirrored his official and private correspondence during the conflict. His most famous wartime expression of this sentiment resides in General Orders No. 9, dated April 10, 1865. Written by staff officer Charles Marshall following a conversation during which Lee's "feelings towards his men were strongly expressed," this order pointed directly to northern manpower and material as the crucial factors in requiring Confederate surrender: "After four years of arduous service, marked by unsurpassed courage and fortitude, the Army of Northern Virginia has been compelled to yield to overwhelming numbers and resources." [2]

In letters to Jubal Early and other former lieutenants shortly after the war, Lee stressed northern numbers and the need to get the Confederate version of the war into print. The question of relative strengths occupied much of Lee's attention, but he also believed northern commanders and their soldiers wantonly had destroyed civilian property and otherwise subjected noncombatants to unnecessary suffering. He planned to write a history of the Army of Northern Virginia that would address what he considered salient features of the conflict, a task complicated by the fact that he had lost many of his official papers during the chaotic retreat from Richmond to Appomattox. He asked Early for information about various battles and campaigns, including "statistics as regards numbers, destruction of private property by the Federal troops, &c." Lee hoped to demonstrate the disparity in strength between the two sides, predicting that it would "be difficult to get the world to understand the odds against which we fought." "My only object," he stated in language that anticipated Early's and Freeman's later writings, "is to transmit, if possible, the truth to posterity, and do justice to our brave Soldiers." Lee himself stood ready to suffer criticism from northerners. "The accusations against myself I have not thought proper to notice, or even to correct misrepresentations of my words & acts," he told Early. "We shall have to be patient, & suffer for awhile at least. . . . At present the public mind is not prepared to receive the truth." Lee assured another of his old subordinates that he had no thought of personal vindication in writing a history of the army: "I want that the world shall know what my poor boys, with their small numbers and scant resources, succeeded in accomplishing."[3]

Such comments about northern numbers and resources should not be interpreted to mean Lee viewed the war as hopeless from the outset. Like Jefferson Davis and other civilian and military leaders, he understood that the weaker side had prevailed in other conflicts such as the American Revolution. Union manpower and material bounty chastened him, but, as the fifth essay in this book suggests, he believed the Confederacy could win by marshaling its men and matériel effectively, winning victories that depressed Union morale, and persuading the North that it would cost too much in lives and treasure to force the seceded states back into the Union. In the end, however, Union will proved sufficient. Lincoln and Grant provided exemplary leadership, and United States armies won victories at critical points (most especially following periods of deep northern pessimism in the spring of 1863 and the late summer of 1864). The

North found leaders who applied their greater resources to excellent effect, and Lee pronounced those resources a decisive factor.[4]

Few men admired Lee more than Jubal Early, who throughout the war exhibited unquestioning devotion to his commander. Lee's letters to Early in 1865 and 1866 helped inspire the latter's dogged effort to create a published record that could convince future generations Lee and his army deserved the highest praise. Early's *Memoir of the Last Year of the War for Independence, in the Confederate States of America*, which appeared in 1866, emphasized points Lee had raised in his letters, highlighting the North's advantage in numbers and detailing Union depredations in the Shenandoah Valley in 1864. Early also may have interpreted Lee's comments about "accusations" and "misrepresentations" as a veiled invitation to defend his old chief against critics. Dismayed by what he considered unfair attacks on Lee, Early decided to persuade the public "to receive the truth," to use Lee's words, about the Confederate commander and his campaigns. In speeches, articles, letters to editors, and a huge correspondence with other ex-Confederates who were writing about the war, Early concentrated on a few crucial themes: that Lee had been a general of unparalleled brilliance, whose army carried the hopes of the Confederacy on its bayonets; that "Stonewall" Jackson (whom Lee had called "my right [arm]" and "this great and good soldier")[5] stood just behind Lee in the southern pantheon; that Lee oversaw military operations that held at bay enormously more powerful Union forces, until finally, at the head of a much diminished army, he capitulated to Grant's well-supplied host at Appomattox; and that, despite defeat, Lee and Jackson offered an ideal of Christian military leadership in which the white South could take continuing pride.

In late 1870, Early pursued the topic of manpower in reaction to Adam Badeau's assertion that Union forces had not enjoyed a significant advantage during the 1864 Overland campaign. A member of Grant's staff during the war, Badeau had published his argument in the *London Standard*, concluding that at the battle of the Wilderness "Lee had about 72,000 engaged, while Grant had 98,000 present for duty." Early's response, offered as a letter to the editor of the *Standard* and later reprinted in the *Southern Historical Society Papers*, insisted that Grant had commanded 141,000 soldiers to Lee's 50,000 and raised the specter of former Federals mounting "a persistent and systematic effort to falsify the truth of history." Early suggested an unflattering explanation for Badeau's figures: "That officers of Grant's army, after witnessing the terrible havoc made in their ranks by the small force opposed to them at the Wilderness, at Spotsylvania C[ourt] H[ouse], and at Cold Harbor, should over estimate the strength of that force, is not to be wondered at." Neither Early's nor Badeau's arithmetic was correct. Grant commanded roughly 120,000 men and Lee 65,000 when their armies first came to grips on May 5, 1864.[6] Yet Early's basic argument, when stripped of hyperbole and antinorthern rhetoric, is difficult to refute. Lee and the Army of Northern Virginia had faced intimidating odds during the 1864 campaign in Virginia.[7]

Early's famous address on the anniversary of Lee's birth in 1872 developed a cluster of durable Lost Cause themes. This speech portrayed Lee as without equal among history's noted captains. "[I]t is a vain work for us to seek anywhere for a parallel to the great character which has won our admiration and love," stated Early. "Our beloved Chief stands, like some lofty column which rears its head among the highest, in grandeur, simple, pure and sublime, needing no borrowed lustre; and he is all our own." The Army of Northern Virginia had fought gallantly, insisted Early, before being "gradually worn down by the combined agencies of numbers, steam-power, railroads, mechanism, and all the resources of physical science." Northern might "had finally produced that exhaustion of our army and resources, and that accumulation of numbers on the other side, which wrought the final disaster." Despite defeat, white southerners could look with pride to Lee and Jackson, "illustrious men, and congenial Christian heroes." "When asked for our vindication," affirmed Early, "we can triumphantly point to the graves of Lee and Jackson and look the world square in the face." Early closed by charging his audience with a "sacred trust" of "cherishing the memory of our leaders and our fallen comrades."[8]

Early's message of Confederate pluck and valor, as well as his direct assaults on Union writings about the war, struck a receptive chord among defeated white southerners. One Mississippian looked to Ireland for a comparative example. "It was the dying wish of Young Emmet, the Irish patriot and martyr, that his epitaph should not be written until his country was free," remarked James F. Trotter in 1866. "The illfated patriot of our own land, General Early, has expressed nearly the same sentiment. . . . [A]fter correcting many gross errors in the official reports of the United States Officers, [he] begs that an impartial world may suspend any fixed judgment of our

THE RELATIVE STRENGTH OF THE ARMIES

OF

GEN'LS LEE AND GRANT.

Reply of Gen. Early to the Letter of Gen. Badeau to the London Standard.

TO THE EDITOR OF THE LONDON STANDARD.

To a people overpowered and crushed in a struggle for their rights, there is still left one resource on earth for the vindication of their conduct and character: that adopted by England's great Philosopher—an appeal to "foreign nations and to the next age." A persistent and systematic effort to falsify the truth of history has been made, since the close of the late war in this country, by the adherents of the United States Government in that conflict; and such a generous desire to vindicate the truth as that evinced by your recent articles upon the death of General Lee, has awakened a deep sense of gratitude in the hearts of all true Confederates. Presuming upon the kind sentiments manifested in your columns, I venture to ask the privilege of correcting, through the same medium, some of the gross errors contained in the letter of General Badeau, the late "military and private secretary to General Grant," which has been extensively copied from your journal into American journals.

In reference to the campaign of 1864 from the Rapidan to James River, General Badeau makes this remarkable statement:

"The calculation that Grant had three times as many men as Lee has been obtained by omitting Longstreet's corps altogether from the estimate, and by giving only Lee's force present for duty on the Rapidan; while in reckoning Grant's numbers, not only the present for duty are counted, but those constituting what, in military parlance, is called the total, which includes the sick, the extra-duty men, and various others, invariably amounting, in any large army, to many thousands. Manifestly, either Lee's total should be compared with Grant's total, or Grant's present for duty with Lee's present for duty. But besides this, in order to make out Grant's army three times as large as Lee's, Grant's two forces in the Valley of Virginia and on the James River (each at least one hundred miles from the Wilderness) are included in the estimate of his strength; while the troops which Lee had in front of these separate forces of Grant are left out of the calculation altogether. I repeat that in the battle of the Wilderness Lee had about 72,000 engaged, while Grant had 98,000 present for duty — according to the confidential field returns made at the time by each General to his own government, when no General would intentionally misstate or mislead."

That officers of Grant's army, after witnessing the terrible havoc made in their ranks by the small force opposed to them at the Wilderness, at Spotsylvania C. H., and at Cold Harbor, should over estimate the strength of that force, is not to be wondered at, but when the report of Mr. Edwin M. Stanton, the United States Secretary of War, made at the opening session of Congress for the years 1865-6, is critically examined, it will be regarded as most surprising that Gen. Badeau should have committed such gross blunders in regard to the strength of Grant's army. In order to expose those blunders, and to enable you to verify the extracts which I shall make from Mr. Stanton's report, I send you an official copy of that report printed under the authority of the United States Congress.

On page 3rd of his report, Mr. Stanton says:—

"The national forces engaged in the Spring campaign of 1864 were organized as armies or distributed in military departments as follows:

"The Army of the Potomac, commanded by Major-General Meade, whose headquarters were on the north side of the Rapidan. This army was confronted by the rebel army of Northern Virginia, stationed on the south side of the Rapidan, under General Robert E. Lee.

"The 9th corps, under Major-General Burnside, was, at the opening of the campaign, a distinct organization, but on the 24th of May, 1864, it was incorporated into the Army of the Potomac.

The first page of Jubal Early's published response to Adam Badeau. (Author's collection) late struggle and its conflict until the time shall come for placing a true history before them." Like Early, Trotter alluded to northern power and celebrated the southern resistance, explaining that Confederates "laid down our arms when we could use them no longer and submitted to our destiny.... We have won true glory, for our struggle for liberty has no parallel in the history of the world."[9]

A determined and able controversialist, Early exerted enormous influence over Confederate historiography in the late nineteenth century. Many of Lee's old soldiers (as well as some who had served in other southern armies) sent their manuscripts to him for approval before publication. Robert Stiles, a former artillerist in the Army of Northern Virginia who published his own reminiscences after Early's death, remarked that as "long as 'the old hero' lived, no man ever took up his pen to write a line about the great conflict without the fear of Jubal Early before his eyes." Early became widely accepted in the postwar South as the leading authority on Lee's army and its campaigns, and upon his death numerous newspapers and camps of the United Confederate Veterans applauded his accomplishments as what one set of UCV resolutions termed "a forceful and truthful writer of history." Among modern historians, Thomas L. Connelly has commented most strongly about Early's impact. Describing him as "the driving force behind the first Lee cult," Connelly characterized Early as "perhaps the most influential figure in nineteenth-century Civil War writing, North or South."[10]

Within twenty-five years after the surrender at Appomattox, Early and other Lost Cause warriors had managed to train the historical focus on Lee and his army rather than on Jefferson Davis and the political history of the Confederacy. They helped create an interpretive framework within which military elements of the Confederate war would receive far more attention than any nonmilitary dimension. This proved immensely useful in presenting the white South's wartime experience in the best possible light. Far more attractive personally than Jefferson Davis, Lee could be examined within a martial setting largely free of the blighting influence of slavery. Lee's brilliance as a soldier, the undeniable odds he faced, and the totality of his eventual defeat invited sympathetic treatment of a type impossible with either the secessionists, whose ringing calls for a slaveholding republic in 1860–61 were problematical in a post-emancipation era, or with the often messy political and social history of the Confederacy.

Jubal Early in old age, a venerable defender of Lee and indefatigable advocate of the Lost Cause. (Courtesy of the Maryland Historical Society)

Douglas Southall Freeman shaped literature about the Confederacy and public understanding of Lee in the 1930s and 1940s much as Early had in the late nineteenth century. The longtime editor of the *Richmond News Leader* and holder of a Ph.D. in history from the Johns Hopkins University (he received his degree in 1908 at the age of twenty-two), Freeman spent much of his boyhood in Lynchburg, Virginia, while General Early lived in the city. The young Freeman absorbed Confederate lore from his father, a veteran of Lee's army who was named national commander in chief of the United Confederate Veterans in 1925. As a seventeen-year-old in 1903, Freeman experienced an epiphany while watching a reenactment of the battle of the Crater. The sight of 2,500 veterans engaged in mock combat at Petersburg, he later explained, inspired him to determine "to preserve from immolating time some of the heroic figures of the Confederacy." Four years after his experience at the Crater, on the centennial of Lee's birth, Freeman expressed his feelings about the general to his mother: "Surely if there is an ideal in the Old South, it is Lee, he stands for all that was best and brightest there." Eighteen years later, in a letter that revealed undiminished admiration for Lee, Freeman spoke of his hopes for the children of a woman who had corresponded with him: "May they grow up to cherish the ideals of Lee! After those of the Saviour Himself, I know of none that are loftier."[11] Publication of his multivolume works *R. E. Lee: A Biography* and *Lee's Lieutenants: A Study in Command*, in 1934–35 and 1942–44 respectively, not only enabled Freeman to make good on his youthful resolution to honor Lee's soldiers but also thrust him into Early's old role as Lee's greatest champion.

Freeman's books reinforced themes that had been central to Lee and Early. Although his work rested on impressive research and took a far more detached approach than Early's speeches and writings, it is easy to imagine that Freeman, laboring on his massive projects, had in mind Lee's expressed hope to "transmit, if possible, the truth to posterity, and do justice to our brave Soldiers." Numbers and resources stood at the center of Freeman's explanation for Confederate defeat in *R. E. Lee:* "Always the odds had been against [Lee], three to two in this campaign, two to one in that. Not once, in a major engagement, had he met the Federals on even terms; not once, after a victory, had his army been strong enough to follow it up. . . . From the moment he undertook to mobilize Virginia until the last volley rolled across the red hills of Appomattox, there had been no single day when he had enjoyed an advantage he had not won with the blood of men he could not replace." Freeman concluded that "[w]ith poverty he faced abundance," and abundance won out. Unlike Early, Freeman admitted that "Lee himself had made mistakes"; those mistakes, however, counted for little when arrayed against the general's accomplishments. "In the evils he prevented, as surely as in his positive military achievements," wrote Freeman, "when seen through the eyes of his subordinates as certainly as when one looks at him across the table in his tent, he is a great soldier and a great man. Twenty years' study of him confirms and deepens every conviction of that."

Freeman seconded Early in placing Stonewall Jackson and the common soldiers who fought in the Army of Northern Virginia near Lee in a Confederate roll of honor. "The greatness of the Army was in its supreme command and in its infantry," Freeman noted. Of all the officers who fought in the Eastern Theater, "only two, Lee, the captain of the host, and his right arm, Jackson, are to be added to those of one's acquaintances, living or dead, real persons or the creation of literature, by whom one's own personal philosophy of life is shaped beyond understanding."[12]

Freeman's books won him a reputation as an unmatched interpreter of Confederate history. The *New York Times Book Review* offered representative praise for *R. E. Lee*. "You rise from the completed work," asserted the reviewer, "with the conviction that here is Lee's monument. . . . Dr. Freeman has left nothing for any aftersculptor to carve." T. Harry Williams, himself an immensely influential historian of the Civil War, observed in 1955 that "Long before his life had ended, Douglas Freeman had become a name and a legend. To him was accorded the rare honor of being accepted, while still alive, as a great historian, as *the* authority in his field and of having his works acclaimed as classics that would endure permanently." Not long after Williams published his comments, Frank E. Vandiver, another major Civil War scholar, pondered "the question of Freeman's place in Civil War history," arguing that "he breathed new life into military and Civil War history, gave them popular as well as academic respectability, and lifted American biography to the level of literature."[13]

Passage of more than four decades since Williams and Vandiver wrote their assessments has done little to diminish Freeman's reputation. He remains the most widely known figure in the field of Con-

Douglas Southall Freeman at "Westbourne," his home in Richmond, Virginia. By the time this photograph was taken, Freeman had achieved eminence as Lee's biographer and the best-known student of the Army of Northern Virginia. (Courtesy of Mary Tyler Freeman McClenahan)

federate military history. Indeed, historians writing books about Lee or the Army of Northern Virginia often include something in their prefaces or introductions similar to what Emory M. Thomas wrote in *Robert E. Lee: A Biography.* "Freeman's four-volume study won a Pulitzer Prize in 1934 and has been 'the definitive Lee' ever since," stated Thomas in 1995. "For a long, long time Lee, essentially Freeman's 'Lee,' has been an American hero. This same Lee has been the patron saint of the American South." [14]

Treatment of Freeman's work in a trio of bibliographies published over a thirty-year span suggests the durability of his reputation. In 1969, Robert W. Johannsen—who rightly appreciated that Freeman was far more even-handed than recent critics would allow but scarcely could be termed a Lost Cause devotee—described *R. E. Lee* as a "classic example of the biographical form; exhaustively researched, vividly written, balanced, judicious and definitive in its portrayal of the Confederacy's greatest soldier." A decade later, Richard B. Harwell, whose sympathies clearly did lie with the South, labeled *R. E. Lee* "a masterpiece of biography and of military history," adding that *Lee's Lieutenants* "stands in its own right as one of the great works of military history." In 1997, David J. Eicher's *The Civil War in Books* lauded both titles. Acknowledging Freeman's open admiration of Lee and his soldiers, Eicher nevertheless termed *R. E. Lee* a "classic work, characterized by brilliant writing," one that is "a necessary part of any Confederate bookshelf." He similarly described *Lee's Lieutenants* as "a masterpiece of Confederate history" that deserves "to be read by all Civil War students." [15]

This evidence of Freeman's continuing influence brings me back to the question of how best to deal with many of the ideas he and Jubal Early put forward. Understandably reluctant to embrace a Lost Cause tradition that includes romantic and self-serving arguments, a number of historians have mounted a major critique of Early and Freeman. Lost Cause interpretations, suggest these scholars, were formulated after Appomattox with the intention of placing Lee and the Confederates in the best possible light and continue to carry undeserved weight in Civil War literature. [16]

Several historians have questioned Early's and Freeman's portrayal of Lee (with Jackson playing the role of his strong right arm) as a supremely gifted soldier who towered above all others in the Confederate high command during the war. Although conceding that Lee possessed considerable military gifts, these scholars have suggested that postwar propagandizing by Jubal Early and a group of like-minded Virginians, rather than wartime accomplishment, accounts for much of the general's current reputation. Thomas L. Connelly and Barbara L. Bellows stated flatly that "Robert E. Lee's reputation as the invincible Confederate general was a postwar phenomenon." During the conflict, wrote Connelly elsewhere, the Confederate people would have lumped Lee together with Albert Sidney Johnston, Joseph E. Johnston, P. G. T. Beauregard, Stonewall Jackson, and others as commanders of approximately the same importance: "Not until the 1880s would Lee be regarded as the South's invincible general, the embodiment of the Confederate cause." William Garrett Piston, a student of Connelly's, followed his mentor in arguing that "When he died on October 12, 1870, Lee was only one of a large number of Confederate heroes and was still second to Stonewall Jackson in the eyes of most Virginians." Carol Reardon's recent study of the image of Pickett's Charge in American history implicitly concurs with this view, alluding to Virginians who "directed postwar efforts to recast Robert E. Lee as the Confederacy's greatest hero." David W. Blight's work on Frederick Douglass and Civil War memory also weighs in on the question of Lee's reputation. Unreconstructed Lost Cause writers, states Blight, most especially "the prototypical unreconstructed rebel" Early, "made Robert E. Lee into a romantic icon" as part of their larger effort to create a pro-Confederate version of the sectional crisis and the war.[17]

No scholar detected more flaws in Early's and Freeman's portraits of Lee than Alan T. Nolan. In *Lee Considered: General Robert E. Lee and Civil War History*, Nolan described what he termed "the manufactured 'history' of the Civil War that began to take form shortly after the fighting ceased" and grew out of "the combination of the war's actual contradictions and traumas and the postwar social rationalizations of the participants." From this process arose a "legend" that substituted "romance in place of realism" and engendered "radical distortions of critical facts." "Exalted himself," insisted Nolan, "Lee is also a visible sign of the elevation of the Lost Cause. The literature on Lee is symbolic of the South's postwar victory and the folk history of the war." Directing some of his sharpest criticism toward Freeman's *R. E. Lee*, Nolan labeled it the "paradigm of the historical treatment of Lee and his times," a "wholly adulatory account . . . setting forth every favorable fact and appealing story that could be reported and rationalizing any act that might be questioned." Selecting a classical allusion for his concluding sentence (and overlooking the fact that Homeric heroes almost always possess major flaws), Nolan wrote that "Robert E. Lee is the Odysseus of an American *Odyssey;* but that *Odyssey*, like Homer's, is myth and legend, not history." [18]

The question of northern manpower and material strength, which loomed so large in Lee's, Early's, and Freeman's thinking, also figures in several recent studies. Gaines Foster contends that Early and his Virginia allies remain important because "their speeches and articles did help establish points that would be accepted by later veterans' movements and become part of the Confederate tradition." One of those points, chosen from an array of possible explanations, was that the South "succumbed only to overwhelming numbers and resources." David W. Blight also attributes to Early and other "die-hard" ex-Confederates a numbers-based strategy to deflect criticism from their war effort: "The Confederacy . . . was never defeated; rather, it was overwhelmed by numbers and betrayed by certain generals at pivotal battles (namely James Long-street at Gettysburg)." A recent article on the Southern Historical Society supports Foster and Blight. "Lost Cause advocates held that the Confederacy had been overwhelmed by superior northern resources," notes Richard D. Starnes. The Society's published *Papers*, over which Jubal Early exerted considerable editorial control, ran a series of pieces in 1876 designed to highlight the relative paucity of southern resources and clinch a key Lost Cause argument; namely, that "Brave southerners fought with great élan, ability, and success, considering the South's much smaller industrial base and its much smaller population."[19]

This scholarship offers a clear alternative to the interpretation of the Confederate war effort that Lee, Early, and Freeman hoped would prevail. It has been useful in illuminating excesses on Early's and Freeman's parts, in demonstrating that a number of ex-Confederates worked very hard to get their version of the war into the historical record as soon as possible, and in underscoring the influence of Freeman's published work.[20] Indeed, in the six decades between Early's first writings and publication of Freeman's massive biography, Lee had assumed a position so elevated as to cry out for revision. Any poll of lay readers almost certainly would have ranked him far ahead of Ulysses S. Grant as the greatest soldier of the Civil War—and perhaps ahead of all other generals in American history. Moreover, Lee had been pictured as an opponent of slavery whose purity of motives raised him above most of his peers, when in fact he owned a few slaves and held quite conventional views about slavery for someone of his time, class, and place. The explicit separation of Lee, who reasonably could be described as the central figure in Confederate history, from the institution of slavery proved invaluable to anyone seeking to offer a flattering assessment of the southern experiment in nation-building. By pursuing a "great man" version of history, Lost Cause warriors played to their strengths and neatly avoided a number of potential pitfalls. The revisionists performed a necessary service in forcing readers to reevaluate Lee's life and Confederate career.

Having said that, I will add that the revisionist scholarship suffers from flaws of its own. Most obviously, it fails to acknowledge the degree to which much of what Lee, Early, and Freeman argued was grounded in wartime fact and accepted by participants on both sides during the conflict and in the half-decade immediately after Appomattox—that is, *before* the Lost Cause literature began to appear in significant bulk.

I will make my final points as succinctly as possible, buttressing each with representative supporting evidence. First, critics of Early's and Freeman's portraits of Lee tend to misrepresent the general's stature during the war. This phenomenon arose in large measure from an understandable effort to combat some of the more extreme claims by Early especially. In Early's discussion of Confederate history, all other political and military figures except Stonewall Jackson seem to be little more than bit players. Yet in efforts to credit other leaders with their just position, a number of historians have misinterpreted Lee's relative importance. By the summer of 1863 at the latest, Lee was the most important southern military figure, and he and the Army of Northern Virginia had become the principal national rallying point of the Confederate people. Moreover, his stature, along with that of his army, grew as the last two years of the war unfolded. The idea that Early and fellow Lost Cause warriors somehow plucked Lee out of a group of wartime peers and made him preeminent, and that Freeman perpetuated and embellished their cunning work, is simply wrong.[21]

Abundant wartime testimony leaves no doubt about Lee's commanding stature in the Confederacy. Four examples will suffice to make this point. A Georgia officer summoned Washington's name in a perceptive evaluation of the relationship between Lee and his soldiers. "General Robt. E. Lee is regarded by his army as nearest approaching the character of the great & good Washington than any man living," wrote Col. Clement A. Evans during the difficult winter of 1864. "He is the only man living in whom they would unreservedly trust all power for the preservation of their independence." In a sentence at odds with the notion that Lee's image of perfection was a Lost Cause fabrication, Evans added, "General Lee has no enemies, and all his actions are so exalted that mirth at his expense is never known." Writing a few weeks after Evans, Lt. Col. William Drayton Rutherford of the 3rd South Carolina described Lee's reviewing the First Corps. "Our venerable military father, Genl Lee, did us the compliment to come down and review us," began Rutherford, who described the event as "the most imposing pageant we have ever witnessed." Lee left the review amid "the shouts and tossing up of hats of the armed multitude. We all feel better after a sight of our grand chieftain. No one can excite their enthusiasm as he does. And no wonder, for such a noble face as he has, and such noble deeds as he has performed deserve admiration."

The *Macon (Ga.) Christian Index* ran a sketch of Lee in July 1864 that understandably highlighted the general's well-known piety. "He is said to be never so busy that he cannot find time to study God's word, and offer earnest prayer for divine guidance and strength," averred this piece. "Gen. Lee (or 'Marse Robert,' as the boys familiarly call him,) is universally loved by the army.... Surely we should thank God for such a leader, while continued prayer ascends that he may be spared to the close of this conflict to reap the rich reward of his priceless services." In March 1865, a British visitor remarked about the degree to which Confederates invested their hopes in Lee: "*Genl R. E. Lee . . .* [is] the idol of his soldiers & the Hope of His country," wrote Thomas Conolly, a member of Parliament. "[T]he prestige which surrounds his person & the almost fanatical belief in his judgement & capacity . . . is the one idea of an entire people."[22]

Many of Lee's opponents also elevated him to a special category among rebel officers. For example, as late as March 24, 1865, with the Army of Northern Virginia manifestly heading for defeat, veteran northern soldier Wilbur Fisk cautioned that "we must bear in mind that we have not yet rendered it impossible for Gen. Lee to win another victory." Perhaps more tellingly, New Englander Stephen Minot Weld struggled to explain to his sister why he found it difficult to celebrate Lee's surrender at Appomattox. She had written several letters complaining of what he termed his "want of enthusiasm" about the climactic Union success. "To tell the truth, we none of us realize even yet that he has actually surrendered," admitted Colonel Weld. "I had a sort of impression that we should fight him all our lives. He was like a ghost to children, something that haunted us so long that we could not realize that he and his army were really out of existence to us. It will take me some months to be conscious of this fact."[23]

My second point concerns northern human and material advantages as a principal cause of Confederate defeat. Far from being a postwar construction by Lost Cause warriors, allusions to northern superiority in these categories abound in wartime Confederate writings. As already noted, Lee frequently addressed this topic during the conflict. On January 10, 1863, for example, he wrote to the secretary of war about "the vast numbers that the enemy is now precipitating upon us." In the wake of Gettysburg, he betrayed deep concern in a letter to Jefferson Davis: "[T]hough conscious that the enemy has been much shattered in the recent battle, I am aware that he can be easily reinforced, while no addition can be made to our numbers." Thirteen months later, with the armies locked in a grinding siege at Petersburg, Lee urged the secretary of war to do everything possible to reinforce the Army of Northern Virginia. "Without some increase of our strength," he warned, "I cannot see how we are to escape the natural military consequences of the enemy's numerical superiority."

Lee understood that Union numbers would tell only if the northern people remained willing to support the war. "[O]ur resources in men are constantly diminishing," he wrote in June 1863, "and the disproportion in this respect between us and our enemies, if they continue united in their effort to subjugate us, is steadily augmenting." If anything, Jubal Early, who faced Union forces two-and-one-half or three times the size of his army in the 1864 Shenandoah Valley campaign, had an even stronger sense of how northern numbers figured in military operations.[24]

Three women's accounts from 1865 suggest that civilians also blamed defeat on northern material advantages. On the Georgia home front, Eliza Francis Andrews learned in late April of Lee's surrender and Joseph E. Johnston's armistice with William Tecumseh Sherman in North Carolina. "It is all over with us now, and there is nothing to do but bow our heads in the dust and let the hateful conquerors trample us under their feet," she wrote in her diary. People no longer talked of "fighting to the last ditch; the last ditch has already been reached." Bitter toward England and France for remaining aloof and watching "a noble nation perish," Andrews explained the war's outcome in a single angry sentence: "We fought nobly and fell bravely, overwhelmed by numbers and resources, with never a hand held out to save us." South Carolinian Harriet R. Palmer focused more specifically on Grant's numerical edge over Lee. "We know that Lee has surrendered," she recorded on May 3; he "had to evacuate Richmond and Petersburg and fought desperately but was outnumbered but not whipped. The Yankees brought nine columns against him. He repulsed eight with a terrible slaughter. Our loss was heavy, too. The ninth column broke through." Having affirmed Confederate resolve against massive odds, Palmer turned to the North's victorious general to clinch her point about numbers: "Grant behaved very nobly towards Gen

Lee. Would not take his sword. Told him he was not whipped but was outnumbered." Catherine Ann Devereux Edmondston, a North Carolinian, echoed Palmer but without any flattering reference to Grant's nobility. "How can I write it? How find the words to tell what has befallen us?" she asked. "*Gen. Lee has surrendered!* Surrendered the remnant of his noble Army to an overwhelming horde of mercenary Yankee knaves & foreigners." [25]

Northerners understood their advantages as well. Abraham Lincoln's sense of frustration at the inability of larger Union armies to vanquish smaller rebel opponents is well known. He worried about Army of the Potomac commander Joseph Hooker in this regard, as evidenced in his comments during a discussion with Hooker and Gen. Darius Couch just before the Chancellorsville campaign. "I want to impress upon you two gentlemen," Lincoln told the officers, "in your next fight, put in all your men." The president clearly believed that proper application of Union resources would yield victory, and he watched with mounting frustration in 1862–63 as one after another of his commanders in the Eastern Theater failed to make effective use of available manpower.[26]

Other northerners explained their triumph as a process of merely grinding down overmatched rebels. Writing on the day of Appomattox, Col. Charles Wainwright, a leading artillerist in the Army of the Potomac, implied that Lee and his army really never had been beaten. "The Army of Northern Virginia under Lee . . . today . . . has surrendered," observed Wainwright, who elaborated in language Early and other Lost Cause writers surely would have applauded. "During three long and hard-fought campaigns it has withstood every effort of the Army of the Potomac; now at the commencement of the fourth, it is obliged to succumb without even one great pitched battle. Could the war have been closed with such a battle as Gettysburg, it would have been more glorious for us. . . . As it is, the rebellion has been worn out rather than suppressed." [27]

Ulysses S. Grant also offered telling testimony on this point. In his final report on operations against the Confederacy, dated June 20, 1865, the Union hero inadvertently bolstered southern arguments about the North's ultimate triumph. "The resources of the enemy, and his numerical strength, was far inferior to ours," stated Grant, though various factors, including the size of the Confederacy and daunting logistical obstacles, helped offset the Union's advantage.

Grant's plan in 1864–65 sought to apply pressure across the strategic board, denying the Confederacy a chance to use its limited manpower to best effect. Grant determined "to use the greatest number of troops practicable against the Armed force of the enemy" and "to hammer continuously at the Armed force of the enemy, and his resources, until by mere attricion, if in no other way, there should be nothing left to him but an equal submission with the loyal section of our common country to the universal law of the land." Thus did Grant frame his orders during the last year of the conflict. How well the resultant campaigns achieved his ends would be for "the public, who have to mourn the loss of friends fallen in the execution, and to pay the pecuniary cost of all this, to say." [28] However the northern people might choose to gauge Grant's performance, his report left little doubt that he believed manpower and resources had been indispensable to success.

How should northern numbers and matériel figure in a consideration of the factors that underlay Confederate defeat? Any such reckoning must recognize the degree to which the war brought debilitating conflict to the southern home front. Conscription, impressment, the tax-in-kind, and other such national measures fanned discontent and exacerbated class tensions. Increasing physical hardship also weakened some people's resolve. Thousands of soldiers deserted, and thousands of civilians behind the lines gave up on the Confederacy as the war dragged on. (Thousands of other white southerners never had supported the Confederacy.) Yet most Confederates remained quite resolute in their determination to win independence at least until the autumn of 1864. They capitulated only when large and well-supplied armies led by Grant, Sherman, and other Union commanders vanquished smaller and less well supplied Confederate armies and proved that they could move across the southern interior virtually at will. Facing an enemy with seemingly endless reserves of well-supplied men commanded by talented officers determined to win, Confederates in and out of uniform grudgingly conceded the North's superiority and abandoned their hopes for independence. [29]

This brings me to the question of why some of Early's and Freeman's interpretations have retained vigor for so long. I believe a major factor is that Early and Freeman, as well as Lee on the question of northern numerical and material advantages, built their arguments on solid foundations. All three men unquestionably had an agenda. Collectively, they hoped to place Lee, the soldiers in his army, and the Confederate nation in the best possible light. But Early and Freeman did not have to stray far beyond any reasonable definition of truth to portray Lee as a gifted general who was pivotal to Confederate hopes for victory; neither did they have to strain the evidence to show that northern resources played a crucial—perhaps *the* crucial—role in defeating the Confederacy. I reiterate that this is not to suggest an inevitability of Union triumph—only to highlight superior numbers and matériel as part of an equation that included sound political and military leadership and continuing commitment on the part of the northern populace.

Both Early and Freeman found a ready audience in the white South. Most former Confederates emerged from the war believing Lee had been an admirable and effective general who led brave troops in a gallant fight against long odds. They proved naturally receptive to Early's writings and speeches, and their descendants were equally quick to embrace Freeman's books.[30]

British readers similarly found the Lost Cause celebration of Lee attractive, as Matthew Arnold noted in his famous review of Grant's memoirs. "General Grant, the central figure of these *Memoirs*," remarked Arnold in his 1886 essay, "is not to the English imagination the hero of the American Civil War; the hero is Lee, and of Lee the *Memoirs* tell us little." Because the *Memoirs* focused on their author rather than on his Confederate antagonist, as well as because of Grant's corrupt presidential administration and failure to engage the British people's interest during a visit to England, explained Arnold, "the *Personal Memoirs* have in England been received with coldness and indifference."[31]

Perhaps more surprising is the degree to which many white northerners during the war and its immediate aftermath expressed favorable interpretations of Lee and Jackson and the men they commanded. During the fall of 1862, for example, the future Lord Acton noted that in northern cities "Stonewall Jackson is the national hero." Just after Jackson's death, the pro-Republican *Washington Daily Morning Chronicle* expressed relief at the removal of a major rebel foe but added that "Every man who possesses the slightest particle of magnanimity must admire the qualities for which Stonewall Jackson was celebrated—his heroism, his bravery, his sublime devotion, his purity of character. He is not the first instance of a good man devoting himself to a bad cause." President Lincoln thanked the editor of the *Daily Morning Chronicle* for the "excellent and manly article . . . on 'Stonewall Jackson.' " [32]

As for Lee and his soldiers, William Swinton's *Campaigns of the Army of the Potomac*, published in 1866, well before most Lost Cause authors had begun to write their works, suggests how generously some northerners treated their former opponents. A wartime newspaper correspondent for the *New York Times*, Swinton praised the Army of Northern Virginia as "that incomparable infantry, . . . which for four years carried the Revolt on its bayonets, opposing a constant front to the mighty concentration of power brought against it." After a heroic struggle, wrote Swinton in a passage that doubtless would have elicited nods of approval from Lee, Early, and Freeman, "the army of Northern Virginia fell before the massive power of the North, yet what vitality had it shown! How terrible had been the struggle!" [33]

Lee received considerable praise from many quarters in the North during the half-decade after the war, which prompted sharp comments from disapproving northerners, who saw him as a traitorous rebel whose activities almost destroyed the Union. The day after Lee's death, George Templeton Strong commented about what he considered distasteful expressions of admiration for the former Confederate commander: "Died in Lexington, Virginia, the ex-Rebel General, Robert E. Lee, whom it is the fashion to laud and magnify as one of the greatest and best of men." Frederick Douglass opposed the northern tendency to forgive former Confederates their sins and reacted more scathingly. "We can scarcely take up a newspaper . . . ," he complained, "that is not filled with *nauseating* flatteries of the late Robert E. Lee. . . . it would seem from this, that the soldier who kills the most men in battle, even in a bad cause, is the greatest Christian, and entitled to the highest place in heaven." [34]

Why so many northerners in the 1860s chose to focus on Lee's and Jackson's piety and other attractive characteristics, as well as on the valor of the men they commanded, would make an excellent topic for another essay. This tendency perplexed and infuriated Frederick Douglass, as it certainly did many thousands of other northerners. [35] For my purposes, it is enough to note that the attitudes so vexing to Douglass were formed *before* Early and the Lost Cause writers began to publish their work on the Confederacy. Like their white southern counterparts, many northerners obviously read the war and the roles of Lee and Jackson in a way that sustained much of what Early and

Freeman would argue. They were not misled by crafty Lost Cause writers who had created a heroic, romantic set of arguments at odds with the facts.

Similarly, modern Americans interested in the Civil War can see that Early's and Freeman's interpretations make sense in many respects. Lee and his army were almost always outnumbered; Lee, with help from Jackson and others, forged a number of spectacular victories; and once Lincoln found Grant, a man who understood how to apply northern resources, the Union's edge in men and matériel almost certainly would win the war if the northern people remained committed to victory. In short, a major reason these elements of the myth of the Lost Cause continue to resonate is that they are not myths at all.

The idea that historians should take elements of the Lost Cause interpretation seriously is unsettling. It places us in the awkward position of having to concede some points to defenders of slavery and disunion. Such concessions might lead to confusion among students and lay readers about Lost Cause arguments that sought to recast the history of antebellum southern society, secession, and the war without slavery as a central factor. More ominously, it might provide fuel to those who find comfort in a vision of the Confederacy divorced from the ugly reality of the peculiar institution. Should we separate the various strands of the Lost Cause fabric in an effort to assess each individually? Or should we treat the whole as a dissembling effort by slaveholders, who had failed in their primary purposes, to salvage what they could by influencing the way in which future generations would define and comprehend the Confederacy?

Although the temptation to follow the latter course might be strong, I believe it is important to engage each part of the Lost Cause interpretation on the merits. Such an approach promises at least two positive results. First, it will yield a better understanding of a compelling example of how Americans have sought to create satisfactory public memories of major events. Second, and perhaps more important, a willingness to point out instances in which authors such as Early advanced arguments well supported by evidence will lend greater power to critiques of Lost Cause interpretations based on blatant twisting of the historical record. Such analysis will not give Lee, Early, and Freeman the last word about the Army of Northern Virginia and its operations, but it will help highlight the complexity of an important and fascinating dimension of the Civil War era.

NOTES

1. See Thomas L. Connelly, *The Marble Man: Robert E. Lee and His Image in American Society* (New York: Knopf, 1977); Connelly and Barbara L. Bellows, *God and General Longstreet: The Lost Cause and the Southern Mind* (Baton Rouge: Louisiana State University Press, 1982); Gaines M. Foster, *Ghosts of the Confederacy: Defeat, the Lost Cause, and the Emergence of the New South* (New York: Oxford University Press, 1987); and Alan T. Nolan, *Lee Considered: General Robert E. Lee and Civil War History* (Chapel Hill: University of North Carolina Press, 1991).

2. Foster, *Ghosts of the Confederacy*, 51; R. E. Lee, *The Wartime Papers of R. E. Lee*, ed. Clifford Dowdey and Louis H. Manarin (Boston: Little, Brown, 1961), 934; Charles Marshall, *An Aide-de-Camp of Lee: Being the Papers of Colonel Charles Marshall, Sometime Aide-de-Camp, Military Secretary, and Assistant Adjutant General on the Staff of Robert E. Lee, 1862–1865*, ed. Sir Frederick Maurice (Boston: Little, Brown, 1927), 275–78. Marshall noted that he "made a draft [of General Orders No. 9] in pencil and took it to General Lee who struck out a paragraph, which he said would tend to keep alive the feeling existing between the North and the South, and made one or two other changes."

3. R. E. Lee to Jubal Early, November 22, 1865, March 15, 1866, George H. and Katherine Davis Collection, Howard-Tilton Memorial Library, Tulane University, New Orleans; J. William Jones, *Personal Reminiscences, Anecdotes, and Letters of Gen. Robert E. Lee* (New York: D. Appleton, 1874), 180. On Lee's plans to write about the war in Virginia, see Allen W. Moger, "General Lee's Unwritten 'History of the Army of Northern Virginia,'" *Virginia Magazine of History and Biography* 71 (July 1963): 341–63.

4. For allusions to the American Revolution as an example for the Confederacy, see Robert E. Lee to Jefferson Davis, September 21, 1862, in U.S. War Department, *The War of the Rebellion: A Compilation of the Official Records of the Union and Confederate Armies*, 127 vols., index, and atlas (Washington: GPO, 1880–1901), ser. 1, vol. 19, pt. 2:143 (hereafter cited as *OR*; all citations are to ser. 1), and Davis's speech at Mobile, Alabama, December 30, 1862, in Jefferson Davis, *The Papers of Jefferson Davis*, ed. Lynda Lasswell Crist et al., 10 vols. to date (Baton Rouge: Louisiana State University Press, 1971–), 8:587–89. For an argument that Lee believed defeat was inevitable, or at least highly likely, by the late summer of 1863, see chapter 6 of Nolan, *Lee Considered*.

5. R. L. Dabney, *Life and Campaigns of Lieut.-Gen. Thomas J. Jackson, (Stonewall Jackson)* (1866; reprint, Harrisonburg, Va.: Sprinkle Publications, 1983), 717; Lee, *Wartime Papers*, 485.

6. Jubal A. Early, *The Relative Strength of the Armies of Gen'ls Lee and Grant: Reply of Gen. Early to the Letter of Gen. Badeau to the London Standard* (n.p.: n.p., [1870]), 1. In reprinting Early's piece in July 1876, the editor of the *Southern Historical Society Papers* termed the "relative strength of the Federal and Confederate armies . . . a matter of great importance. . . . Even our own people are in profound ignorance of the great odds against which we fought, while Northern writers have persistently misrepresented the facts." J. William Jones et al., eds., *Southern Historical Society Papers*, 52 vols. (1876–1959; reprint with 3-vol. index, Wilmington, N.C.: Broadfoot, 1990–92), 2:6–7 (set hereafter cited as *SHSP*). For the armies' strengths in early May 1864, see Gordon C. Rhea, *The Battle of the Wilderness: May 5–6, 1864* (Baton Rouge: Louisiana State University Press, 1994), 21, 34. On the exchange between Early and Badeau, see William A. Blair, "Grant's Second Civil War: The Battle for Historical Memory," in Gary W. Gallagher, ed., *The Spotsylvania Campaign* (Chapel Hill: University of North Carolina Press, 1998), 230–36.

7. Among other ex-Confederates who pursued the subject of numbers, Walter H. Taylor of Lee's staff stands out as particularly indefatigable. See especially his *Four Years with General Lee* (1877; reprint, Bloomington: Indiana University Press, 1962), 162–89. "Having for a long time supervised the preparation of the official returns of the Army of Northern Virginia, and having been permitted to make a recent examination of a number of those returns, now on file in the archive-office of the War Department at Washington," wrote Taylor in his preface, "I am enabled to speak with confidence of the numerical strength of the Confederate forces; my information concerning that of the Federal forces is derived from official documents emanating from the officers and authorities of the United States Government." Although Taylor's figures for the Army of Northern Virginia generally fell below the totals now accepted by scholars, he easily demonstrated that Lee frequently had fought at a striking numerical disadvantage. "Startling to some as the disparity in numbers between the two armies on certain occasions may appear," he observed in vintage Lost Cause language, "it is nevertheless established upon incontrovertible evidence, and makes pardonable the emotions of pride with which the soldier of the Army of Northern Virginia points to the achievements of that incomparable body of soldiery, under its peerless and immortal leader" (p. 188). Grant also wrote about relative strengths, seeking in his memoirs and elsewhere to refute the idea that Lee had fought at a huge disadvantage. See Blair, "Grant's Second Civil War: The Battle for Historical Memory," 223–54. On the broader topic of Grant and Lost Cause writers, see Brooks D. Simpson, "Continu-

ous Hammering and Mere Attrition: Lost Cause Critics and the Military Reputation of Ulysses S. Grant," in Gary W. Gallagher and Alan T. Nolan, eds., *The Myth of the Lost Cause and Civil War History* (Bloomington: Indiana University Press, 2000), 147–69.

8. Jubal A. Early, *The Campaigns of Gen. Robert E. Lee: An Address by Lieut. General Jubal A. Early, before Washington and Lee University, January 19th, 1872* (Baltimore: John Murphy, 1872), 45, 40, 44, 46.

9. James F. Trotter, "The Last Charge to the Court in Desota County, Miss., 1866," typed copy (made from document in possession of Mr. Frank Hopkins, Holly Springs, Miss., April 1945), Southern Historical Collection, Wilson Library, University of North Carolina, Chapel Hill.

10. Robert Stiles, *Four Years under Marse Robert* (1903; reprint, Dayton, Ohio: Morningside, 1977), 190–91; resolution from UCV camp in Jedediah Hotchkiss Papers, reel 36, frames 234–35, Library of Congress, Washington, D.C.; Connelly, *Marble Man*, 51.

11. Keith Dean Dickson, "The Divided Mind of Douglas Southall Freeman and the Transmission of Southern Memory" (Ph.D. diss., University of Virginia, 1998), 36, 38; Mary Tyler Freeman Cheek, "A High Calling: Douglas Southall Freeman and Robert E. Lee," in Robert A. Armour, ed., *Douglas Southall Freeman: Reflections by His Daughter, His Research Associate, and a Historian* (Richmond, Va.: Friends of the Richmond Public Library, 1986), 8; Douglas Southall Freeman to Ruth Davenport Deiss, December 14, 1935, collection of Jon Lowry (who kindly gave permission to quote from the letter).

12. Freeman, *R. E. Lee*, 4:165–66, 167–69; Freeman, *Lee's Lieutenants*, 3:xxiii, xxv.

13. Dickson, "Douglas Southall Freeman," 118; T. Harry Williams, "Freeman, Historian of the Civil War: An Appraisal," in Williams, *The Selected Essays of T. Harry Williams* (Baton Rouge: Louisiana State University Press, 1983), 185 (this piece first appeared in *Journal of Southern History* 21 [February 1955]: 91–100); Frank E. Vandiver, "Douglas Southall Freeman, May 16, 1886–June 13, 1953," in *SHSP* 52:xiv.

14. Emory M. Thomas, *Robert E. Lee: A Biography* (New York: Norton, 1995), 13. Thirty years before Thomas published his life of Lee, Clifford Dowdey had admitted in the foreword to his *Lee* (Boston: Little, Brown, 1965), x, that he "was awed at the prospect of trying to offer any supplement to Douglas Southall Freeman's definitive biography."

15. Allan Nevins, Bell I. Wiley, and James I. Robertson Jr., eds., *Civil War Books: A Critical Bibliography*, 2 vols. (Baton Rouge: Louisiana State University Press, 1967, 1969), 2:57; Richard Barksdale Harwell, *In Tall Cot-*

ton: *The 200 Most Important Confederate Books for the Reader, Researcher and Collector* (Austin, Tex.: Jenkins Publishing Company, 1978), 21; David J. Eicher, *The Civil War in Books: An Analytical Bibliography* (Urbana: University of Illinois Press, 1997), 91, 333–34.

16. On the persistence of Lost Cause arguments, see Alan T. Nolan's essay in Gallagher and Nolan, eds., *The Myth of the Lost Cause and Civil War History.*

17. Connelly and Bellows, *God and General Longstreet*, 25–26; Connelly, *Marble Man*, 25–26; William Garrett Piston, *Lee's Tarnished Lieutenant: James Longstreet and His Place in Southern History* (Athens: University of Georgia Press, 1987), 117; Carol Reardon, *Pickett's Charge in History and Memory* (Chapel Hill: University of North Carolina Press, 1997), 84; David W. Blight, "'For Something beyond the Battlefield': Frederick Douglass and the Struggle for the Memory of the Civil War," in David Thelen, ed., *Memory and American History* (Bloomington: Indiana University Press, 1990), 37–38. For a pair of less impressive works that make comparable arguments about postwar efforts to build Lee's reputation, see Edward H. Bonekemper III, *How Robert E. Lee Lost the Civil War* (Fredericksburg, Va.: Sergeant Kirkland's Press, 1997), and John D. McKenzie, *Uncertain Glory: Lee's Generalship Re-Examined* (New York: Hippocrene Books, 1997).

18. Nolan, *Lee Considered*, 171, 7, 174.

19. Foster, *Ghosts of the Confederacy*, 58, 62; Blight, "For Something beyond the Battlefield," 37–38; Richard D. Starnes, "Forever Faithful: The Southern Historical Society and Confederate Historical Memory," *Southern Cultures* 2 (Winter 1996): 183.

20. That Freeman's multivolume works never have gone out of print suggests the degree to which they continue to influence readers. Both *R. E. Lee* and *Lee's Lieutenants* also have appeared in one-volume abridgments (the former in 1961 and again in 1991, the latter in 1998; James M. McPherson introduced the 1991 and 1998 editions), and Scribner's issued a three-volume paperback edition of *Lee's Lieutenants* in the late 1980s.

21. I have expanded on this point in much greater detail elsewhere, and there is no reason to reprise my full argument. See Gary W. Gallagher, *The Confederate War* (Cambridge, Mass.: Harvard University Press, 1997), especially chapter 3; and "The Idol of His Soldiers and the Hope of His Country: Lee and the Confederate People," in Gallagher, *Lee and His Generals in War and Memory* (Baton Rouge: Louisiana State University Press, 1998), 3–20.

22. Robert Grier Stephens Jr., ed., *Intrepid Warrior: Clement Anselm Evans, Confederate General from Georgia; Life, Letters, and Diaries of the*

War Years (Dayton, Ohio: Morningside, 1992), 342–43; William Drayton Rutherford to "My own sweet one," April 30, 1864, typescript at Fredericksburg and Spotsylvania National Military Park Library, Fredericksburg, Va.; *Macon (Ga.) Christian Index*, July 1, 1864; Thomas Conolly, *An Irishman in Dixie: Thomas Conolly's Diary of the Fall of the Confederacy*, ed. Nelson D. Lankford (Columbia: University of South Carolina Press, 1988), 52.

23. Wilbur Fisk, *Hard Marching Every Day: The Civil War Letters of Wilbur Fisk*, ed. Emil and Ruth Rosenblatt (Lawrence: University Press of Kansas, 1992), 318–19; Stephen Minot Weld, *War Diary and Letters of Stephen Minot Weld, 1861–1865* (1912; reprint, Boston: Massachusetts Historical Society, 1979), 396.

24. Lee, *Wartime Papers*, 388, 544, 844; *OR* 27(3):881.

25. Eliza Francis Andrews, *The War-Time Journal of a Georgia Girl*, ed. Spencer Bidwell Jr. (1908; reprint, Atlanta, Ga.: Cherokee Publishing, 1976), 171 (entry for April 21, 1865); Louis P. Towles, ed., *A World Turned Upside Down: The Palmers of South Santee, 1818–1881* (Columbia: University of South Carolina Press, 1996), 473–74; Catherine Ann Devereux Edmondston, *"Journal of a Secesh Lady": The Diary of Catherine Ann Devereux Edmondston, 1860–1866*, ed. Beth Gilbert Crabtree and James W. Patton (Raleigh: North Carolina Division of Archives and History, 1979), 694 (entry for April 16, 1865).

26. Darius N. Couch, "The Chancellorsville Campaign," in Robert Underwood Johnson and Clarence Clough Buel, eds., *Battles and Leaders of the Civil War*, 4 vols. (New York: Century Company, 1887–88), 3:155.

27. Charles S. Wainwright, *A Diary of Battle: The Personal Journals of Colonel Charles S. Wainwright, 1861–1865*, ed. Allan Nevins (New York: Harcourt, Brace & World, 1962), 520–21.

28. Ulysses S. Grant, *The Papers of Ulysses S. Grant*, ed. John Y. Simon, 21 vols. to date (Carbondale: Southern Illinois University Press, 1967–), 15:165–66.

29. For a fuller explication of the arguments in this paragraph, see Gallagher, *The Confederate War*, especially chapters 1 and 4.

30. On the receptivity of late-nineteenth- and twentieth-century Americans outside the South to Early's arguments, see Connelly's *The Marble Man*, especially chapters 4 and 6.

31. John Y. Simon, ed., *General Grant by Matthew Arnold, with a Rejoinder by Mark Twain* (Kent, Ohio: Kent State University Press, 1995), 11–12.

32. Mark E. Neely Jr., Harold Holzer, and Gabor S. Boritt, *The Confederate Image: Prints of the Lost Cause* (Chapel Hill: University of North

Carolina Press, 1987), 107 (quoting Lord Acton); *Washington Daily Morning Chronicle,* May 13, 1863; Abraham Lincoln, *The Collected Works of Abraham Lincoln,* ed. Roy P. Basler et al., 9 vols. (New Brunswick, N.J.: Rutgers University Press, 1953), 6:214.

33. William Swinton, *Campaigns of the Army of the Potomac: A Critical History of Operations in Virginia, Maryland and Pennsylvania from the Commencement to the Close of the War, 1861–5* (1866; reprint, Secaucus, N.J.: Blue and Grey Press, 1988), 16, 621–22.

34. George Templeton Strong, *The Diary of George Templeton Strong,* ed. Allan Nevins and Milton Halsey Thomas, 4 vols. (New York: Macmillan, 1952), 4:316; David W. Blight, *Frederick Douglass' Civil War: Keeping Faith in Jubilee* (Baton Rouge: Louisiana State University Press, 1989), 229.

35. On this point, see chapter 10 of Blight, *Frederick Douglass' Civil War.*

INDEX

Abbot, Henry L., 79 (n. 33)
Acton, Lord, 274
Adams, Charles F., 155, 180, 183
   (n. 5)
Aiken, David W., 96
Alabama units: 5th Infantry Regiment, 66, 85; 9th Infantry Regiment, 16, 123; 47th Infantry Regiment, 30
Alexander, Bevin, 162
Alexander, Edward Porter, 80
   (n. 40), 97, 131, 192, 233
Alexander, Peter W., 9, 14, 88
Alexander, William, 117
Allan, William, 169, 201, 202, 205, 207, 218 (n. 27), 244, 245
Allen, Ujanirtus, 26–28
Alum Spring Mill, 233, 235, 236
The American Way of War, 159, 160
Amherst Artillery, 94
Anderson, Archer, 153, 155
Anderson, "Bloody Bill," 190 (n. 52)
Anderson, George T., 57
Anderson, Richard H.: and Spotsylvania Court House, 197, 207–9, 211–12; during siege of Petersburg and Richmond, 213, 214 (n. 6), 219 (n. 35); and Chancellorsville campaign, 222, 233, 235–37, 244; Anderson's Corps. *See* First Corps, Army of Northern Virginia
Andrews, Eliza F., 271
Andrews, R. Snowden, 225, 230
Antietam campaign, x, xi, 6–50, 57, 73, 74, 221; and Confederate straggling, 11, 29–31, 36
Appalachian Mountains, 160

Appomattox, Va., xi, 173, 257, 258, 261, 263, 266, 269, 270
Archer, James J., 67
Arlington, Va., 155
Army of Northern Virginia, ix, x, xi, 167, 168, 171–75, 272, 278 (n. 7); attitudes toward Robert E. Lee, 5, 25–28, 33–34, 39, 62–64, 68, 85, 92, 93, 96, 98, 99, 105, 106, 115, 129, 134, 135, 137, 180, 181, 269, 270; and 1862 Maryland campaign, 6, 8, 9, 14, 18, 24, 36, 38, 39; supply situation in, 10, 26, 29, 30, 31, 35, 36, 97, 98, 101–3, 115, 121, 122, 128, 129, 138, 171, 180; and Fredericksburg campaign, 53, 57, 62–64, 67, 71, 73; and Gettysburg campaign, 83–86, 89, 91, 92, 94, 96, 100–102, 173; in spring 1864, 115, 121, 123, 124, 126, 132, 135, 137, 139; and Lost Cause, 152, 155, 160, 167, 168, 171–75, 178, 256–59, 261, 264, 265, 269, 271, 275; and Spotsylvania campaign, 191, 194, 213; Cavalry Corps, 208; and Chancellorsville campaign, 221, 222, 225, 243, 250 (n. 41)
Army of Tennessee, 139, 168
Army of the Potomac, xi, 10, 20, 31, 35, 172, 188 (n. 37); and Fredericksburg campaign, 51, 54, 55, 57, 60, 61, 64, 66, 67, 71, 72, 76 (n. 22), 79 (n. 33); and Gettysburg campaign, 87, 94, 96, 101, 102, 104; in spring 1864, 132–34, 146 (n. 35); and Chancellorsville

Hahn, Steven, 140 (n. 1)
Hale, Samuel, 224, 229
Hall, Matthew R., 216 (n. 16)
Hamilton's Crossing, 223, 225, 229, 230, 235
Hampton, Wade, 85, 133
Hancock, Winfield S., 193, 194, 197
Harpers Ferry, Va., 6, 8–11, 14, 16–18, 26, 27, 39, 41 (n. 9), 58
Harrisburg, Pa., 84
Harris Farm, engagement at, 192, 205
Harsh, Joseph L., 162
Harwell, Richard B., 112 (n. 33), 265
Haskell, Alexander C., 30, 31, 140
Hays, Harry T., 97, 203, 208, 224, 228, 230, 232, 233, 235, 236, 239, 240, 242, 244, 249 (n. 37)
Hazel Grove, 238
Hazel Run, 225, 231, 232, 235, 236, 241
Henry, Robert S., 6
Heth, Henry, 70, 103, 196–98
Hill, Ambrose P., 94, 124, 214 (n. 6), 222; and 1862 Maryland campaign, 8, 9, 16; and Fredericksburg campaign, 63, 67; and Overland campaign, 191, 194, 196–201, 206, 208, 210–12, 216–17 (n. 16)
Hill, Daniel H., 41 (n. 9), 47 (n. 47), 67, 210
Hilton, Joseph, 101
Hoke, Robert F., 116, 120, 139, 225, 230–33, 235, 236, 240, 242, 244
Holden, William W., 86, 118, 123–26
Holmes, Emma, 88, 124
Holmes, Theophilus H., 193, 210
Hooker, Joseph, 72, 101, 102, 132, 177, 222, 224–26, 228, 231, 238, 244, 272
Hosford, John W., 137, 138
Hotchkiss, Jedediah, 133, 192, 196, 200, 224, 244, 245
Houston Tri-Weekly Telegraph, 87
Howard, Francis M., 128

Howison's Hill, 226, 240
Huger, Benjamin, 193, 210
Humphreys, Benjamin G., 229, 244
Hunter, Andrew, 169, 170, 187 (n. 32)

Illustrated London News, 90
Impressment, 129, 170, 171, 273
Industrial Revolution, 157
Ireland, 259
Iron Brigade, 79 (n. 35)
Island No. 10, 58
Iverson, Alfred, Jr., 107 (n. 8)

Jackson, Thomas J. "Stonewall," 169, 191, 193, 194, 196, 200, 201, 211–13, 214 (n. 6), 217 (n. 18), 246 (n. 4); and 1862 Maryland campaign, 8, 16–18, 22, 23, 25, 32, 33, 36; and Fredericksburg campaign, 62–64, 69, 76 (n. 22); and Lost Cause, 157, 161, 258, 259, 264, 266, 269, 274–76; and Chancellorsville campaign, 221, 222, 226, 238
Jenkins, Micah, 135
Jericho Mills, battle of, 200
Johannsen, Robert W., 265
Johns Hopkins University, 263
Johnson, Edward "Allegheny," 193, 208
Johnston, Albert S., 179, 266
Johnston, Joseph E., 32, 33, 73, 145 (n. 28), 164, 179, 266, 271
Johnston, Robert D., 139, 208
Johnston, William P., 169, 197, 198
Jones, Benjamin F., 27, 28
Jones, Edward, 27
Jones, John B., 18, 20, 22, 58, 60, 73, 84, 186 (n. 29)
Jones, Mary, 59

Kantor, MacKinlay, 156
Kean, Robert G. H., 23, 44 (n. 34), 48 (n. 55), 61, 84, 85, 118, 134, 135
Keever, James E., 7
Kelly, William Aiken, 93

Southern Historical Society, 268
Southern Historical Society Papers,
    258, 268, 278 (n. 6)
Southern History of the War, 52, 116
Southern Illustrated News, 21, 195,
    204, 237
South Mountain, 6, 23, 41 (n. 9)
Spotsylvania campaign, xii, 139,
    191–93, 198, 202–5, 208–12, 259
Spotsylvania County, Va., 140
Spotsylvania Court House, Va., 228
Stafford, Leroy, 208
Stafford Heights, 53, 54, 64, 68, 70,
    81 (n. 46)
Stansbury's Hill, 226, 230
Stanton, Edwin M., 60, 61, 77 (n. 24)
Starnes, Richard D., 268
Steger, O. H., 132
Stephens, Alexander H., 11, 118, 124,
    125, 128
Steuart, George H., 100
Stiles, Robert, 153, 222, 261
Stillwell, William, 30
Stone, Kate, 91
Stonewall Brigade, 63, 67, 122, 127,
    134
Strong, George T., 77 (n. 24), 275
Stuart, James Ewell Brown "Jeb," 18,
    64, 68, 98, 123, 124, 153, 208
Stuart, Margaret, 103, 104
Suffolk, Va., 246 (n. 4)
Sumner, Charles, 77 (n. 23)
Sumter (S.C.) Tri-Weekly Watchman,
    56
Sunken Road, 47 (n. 47), 62, 230, 232
Swinton, William, 275

Tapp farm, 211
Taylor, Walter H., 27, 32, 38, 129,
    131–33, 137, 139, 194, 209, 278
    (n. 7)
Taylor, William B., 93, 94
Taylor's Hill, 225, 226, 230, 232,
    233, 235, 236, 240

Telegraph Road, 230, 232, 235, 239
Tennessee, 58, 134, 172
Texas, 18
Texas Brigade, 27, 122
Texas units: 10th Infantry Regi-
    ment, 18
Third Corps, Army of Northern Vir-
    ginia, 191, 194, 196, 198, 206, 208,
    209, 214 (n. 6)
Thomas, Edward L., 63
Thomas, Emory M., 83, 265
Time-Life Books, 157
Traveller, 131
Trent affair, 165
Trotter, James F., 259, 261
Tullahoma, Tenn., 83
Twelfth Corps, Army of the Poto-
    mac, 139
*Two Great Rebel Armies: An Essay in
    Confederate Military History*, 187
    (n. 37)

United Confederate Veterans, 261,
    263
United States, popular morale in,
    xi, 159, 163, 172–75, 177, 178, 188
    (n. 39), 189 (n. 46), 257, 271, 273,
    274, 276; during winter of 1862–
    63, 51, 54, 55, 59, 61, 64, 66, 71,
    72, 76 (n. 20); in spring 1864, 115,
    119, 134
United States Army, 152, 163; and
    emancipation, 20
United States Capitol, 155
United States Congress, 134, 135,
    166
U.S. Engineers, 192
United States Military Academy. *See*
    West Point
United States Senate, 61
University of Chicago, 155

Valley Forge, Pa., 14
Vance, Zebulon B., 124, 125, 167

Vandiver, Frank E., 54, 264
Van Dorn, Earl, 22, 40 (n. 20), 44 (n. 33)
Venable, Charles, 114 (n. 54), 198, 212
Vera Cruz, Mexico, siege of, 178
Verdery, James P., 216 (n. 16)
Vicksburg, Miss., 58, 59, 61, 67, 74, 83–89, 91, 92, 100, 105, 114 (n. 55), 116, 172, 178, 179, 192
Virginia, 22, 35, 87, 102, 138, 158, 159, 161–63, 166, 167, 179, 181
Virginia units: 12th Cavalry Regiment, 129; 13th Cavalry Regiment, 66; 4th Infantry Regiment, 134; 5th Infantry Regiment, 123; 8th Infantry Regiment, 108 (n. 8); 10th Infantry Regiment, 62; 12th Infantry Regiment, 99, 123; 13th Infantry Regiment, 145 (n. 28), 249 (n. 31); 16th Infantry Regiment, 123; 21st Infantry Regiment, 132; 41st Infantry Regiment, 122; 47th Infantry Regiment, 137; 56th Infantry Regiment, 25; 58th Infantry Regiment, 249 (n. 31)
Vizetelly, Frank, 90
Von Borcke, Heros, 64, 67

Wainwright, Charles S., 79 (n. 33), 272
War Memoirs, 246
Warrenton, Va., 22, 57, 120
The Warrior Generals: Combat Leadership in the Civil War, 184 (n. 17)
Washburne, Elihu, 76
Washington, George, 14, 59, 129, 153, 157, 172, 175, 189 (n. 46), 269
Washington, D.C., 11, 41 (n. 9), 61, 79 (n. 33), 92, 98, 101, 104, 120, 188 (n. 37)
Washington and Lee University, 152, 153, 169, 183 (n. 5)

Washington Artillery, 225
Washington College. *See* Washington and Lee University
Washington Daily Morning Chronicle, 274
Watson, John W., 137
Wearing of the Gray, 153
Weigley, Russell F., 158–61
Welch, Spencer G., 94, 95, 99, 134
Welch, Stephen E., 135
Weld, Stephen M., 270
"Westbourne" (Freeman home), 265
Western Theater of Civil War, 18, 22, 58, 59, 67, 83, 89, 92, 132, 134, 138, 139, 161, 172, 187 (n. 37)
West Point, 192, 200, 208, 216 (n. 14)
Whelchel, Francis M., 131
Whiting, W. H. C., 193
Why the South Lost the Civil War, 116
Wilcox, Cadmus M., 16, 196–98, 200, 229, 231, 239, 240
Wilderness, battle of the, 140, 194, 196, 202, 208, 211, 212, 216 (n. 14), 258, 259
Wiley, Bell I., 40 (n. 6), 115, 117
Williams, T. Harry, 158, 161, 173, 183 (n. 11), 264
Williamsport, Md., 37, 102
Willis's Hill, 226
Wilson, William L., 129, 137
Winchester, Va., 14, 20, 22, 32, 39, 59; second battle of, 201
Wofford, William T., 92, 101, 233
Wood, Fernando, 134
Wright, Ambrose R., 98, 198, 200, 216–17 (n. 16), 236

Yazoo River, 61
Yellow Tavern, Va., engagement at, 208
York, Richard W., 235
Young, Abram H., 125–27